An historical, geographical, and philosophical view of the Chinese empire; ... By W. Winterbotham. To which is added, a copious account of Lord Macartney's embassy, ... Second edition.

An historical, geographical, and philosophical view of the Chinese empire; ... By W. Winterbotham. To which is added, a copious account of Lord Macartney's embassy, ... Second edition.
Multiple Contributors, See Notes
ESTCID: N017774
Reproduction from Harvard University Libraries
Edited by William Winterbotham. The narrative of the Embassy to China has separate pagination and register.
London : printed for, and sold by the editor; J. Ridgway; and W. Button, [1795?]
[10],435,[1];114p.,plates : map ; 8°

Gale ECCO Print Editions

Relive history with *Eighteenth Century Collections Online*, now available in print for the independent historian and collector. This series includes the most significant English-language and foreign-language works printed in Great Britain during the eighteenth century, and is organized in seven different subject areas including literature and language; medicine, science, and technology; and religion and philosophy. The collection also includes thousands of important works from the Americas.

The eighteenth century has been called "The Age of Enlightenment." It was a period of rapid advance in print culture and publishing, in world exploration, and in the rapid growth of science and technology – all of which had a profound impact on the political and cultural landscape. At the end of the century the American Revolution, French Revolution and Industrial Revolution, perhaps three of the most significant events in modern history, set in motion developments that eventually dominated world political, economic, and social life.

In a groundbreaking effort, Gale initiated a revolution of its own: digitization of epic proportions to preserve these invaluable works in the largest online archive of its kind. Contributions from major world libraries constitute over 175,000 original printed works. Scanned images of the actual pages, rather than transcriptions, recreate the works ***as they first appeared.***

Now for the first time, these high-quality digital scans of original works are available via print-on-demand, making them readily accessible to libraries, students, independent scholars, and readers of all ages.

For our initial release we have created seven robust collections to form one the world's most comprehensive catalogs of 18th century works.

Initial Gale ECCO Print Editions collections include:

History and Geography
Rich in titles on English life and social history, this collection spans the world as it was known to eighteenth-century historians and explorers. Titles include a wealth of travel accounts and diaries, histories of nations from throughout the world, and maps and charts of a world that was still being discovered. Students of the War of American Independence will find fascinating accounts from the British side of conflict.

Social Science

Delve into what it was like to live during the eighteenth century by reading the first-hand accounts of everyday people, including city dwellers and farmers, businessmen and bankers, artisans and merchants, artists and their patrons, politicians and their constituents. Original texts make the American, French, and Industrial revolutions vividly contemporary.

Medicine, Science and Technology

Medical theory and practice of the 1700s developed rapidly, as is evidenced by the extensive collection, which includes descriptions of diseases, their conditions, and treatments. Books on science and technology, agriculture, military technology, natural philosophy, even cookbooks, are all contained here.

Literature and Language

Western literary study flows out of eighteenth-century works by Alexander Pope, Daniel Defoe, Henry Fielding, Frances Burney, Denis Diderot, Johann Gottfried Herder, Johann Wolfgang von Goethe, and others. Experience the birth of the modern novel, or compare the development of language using dictionaries and grammar discourses.

Religion and Philosophy

The Age of Enlightenment profoundly enriched religious and philosophical understanding and continues to influence present-day thinking. Works collected here include masterpieces by David Hume, Immanuel Kant, and Jean-Jacques Rousseau, as well as religious sermons and moral debates on the issues of the day, such as the slave trade. The Age of Reason saw conflict between Protestantism and Catholicism transformed into one between faith and logic -- a debate that continues in the twenty-first century.

Law and Reference

This collection reveals the history of English common law and Empire law in a vastly changing world of British expansion. Dominating the legal field is the *Commentaries of the Law of England* by Sir William Blackstone, which first appeared in 1765. Reference works such as almanacs and catalogues continue to educate us by revealing the day-to-day workings of society.

Fine Arts

The eighteenth-century fascination with Greek and Roman antiquity followed the systematic excavation of the ruins at Pompeii and Herculaneum in southern Italy; and after 1750 a neoclassical style dominated all artistic fields. The titles here trace developments in mostly English-language works on painting, sculpture, architecture, music, theater, and other disciplines. Instructional works on musical instruments, catalogs of art objects, comic operas, and more are also included.

biblio life
old books, new life.

AN

HISTORICAL, GEOGRAPHICAL,

AND

PHILOSOPHICAL

VIEW

OF THE

CHINESE EMPIRE;

COMPREHENDING

A DESCRIPTION OF THE FIFTEEN PROVINCES OF CHINA, CHINESE TARTARY, TRIBUTARY STATES, NATURAL HISTORY OF CHINA, GOVERNMENT, RELIGION, LAWS, MANNERS AND CUSTOMS, LITERATURE, ARTS, SCIENCES, MANUFACTURES, &c.

BY

W. WINTERBOTHAM.

To which is added,

A COPIOUS ACCOUNT

OF

LORD MACARTNEY's EMBASSY,

COMPILED FROM ORIGINAL COMMUNICATIONS.

SECOND EDITION.

LONDON:

PRINTED FOR, AND SOLD BY THE EDITOR, J. RIDGWAY, YORK-STREET, AND W BUTTON, PATERNOSTER-ROW.

ADVERTISEMENT.

FROM the expenſive preparations made for the late Embaſſy to China, the Britiſh nation was certainly led to expect that a commercial intercourſe would have been opened between the two nations, which might have proved of the utmoſt importance to both. Theſe hopes have, however, been fruſtrated and diſappointed for the preſent, but the Embaſſy has given riſe to a laudable ſpirit of inquiry with reſpect to the Chineſe empire, which we have no doubt will ultimately prove advantageous to Britiſh commerce. To aid the inquirer in his purſuit, and to furniſh the public at large with the means of obtaining a general knowledge of China, as well as to gratify their curioſity with reſpect to the Embaſſy itſelf, this volume was compiled.

The propriety of blending theſe two objects will be readily admitted, when it is conſidered, that whatever may have been the abilities of the perſons who attended the embaſſy, or however copious the accounts given of it by them, it was impoſſible for them to obtain any proper idea, or furniſh any information of the Chineſe empire, in general, from their own obſervation. This, their ſituation abſolutely precluded, having, to uſe the language of Mr Anderſon in his account of that Embaſſy, "entered it like paupers, re-"mained in it like priſoners, and quitted it like "vagrants."

The Editor has only to add, that in compiling this work, he has investigated different accounts with impartiality, stripped the accounts of visionary missionaries of their absurdities, and by collecting facts respecting the natural history, population, government, laws, customs, religion, literature, sciences, manufactures, &c of the Chinese empire, he hopes he has enabled the reader to form a pretty correct opinion of a nation, in many instances the most astonishing of any recorded in the page of history.

With respect to the account of the Embassy, he has only to say, the materials from which it was compiled, were furnished to the publisher by one who formed a part of the suite attendant on the Embassy, and has every proof that the author was an attentive observer

The map is laid down from the Jesuits maps, made from actual surveys, and includes the whole of China, Chinese Tartary, and the tributary kingdoms.

CONTENTS.

I.—GENERAL HISTORY OF CHINA.

II.—GENERAL DESCRIPTION OF THE CHINESE EMPIRE.

III.—GENERAL DESCRIPTION OF CHINESE TARTARY.

IV.—STATES TRIBUTARY TO CHINA.

V.—NATURAL HISTORY OF CHINA

CONTENTS

I.—ACCOUNT OF THE EMBASSY.

CONTENTS.

DIRECTIONS TO THE BINDER.

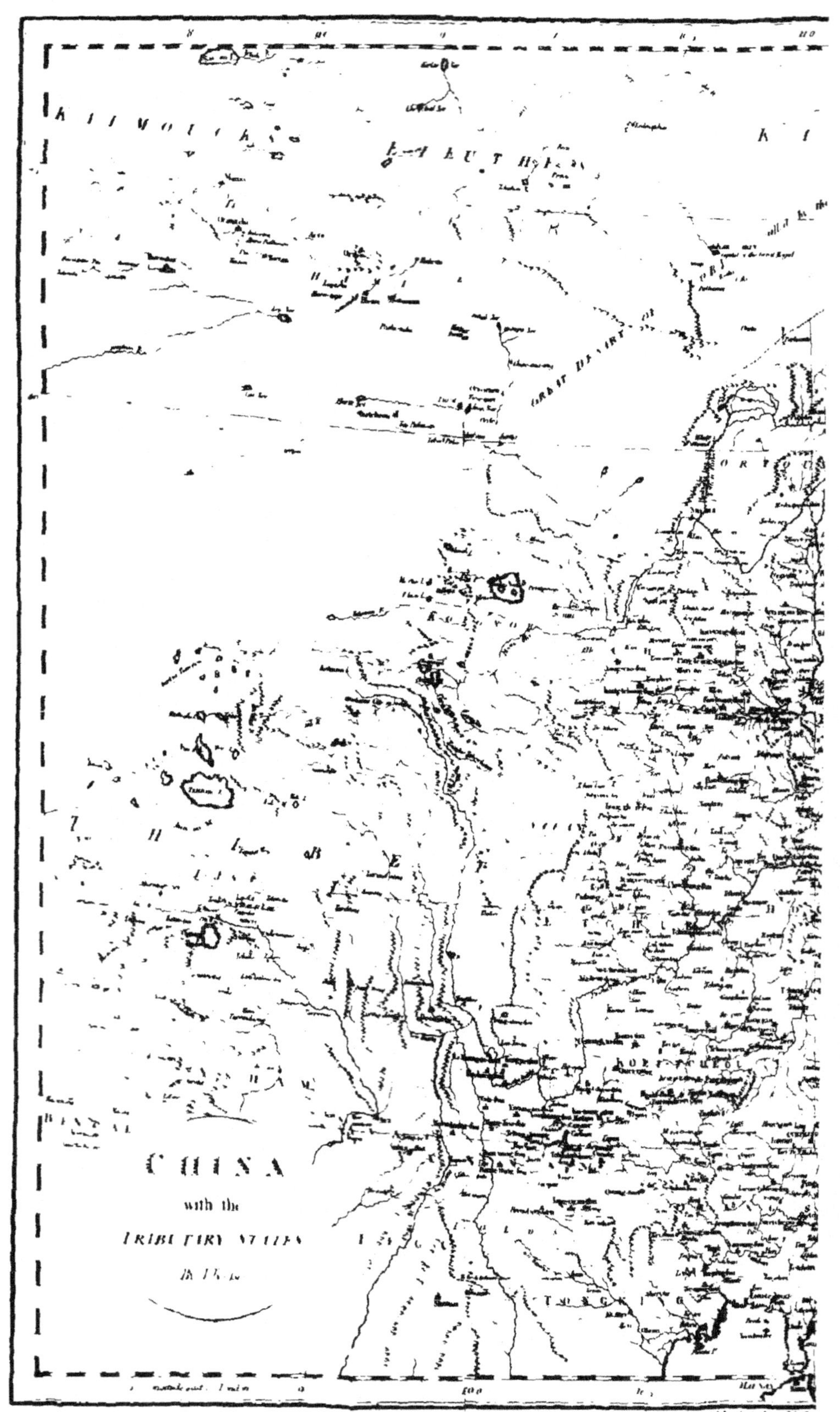
CHINA
with the
TRIBUTARY STATES

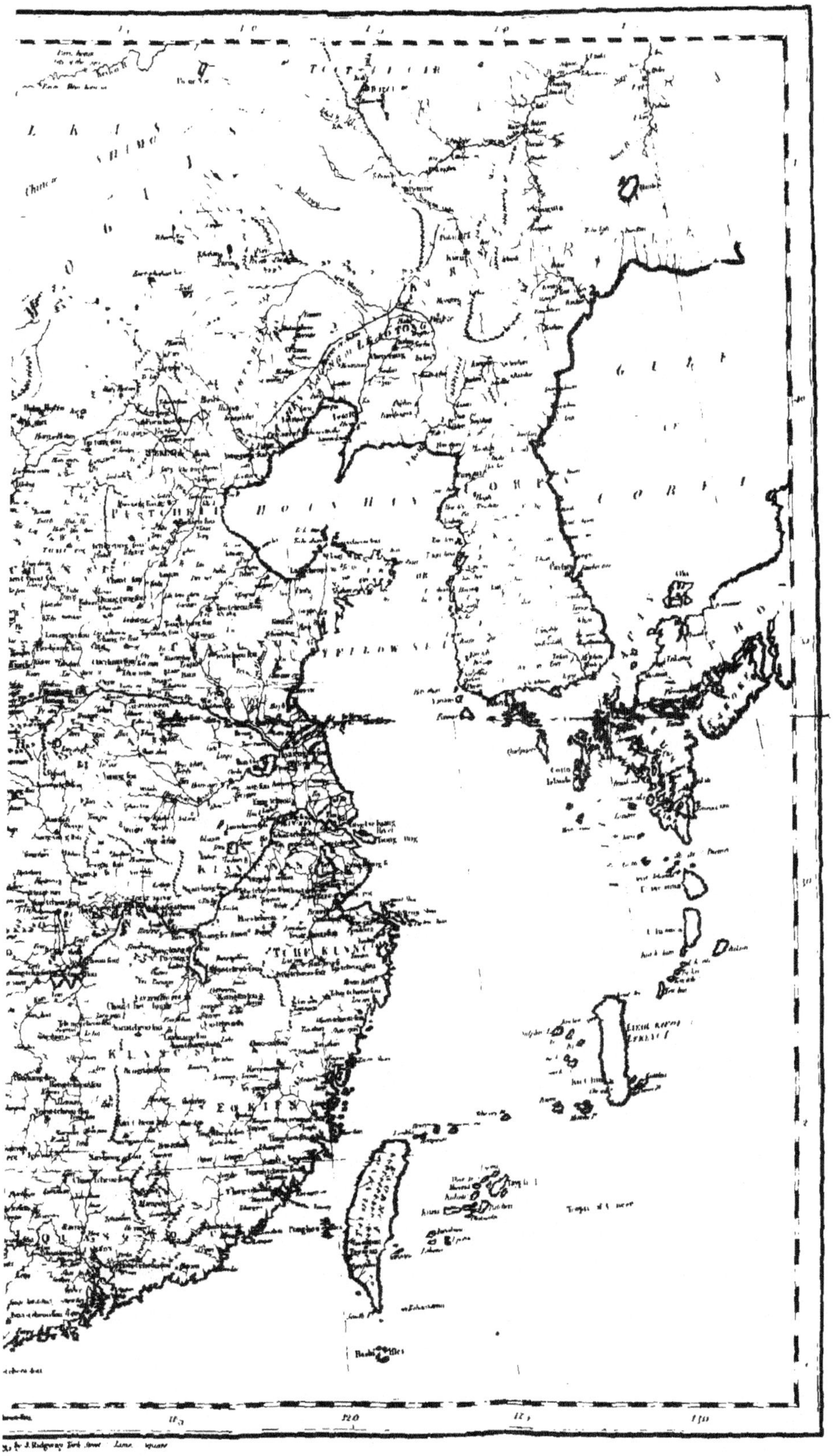

by J. Ridgway York Street Lane square

GENERAL HISTORY

OF

CHINA.

THE origin of all nations is involved in obscurity and fable, but that of the Chinese perhaps much more so than any other. Every nation is inclined to assume too high an antiquity to itself, but the Chinese carry theirs beyond all bounds. Indeed, though no people on earth are more exact in keeping records of every memorable transaction, yet such is the genius of the Chinese for superstition and fable, that the first part of their history is deservedly contemned by every rational person. What contributes more to this uncertainty of the Chinese history is, that neither we, nor they themselves, have any thing but fragments of the ancient historical books, for about two hundred and thirteen years before the Christian era, the reigning emperor Si-hoang-ti caused all the books in the empire to be burned, except those written by lawyers and physicians. Nay, the more effectually to destroy the memory of every thing contained in them, he commanded a great number of learned men to be buried alive, lest, from their memories, they should commit to writing something of the true memoirs of the empire. The inaccuracy of the Chinese annals is complained of even by their most respected author Confucius himself, who also affirms, that before his time many of the oldest materials for writing such annals had been destroyed.

According to the Chinese histories, the first monarch of the whole universe (that is, of China), was called PUON-KU, or PUEN-CU This, according to some, was the first man; but according to Bayer and Menzelius, two of the greatest critics in Chinese literature that have hitherto appeared, the word signifies *the highest antiquity*. PUON-KU was succeeded by TIENE-HOANG, which signifies *the emperor of heaven*. They call him also the intelligent heaven, the supreme king of the middle heaven, *&c*. According to some of their historians, he was the inventor of letters, and of the Cyclic characters by which they determine the place of the year, *&c*. Tiene-hoang was succeeded by TI-HOANG, *the emperor of the earth*, who divided the day and night, appointing thirty days to make one moon, and fixed the winter solstice to the eleventh moon. Ti-hoang was succeeded by GINE-HOANG, *sovereign of men*, who with his nine brothers shared the government among them. They built cities, and surrounded them with walls, made a distinction between the sovereign and subjects, instituted marriage, *&c*.

The reigns of these four emperors make up one of what the Chinese called *ki*, "ages," or "periods," of which there were nine before FO-HI, whom the most sensible writers acknowledge as the founder of their empire.

The history of the second *ki* contradicts almost every thing said of the first; for though we have but just now been told that Gine-hoang and his brethren built cities surrounded with walls; yet, in the succeeding age, the people dwelt in caves, or perched upon trees as it were in nests. Of the third *ki* we hear nothing, and in the fourth, it seems matters had been still worse, as we are told that men were then only taught to retire into the hollows of rocks. Of the fifth and sixth we have no accounts. These six periods, according to some writers, contained ninety thousand years, according to others, one million one hundred thousand seven hundred and fifty.

In the ſeventh and eighth *ki*, they tell us over again what they had ſaid of the firſt, namely, that men began to leave their caves and dwell in houſes, and were taught to prepare clothes, &c. TCHINE-FANG, the firſt monarch of the eighth *ki*, taught his ſubjects to take off the hair from ſkins with rollers of wood, and cover themſelves with the ſkins ſo prepared. He taught them alſo to make a kind of web of their hair, to ſerve as a covering to their heads againſt rain They obeyed his orders with joy, and he called his ſubjects *people clothed with ſkins* His reign is ſaid to have laſted three hundred and fifty years, that of one of his ſucceſſors, alſo, named YEOU-TSAO-CHI, laſted more than three hundred, and his family continued for twelve or eighteen thouſand years. But what is very ſurpriſing, all theſe thouſands and millions of years had elapſed without mankind's having any knowledge of fire. This was not diſcovered till towards the cloſe of this period, by one SOUIGINE. After ſo uſeful a diſcovery, he taught the people to dreſs their victuals, whereas before, they had devoured the fleſh of animals quite raw, drunk their blood, and ſwallowed even their hair and feathers. He is alſo ſaid to have been the inventor of fiſhing, letters, &c.

In the ninth period we find the invention, or at leaſt the origin of letters, attributed to one TSANG-HIE, who received them from a divine tortoiſe that carried them on his ſhell, and delivered them into the hands of TSANG-HIE. During this period alſo, muſic, money, carriages, merchandize, commerce, &c. were invented. There are various calculations of the length of theſe *ki* or periods. Some make the time from Puan-ku to Confucius, who flouriſhed about four hundred and ſeventy-nine years before Chriſt, to contain two hundred and ſeventy-nine thouſand years, others, two millions two hundred and ſeventy-ſix thouſand, ſome, two millions ſeven hundred and fifty-nine thouſand eight hundred and ſixty years; others, three millions, two hundred and ſeventy-ſix thouſand, and ſome no leſs than ninety-ſix millions nine hundred and ſixty-one thouſand, ſeven hundred and forty years.

Theſe extravagant accounts are by ſome thought to contain obſcure and imperfect hints concerning the coſmogony and creation of the world, &c. Puon-ku, the firſt emperor, they think, repreſents eternity preceding the duration of the world. The ſucceeding ones, Tiene-hoang, Ti-hoang, and Gine-hoang, they imagine ſignify the creation of the heavens and earth, and the formation of man. The ten ki, or ages, nine of which preceded Fo-hi, mean the ten generations preceding Noah.

What we have now related contains the ſubſtance of that part of the Chineſe hiſtory which is entirely fabulous. After the nine ki, or ages, already taken notice of, the tenth commenced with Fo-hi, and the hiſtory, though ſtill dark, obſcure, and fabulous, begins to grow ſomewhat more conſiſtent and intelligible. Fo-hi is ſaid to have been born in the province of Shenſi. His mother, walking upon the bank of a lake in that province, ſaw a very large print of a man's foot in the ſand, and being ſurrounded by a rainbow, became impregnated. The child was named Fo-hi, and, when he grew up, was by his countrymen elected king, on account of his ſuperior merit, and ſtiled Tien-tſe, that is, "*the ſon of heaven.*" He is ſaid to have invented the eight *qua*, or ſymbols, conſiſting of three lines each, which, differently combined, formed ſixty-four characters that were made uſe of to expreſs every thing. To give theſe the greater credit, he pretended that he had ſeen them inſcribed on the back of a dragon-horſe, an animal ſhaped like a horſe, with the wings and ſcales of a dragon, which aroſe from the bottom of a lake. Having gained great reputation among his countrymen by this prodigy, he is ſaid to have created mandarines or officers, under the name of *dragons*. Hence we may aſſign a reaſon why the emperors of China always carry a dragon in their banners. He alſo inſtituted marriage, invented music, regulated the dress of the sexes, &c. Having established a prime minister, he divided the government of his dominions among four mandarines, and died after a reign of one hundred and fifteen years.

After Fo-hi followed a succession of emperors, of whom nothing remarkable is recorded, except that in the reign of YAU, the seventh after Fo-hi, the sun did not set for ten days, so that the Chinese were afraid of a general conflagration. This event the compilers of the Universal History take to be the same with that mentioned in the book of Joshua, when the sun and moon stood still for about the space of a day. Fo-hi they will have to be the same with Noah. They imagine, that after the deluge this patriarch remained some time with his descendants, but on their wicked combination to build the tower of Babel, he separated himself from them, with as many as he could persuade to go along with him, and that, still travelling eastward, he at last entered the fertile country of China, and laid the foundation of that vast empire.—But, leaving these fabulous and conjectural times, we shall proceed to give some account of that part of the Chinese history which may be more certainly depended on.

As the Chinese, contrary to the practice of almost all nations, have never sought to conquer other countries, but rather to improve and content themselves with their own, their history for many ages furnishes nothing remarkable. The whole of their emperors, abstracted from those who are said to have reigned in the fabulous times, are comprehended in twenty-two dynasties, mentioned in the following table.

		Emperors	Before Christ.
1	*Hya*, containing	17	2207.
2	*Shang*, or *Ing*,	28	1766
3	*Chew*,	35	1122
4	*Tsin*,	4	248.
5	*Han*,	25	206

Emperors			After Christ.
6	*Heu-han*,	2	220
7	*Tsin*,	15	465
8	*Song*,	8	22c
9	*Tsi*,	5	479
10	*Leang*,	4	502.
11	[illegible]	4	557
12	[illegible]	3	
13	*Tang*,	20	618
14	*Heu-leang*,	2	907
15	[illegible]	4	9-5
16	[illegible]	2	936
17	[illegible]	2	947
18	[illegible]	3	951
19	*Song*,	18	960
20	*Iuen*,	9	1280
21	*Ming*,	16	1368.
22	*Tsing*,		1645

This table is formed according to the accounts of the Jesuit Du Halde, and is commonly reckoned to be the most authentic; but according to the above mentioned hypothesis of the compilers of the Universal History, who make a different era from the Jesuits, the dynasty of *Hya* did not commence until the year before Christ 1357, and to accommodate the history to their hypothesis, great alterations must be made in the duration of the dynasties.

The most interesting particulars of the Chinese history relate chiefly to the incursions of the Tartars, who at last conquered the whole empire, and who still continue to hold the sovereignty, though by transferring the seat of the empire to Pekin, and adopting the Chinese language, manners, &c. the Tartars would seem rather to have been conquered by China, than China by Tartary. These incursions are said to have begun very early, even in the time of the emperor SHUN, successor to YAU above mentioned, in whose reign the miraculous solstice happened. At this time, the Tartars were repulsed, and obliged to retire into their own territories. From time to time, however, they continued to threaten the empire with invasions, and the northern provinces were often actually ravaged by the Tartars in the neighbourhood. About two hundred and thirteen years before the Christian æra, SHI-HOANG-TI, having fully subdued all the princes, or kings as they were called, of the different provinces, became emperor of China with unlimited power. He divided the whole empire into thirty six provinces, and finding the northern part of his dominions much incommoded by the invasions of the neighbouring barbarians, he sent a formidable army against them, which drove them far beyond the boundaries of China, and to prevent their return, he built the famous wall which separates China from Tartary. After this, being elated with his own exploits, he formed the design of making posterity believe that he himself had been the first Chinese emperor that ever sat on the throne, and for this purpose, ordered all the historical writings to be burnt, and caused many of the learned to be put to death, as already mentioned.

What effect the great wall for some time had in preventing the invasions of the Tartars, we are not told; but in the tenth century of the Christian æra, those of Kitan or Lyau got a footing in China. The Kitan were a people of western Tartary, who dwelt to the north and north-east of the province of Pecheli in China, particularly in that of Lyau-tong lying without the great wall. These people having subdued the country between Korea and Kashgar, became much more troublesome to the Chinese than all the other Tartars. Their empire commenced about the year 916, in the fourth year of MO-TI-KYAN-TI, second emperor of the 13th Chinese dynasty called HEW LYANG

In 936, MINGT-SONG, second emperor of the fifteenth dynasty, being dead, Shi-king-tang, his son-in-law, rebelled against [illegible], his son and successor, whom he deprived of his crown and life. This he accomplished by means of an army of fifty thousand men furnished by the Kitan. The descendant of Mingt-song, being unable to resist the conqueror, fled to the city Gnei-chew, where shutting himself up with his family and all his valuable effects, he set fire to the palace and was burnt to ashes. On his death, SHI-KING-TANG assumed the title of emperor, founded the [illegible] dynasty, and changed his name to that of [illegible]. But the Kitan general refusing to acknowledge him, he was obliged to purchase a peace by yielding up to the Tartars sixteen cities in the province of Peche-li, besides a yearly present of three hundred thousand pieces of silk.

This submission served only to inflame the avarice and ambition of the Kitan. In 959, they broke the treaty when least expected, and invaded the empire afresh. TSI-VANG, the emperor at that time, opposed them with a formidable army; but through the treachery of his general Lyew-chi-ywen, the Tartars were allowed to take him prisoner. On this, Tsi-vang was glad to recover his liberty, by accepting of a small principality, while the traitor became emperor of all China, and, changing his name to KAUT-SU, founded the 17th dynasty. The Tartars, in the mean time, ravaged all the northern provinces without opposition, and then marched into the southern. But being here stopped by some bodies of Chinese troops, the general thought proper to retire with his booty into Tartary. In 962, Kaut-su dying was succeeded by his son IN-TI. The youth of this prince gave an opportunity to the eunuchs to raise commotions, especially as the army was employed at a distance in repelling the invasions of the Tartars. This army was commanded by Ko ghey, who defeated the enemy in ſeveral battles, and thus reſtored peace to the northern provinces In the mean time, In ti was ſlain by his eunuchs, and the empreſs placed his brother on the throne but Ko-ghey returning in triumph, was ſaluted emperor by his victorious army, and the empreſs being unable to ſupport the rights of her ſon, was obliged to ſubmit, while Ko-ghey, aſſuming the name of TAY-TSU, founded the eighteenth dynaſty. Nine years after this, however, the grandees of the empire, ſetting aſide Kong-ti, the third in ſucceſſion from Tay-tſu, on account of his non-age, proclaimed his guardian, named *Chau-quang-yu*, emperor, who aſſuming the name of KAU-TSU, founded the nineteenth dynaſty, called *Song* or *Tſong*.

Under this monarch the empire began to recover itſelf, but the Kitan ſtill continued their incurſions The ſucceſſors of Kau-tſu oppoſed them with various ſucceſs, but at laſt, in 978, the barbarians became ſo ſtrong as to lay ſiege to a conſiderable city TAY-TSONG, ſucceſſor to Kau-tſu, detached three hundred ſoldiers, each carrying a light in his hand, againſt them in the night time, with orders to approach as near as poſſible to the Tartar camp The barbarians, imagining, by the number of lights, that the whole Chineſe army was at hand, immediately fled, and, falling into the ambuſcades laid for them by the Chineſe general, were almoſt all cut to pieces.

This check, however, did not long put a ſtop to the ravages of the Kitan In the year 999, they laid ſiege to a city in the province of Pecheli, but CHING-TSONG, ſucceſſor to Tay-tſong, came upon them with his army ſo ſuddenly, that they betook themſelves to flight The emperor was adviſed to take advantage of their conſternation, and recover the country which had been yielded to them, but inſtead of purſuing his victory, he bought a peace, by conſenting to pay annually one hundred thouſand tael, about thirty four thouſand pounds, and two hundred thousand pieces of silk The youth and pacific disposition of JIN-TSONG, successor to Ching-tsong, revived the courage of the Kitan, and, in 1035, war would have been renewed, had not the emperor condescended to as shameful a treaty as that concluded by his father Two years after, the Tartars demanded restitution of ten cities in the province of Peche-li, which had been taken by Ko-ghey, founder of the eighteenth dynasty, upon which Jin tsong engaged to pay them an annual tribute of two hundred thousand taels of silver, and three hundred thousand pieces of silk, in lieu of these cities.

From this time the Kitan remained in peaceable possession of their Chinese dominions till the year 1117. Whey-tsong, at that time emperor, being able neither to bear their ravages, nor by himself to put a stop to them, resolved upon a remedy which at last proved worse than the disease This was to call in the Nu che, Nyu-che, or Eastern Tartars, to destroy the kingdom of the Kitan. From this he was dissuaded by the king of Korea, and most of his own ministers, but, disregarding their salutary advice, he joined his forces to those of the Nu-che The Kitan were then every where defeated, and at last reduced to such extremity, that those who remained were forced to leave their country, and fly to the mountains of the west

Thus the empire of the Kitan was totally destroyed, but nothing to the advantage of the Chinese, for the Tartar general, elated with his conquest, gave the name of KIN to his new dominion, assumed the title of emperor, and began to think of aggrandizing himself and enlarging his empire For this purpose, he immediately broke the treaties concluded with the Chinese emperor, and, invading the provinces of Peche-li and Shen-si, made himself master of the greater part of them Whey-tsong, finding himself in danger of losing his dominions, made ſeveral advantageous propoſals to the Tartar, who, ſeeming to comply with them, invited him to come and ſettle matters by a perſonal conference The Chineſe monarch complied but, on his return, the terms agreed on ſeemed ſo intolerable to his miniſters, that they told him the treaty could not ſubſiſt, and that the moſt cruel war was preferable to ſuch an ignominious peace The Kin monarch, being informed of all that paſſed, had recourſe to arms, and took ſeveral cities Whey-tſong was weak enough to go in perſon to hold a ſecond conference, but, on his arrival, was immediately ſeized by the Tartar He was kept priſoner under a ſtrong guard during the remaining part of his life; and ended his days in 1126, in the deſert of Shamo, having nominated his eldeſt ſon Kin-tſong to ſucceed him.

KIN-TSONG began his reign with putting to death ſix miniſters of ſtate, who had betrayed his father into the hands of the Kin Tartars. The barbarians in the mean time purſued their conqueſts without oppoſition. They croſſed the Hoang-ho, or Yellow River, which an handful of troops might have prevented, and marching directly towards the imperial city, took and plundered it Then ſeizing the emperor and his conſort, they carried them away captives but many of the principal lords, and ſeveral of the miniſters, preferring death to an ignominious bondage, killed themſelves The Kin being informed by the empreſs *Mang* that ſhe had been divorced, they left her behind This proved the means of ſaving the empire, for by her wiſdom and prudence ſhe got the crown placed on the head of Kau-tſong, ninth ſon of the emperor Whey-tſong by his divorced empreſs

KAU-TSONG fixed his court at Nankin, the capital of Kyang-nan, but ſoon after was obliged to remove it to King-chew in Che-kyang He made ſeveral efforts to recover ſome of his provinces from the Kin, but without effect ILI-TSONG *the Kin monarch*, in the mean time, endeavoured to gain the esteem of his Chinese subjects by paying a regard to their learning and learned men, and honouring the memory of Confucius. Some time after, he advanced to Nan-king, from whence Kau-tsong had retired, and took it: but, receiving advice that Yo-fi, general of the Song, or southern Chinese, was advancing by long marches to the relief of that city, they set fire to the palace and retired northward. However, Yo-fi arrived time enough to fall upon their rear-guard, which suffered very much; and from this time the Kin never dared to cross the river Kyang. In a few years afterwards the Chinese emperor submitted to become tributary to the Kin, and concluded a peace with them upon very dishonourable terms. This submission, however, was of little avail: for, in 1163, the Tartars broke the peace, and, invading the southern province with a formidable army, took the city of Yang-chew. The king, having approached the river Kyang, near its mouth, where it is widest as well as most rapid, commanded his troops to cross it, threatening with his drawn sword to kill those who refused. On receiving such an unreasonable command, the whole army mutinied; and the king being killed in the beginning of the tumult, the army immediately retired.

From this time to the year 1210, nothing remarkable occurs in the Chinese history; this year, JENGHIZ-KHAN, chief of the western Tartars, *Mogols* or *Mungls*, quarrelled with Yong-tsi, emperor of the Kin, and at the same time the king of Hya, disgusted at being refused assistance against Jenghiz-khan, threatened him with an invasion on the west side. Yong-tsi prepared for his defence, but in 1211, receiving news that Jenghiz-khan was advancing southward with his whole army, he was seized with fear, and made proposals of peace, which were rejected. In 1212, the Mogul generals forced the great wall, or, according to some writers, had one of the gates treacherously opened to them, to the north of Shen-si, and made incursions as far as Pekin, the capital of the Kin empire. At the same time the province of Lyau-tong was almost totally reduced by several Kitan lords who had joined Jenghiz-khan, several strong places were taken, and an army of three hundred thousand Kin defeated by the Moguls. In autumn they laid siege to the city of Tay-tong-fou, where, although the governor Hujaku fled, yet Jenghiz-khan met with considerable resistance Having lost a vast number of men, and being himself wounded by an arrow, he was obliged to raise the siege and retire into Tartary, after which the Kin retook several cities. The next year, however, Jenghiz-khan re-entered China, retook the cities which the Kin had reduced the year before, and overthrew their armies in two bloody battles, in one of which the ground was strewed with dead bodies for upwards of four leagues

The same year Yong-tsi was slain by his general Hujaku; and Sun, a prince of the blood, advanced in his room After this the Moguls, attacking the empire with four armies at once, laid waste the provinces of Shen-si, Ho-nan, Peche-li, and Shan-tong In 1214 Jenghiz-khan sat down before Pekin, but instead of assaulting the city, offered terms of peace, which were accepted, and the Moguls retired into Tartary After their departure, the emperor, leaving his son at Pekin, removed his court to Pyen-lyang near Kay-fong-fou, the capital of Ho-nan At this Jenghiz-khan being offended, immediately sent troops to besiege Pekin The city held out to the fifth month of the year 1215, and then surrendered. At the same time the Moguls finished the conquest of Lyau-tong, and the Song refused to pay the usual tribute to the Kin.

In 1216, Jenghiz-khan returned to pursue his conquest in the west of Asia, where he staid seven years, during which time his general MUHULI made great progress in China against the Kin emperor He was greatly assisted by the motions of NING-TSONG, emperor of the Song, or southern China, who, incensed by the frequent perfidies of the Kin, had declared war against them, and would hearken to no terms of peace, though very advantageous proposals were made. Notwithstanding this, however, in 12[illegible]0, the Kin, exerting themselves, raised two great armies, one in Shen-[illegible], and the other in Shang-tong. The former [illegible] the [illegible] of H[illegible], who had [illegible] no fewer than [illegible], were [illegible] defeated by Muhuli. In 1221, [illegible] Ho[illegible], and died after [illegible].

In 122[illegible], the Kin emperor died, and was succeeded by his son Tiheu, who made peace with the king of Hia. But next year, that kingdom was entirely destroyed by Jenghiz-khan. In 1226, Oktay, son to Jenghiz-khan, marched into Ho-nan, and besieged Kay-fong-fou, capital of the Kin empire, but was obliged to withdraw into Shen-si, where he took several cities, and cut in pieces an army of thirty thousand men. In 1227 Jenghiz-khan died, after having desired his sons to demand a passage for their army through the dominions of the Song, without which he said they could not easily vanquish the Kin.

After the death of that great conqueror, the war was carried on with various success; but though the Moguls took above sixty important posts in the province of Shen-si, they found it impossible to force Ton-quan, which it behoved them to do in order to penetrate effectually into Ho-nan. In April 1231 they took the capital of Shen-si, and defeated the Kin army which came to its relief. Here one of the officers desired prince Tolo to demand a passage from the Song through the country of Han-chong-fou. This proposal Tolo communicated to his brother Oktay, who approved of it, as being conformable to the dying advice of Jenghiz-khan. Hereupon Tolo, having assembled all his forces, sent a messenger to the Song generals to demand a passage through their territories. This, however, they not only refuſed, but put the meſſenger to death, which ſo enraged Toley that he ſwore to make them repent of it, and was ſoon as good as his word. He decamped in Auguſt 1231, and having forced the paſſages, put to the ſword the inhabitants of Hoa-yang and Fong-chew, two cities in the diſtrict of Han-chong fou. Then having cut down rocks to fill up deep abyſſes, and made roads through places almoſt innacceſſible, he came and beſieged the city of Han-chong-fou itſelf. The miſerable inhabitants fled to the mountains on his approach, and more than one hundred thouſand of them periſhed. After this, Toley divided his forces, conſiſting of thirty thouſand horſe, into two bodies. One of theſe went weſtward to Myen-chew, from thence, after opening the paſſages of the mountains, they arrived at the river Kyaling, which runs into the great Kyang. This they croſſed on rafts made of the wood of demoliſhed houſes, and then, marching along its banks, ſeized many important poſts. At laſt, having deſtroyed more than one hundred and forty cities, towns, or fortreſſes, they returned to the army. The ſecond detachment ſeized an important poſt in the mountains, called Tau-tong, ſix or ſeven leagues to the eaſtward of Han-chong-fou. On the other ſide Oktay advanced, in October, towards Pu-chew, a city of Shan-ſi, which being taken after a vigorous defence, he prepared to paſs the Hoang-ho. Toley, after ſurmounting incredible difficulties, arrived in December on the borders of Ho-nan, and made a ſhew as if he deſigned to attack the capital of the Kin empire. On his firſt appearance in Ho-nan through a paſſage ſo little ſuſpected, every body was filled with terror and aſtoniſhment, ſo that he proceeded for ſome time without oppoſition. At laſt the emperor ordered his generals, Hota, Hapua, and others, to march againſt the enemy. Toley boldly attacked them, but was obliged to retire, which he did in good order. Hota was for pursuing him, saying that the Mogul army did not exceed thirty thousand men, and that they seemed not to have eaten any thing for two or three days. Hapua, however, was of opinion that there was no occasion for being so hasty, as the Moguls were inclosed between the rivers Han and Hoang-ho, so that they could not escape. This negligence they soon had occasion to repent of; for Toley, by a stratagem, made himself master of their heavy baggage, which accident obliged them to retire to Tang-chew. From thence they sent a messenger to acquaint the emperor that they had gained the battle, but concealed the loss of their baggage. This good news filled the court with joy, and the people who had retired into the capital for its defence, left it again, and went into the country: but, in a few days after, the vanguard of the Moguls, who had been sent by the emperor Oktay, appeared in the field, and carried off a great number of those that had quitted the city.

In January, 1232, Oktay passing the Hoang-ho, encamped in the district of Kay-fong-fou, capital of the Kin empire, and sent his general Suputay to besiege the city. At that time the place was near thirty miles in circumference: but having only forty thousand soldiers to defend it, as many more from the neighbouring cities, and twenty thousand peasants, were ordered into it, while the emperor published an affecting declaration, animating the people to defend it to the last extremity. Oktay, having heard with joy of Toley's entrance into Ho-nan, ordered him to send succours to Suputay. On the other hand, the Kin generals advanced with one hundred and fifty thousand men to relieve the city, but being obliged to divide their forces in order to avoid in part the great road which Toley had obstructed with trees, they were attacked by him in a place of a disadvantage, and, after a faint resistance, defeated with great slaughter, and the loss of both their generals, one killed and the other taken The emperor now ordered the army at Tong-quan and other fortified places to march to the relief of Kay-fong-fou They assembled accordingly, to the number of one hundred and ten thousand foot and fifteen thousand horse, and were followed by vast numbers of people, who expected by their means to be protected from the enemy But many of these troops having deserted, and the rest being enfeebled by the fatigues of their march, they dispersed on the approach of their pursuers, who killed all they found in the highways After this the Moguls took Tong-quan and some other considerable posts; but were obliged to raise the sieges of Quey-te-fou and Loy-ang by the bravery of the governors Kyang-shin, governor of Loy-ang, had only three or four thousand soldiers under him, while his enemies were thirty thousand strong. He placed his worst soldiers on the walls, putting himself at the head of four hundred brave men, whom he ordered to go naked, and whom he led to all dangerous attacks. He invented engines to cast large stones, which required but few hands to play them, and aimed so true as to hit at an hundred paces distance When their arrows failed, he cut those shot by the enemy into four pieces, pointed them with pieces of brass coin, and discharged them from wooden tubes with as much force as bullets are from a musket. Thus he harrassed the Moguls for three months so grievously, that they were obliged, notwithstanding their numbers, to abandon the enterprize

Oktay, at last, notwithstanding his successes, resolved to return to Tartary, and offered the Kin emperor peace, provided he became tributary, and delivered up to him twenty-seven families which he named. These offers were very agreeable to the emperor, but Suputay, taking no notice of the treaty, pushed on the siege of the capital with more vigour than ever By the help of the Chinese slaves in his army, the Mogul general soon filled the ditch;

... his efforts seemed only to inspire the besieged with ... vigour. The Moguls at that time made use of artillery, but were unable to make the least impression upon the city walls. They raised walls round those they besieged, which they fortified with ditches, towers, and battlements. They proceeded also to sap the walls of the city, but were very much annoyed by the artillery of the besieged, especially their bombs, which sinking into the galleries, and burning underground, made great havock among the miners. For fifteen days and nights the attack continued without intermission, during which time an incredible number of men perished on both sides; at length, Supotay, finding that he could not take the city, withdrew his troops, under pretence of conferences being on foot. Soon after the plague began in Kay-fong-fou, and raged with such violence, that, in fifty days, nine hundred thousand biers were carried out, besides a vast multitude of the poorer sort who could not afford any.

In a short time, two unlucky accidents occasioned a renewal of the war, which now put an end to the empire of the Kin. Gan-yong, a young Mogul lord, having usurped the government of some cities in Kyang-nan, and killed the officer sent to take possession of them, declared for the Kin. The emperor unwillingly took Gan-young into his service, and gave him the title of Prince. Upon this Oktay sent an envoy, attended by thirty other persons, to enquire into the affair; but the Kin officers killed them all, without being punished by the emperor. Supotay having informed his master of all these proceedings, was ordered to continue the war in Ho-nan. Shew-su now commanded his officers to collect troops for the defence of the capital; but before his orders could be executed, they were attacked and defeated, one after another, by the Moguls. This obliged him to raise soldiers from among the peasants, for whose [illegible] the people were taxed three tenths of the rice they possessed The city began now to be distressed for want of provisions, and as it was but in a bad posture of defence, the emperor marched with an army against the Moguls His expedition proved unfortunate, for, sending part of his army to besiege a city called Wy-chew, it was totally cut in pieces, and Suputay a second time sat down before the capital

On hearing this news, the emperor repassed the Hoang-ho, and retired to Quey-te-fou. Here he had not been long before the capital was delivered up by treachery, and Suputay put all the males of the imperial race to death, but, by the express command of Oktay, spared the inhabitants, who are said to have amounted to one million and four hundred thousand families After this disaster the unhappy monarch left his troops at Quey-te-fou, and retired to Juning-fou, a city in the southern part of Ho nan, attended only by four hundred persons. Here the distance of the Moguls made him think of living at ease, but while he flattered himself with these vain hopes, the enemy's army arrived before the city and invested it. The garrison were terrified at their approach, but were encouraged by the emperor, and his brave general Hu-sye-hu, to hold out to the last As there were not in the city a sufficient number of men, the women, dressed in mens clothes, were employed to carry wood, stones, and other necessary materials to the walls All their efforts, however, were ineffectual. They were reduced to such extremities, that for three months they fed on human flesh, killing the old and feeble, as well as many prisoners, for food This being known to the Moguls, they made a general assault in January 1234 The attack continued from morning till night, but at last the assailants were repulsed. In this action, however, the Kin lost all their best officers, upon which the emperor resigned the crown to Cheng-lin a prince of the blood Next morning, while the ceremony of investing the new emperor was performing, the enemy mounted the south walls, which were defended only by two hundred men; and the south gate being at the same time abandoned, the whole army broke in. They were opposed, however, by Hu-sye-hu, who, with a thousand soldiers, continued to fight with amazing intrepidity. In the mean time Shew-su, seeing every thing irreparably lost, lodged the seal of the empire in a house, and then causing sheaves of straw to be set round it, ordered it to be set on fire as soon as he was dead. After giving this order he hanged himself, and his commands were executed by his domestics. Hu-sye-hu, who still continued fighting with great bravery, no sooner heard of the tragical death of the emperor, than he drowned himself in the river Ju, as did also five hundred of his most resolute soldiers. The same day the new emperor, Cheng-lin, was slain in a tumult, and thus an end was put to the dominion of the Kin Tartars in China.

The empire of China was now to be shared between the Song, or southern Chinese, and the Moguls. It had been agreed upon, that the province of Ho-nan should be delivered up to the Song as soon as the war was finished. But they, without waiting for the expiration of the term, or giving Oktay notice of their proceedings, introduced their troops into Kay-fong-fou, Lo-yang, and other considerable cities. On this the Mogul general resolved to attack them, and crossing the Hoang-ho, cut in pieces part of the garrison of Lo-yang, while they were out in search of provisions. The garrison of Kay-fong-fou likewise abandoned that place; and the Song emperor degraded the officers who had been guilty of those irregularities, sending ambassadors to Oktay, at the same time, to desire a continuance of the peace. What Oktay's answer was we are not told; but the event showed that he was not satisfied; for in 1235 he ordered his second ſon prince Kotovan, and his general Chahav, to attack the Song in Se-chwen, while others marched towards the borders of Kyang-nan.

In 1236, the Moguls made great progreſs in the province of Hu-quang, where they took ſeveral cities, and put vaſt numbers to the ſword. This year they introduced paper or ſilk money, which had formerly been uſed by Ching-tſong, ſixth emperor of the Kin. Prince Kotovan forced the paſſages into the diſtrict of Hang-chong-fou in the province of Shen-ſi, which he entered with an army of five hundred thouſand men. Here a terrible battle was fought between the vaſt army of the Moguls and the Chineſe troops, who had been driven from the paſſages they defended. The latter conſiſted only of ten thouſand horſe and foot, who were almoſt entirely cut off, and the Moguls loſt ſuch a number of men, that the blood is ſaid to have run for two leagues together. After this victory the Moguls entered Se-chwen, which they almoſt entirely reduced, committing ſuch barbarities, that, in one city, forty thouſand people choſe rather to put an end to their own lives than ſubmit to ſuch cruel conquerors.

In 1237, the Moguls received a conſiderable check before the city of Gintong in Kyang-nan, the ſiege of which they were obliged to raiſe with loſs. In 1238 they beſieged Lu-chew, another city in the ſame province. They ſurrounded it with a rampart of earth and a double ditch, but the Chineſe general ordered their intrenchments to be filled with immenſe quantities of herbs ſteeped in oil, and then ſet on fire, while he ſhot ſtones upon them from a tower ſeven ſtories high. At the ſame time a vigorous ſally was made, and the Mogul army being thrown into the utmoſt diſorder, were obliged finally to abandon the ſiege, and retire northwards.

In 1239, theſe barbarians were oppoſed by a general called Meng-kong, with great ſucceſs, who, this and the following year, gained great honour by his exploits. While he lived, the Moguls were never able to make any considerable progress, but his death, in 12[illegible]6, proved of the greatest detriment to the Chinese affairs, and soon after the Tartars renewed the war with more vigour and success than ever. In 1255, they re-entered the province of Se-chuen, but still met with vigorous opposition in this quarter, because the Chinese took care to have Se-chuen furnished with good troops and generals. Though these were always beaten, being greatly inferior in number to their enemies, yet they generally retook the cities the Moguls had reduced, as the latter were commonly obliged to withdraw for want of provisions and forage. In 1259 they undertook the siege of Ho-chew, a strong city to the west of Pe-kin, defended by Vang-kyen, a very able officer, who commanded a numerous garrison. The siege continued from the month of February till August, during which time the Moguls lost an immense number of men. On the 10th of August they made a general assault in the night. They mounted the walls before the governor had intelligence, but were soon attacked by him with the utmost fury. The Mogul emperor Meng-ko, himself came to the scalade, but his presence was not sufficient to overcome the valour of Vang-kyen. At the same time the scaling-ladders of the Moguls were blown down by a storm, upon which a terrible slaughter ensued, and among the rest fell the emperor himself. Upon this disaster the Mogul generals agreed to raise the siege, and retire towards Shen-si.

On the death of Meng-ko, Hupilay, or Kublay Khan, who succeeded him, laid siege to Vu-chang-fou, a city not far distant from the capital of the Song empire.

At this the emperor being greatly alarmed, distributed immense sums among his troops, and, having raised a great army, marched to the relief of Vu-chang-fou.

Unfortunately the command of this army was committed to the care of Kya-tse tau, a man without either courage or experience in war. He was besides very vain and vindictive in his temper, often using the best officers ill, and entirely overlooking their merit, which caused many of them to go over to the Moguls. The siege of Vu-chang fou was commenced, and had continued a considerable time, when Kya-tse tau, afraid of its being lost, and at the same time not daring to take any effectual step for its relief, made proposals of peace. A treaty was accordingly concluded, by which Kya-tse-tau engaged for the emperor to pay an annual tribute of about fifty thousand pounds in silver and as much in silk, acknowledging likewise the sovereignty of the Moguls over the Song empire. In consequence of this treaty, the Moguls retreated after the boundaries of the two empires had been fixed, and repassed the Kyang, but one hundred and seventy of them having staid on the other side of the river, were put to death by Kya-tse-tau.

This minister totally concealed from the emperor his having made such a shameful treaty with the Moguls; and the hundred and seventy soldiers massacred by his order, gave occasion to report that the enemy had been defeated, so that the Song court believed that they had been compelled to retreat by the superior valour and wisdom of Kya-tse-tau. This proved the ruin of the empire, for, in 1260, the Mogul emperor sent an officer to the Chinese court to execute the treaty according to the terms agreed on with Kya-tse tau. The minister dreading the arrival of this envoy, imprisoned him near Nankin, and took all possible care that neither Hupilay, nor Li-tsong the Chinese emperor, should ever hear any thing of him.

It was impossible such unparalleled conduct could fail to produce a new war. Hupilay's courtiers accordingly pressed him to revenge himself on the Song for their treacherous behaviour, and he soon published a manifesto against them, which was followed by a renewal of hostilities in 1268. The Mogul army amounted to three hundred thousand men, but notwithstanding their numbers, little progress was made till the year 1271. Syan-yang and Fan-ching, cities in the province of Se-chew, had been besieged for a long time ineffectually, but this year an *Igur* lord advised Hupilay to send for several of those engineers out of the west, who knew how to cast stones of an hundred and fifty pounds weight out of their engines which made holes of seven or eight feet wide in the strongest walls. Two of these engineers were accordingly sent for, and after giving a specimen of their art before Hupilay, were sent to the army in 1272. In the beginning of 1273 they planted their engines against the city of Fan-ching, and presently made a breach in the walls. After a bloody conflict the suburbs were taken, and soon after the Moguls made themselves masters of the walls and gates of the city. Nevertheless, a Chinese officer, with only an hundred soldiers, resolved to fight from street to street. This he did for a long time with the greatest obstinacy, killing vast numbers of the Moguls, and both parties are said to have been so much overcome with thirst, that they drank human blood to quench it. The Chinese set fire to the houses, that the great beams falling down, might embarrass the way of their pursuers, but at last being quite wearied out, and filled with despair, they put an end to their own lives. After the taking of Fan-ching, all the materials which had served at the siege were transported to Syen-yang. The two engineers posted themselves against a wooden retrenchment raised on the ramparts. This they quickly demolished, and the besieged were so intimidated by the noise and havock made by the stones cast from these terrible engines, that they immediately surrendered.

In 1247, Pe-yen, an officer of great valour, and endowed with many other good qualities, was promoted to the command of the Mogul army. His firft exploits were the taking of two ftrong cities. after which he paffed the great river Ky-ang, defeated the Song army, and laid fiege to Vu-chang-fou This city was foon intimidated into a furrender, and Pe-yen, by reftraining the barbarity of his foldiers, whom he would not allow to injure any one, foon gained the hearts of the Chinefe fo much, that feveral cities furrendered to him on the firft fummons. In the mean time the treacherous Kya-tfe-tau, who was fent to oppofe Pe-yen, was not afhamed to propofe peace on the terms he had formerly concluded with Hupilay, but thefe being rejected, he was obliged at length to come to an engagement. In this he was defeated, and Pe-yen continued his conquefts with great rapidity Having taken the city of Nankin, and fome others, he marched towards Hang-chew-fou, the capital of the Song empire. Peace was now again propofed, but rejected by the Mogul general, and at laft the emprefs was conftrained to put herfelf, with her fon, then an infant, into the hands of Pe-yen, who immediately fent them to Hupilay

The fubmiffion of the emprefs did not yet put an end to the war. Many of the chief officers fwore to do their utmoft to refcue her from the hands of her enemies. In confequence of this refolution they diftributed their money among the foldiers, and foon got together an army of forty thoufand men. This army attacked the city where the young emperor Kong-tfong was lodged, but without fuccefs, after which, and feveral other vain attempts, they raifed one of his brothers to the throne, who then took upon him the name of TWON-TSONG. He was but nine years of age when he was raifed to the imperial dignity, and enjoyed it but a very fhort time. In 1277 he was in greater danger of perifhing, by reafon of the fhip on board which he then was being caft away. A great part of his troops periſhed at that time, and he ſoon after made offers of ſubmiſſion to Hupila. Theſe, however, were not accepted, for, in 1278, the unhappy Twon-tſong was obliged to retire into a little deſert iſland on the coaſt of Quan-tong, where he died in the eleventh year of his age.

Notwithſtanding the progreſs of the Moguls, vaſt territories ſtill remained to be ſubdued before they could become maſters of all the Chineſe empire. On the death of Twon-tſong, therefore, the mandarins raiſed to the throne his brother, named TE-PING, at that time but eight years of age. His army conſiſted of no fewer than two hundred thouſand men, but being utterly void of diſcipline, and entirely ignorant of the art of war, they were defeated by twenty thouſand Mogul troops. Nor was the fleet more ſucceſsful, for being put in confuſion by that of the Moguls, and the emperor in danger of falling into their hands, one of the officers taking him on his ſhoulders, jumped with him into the ſea, where they were both drowned. Moſt of the mandarins followed this example, as did alſo the miniſter, all the ladies and maids of honour, and multitudes of others, inſomuch that one hundred thouſand people are thought to have periſhed on that day. Thus ended the Chineſe race of emperors, and the Mogul dynaſty, known by the name of *Tuen*, commenced.

Though no race of men that ever exiſted were in general more remarkable for cruelty and barbarity than the Moguls, yet it doth not appear that the emperors of the Ywen dynaſty were in any reſpect worſe than their predeceſſors. On the contrary, HUPILAY, by the Chineſe called SHI-TSI, found the way of reconciling the people to his government, and even of endearing himſelf to them ſo much, that the reign of his family is to this day ſtyled by the Chineſe *the wiſe government*. This he accompliſhed by keeping as cloſe as poſſible to their ancient laws and cuſtoms, by his mild and juſt government, and by his regard for their learned men. He was indeed aſhamed of the ignorance and barbarity of his Mogul ſubjects, when compared with the Chineſe. The whole knowledge of the former was ſummed up in their ſkill in managing their arms and horſes, being perfectly deſtitute of every art or ſcience, or even of the knowledge of letters. In 1269, he had cauſed the Mogul characters to be contrived. In 1280, he cauſed ſome mathematicians to ſearch for the ſource of the river Hoang-ho, which at that time was unknown to the Chineſe themſelves. In four months time they arrived in the country where it riſes, and formed a map of it, which they preſented to his majeſty. The ſame year a treatiſe on aſtronomy was publiſhed by his order; and, in 1282, he ordered the learned men to repair from all parts of the empire to examine the ſtate of literature, and take meaſures for its advancement.

At his firſt acceſſion to the crown he fixed his reſidence at Tay-ywen-fou, the capital of Shen-ſi, but thought proper afterwards to remove it to Pe-kin. Here, being informed that the barks which brought to court the tribute of the ſouthern provinces, or carried on the trade of the empire, were obliged to come by ſea, and often ſuffered ſhipwreck, he cauſed that celebrated canal to be made, which is at preſent one of the wonders of the Chineſe empire, being three hundred leagues in length. By this canal above nine thouſand imperial barks tranſport with eaſe, and at ſmall expence, the tribute of grain, rice, ſilks, *&c.* which is annually paid to the court. In the third year of his reign Shi-tſu formed a deſign of reducing the iſlands of Japan, and the kingdoms of Tonquin and Cochin-china. Both theſe enterpriſes ended unfortunately, but the firſt remarkably ſo, for of one hundred thouſand perſons employed in it, only four or five eſcaped with the melancholy news of the deſtruction of the reſt, who all periſhed by ſhipwreck. Shi-tſu reigned fifteen years, died in the eightieth year of his age, and was ſucceeded by his grandſon. The throne continued in the Ywen family till the year 1367, when SHUN-TI, the last of that dynasty, was driven out by a Chinese named CHU During the above period the Tartars had become enervated by long prosperity, and the Chinese had been roused into valour by their subjection Shun-ti, the reigning prince, was quite sunk in sloth and debauchery, and the empire was oppressed by a tyrannic minister named Ama. In June 1355, Chu, a Chinese of mean extraction, and head of a small party, set out from How-chew, passed the Kyang, and took Tay-ping. He then associated himself with some other mal-contents, at the head of whom he reduced the town of Tu-chew, in Kyang-nan Soon after he made himself master of Nankin, having defeated the Moguls who came to its relief In December 1356, he was able to raise an hundred thousand men, at the head of whom he took the city of U-chew, in the east borders of Quang-si, and here, assembling his generals, it was resolved neither to commit slaughters nor to plunder The most formidable enemy he had to deal with was *Chen-yew-lyang*, styled "emperor of the Han This man being grieved at the progress made by Chu, equipped a fleet, and raised a formidable army, in order to reduce Nan-chang-fou, a city of Kyang-si, which his antagonist had made himself master of The governor, however, found means to inform Chu of his danger, upon which that chief caused a fleet to be fitted out at Nankin, in which he embarked two hundred thousand soldiers As soon as Chen-yew-ylang was informed of his enemy's approach, he raised the siege of Nan-chang-fou, and gave orders for attacking Chu's naval force An engagement ensued between a part of the fleets, in which Chu proved victorious, and next day, all the squadrons having joined in order to come to a general engagement, Chu gained a second victory, and burnt an hundred of the enemy's vessels A third and fourth engagement happened, in which Chu was victorious, and in the last, Chen-yew-lyang himself was killed, his ſon taken priſoner, and his generals obliged to ſurrender themſelves, with all their forces and veſſels.

In January 1364, Chu's generals propoſed to have him proclaimed emperor, but this he declined, and at firſt contented himſelf with the title of king of *U*. In February he made himſelf maſter of Vu-chang-fou, capital of Hu-quang, where with his uſual humanity, he relieved thoſe in diſtreſs, encouraged the literati, and would allow his troops neither to plunder nor deſtroy This wiſe conduct procured him an eaſy conqueſt both of Kyang-ſi and Hu-quang. The Chineſe ſubmitted to him in crowds, and profeſſed the greateſt veneration and reſpect for his perſon and government.

All this time Shun-ti, with an unaccountable negligence, never thought of exerting himſelf againſt Chu, but continued to employ his forces againſt the rebels who had taken up arms in various parts of the empire, ſo that Chu found himſelf in a condition to aſſume the title of emperor. This he choſe to do at Nankin on the firſt day of the year 1368 After this his troops entered the province of Ho-nan, which they preſently reduced. In the third month, Chu, who had now taken the title of *Hong-vou*, or *Tay-tſu*, reduced the fortreſs of Tong-quan, after which his troops entered Pe-cheli from Ho-nan on the one ſide, and Shan-tong on the other. Here his generals defeated and killed one of Shun-ti's officers, after which they took the city of Tong-chew, and then prepared to attack the capital, from which they were now but twelve miles diſtant On their approach the emperor fled with all his family beyond the great wall, and thus put an end to the dynaſty of Ywen In 1370 he died, and was ſucceeded by his ſon, whom the ſucceſſor of Hong-vou drove beyond the Kobi or Great Deſert, which ſeparates China from Tartary. They continued their incurſions, however, for many years; nor did they ceaſe their attempts till 1583, when vaſt numbers of them were cut in pieces by the Chineſe troops.

The twenty-first dynasty of Chinese emperors, founded in 1368 by Chu, continued till the year 1644, when they were again expelled by the Tartars. The last Chinese emperor was named Whay-tsong, and ascended the throne in 1628. He was a great lover of the sciences, and a favourer of the Christians, though much addicted to the superstitions of the Bonzes. He found himself engaged in a war with the Tartars, and a number of rebels in different provinces. That he might more effectually suppress the latter, he resolved to make peace with the former, and for that end sent one of his generals, named Ywen, into Tartary, at the head of an army, with full power to negociate a peace, but that traitor made one [illegible] on such shameful terms, that the emperor refused to ratify it. Ywen, in order to oblige his master to comply with the terms made by himself, poisoned his best and most faithful general, named Mau-wen-long, and then desired the Tartars to march directly to Pe-kin, by a road different from that which he took with his army. This they accordingly did, and laid siege to the capital. Ywen was ordered to come to its relief, but, on his arrival, was put to the torture and strangled, of which the Tartars were no sooner informed, than they raised the siege, and returned to their own country. In 1636 the rebels above-mentioned composed four great armies, commanded by as many generals; which, however, were soon reduced to two, commanded by Li and Chang. These agreed to divide the empire between them; Chang taking the western provinces, and Li the eastern ones. The latter seized on part of Shen-si, and then of Ho-nan, whose capital, named Kay-fong-fou, he laid siege to, but was repulsed with loss. He renewed it six months after, but without success, the besieged choosing rather to feed on human flesh than surrender. The imperial forces coming [illegible] after to its assistance, the general made no doubt [illegible] being [illegible] to destroy the rebels at once, by breaking [illegible] the Yellow River, but unfortunately the rebels escaped to the mountains, while the city was quite overflowed, and three hundred thousand of the inhabitants perished.

After this disaster, Li marched into the provinces of Shen-si and Ho-nan, where he put to death all the mandarines, exacted great sums from the officers in place, and showed no favour to any but the populace, whom he freed from all taxes by this means he drew so many to his interest, that he thought himself strong enough to assume the title of emperor. He next advanced towards the capital, which, though well garrisoned, was divided into factions. Li had taken care to introduce before hand a number of his men in disguise, and by these the gates were opened to him the third day after his arrival. He entered the city in triumph at the head of three hundred thousand men; whilst the emperor kept himself shut up in his palace, busied only with his superstitions It was not long, however, before he found himself betrayed and, under the greatest consternation, made an effort to get out of the palace, attended by about six hundred of his guards. He was still more surprised to see himself treacherously abandoned by them, and deprived of all hopes of escaping the insults of his subjects Upon this, preferring death to falling alive into their hands, he immediately retired with his empress, whom he tenderly loved, and the princess her daughter, into a private part of the garden His grief was so great that he was not able to utter a word; but she soon understood his meaning, and, after a few silent embraces, hanged herself on a tree in a silken string. Her husband staid only to write these words on the border of his vest "I have been basely deserted by my subjects, do "what you will with me, but spare my people" He then cut off the young princess's head with one stroke of his scymitar, and hanged himself on another tree, in the seventeenth year of his reign, and thirty-sixth of his age His prime minister, queens, and eunuchs, followed his example;

and thus ended the Chinese monarchy, to give place to that of the Tartars, which hath continued ever since

It was some time before the body of the unfortunate monarch was found At last it was brought before the rebel Li, and by him treated with the utmost indignity; after which he caused two of Whey-tsong's sons, and all his ministers, to be beheaded, but his eldest son happily escaped by flight The whole empire submitted peaceably to the usurper, except prince U-san-ghey, who commanded the imperial forces in the province of Lyau-tong This brave prince, finding himself unable to cope with the usurper, invited the Tartars to his assistance, and Tsong-te, their king, immediately joined him with an army of eighty thousand men Upon this the usurper marched directly to Pe-kin, but not thinking himself safe there, plundered and burnt the palace, and then fled with the immense treasure he had got What became of him afterwards we are not told, but the young Tartar monarch was immediately declared emperor of China, his father Tsong-te having died almost as soon as he set his foot in that empire.

The new emperor, named SHUN-CHI, or XUN-CHI, began his reign with rewarding U-san-ghey, by conferring upon him the title of King, and assigned him the city of Si-gnan-fu, capital of Shen-si, for his residence This, however, did not hinder U-san-ghey from repenting of his error in calling in the Tartars, or, as he himself used to phrase it, "in sending for lions to drive away dogs" In 1674, he formed a very strong alliance against them, and had probably prevailed if his allies had been faithful; but they treacherously deserted him one after another. which so affected him, that he died soon after In 1681 Hong-wha, son to U-san-ghey, who continued his efforts against the Tartars, was reduced to such straits that he put an end to his own life.

During this ſpace, there had been ſome reſiſtance made to the Tartars in many of the provinces. Two princes of Chineſe extraction had at different times been proclaimed emperors, but both of them were overcome and put to death. In 1682, the whole fifteen provinces were ſo effectually ſubdued, that the emperor KANG-HI, ſucceſſor to Shun-chi, determined on a viſit to his native dominions of Tartary. He was accompanied by an army of ſeventy thouſand men, and continued for ſome months taking the diverſion of hunting. This he continued to do for ſome years, and in his journeys took father Verbeiſt along with him, by which means we have a better deſcription of theſe countries than could poſſibly have been otherwiſe obtained. This prince was a great encourager of learning and of the Chriſtian religion, in favour of which laſt he publiſhed a decree, dated in 1692. In 1716, however, he revived ſome obſolete laws againſt the Chriſtians, nor could the Jeſuits with all their art preſerve the footing they had got in China. The cauſes of this alteration in the emperor are, by the miſſionaries, ſaid to have been the ſlanders of the mandarins, but from the known character of the Jeſuits, it will readily be believed, that there were other cauſes for this conduct. This emperor died in 1722, and was ſucceeded by his ſon Yon-ching, who not only gave no encouragement to the miſſionaries, but perſecuted all Chriſtians of whatever denomination, not excepting even thoſe of the imperial race. At the beginning of his reign he baniſhed all the Jeſuits into the city of Canton, and in 1732 they were baniſhed from thence into Ma-kau, a little iſland inhabited by the Portugueſe, but ſubject to China.

He died in 1736, and was ſucceeded by the preſent emperor, from whom the Jeſuits flattered themſelves with meeting with different treatment, but we believe, they have not yet had their expectations realized, nor does it appear probable that they will.

Having thus ſketched the moſt material tranſactions recorded in the Chineſe Hiſtory, we ſhall proceed to deſcribe the preſent ſtate of the empire, its dependencies, and inhabitants, according to the beſt and lateſt accounts we are in poſſeſſion of.

GENERAL DESCRIPTION

OF THE

CHINESE EMPIRE.

IN attempting a general description of this vast empire, we shall pursue the following arrangement 1 CHINA PROPER—2. CHINESE TARTARY—3. THE STATES TRIBUTARY TO CHINA

CHINA PROPER.

ORIGIN OF ITS NAME.

The western Moguls call this kingdom CATAY—the Mantchew Tartars call it NICAN-COURANE,—the Japanese THAU, and the people of Cochin-china, and Siam CIN From this latter appellation it is most probable the name CHINA is derived, for according to the Chinese history, the first imperial family that carried their arms toward the west, assumed the name of *Tsin*, or *Tai sin* And the armament, sent by the Emperor Tsin-chi-hoang as far as Bengal, must have brought the people of India acquainted with the name of Tsin, whose formidable power had been so severely felt This name passing from India, perhaps to Persia, or Egypt, might lay the ground for *China* this is the opinion of Du Halde, and Grosier,

But according to Navarrete, the name has its origin in India, or Persia, from a species of silk called Chin, from whence it was brought to Europe by the Portuguese. The Chinese themselves, however, call it TCHONG-KOUE, or CHONG-QUE, that is the middle kingdom, for till their intercourse with Europeans had rectified their geography, they imagined that their country was situated in the centre of the earth, and that all other kingdoms lay scattered around it.

EXTENT, BOUNDARIES, &c.

China, properly so called, according to Grosier and Duhalde, comprehends from north to south eighteen degrees; its extent from east to west being somewhat less. The adjacent countries subjected to the Chinese government, such as the islands of Hainan and Formosa, Tartary, &c. are not included in this estimation; for, reckoning from the most southern point of the island of Hainan to the northern extremity of Tartary which is under the dominion of China, we shall find that the territories of this emperor are more than nine hundred leagues in extent from north to south, and about fifteen hundred from east to west, reckoning from the eastern sea as far as the country of *Casgar*, conquered by the Chinese in 1759. According to Guthrie, China is situated between 20° and 42° N. latitude, and 98° and 123° E. longitude. It is bounded on the north by Tartary, from which it is separated by a wall five hundred leagues in length, on the east by the sea, on the west by lofty mountains and desarts, and towards the south by the ocean, the kingdoms of Tong-king, Laos, and Cochin-china. It is divided into fifteen provinces, the northern are CHEN-SI, CHAN-SI and PE-TCHELI. CHAN-TONG, KIANG-NAN, TCHE-KIANG and FO-KIEN extend along the shore of the eastern sea. The provinces of QUANG-TONG, QUANG-SI, YUN-NAN and SE-TCHUEN terminate the empire on the south and north. HO-NAN, HOU-QUANG,

KOEI-TCHOU and KIANG-SI occupy the middle ſpace. Of each of theſe provinces we ſhall now proceed to give a general account.

PROVINCE OF PE-TCHELI.

Pe-tcheli, T-cheli, or Li-pa-fou, is the principal province of the whole empire, and its capital, Pe-king or Pekin, is become the ordinary reſidence of the imperial court It approaches the form of a right-angled triangle, and is bounded on the north by the great wall and part of Tartary, on the eaſt by the ſea, on the ſouth by the provinces of Chang-tong and Ho-nan, and towards the weſt by the mountains of Chan-ſi

This province contains nine counties, each of which has a city of the firſt claſs, which have ſeveral others under their juriſdiction, theſe are about forty in number, leſs conſiderable indeed, but all ſurrounded with walls and ditches, beſides numerous boroughs and villages without walls

PE-KIN.

Pe-kin is the capital of the empire, is ſituated in a very fertile plain, twenty leagues diſtant from the great wall, this name, which ſignifies the *Northern Court*, was given to diſtinguiſh it from another conſiderable city called Nan-king, or the *Southern Court* The emperor formerly reſided in the latter, till the Tartars, a reſtleſs and warlike people, obliged him to remove his court to the northern provinces, that he might more effectually repel the incurſions of thoſe barbarians

This capital forms an exact ſquare, and is divided into two cities, the firſt, where the emperor's palace is built, is called SIN-CHING, or the New City, and is inhabited chiefly by Tartars, and therefore called alſo the Tartar City The ſecond is called LAU-CHING, or the Old City, and inhabited chiefly by Chineſe. Theſe two cities, without including the ſuburbs, are eighteen miles in circumference, according to the most accurate measurement made by the express order of the emperor

The height and enormous thickness of the walls of the Tartar city excite admiration, twelve horsemen might easily ride abreast upon them, they have spacious towers raised at intervals, a bow-shot distant from one another, and large enough to contain bodies of reserve in case of necessity.

The city has nine gates, which are lofty and well arched, over them are large pavilion-roofed towers divided into nine stories, each having several apertures or port-holes, the lower story forms a hall for the use of the soldiers and officers who quit guard, and those appointed to relieve them Before each gate a space is left of more than three hundred and sixty feet, this is a kind of place of arms, enclosed by a semicircular wall equal in height and thickness to that surrounding the city The great road, which ends here, is commanded by a pavilion roofed tower like the first, in such a manner, that, as the cannon of the former can batter the houses of the city, those of the latter can sweep the adjacent country

The streets of Pe-kin are straight, about an hundred and twenty feet wide, a full league in length, and bordered with shops, but the houses being low make a mean appearance. An immense concourse of people continually fill the streets, and the confusion caused by the number of horses, camels, mules and carriages, which cross or meet each other is prodigious Besides this inconvenience passengers are every now and then stopped by crowds who stand listening to fortune-tellers, jugglers, ballad singers, and a thousand other mountebanks and buffoons, who read and relate stories calculated to promote mirth and laughter, or distribute medicines, the wonderful effects of which they explain with all the eloquence peculiar to them

People of diftinction oblige all their dependants to follow them A mandarin of the firft rank is always accompanied in his walks by his whole tribunal, and to augment his equipage, each of the inferior mandarins in his fuit is generally attended by feveral domeftics. The nobility of the court, and princes of the blood, never appear in public without being furrounded by a large body of cavalry, and as their prefence is required at the palace every day, their train alone is fufficient to create confufion in the city. In all this prodigious concourfe, no women are ever feen. hence we may judge how great the population of China muft be, fince the number of females in this country, as well as every where elfe, is fuperior to that of the other fex.

As there is a continual influx of the riches and merchandife of the whole empire into this city, the number of ftrangers that refort to it is immenfe, they are carried in chairs, or ride on horfeback always attended by a guide acquainted with the ftreets, and who knows the houfes of the nobility and principal people of the city They are alfo provided with a book containing an account of the different quarters, fquares, remarkable places, and of the refidence of thofe in public offices In fummer there are to be feen fmall temporary fhops where people are ferved with water cooled by means of ice, and every where eating-houfes, with refrefhments of tea and fruits are found. Each kind of provifion has a certain day and place appointed for its being expofed to fale.

The governor of Pe-kin, who is a Mantchew Tartar, is ftyled Governor of the Nine Gates, his jurifdiction extends not only over the foldiers, but alfo over the people in every thing that concerns the police No police can be more active It is rare, in a number of years, to hear of houfes being robbed, or people affaffinated; all the principal ftreets have guard-rooms, and foldiers patrole night and day, each having a ſabre hanging from his girdle, and a whip in his hand, to correct, without diſtinction, thoſe who excite quarrels or cauſe diſorder.

The lanes are guarded in the ſame manner, and have latticed gates which do not prevent thoſe from being ſeen who walk in them; they are always kept ſhut during the night, and ſeldom opened even to thoſe who are known if they are, the perſon to whom this indulgence is granted muſt carry a lanthorn, and give a ſufficient reaſon for his going out

In the evening, as ſoon as the ſoldiers are warned to their quarters by beat of drum, two ſentinels go and come from one guard-room to another, making a continual noiſe with a kind of caſtanet, to ſhew that they are not aſleep They permit no one to walk abroad in the night time They even examine thoſe whom the emperor diſpatches on buſineſs, and if their reply gives the leaſt cauſe of ſuſpicion, they have a right to convey them to the guard-room The ſoldiers in each of the guard-rooms are obliged to anſwer every time the ſentinels on duty call out

It is by theſe regulations, obſerved with the greateſt ſtrictneſs, that peace, ſilence, and ſafety reign throughout the whole city The governor is alſo obliged to go the round, and the officers ſtationed on the walls and in the towers over the gates, in which are kept large kettle-drums, that are beat every time the guard is relieved, are continually diſpatching ſubalterns to examine the quarters belonging to the gates where they are poſted The leaſt neglect is puniſhed next morning, and the officer who was on guard is cashiered This police, which prevents nocturnal aſſemblies, would appear no doubt extraordinary in Europe, and, in all probability, would not be much reliſhed by our young men of fortune and ladies of quality But the Chineſe think juſtly, they conſider it to be the duty of the magiſtrates of a city, to prefer good order and public tranquility, to vain amuſements, which generally occasion many attempts against the lives and property of the citizens. It is true, the support of this police costs the emperor a great deal; part of the soldiers we have mentioned being maintained for this purpose only They are all infantry, and their pay is generally very high, their employment consists not only in watching for those who may occasion disturbance in the day time, or walk abroad during the night, they must also take care that the streets are kept clean and swept every day, that they are watered morning and evening in time of dry weather, and that every nuisance is removed, they have orders also to assist in this labour themselves, and to clear the kennels, that the water may have a free course.

The emperor's palace stands in the middle of the Tartar city. It presents a prodigious assemblage of vast buildings, extensive courts and magnificent gardens, and is shut up on all sides by a double wall, the intervening space being occupied by houses belonging to the officers of the court, eunuchs, and different tribunals. To some of these is assigned the care of providing necessaries for the use of the emperor, others are for determining disputes, and punishing faults committed by the domestics of the imperial family. The exterior circumference of this immense palace is reckoned at about seven English miles

The imperial palace of Pe-kin does not fail to strike beholders by its extent, grandeur, and the regular disposition of its apartments, and by the singular structure of its pavilion-roofs, ornamented at each corner with a carved plat-band, the lower extremity of which is turned upwards, these roofs are covered with varnished tiles of so beautiful a yellow colour, that, at a distance, they make as splendid an appearance as if they were gilded. Below the upper roof, there is another of equal brilliancy, which hangs sloping from the wall, supported by a great number of beams, daubed over with green varnish, and interspersed with gilt figures. This second roof, with the projection of the first, forms a kind of crown to the whole edifice, and gives it a good effect

The palace is a small distance from the south gate of the Tartar city, the entrance to it is through a spacious court, to which there is a descent by a marble staircase, ornamented with two large copper lions, and a balustrade of white marble This balustrade runs in the form of a horse-shoe, along the banks of a rivulet, that winds across the palace with a serpentine course, the bridges over which are of marble. At the bottom of this first court arises a façade with three doors that in the middle is for the emperor only, the mandarins and nobles pass through those on each side These doors conduct to a second court, which is the largest of the palace, it is about three hundred feet in length, and fifty in breadth, an immense gallery runs round it, containing the rich effects, which belong to the emperor as his private property, for the public treasure is entrusted to a sovereign tribunal, called *Hou-pou*

The royal hall, called Tai-hotien, or the *Hall of the Grand Union*, is in this second court, it is built upon a terrace about eighteen feet in height, incrusted with white marble, and ornamented with balustrades of excellent workmanship Before this hall all the mandarins range themselves, when they go, on certain days, to renew their homage, and perform those ceremonies that are appointed by the laws of the empire

This hall is almost square, and about one hundred and thirty feet in length The ceiling is carved, varnished green, and loaded with gilt dragons The pillars which support the roof within, are six feet in circumference towards the base and are coated with a kind of mastich varnished red, the floor is partly covered with coarse carpets, after the Turkish manner, but the walls have no kind of ornament, neither tapestry, lustres, nor paintings.

The throne, which is in the middle of the hall, consists of a pretty high alcove, exceedingly neat It has no inscription but the character *Ching*, a word answering to the English words *holy*, *excellent*, *perfect*, *most wise*. Upon the platform opposite to this hall, stand large vessels of bronze, in which incense is burnt when any ceremony is performing There are also chandeliers shaped like birds and painted different colours, as well as the wax-candles that are lighted up in them.

This platform is extended towards the north, and has on it two lesser halls, one of them is a rotunda that glitters with varnish, and is lighted by a number of windows. Here the emperor changes his dress before or after any ceremony. The other is a saloon, the door of which opens to the north, through this door the emperor must pass, when he goes from his apartment, to receive on his throne the homage of the nobility, he is then carried in a chair, by officers dressed in long red robes bordered with silk, and caps ornamented with plumes of feathers It is perhaps impossible to give an exact description of the interior apartments which properly form the palace of the emperor, and are set apart for the use of his family, as few are permitted to enter them but women and eunuchs.

PAO-TING-FOU

Pao-ting-fou is the most considerable city in the province next to Pe-kin, and here it is the viceroy resides. It has twenty others under its jurisdiction, three of the second and seventeen of the third class In the midst of the city is a beautiful small lake, famous for the great quantities of water lilies produced there, and called by the Chinese Lyen-wha. This flower, so little esteemed in Europe, is a favourite of the Chinese, and, owing either to the climate or the care they take of it, generally blows there double The country around is pleasant, and inferior in fertility to no part of China. It is necessary to paſs this city in going from Pe-kin to the province of Chan-ſi

HOKIEN-FOU

Ho-kien-fou is the next in order; it has two cities of the ſecond, and fifteen of the third claſs in its diſtrict, and is remarkable for nothing but the neatneſs of its ſtreets and its ſituation between two rivers, from whence it derives its name.

ICHIN-TING-FOU.

Ichin-ting-fou is a large city about four miles in circumference. its figure an oblong ſquare. Its juriſdiction is very extenſive, comprehending thirty-two cities, five of which are of the ſecond, and twenty ſeven of the third claſs Northward from it lie ſeveral mountains, where, the Chineſe ſay, many ſimples and curious plants are to be found. On theſe mountains there are alſo ſeveral monuments or temples erected in honour of deceaſed heroes, among which is one conſecrated to the memory of the firſt emperor of the dynaſty of Han.

CHUN-TE-FOU.

Chun-te-fou has but a ſmall diſtrict, for there are only nine cities of the third claſs under its juriſdiction; but all very populous The adjacent country is pleaſant and fertile, owing to the number of rivers and lakes that water and refreſh it. Its fiſh are various, and its craw-fiſh are celebrated, it produces a fine delicate kind of ſand, uſed in the manufacture of an inferior kind of China-ware, and in poliſhing precious ſtones. It abounds alſo with touch-ſtones for gold, reckoned the beſt in the empire.

QUANG-PING-FOU.

Quang-ping-fou is ſituated in the northern part of Pe-tcheli, between the provinces of Chang-tong and Honan, and has nine cities of the third claſs dependent on it; all its plains are well watered by rivers. Among its temples, there is one dedicated to thoſe men, who, as the Chinese pretend, discovered the secret of rendering themselves immortal The country is agreeable around it, and its waters are well stored with fish.

TAI-MING-FOU.

Tai-ming-fou has one city of the second class and eighteen of the third, in its district. It presents nothing remarkable. It lies near to Quang-ping-fou, and the country around it is peculiarly fruitful and agreeable.

YUNG-PING-FOU.

Yung-ping-fou is very advantageously situated in the neighbourhood of the sea. The surrounding mountains produce abundance of tin. But its soil is not very fertile. Here is a paper manufactory, and not far from the city is a fortress named Chan-hai, which may be called the key of the province of Leao-tong. This fortress is near the great wall. Yung-ping fou reckons in its district only one city of the second, and five of the third class.

FUEN-HOA-FOU.

Fuen-hoa-fou is a city celebrated for its extent and the number of its inhabitants, as well as for the beauty of its streets and triumphal arches. It is situated near the great wall, amidst mountains, and has under its jurisdiction, besides two cities of the second, and eight of the third class, a great number of fortresses, which bar the entrance of China against the Tartars.

It would be unnecessary if not tiresome to the reader to enter into a description of the cities of the second class, but there is one which though without any jurisdiction over others, is beyond comparison more populous and rich, and has a greater trade than any of those we have mentioned, It is seated on the spot where the Royal Canal which comes from Lin-tsin-chew, joins the river of Pe-kin, and is called Tyen-sing-wey Here the great mandarin resides, on whom the officers who superintend the salt made along the coasts of Pe-tcheli and Chang-ton depend, and at this port all the ships which fetch timber from Eastern Tartary unload

Pe-tcheli has few mountains Its soil is sandy, and produces very little rice when compared with the southern provinces, owing to its small number of canals, but all other kinds of grain abound, as well as the greater part of the fruit-trees we have in Europe Cattle are also in great plenty, and the rivers are full of fish It pays an annual tribute to the emperor, which, according to Father Martini, consists of six hundred and one thousand one hundred and fifty three bags of rice, wheat, and millet, two hundred and twenty four pounds of linseed, forty five thousand one hundred and thirty five pounds of spun silk, thirteen thousand seven hundred and forty eight pounds of cotton, eight million seven hundred and thirty seven thousand two hundred and forty eight trusses of straw for the horses belonging to the court, and one hundred and eighty thousand eight hundred and seventy measures of salt, each containing one hundred and twenty four pounds This tribute is proportionally much inferior to that paid by other provinces

The face of the country here being flat and level, permits the use of a kind of carriage, the construction of which appears to be rather singular Father Martini, one of the first missionaries in China, thus describes it. "They use," in the province of Pe-tcheli, "a kind of "chariot with one wheel, and constructed in such a manner, that there is room in the middle for only one person, who sits as if on horseback, the driver pushes behind, and by means of wooden levers, makes the chariot advance with safety and expedition This has perhaps given rise to the report of chariots driven in that

" country by the wind, which the Chineſe direct over " land with ſails, as they do ſhips at ſea " A French miſſionary, who traverſed this province in 1768, ſeems to have made uſe of the ſame kind of carriage. " We " quitted the canal," ſays he, " to travel in carts, which is " cuſtomary in this part of China, but it is diſagreeable " beyond deſcription The cart is amazingly clumſy, and " has a great reſemblance to the carriage of a gun, there " is room in it for only one perſon, who is frequently " obliged to ſit croſs-legged, as our taylors do in Europe, " it jolts prodigiouſly, and, while the traveller is expoſed " to the ſcorching rays of the ſun, ſuch clouds of duſt " ſometimes ariſe as almoſt ſuffocate him "

Among the animals of this country, the moſt remarkable are yellow rats, they are much larger than thoſe ſeen in Europe, and their ſkins are highly valued by the Chineſe Chryſtal, marble, and porphyry are dug from the mountains of Pe-tcheli

The temperature of the air of this province does not ſeem to agree with its latitude Although Pe-tcheli extends no farther than to the forty ſecond degree of north latitude, yet all the rivers there are ſo much frozen during four months in the year, that horſes and waggons with the heavieſt loads, may ſafely paſs them, and it is remarkable that the whole body of ice is formed in one day, though ſeveral are neceſſary to thaw only the ſurface What may appear no leſs extraordinary is, that during theſe ſevere froſts, that ſharp and pinching cold which accompanies the production of ice in Europe, is not felt in this province Theſe phenomena cannot be accounted for, but by attributing them to the great quantity of nitre which is found diſperſed throughout this province, and to the ſerenity of the ſky, which, even during winter, is ſeldom obſcured by a cloud. This phyſical explanation appears to be confirmed by experiments made by Father

Amiot at Pe-kin *, which convinced him, that in this capital and neighbourhood, as far as seven or eight leagues around, the water, air and earth equally abound with nitre.

With regard to the water, the facility with which it freezes, the solidity of the ice and its duration, evidently announce the presence of nitre. " A tub filled with water, placed " near one of Reaumur's thermometers, had its surface immediately frozen, when the mercury stood only one " degree above the freezing point, and when it stood " three degrees below freezing, the water became a solid " mass of ice, if the diameter of the vessel did not exceed " a foot and a half, and the depth of the water four or " five inches. This water, when the weather was fine, " continued in the same state of congelation, as long as " the mercury in the thermometer did not rise higher " than three degrees above (o), when the mercury rose " higher, it then began to dissolve, but so slowly, that " two or three days were scarcely sufficient to restore it " to its former fluidity " To this experiment, Father Amiot adds another, made in the summer of the year 1777, which appears to have been attended to with the greatest possible accuracy It may be proper to observe, before we relate it, that during the year 1777, there was a longer continuance of hot weather than is generally observed at Pe kin In the course of the months of June and July, the thermometer continually rose from the twenty sixth to the thirty second and thirty third degrees above *Zero*, on the 23d of July, at three in the afternoon, the thermometer rose to thirty four degrees, and remained at that height until half past four on the 24th of the same month, it rose, about three o'clock, to thirty three degrees, half an hour after, the sky became over-cast, and a strong wind arose, accompanied with thick clouds of

* The latitude of Pe-kin is 39° 52′ 55″.

duſt, which continued half an hour, during this time, the thermometer began to fall, at four the wind ceaſed, and ſome rain fell, the thermometer then ſtood at thirty three degrees, the 25th and 26th of July it roſe to twenty nine degrees, and the 28th to thirty three degrees, owing to a northerly wind

On the 29th of July, Father Amiot put into a ſmall net, made of ſtrong pack-thread, a block of ice of an irregular figure, and ſuſpended it from a balance placed in the open air and expoſed to the wind and rays of the ſun.

At ſix in the morning, a thermometer, expoſed to the north, being at 26½ degrees, the ice was weighed, its weight was found to be fifty pounds

At 7	the therm.	27°¼	weight of the ice	46 lb.
At 8	- - -	27¾	- - - - -	40
At 9	- - -	30	- - - - -	32
At 10	- - -	31½	- - - - -	25

It is to be obſerved, that during this time, the wind was north, and ſtronger than it had been for ſome time before.

At 11	the therm.	32°	weight of the ice	19 lb.
At 12	- - -	33	- - - - -	15
At 1	- - -	33¼	- - - - -	10
At 2	- - -	33¼	- - - - -	7
At 3	- - -	33¼	- - - - -	5
At 4	- - -	33	- - - - -	3
At 5	- - -	33¾	- - - - -	1½

It muſt be obſerved, that during the laſt four hours, the ice had been in the ſhade.

At 6 the therm. ſtood at 32½ the weight of the ice 1lb. 4oz

At 7 the ice was not weighed.

At 8 ſome of it ſtill remained.

At 9 there remained only a bit of the ſize of a nut, fifteen hours were therefore neceſſary to diſſolve this piece of ice, weighing fifty pounds, even when exposed to the wind and scorching rays of the sun

It is to be further observed, that this ice had already been three or four days from the ice-house, for Father Amiot relates, that he purchased it from one of those people who are employed by the emperor to give fresh water, gratis, to all who ask for it Ice, when first taken from the ice-house, dissolves with difficulty, it is transported to Pe-kin, and from one place to another, during the greatest heats of summer, in open wheel-barrows, with as little precaution as if it were brick or flint, yet it leaves no other traces along the road behind it, but a few drops that fall here and there From these observations it appears evidently, that the reason why this ice is so long in dissolving is, because of its impregnation with nitrous particles, which preserve it a long while in its state of congelation

Father Amiot also tells us, that every kind of water at Pe-kin, whether taken from springs or rivers, has a very singular quality, it leaves a kind of tartar in those vessels in which it has been kept and in those in which it has been boiled. The Chinese call this kind of tartar *kien*, it is white when produced by water which has not been subjected to the action of fire, and yellowish when it is left by that which has been boiled This *kien* has neither smell nor taste, nor is it good for any thing. "The first opportunity I had of being acquainted with it," says Father Amiot, "was by accident I caused a small porcelain vessel to be filled every evening with fresh spring-water; this vessel had a cover, which I always shut very carefully, to prevent insects and dirt from getting into my water After some months, I perceived that there was formed in the bottom and sides of the vessel, a crust, of the thickness of a leaf of paper, which adhered so closely, that it was necessary to make use of the point of "a knife to detach it. Upon this occasion, being desirous of giving a lesson of cleanliness to my servant, he told me, that what I saw had nothing in it to occasion disgust, that it was what was generally left by the water of the country, and that I should be much more surprised, if I should see how this *kien* incrusted the insides of sauce-pans, and other kitchen utensils, in which water had been boiled. I immediately ordered some to be brought, and was convinced, by my own eyes, that my Chinese had told me truth. A yellow crust, about four or five tenths of an inch in thickness, covered the whole inside of the vessel, in the same manner as tartar covers the inside of an old cask. I detached some of it, which I applied to my nose and mouth, and examined with the greatest care, but I found nothing in it which enabled me to define it. May it not have been a depraved salt (*infatuatum*) or dead nitre, which might have been revived by means of air or fire? I am no chemist, I express myself as I can, on a subject which I do not understand."

If the waters of the province of Pe-tcheli contain much nitre, it is no less certain, that the air there is abundantly impregnated with it. The Abbé Grosier adduces the following as indubitable proofs of it. "1st. Notwithstanding unwholesome food, such as the flesh of the greater part of domestic animals that have died of old age or disease, which the people of this province greedily devour, notwithstanding filth and all the inconveniences resulting from low, damp and confined lodgings, where all the individuals of the same family are, as it were, heaped one upon another, the plague never makes its appearance in Pe-tcheli, and the people are seldom attacked by any of those epidemical distempers which are so common in Europe. 2dly. Provisions of every kind may be kept at Pe-kin a long while, without being subject to corruption,

Raisins are eaten there fresh even in May, apples and pears till Midsummer, wild boars, stags, deer, roe-bucks, rabbits, hares, pheasants, ducks, geese, and all kinds of game brought from Tartary to Pe-kin after the commencement of winter, fish of every species, transported from the rivers of Leao-tong, will keep without the assistance of salt, in their state of congelation, for two or three months, although they are exposed every day in the markets, carried from the markets to private houses, and from private houses brought back to the markets, until they are all sold, which does not happen before the end of March It is certain, that these facts announce an antiseptic quality in the air, which must undoubtedly proceed from the great quantity of nitre contained in it"

The earth which forms the soil of Pe-tcheli abounds no less with nitre, whole fields may be seen in the neighbourhood of Pe-kin which are covered with it Every morning at sun-rise, the country in certain cantons, appears as white as if sprinkled by a gentle fall of snow. If a quantity of this substance be swept together, a great deal of *kien*, nitre, and salt may be extracted from it. The Chinese pretend, that this salt may be substituted for common salt, however this may be, it is certain, that, in the extremity of the province, towards Siuen-hoa-fou, poor people and the greater part of the peasants make use of no other Although the land of Pe-tcheli is replete with nitrous particles, it does not, however, form dry desarts, it is cultivated with care, and becomes fruitful by labour The earth is frozen in winter to the depth of two or three feet, and does not become soft before the end of March. This may sufficiently explain, why the frost kills plants in the neighbourhood of Pe-kin, which Linnæus raised in Sweden, although it is twenty degrees farther north than the capital of the Chinese empire.

PROVINCE OF KIANG-NAN.

KIANG-NAN is the ſecond province of the empire, and is undoubtedly one of the moſt fertile, commercial, and conſequently one of the richeſt in China. It is bounded on the weſt by the provinces of Ho-nan and Hou-quang; on the ſouth by Tche-kiang and Kiang-ſi, and on the eaſt by the gulph of Nan-kin, the reſt borders on the province of Chan-tong

The emperors long kept their court in this province; but reaſons of ſtate having obliged them to move nearer to Tartary, they made choice of Pe-kin for the place of their reſidence. The province is of vaſt extent, it contains fourteen cities of the firſt claſs, and ninety-three of the ſecond and third. Theſe cities are very populous, and there is ſcarcely one of them which may not be called a place of trade Large barks can go to them from all parts, for the whole country is interſected by lakes, rivers and canals, which have a communication with the great river Yang-tſe-kiang, which runs through the middle of the province Silk-ſtuffs, lacquer-ware, ink, paper, and, in general, every thing that comes from Nan-kin, as well as from the other cities of this province, are much more eſteemed, and fetch a higher price than thoſe brought from the neighbouring provinces, In the town Chang-hai alone, and the villages dependent on it, there are reckoned to be more than two hundred thouſand weavers of calicoes and other common cotton cloths The manufacturing of theſe cloths gives employment to the greater part of the women.

In ſeveral places on the ſea coaſt there are found many ſalt-pits, the ſalt of which is diſtributed all over the empire, a great quantity of marble is alſo found here. In ſhort, this province is ſo abundant and opulent, that it brings every year into the emperor's treaſury, about thirty-two million taels*, exclusive of the duties upon every thing exported or imported, for the receiving of which several offices are established.

The inhabitants of this province are civil and ingenious, and acquire the sciences with great facility; hence many of them become eminent in literature, and rise to offices of importance by their abilities alone.

This province is divided into two parts, each of which has a distinct governor. The governor of the eastern part resides at Sou-tcheou-fou, and the governor of the western at Ngan-king-fou. Each of these governors has under his jurisdiction [illegible] *fou*, or cities of the first class.

NAN-KIN.

Kiang-ning-fou, or Nan-kin, is the capital of this province, and, by the ancient Chinese, it is said to have been one of the most beautiful and flourishing cities in the world. When they speak of its extent, they say, if two horsemen should go out by the same gate in the morning, and ride round it on full speed, taking different directions, they would not meet before the evening. This account is evidently exaggerated; but it is certain, that Nan-kin surpasses in extent all the other cities of China. Its walls are [illegible] fifteen leagues and a half in circumference. A French missionary, lately arrived from China, speaks of this celebrated city in the following manner: "We arrived at Nan-kin on the 2d of June. I was very desirous of seeing this city, which is reckoned the largest in the world. The suburbs through which we passed are very long, but not populous; the houses stand at some distance from each other, having reeds, pools of water, or plantations of bamboo between them. We took a view of the city from the fifth story of the porcelain tower, which commands an extensive prospect; but it did not appear to us,

* [illegible] an ounce of silver, which in China is worth [illegible]

" to be above two thirds as large as Paris. We could not " reconcile this with the accounts generally given of its " immense extent, but the next morning explained the mat- " ter. We had travelled a full league from Nan-kin, when " we perceived, on a sudden, the walls of a city rising amidst " mountains, and appearing as if cemented to the rocks. " These were the walls of Nan-kin, which, leaving the " city where it now stands, have, as it were, retired thither, " and inclose a space of fifteen or sixteen leagues, twelve or " thirteen of which are not inhabited."

Nan-kin is situated at the distance of a league from the river Yang-tse-kiang, from whence barks come up to it by means of canals; it is of an irregular figure, the mountains which are within its circumference having prevented its being built on a regular plan. It was formerly the imperial city, and for this reason, it was called Nan-kin, which signifies *The Southern Court*; but since the six grand tribunals have been transferred from hence to Pe-kin, it is called Kiang-ning-fou in all the public acts.

This city has lost much of its ancient splendour; it had formerly a magnificent palace, no vestige of which is now to be seen. Its observatory is neglected, and almost destroyed; of its temples, tombs of the emperors, and other superb monuments, nothing remains but the remembrance, being all demolished by the Tartars, who first invaded the empire. A third of the city is deserted, but the rest is well inhabited. Some quarters of it are extremely populous and full of business. The streets are not so broad as those of Pe-kin; they are, however, very beautiful and well paved, and abound with shops richly furnished.

In this city resides one of those great mandarins called Tsong-tou, who takes cognizance of all important affairs, on appeal from the tribunals of both the governments of the province, and also from those of the province of Kiang-si. The Tartars have a numerous garrison here, commanded by a general of their own nation, and they occupy a quarter of the city, separated from the rest by a single wall

The palaces of the mandarins here are neither so large, nor so well built as those in the capital cities of other provinces. Nor are there here any public edifices corresponding to the reputation of so celebrated a city, excepting its gates, which are beautiful, and some idol temples, among which is the famous porcelain tower. It is of an octagonal figure, each side being fifteen feet in front, it it is two hundred feet high, and divided into nine stories by single floors within, and without by cornices at the rise of the arches and small projections covered with green-varnished tiles There is an ascent of forty steps to the first story, and between each of the others there are twenty-one The tower is the tallest and most beautiful of all those to be seen in China.

The breadth and depth of the river Yang-tse-kiang formerly rendered the port of Nan-kin very commodious; but at present large barks, or rather Chinese junks, never enter it, whether it be, that it is shut up by sand-banks, or that the Chinese, out of policy, forego the use of it, in order that navigators may insensibly lose all knowledge of it.

In the months of April and May a great number of excellent fish are caught in this river, near the city, which are sent to the emperor's court, they are covered with ice, and transported in that manner by barks kept entirely on purpose. And though Nan-kin is more than two hundred leagues from Pe-kin, these boats make such expedition, that they arrive there in eight or ten days. All the way there are stages where the men are relieved, during the fishing season Nan-kin, though the capital of the province, has under its particular jurisdiction only eight cities of the third class.

SOU-TCHEOU.

Sou-tcheou is the second city in this province, it is one of the most agreeable in China, and by those Europeans who have seen it, has been compared to Venice, with this difference, that the latter is built as it were in the sea, and Sou-tcheou is intersected by canals of fresh water, so that you may pass through the streets by water as well as by land. The branches of the river and canals are almost all capable of bearing the largest barks, which, according to Du Halde, may sail through the city to the ocean in two days From this city a trade is carried on, not only with all the provinces of the empire, but with Japan.

There is not, perhaps, in the universe, a country more delightful, either from the pleasantness of its situation, or the mildness of its climate, the air is temperate, provisions plentiful, the soil fruitful and well improved, and the manners of the people gentle, so that the city is considered as a place of pleasure, and the paradise of China. *Above*, says the Chinese authors, *is the celestial paradise; but the paradise of this world is Sou-tcheou* The brocades and embroideries made here are in great request throughout the whole empire Its jurisdiction extends over only eight cities, one of which is of the second class, and the rest of the third, but all these cities are beautiful, and about two or three leagues in circumference each.

SONG-KIANG-FOU.

This city is built close to the water, the prodigious quantity of cotton cloth here made, is very fine, and with which it supplies, not only the empire, but also foreign countries, renders it very celebrated, and causes it to be much frequented. This city has only four others under its jurisdiction, but which for magnitude and commerce may compare with most in China.

TCHIN-TCHEOU-FOU.

Tchin-tcheou fou is situated near the canal through which all barks going from Sou-tcheou to Kiang must pass According to Du Halde, it is adorned with triumphant arches, and the sides of the canal leading to it are lined with hewn stone It is celebrated on account of its trade and waters, which are said to give to tea an agreeable and pleasant taste, it has dependant on it five cities of the third class, in some of which a particular kind of earthen-ware is made, which the Chinese highly value Pretending that tea prepared in these vessels acquires a superior quality, hence they prefer this plain earthen-ware to the most elegant porcelain.

TCHIN-KIANG-FOU.

Tchin kiang-fou is the key of the empire on the sea coast, here a numerous garrison is always kept, and though it is small, compared with some cities we have described, its situation, trade, and the beauty of its walls give it a pre-eminence over the others of this province, but its jurisdiction is very confined, for it has authority over only three cities of the third class.

It stands on the sides of the Ta-kiang, which is here a mile and a half over, and a little to the east of a canal cut as far as the river Six paces from the bank in the river stands a hill, called Kin-shan, or golden-hill, on the top of it is a tower several stories high, and its shores are beset with idol temples and houses of bonzes On the opposite side of the river stands *Qua-chew*, which, though simply denominated a place of trade, may yet rank with many cities.

HOAI-NGAN-FOU.

Hoai-ngan-fou is situated in a marsh, and enclosed by a triple wall: as the ground on which it stands is lower than the bed of the canal, and in many parts only supported by a bank of earth, the inhabitants live in continual danger of an inundation. The suburbs extend to the distance of a league on each side of the canal, and form at their extremity a kind of port on the river Hoang-ho. This place is very populous, and every thing in it announces an active and brisk trade. A mandarin who has the inspection of the canals and navigation, and who is one of those obliged to supply the court with necessary provisions, resides here; he has a number of officers under him who have here proper stations allotted to them. This city has eleven others under its jurisdiction, two of which are of the second, and nine of the third class.

YANG-TCHEOU.

This city enjoys a mild and temperate air, and the country around is pleasant and fertile. It is populous, and two leagues in circumference, built on the side of the royal canal, which extends from the Ta-kyang and runs northward to the Hoang-ho or Yellow River. As it is intersected by a number of canals, it has twenty-four stone bridges, each of which consists of several arches. There is always so great a crowd on the bridge which forms a communication with the eastern suburbs, that it has been found too narrow; and a ferry-boat has been established at a small distance, which is scarce sufficient for the confluence of passengers, although the breadth of the canal is only thirty paces.

The inhabitants of this city are accounted very voluptuous, and it is said that they carry on a traffic in women; they educate with great care a certain number of young girls, who are taught music, singing, drawing, and every branch of education ſuitable to their ſex, theſe are afterwards ſold at a high price to ſome of the principal nobility, who add them to the number of their concubines. The author quoted, when ſpeaking of Nan-kin, thus expreſſes himſelf of Yang-tcheou. "It is one of the "moſt beautiful and largeſt cities I ever beheld. The "farmers of the ſalt revenue have built here a pleaſure-"houſe for the emperor, which ſtrikes with more aſto-"niſhment, as nothing has been ſeen hitherto equivalent "to it; it is built after the model of Hai-tien, another "country-houſe, two leagues diſtant from Pe-kin, where "the emperor commonly reſides. The palace of Yang-"tcheou occupies more ground than a moderate city; it "is a collection of artificial mounts and rocks formed by art, "of valleys and canals, ſometimes broad and ſometimes "narrow, bordered in ſome places with cut ſtone, in others "with rocks ſcattered promiſcuouſly, a vaſt aſſemblage of "buildings, each different from another, of halls, courts "and galleries both open and encloſed, gardens, parterres, "caſcades, elegant bridges, pavilions, groves and triumphal "arches. Each piece, taken ſeparately, is neither beau-"tiful nor laid out with taſte, but the multiplicity of "objects is ſtriking, and makes the beholder at laſt ex-"claim, *This is the habitation of a powerful ruler!*"

NGAN-KING-FOU.

Ngan-king-fou is the capital of the weſtern part of the province; its ſituation is delightful. It is governed by a mandarin as a particular viceroy, who keeps a large garriſon in a fort built on the banks of the river Yang-tſe-kiang, and which commands the lake Poy-ang. The commerce and riches of this city render it very conſiderable, and every thing that goes from the ſouthern part of China to Nan-kin muſt paſs through it. The country belonging to it is level, pleaſant and fertile; but under its juriſdiction there are only ſix cities of the third claſs.

HOEI-TSHEOU.

This is the moſt ſouthern city of the province, and one of the richeſt of the empire, the people are economical and temperate, active and enterpriſing, and they boaſt of their tea, varniſh, ink, engravings, and earth for China ware, which are indeed the moſt eſteemed in China. It has ſix cities of the third claſs dependent on it, and the mountains which ſurround this canton contain gold, ſilver and copper mines.

NING-KOUE-FOU.

Ning-koue-fou is ſituated on a river that falls into the Yang-tſe-kyang has nothing remarkable but its manufactories of paper, which is made of a ſpecies of reed, of which there are ſeveral. It has under its juriſdiction ſix cities of the third claſs

TCHI-TCHEOU-FOU.

Tchi-tcheou-fou is ſurrounded by a hilly country, its principal reſource is in its ſituation on the river Yank-tſe-kiang, by which it can either furniſh or draw from the other provinces every neceſſary or luxury. It has ſix cities of the third claſs belonging to its diſtrict, but of no great note.

TAY-PING-FOU

Tay-ping-fou is alſo built upon the banks of the Yang-tſe-kiang, and its plains are watered by a number of navigable rivers, which almoſt incloſe it, and render it very opulent. Its juriſdiction extends over only three cities, of which Vou-hou-hien is the moſt conſiderable in point of opulence.

FONG-YANG-FOU.

This city is ſituated on a mountain near the Yellow river, and encloſes with its walls ſeveral fertile little hills. Its juriſdiction is very entenſive, being eighty leagues from eaſt to weſt, and ſixty from north to ſouth, comprehending eighteen cities, five of which are of the ſecond and thirteen of the third claſs, beſides a number of villages, or rather places of trade, ſettled on the river for the convenience of merchants and collecting of dues. As this was the birth-place of the emperor Hong-vou, chief of the preceding dynaſty, this prince formed a deſign of rendering it a magnificent city, in order to make it the ſeat of empire. After having expelled the weſtern Tartars, who had taken poſſeſſion of China eighty ſeven years, he transferred his court thither, and named the city Fong-yang, that is to ſay, *The place of the Eagle's Splendor*. His intention was to beautify and enlarge it, but the inequality of the ground, the ſcarcity of freſh water, and the vicinity of his father's tomb, made him change his deſign, and by the unanimous advice of his principal officers, this prince eſtabliſhed his court at Nan-kin. When he had formed this reſolution, a ſtop was put to the intended works, the imperial palace, which was to have been encloſed by a triple wall, the walls of the city, to which a circumference of nine leagues were aſſigned, the canals that were marked out and begun, all were abandoned, and nothing was finiſhed but three monuments, which ſtill remain, their extent and magnificence ſufficiently ſhew what this city would have been, had the emperor purſued his original deſign.

The firſt of theſe monuments is the tomb of the father of Hong-vou, to decorate which no expence was ſpared, nor any thing which filial affection could invent; it is called *Hoang-lin*, or the *Royal Tomb*. The ſecond is a tower built in the middle of the city, which is of an oblong form, an hundred feet high, and divided into four ſtories raiſed on a maſſive pile of brick work. The third is a magnificent temple erected to the idol Fo. At firſt it was only a little pagod, to which Hong-vou, at the age of ſeventeen, retired after having loſt his parents, and where he was admitted as an inferior domeſtic, but having ſoon become weary of this kind of life, he enliſted with the chief of a band of robbers who had revolted from the Tartars, where he soon gave proof of his valour and talents As he was bold and enterprising, the general whose esteem he had gained, made choice of him for his son-in-law, and soon after he was declared his successor by the unanimous voice of the troops. The new chief, seeing himself at the head of a large party, had the presumption to aspire to the throne, and having gained a numerous party to his interest, took his measures accordingly. The Tartars, informed of the progress of his arms, sent a numerous army into the field, but he surprised and attacked them with so much impetuosity, that they were obliged to fly, and, though they several times returned to the charge, they were still defeated, and at length, after a close pursuit, driven entirely out of China

Soon after he mounted the throne, he caused the superb temple which we have mentioned to be raised, out of gratitude to the bonzes, who had received him in his distress, and assigned them a revenue sufficient for the maintenance of three hundred persons, under a chief of their own sect, whom he constituted a mandarin, with power of governing them, independent of the officers of the city

This pagod, called Long-hing-oe, was supported as long as the preceding dynasty lasted, but that of the eastern Tartars, which has succeeded have suffered it to fall to ruins, at present there are to be seen here only about a score of priests, who are almost reduced to beggary.

LIN-TCHEOU-FOU.

Lin-tcheou-fou, is the last city of the first class, it has nothing to distinguish it from others, but the excellence of the grain and fruits with which it abounds. Its mountains are covered with excellent timber, and its jurisdiction comprehends eight cities, two of which are of the second, and six of the third class

ISLAND OF TSONG-MING.

The iſland of Tſong-ming belongs alſo to the province of Kiang-nan, from which it is ſeparated only by an arm of the ſea, about five or ſix leagues broad.

Formerly this country was a ſandy deſart, to which criminals were baniſhed. Thoſe who firſt landed on it began to till the earth, that they might not periſh with hunger; and ſome poor Chineſe families emigrating thither, divided the iſland among them; they afterwards invited others to ſettle, and gave them part of the land, on condition of an annual rent of the produce: ſo that in leſs than in ten years the iſland was peopled and cultivated. It now contains one city of the third rank, and ſeveral villages.

Some parts of it produce wheat, rice, barley, cotton, citrons and ſeveral other fruits; but its principal revenue ariſes from ſalt, which is made in ſuch abundance, that the iſland can ſupply moſt of the neighbouring countries. This ſalt is extracted from a kind of grey earth, which is found diſperſed by acres in different parts of the iſland, eſpecially in the north.

The method of making this ſalt, according to the accounts we have, is curious. "The earth is ſmoothed, and "raiſed in a ſloping form, that the water may not ſettle "upon it. When the ſun has dried its ſurface, it is "carried off, and laid in heaps, which are carefully beat "on every ſide; this earth is afterwards ſpread out on "large tables a little inclined, and a quantity of freſh "water is poured over it, which, as it runs off, carries "with it the ſaline particles into a large earthen veſſel, "into which it falls, drop by drop, from a ſmall canal "made on purpoſe. The earth, being thus freed from "its ſalt, is placed apart, and when dry is pulveriſed, "after which it is ſpread over the ſoil from which it was "taken; and at the end of ſome days it is found im-"pregnated, as before, with a great quantity of ſaline par-

" ticles which are a second time extracted in the same " manner."

" While the men are labouring in the field, the women " and children are employed in boiling the salt water, " they fill large iron basons with it, in which it thickens " and changes gradually into a very white salt, which " they keep continually stirring with an iron spatula, until " the aqueous part is entirely evaporated."

Other parts of the island yield the inhabitants two crops per annum, one of corn in the month of May, and the other of rice and cotton in September.

The air in this part is healthful and temperate, the country delightful, and intersected by a great number of canals, which are carefully kept in repair.

There are a great number of mandarins in this country, but the governor is one of those who are called *literati*, he administers justice, receives the tribute paid to the emperor, gives passports to ships, and passes sentence of death on criminals. When the people have occasion for rain, or fine weather, he proclaims a general fast, butchers and inn-keepers are then forbid to sell any thing under the severest penalties, they however in general take care to get rid of their provisions, by privately bribing the officers of the tribunal, whose business it is to enforce the observance of this order. The mandarin afterwards walks in procession, accompanied by his subalterns, to the temple of the idol whom they intend to invoke, he kindles on the altar two or three small aromatic twigs, which being done they then all sit down and pass the time in drinking tea, smoking and conversation, for an hour or two, after which they retire.

Father Jacquemin relates, that in his time the viceroy of one of the provinces, becoming impatient because rain had not been granted to his repeated requests, sent an inferior mandarin to tell the idol from him, that if it did not [illegible] a certain day, he would drive him from the city, and cause his temple to be rased. No rain having fallen before the day mentioned, the viceroy, in a great passion, forbade the people to carry, according to custom, their offerings to the idol, and ordered the temple to be shut and the gates sealed up, which was immediately executed.

This island extends from south-east to north-west, and is about twenty leagues in length, and five or six in breadth.

PROVINCE OF KIANG-SI.

This province is bounded on the north by that of Kiang-nan, on the west by Hou-quang, on the south by Quang-tong, and on the east by Fo-kien and Tche-kiang. The country is extremely fertile, but it is so populous, that it can scarcely supply the wants of its inhabitants: on this account, they are very economical and sordid, which exposes them to the sarcasms and raillery of the Chinese of the other provinces; however, they have the character of being a people of great solidity and acuteness, and have the *talent of rising rapidly to the dignities of the state.*

The mountains of this province are covered with simples, and contain in their bowels mines of gold, silver, lead, iron and tin; the rice it produces is exceedingly fine, and the wine made here is, by the Chinese reckoned among the best in the country. The porcelain made here is also the finest and most valuable of any in the empire.

The river Kan-kiang divides this province, which contains thirteen cities of the first class, and seventy-eight of the second and third.

NAN-TCHANG-FOU.

This city is the capital of the province, has no trade but that of porcelain, which is made in the neighbourhood of Jao-tcheou, and exceeding good. It is the residence of a viceroy, and comprehends in its district eight cities, ſeven of which are of the third claſs, and only one of the ſecond. So much of the country around is cultivated, that the paſtures left are ſcarcely ſufficient for the flocks.

JAO-TCHEOU-FOU

Jao-tcheou-fou is ſituated on the northern bank of the river Po, which diſcharges itſelf at a ſmall diſtance into the lake Po-yang It commands ſeven other cities of the third claſs, and is particularly famous on account of the beautiful porcelain made in a village belonging to its diſtrict, called King-te-tching, in which are collected the beſt workmen in porcelain, this village is as populous as the largeſt cities of China It is reckoned to contain a million of inhabitants, who conſume every day more than ten thouſand loads of rice It extends a league and a half along the banks of a beautiful river, and is not, like many others, a collection of ſtraggling houſes intermixed with ſpots of ground, on the contrary, the people complain that the buildings are too crowded, and that the long ſtreets which they form are too narrow; thoſe who paſs through them imagine themſelves tranſported into the midſt of a fair, where nothing is heard around, but the noiſe of porters calling out to make way Proviſions are here exceedingly dear, becauſe every thing conſumed is brought from a great diſtance, even wood, ſo neceſſary for the furnaces, is actually tranſported from the diſtance of an hundred leagues. This village, notwithſtanding the high price of proviſions, is an aſylum for a great number of poor families, who have no means of ſubſiſting in the neighbouring towns Children and invalids find employment, and the blind gain a livelihood by pounding colours. The river in this place forms a kind of harbour of about a league in circumference, and two or three rows of barks placed in a line, ſometimes border the whole extent of this vaſt baſon

King-te-ching contains about five hundred furnaces for making porcelain, all employed the flames and clouds of ſmoke, which riſe from them in different places, ſhew at a diſtance the extent and ſize of this celebrated village. Strangers are with difficulty permitted to ſleep here, they muſt either paſs the night in the barks which brought them hither, or lodge with their friends, who are obliged in ſuch caſe to anſwer for their conduct Thus they maintain order and ſafety in a place, the riches of which might otherwiſe excite the avidity of a number of banditti

KOANG-FIN-FOU.

Koang-fin-fou is ſurrounded by mountains, the greater part of which are lofty, and abound with fine cryſtal, others are divided into ploughed lands, many of which are but little inferior to the valleys, and ſome are covered with foreſts. There is ſome good paper made in this city, and the candles here are deemed the beſt in the empire Its juriſdiction extends over ſeven cities of the third claſs

NANG-KANG-FOU, KIEOU-KIANG-FOU, KIEN-TCHANG-FOU

Theſe cities have nothing remarkable but their ſituation. The firſt is built on the banks of the lake Po-yang, the ſecond on the ſouth ſide of the river Yang-tſe-kiang, and the third on the frontiers of the province of Fo-kien. The firſt has four others of the third claſs under its juriſdiction, and the two laſt have five At Nang-kang-fou and Kieou-kiang-fou they manufacture ſlight ſummer cloathing from a ſpecies of hemp that grows near them, and the country in general, produces plenty of rice, fruits, wheat, &c though the former is not very good.

VOU-TCHEOU-FOU.

This city was formerly one of the moſt beautiful in China, but ſince the invaſion of the Tartars it has been a heap of ruins, which however ſerve to convey ſome idea of its ancient magnificence. The air here is pure, the people are active and induſtrious, and the fields well cultivated. Its diſtrict is about twenty-five leagues in extent, and its government embraces ſix cities of the third claſs.

LIN-KIANG-FOU

Lin-kiang-fou is ſituated on the banks of the river Yu ho; its ſoil is good, and the climate is healthful, but it is much deſerted, and the inhabitants live very poor, ſo that the Chineſe ſay, by way of ſneer, *one hog would be ſufficient to maintain the whole city two days.* It has four cities of the third claſs belonging to its diſtrict. One of its villages, at about three leagues diſtant on the banks of the river Kan-kyang, is the general mart for all the drugs ſold in the empire; this makes it a place of ſome note.

KI-NGNAN-FOU, CHOUI-TCHFOU-FOU AND YUEN-TCHEOU-FOU.

Theſe are cities very commodiouſly ſituated upon the banks of different rivers, and in cantons equally fertile. The mountains of the firſt contain gold and ſilver mines, and nine cities of the third rank are within its diſtrict, the diſtrict of the ſecond reaches over three cities of the third claſs, and in its mountains are found the lapis lazuli, and the third furniſhes the reſt of China with abundance of vitriol and alum, while its diſtrict extends over four cities of the third claſs.

KAN-TCHEOU-FOU.

Kan-tcheou-fou has every appearance of a flouriſhing trade, and its rivers, port, riches and population, all contribute to attract ſtrangers. A day's journey from this city the river forms a rapid current, almoſt twenty leagues in length, flowing with great impetuoſity over a number of ſcattered rocks that are level with the water. So that travellers here are in great danger of being loſt, unleſs they are conducted by a pilot of the country, after this paſſage the river becomes three or four times as large as the Seine at Rouen, and is continually covered with loaded barks and other vessels under sail.

Near the walls of the city is a very long bridge, composed of an hundred and thirty boats joined together by strong iron chains The custom-house is near this bridge, where a receiver constantly resides, to visit all barks, and examine if they have paid the duties imposed on the commodities with which they are loaded Two or three moveable boats are so placed, that by their means the bridge can be opened or shut, to give or refuse a passage, and no barks are ever permitted to pass until they have been examined In the territory belonging to this city, a great number of those valuable trees grow, from which varnish distils Its district is extensive, containing twelve cities of the third class.

NAN-NGAN-FOU

This city is situated in the most southern part of the province, it is beautiful, populous, and commercial, for here all the merchandise must be landed that goes to, or comes from the province of QUANG-TONG, and is much frequented It has dependant on it four cities of the third class.

PROVINCE OF FO-KIEN

The province of Fokien is not very extensive, but its riches entitle it to be ranked among the most flourishing of the empire Its climate is warm, but the air is so pure, owing to the sea breezes, that no contagious disease was ever known to prevail here

It is bounded on the north by the province of Tche-kiang, on the west by Kiang-si, on the south by Quang-tong, and on the east by the Chinese sea Its productions are musk in abundance, precious stones, quick-silver, iron, and tin. Tools of steel necessary for every art, silk stuffs, cotton and linen, and cloths of surprising fineness and beauty are made here The mountains of this province are likewise said to contain tin, gold, and silver mines; but the latter are forbid to be opened, under pain of death.

It has few plains, but industry has fertilized the mountains, the greater part of which are disposed in the form of amphitheatres, and cut into terraces that rise one above another, and which have to an European a very novel appearance. The valleys are watered by rivers and springs, which fall from the mountains, which the Chinese husbandman distributes with great skill, on his rice, they likewise raise the water to the tops of the mountains, and convey it from one side to another, by pipes of bamboo, plenty of which are found in this province Most of the grains and fruits of the other provinces are likewise found here.

The inhabitants of Fo-kien carry on a considerable trade with Japan, the Philippines, Java, Camboya, Siam, and the isle of Formosa, which renders this country extremely opulent. It contains nine *fou*, or cities of the first class, and sixty *hien*, or cities of the third class among the former they reckon Tay-wan, the capital of the island of Formosa, as well as the isles of Pong-hu, between Formosa and the port of Hya-men, which is also in its district

FOU-TCHEOU-FOU

Fou-tcheou-fou is one of the most considerable cities in the province, with respect to the beauty of its situation, goodness of its soil, the extensiveness of its trade, the number of its literati, the convenience of its rivers and port, and the magnificence of its principal bridge, which has more than an hundred arches, constructed of white stone, and ornamented with a double balustrade throughout This city is the residence of a viceroy, and it has under its jurisdiction nine cities of the third class

TSUEN-TCHEOU-FOU

This city is little inferior to the preceding, its situation, trade, extent, triumphal arches, temples, &c. secure it a distinguished rank among the most beautiful cities of China. Within its district are seven cities of the third class. Not far from this city is a bridge remarkable for its extraordinary size and the singularity of its construction, which was built at the expence of one of its governors. Father Martini speaks of it in the following words: "I saw it twice, and always "with astonishment. It is built entirely of the same kind "of blackish stone, and has no arches, but above three "hundred large stone pillars, which terminate on each side "in an acute angle, to break the violence of the current "with greater facility. Five stones of equal size, laid "transversely from one pillar to another, form the breadth of "the bridge, each of which, according to the measurement "I made in walking, were eighteen of my ordinary steps "in length; there are one thousand of them, all of the same "size and figure: a wonderful work, when one considers "the great number of these heavy stones, and the manner "in which they are supported between the pillars! On "each side there are buttresses or props, constructed of the "same kind of stone; on the tops of which are placed lions "on pedestals, and other ornaments of the like nature. "It is to be observed, that in this description, I speak only of one part of the work (that which is between the "small city of Lo-yang and the castle built upon the bridge); "for, beyond the castle, there is another part equally stupendous as the first."

KIEN-NING-FOU.

This is one of those common cities which presents nothing remarkable. It stands on the side of the river Minho, and has a pretty good trade, lying in the way of all ships that pass up and down. At the time of the conquest of China by the Tartars, it sustained two sieges, and resolutely refused to submit; but, some time after, being taken, all the inhabitants were put to the sword. Having been since re-established by the same Tartars who destroyed it, it is now ranked amongst cities of the first class, which is the more astonishing, as it has nothing to distinguish it from ordinary cities. Eight cities of the third class belong to its district

YEN-PING-FOU

This city rises in the form of an amphitheatre, upon the brow of a mountain washed by the river Min-ho, it is fortified by inaccessible mountains, which cover it on every side, and all the barks of the province pass by the foot of its walls, to go to their different places of destination. The water of the mountains is conveyed by canals into every house, which few other cities can boast It has under its jurisdiction seven cities of the third class, among which is Cha-hien, commonly called *The Silver City*, on account of the plenty occasioned by the fertility of its lands.

TING-CHEOU-FOU, HING-HOA-FOU AND CHAO-OU-FOU.

These cities present nothing curious to the traveller. Seven cities of the third class depend on the former, two on the second, and four on the third, which is a place of strength, and one of the keys of the province Hing-hoa-fou, though it has but two cities within its district, has a number of villages, and pays the most considerable tribute of rice of any other city in the province.

TCHANG-TCHEOU-FOU

Tchang-tcheou-fou is a city very considerable on account of its trade with the isles of *Emouy*, *Pong-hou*, and *Formosa* The missionaries found here some vestiges of the Christian religion, and Father Martini says he saw in the house of one of the literati an old parchment book written in Gothic characters, which contained in Latin the greater part of the scriptures This Jesuit offered a sum of money for it, but the owner refused to part with it, though he had no knowledge of christianity, because it was a book which had been long preserved in his family, and which he said his ancestors had always considered as a very great curiosity.—This city, which is the most southern in the province, has ten cities of the third rank in its district, the inhabitants of which, for the most part, have a considerable talent for commerce.

Besides these cities and a number of forts belonging to them, this province has under its jurisdiction a celebrated port, commonly called *Hia-men*, or *Emouy*, and the isles of *Pong-hu*, and *Tay-uan*, or *Formosa*

ISLAND OF EMOUY.

The port of Emouy is properly but an anchoring-place for ships, inclosed on one side by the island from which takes its name, and on the other by the main land, but it is so extensive, that it can contain several thousands of vessels, and the depth of its water is so great, that the largest ships may lie close to the shore without danger

In the beginning of the present century it was much frequented by European vessels, but at present few visit it, the trade being carried to *Canton* Here, however, the emperor keeps a garrison of six or seven thousand men, commanded by a Chinese general

A large rock which stands at the mouth of the road divides it almost as the *Mingant* divides the harbour of Brest. It is visible, and rises several feet above the surface of the water About three leagues distant is a small island, with a natural arch in the middle which admits light from the opposite side from this circumstance it is named *The Perforated Island*

The island of Emouy is celebrated on account of its principal pagod, consecrated to the deity *Fo* This temple is situated in a plain, terminated on one side by the sea, and on the other by a lofty mountain Before it the sea, flowing through different channels, forms a large sheet of water, bordered with turf of the most beautiful verdure. The front of this edifice is one hundred and eighty feet in length, and its gate is adorned with figures in relief, the usual ornaments of the Chinese architecture. On entering, a vast portico presents itself, with an altar in the middle, on which is a gigantic statue of gilt brass, representing the god *Fo*, sitting cross-legged There are four other statues at the corners of this portico, eighteen feet high, although they represent people sitting. These statues are each formed from a single block of stone, and they bear in their hands different symbols, which mark their attributes, as formerly in Athens and Rome the trident and caduceus distinguished Neptune and Mercury. One holds a serpent in its arms, which is twisted round its body in several folds, another has a bent bow and quiver, a third presents a battle-axe, and the other a guitar, or instrument of the same kind.

Crossing this portico, there is an entrance to a square outer court, paved with large grey stones, the least ten feet in length and four in breadth. At the four sides of this court arise pavilions, which terminate in domes, and have a communication with one another by means of a gallery which runs quite round One of these contains a bell ten feet in diameter, in the other is a drum of an enormous size, which the bonzes use to proclaim the days of new and full moon The two other pavilions contain the ornaments of the temple, and often serve for the accommodation of travellers, whom the bonzes are obliged to receive

In the middle of this court is a large tower, which stands by itself, and terminates in a dome, to which the ascent is by a beautiful stone staircase that winds round it. This dome contains a remarkably neat temple, the ceiling of which, is ornamented with mosaic work, and the walls covered with stone figures in relief, representing animals and monsters. The pillars which support the roof of this edifice are of varnished wood, which on festivals are ornamented with ſmall flags of different colours The pavement is formed of little ſhells, and its different compartments preſent birds, butterflies, flowers, &c.

The bonzes continually burn incenſe upon the altar, and keep the lamps lighted, which hang from the ceiling At one extremity of the altar is a brazen urn, which when ſtruck ſends forth a mournful ſound, and on the oppoſite ſide is a hollow machine of wood, of an oval form, for the ſame purpoſe, viz to accompany with its ſound their voices when they ſing in praiſe of the tutelary idol of the pagod

The idol *Pouſſa* is placed on the middle of this altar, on a flower of gilt braſs, which ſerves as a baſe He holds a young child in his arms, and ſeveral ſubaltern deities are ranged around him, who ſhew by their attitudes their reſpect and veneration

The bonzes have traced on the walls of this temple ſeveral hieroglyphical characters in praiſe of *Pouſſa*, there is alſo an hiſtorical or allegorical painting in freſco, repreſenting a burning lake, in which ſeveral men appear to be ſwimming, ſome carried by monſters, others ſurrounded by dragons and winged ſerpents. In the middle of the gulph riſes a ſteep rock, on the top of which the god is ſeated, holding in his arms a child, who ſeems to call out to thoſe who are in the flames of the lake, but an old man, with hanging ears and horns on his head, prevents them from climbing to the ſummit of the rock, and threatens to drive them back with a large club Behind the altar is a library, containing books which treat of the worſhip of idols

Croſſing the court there is an entrance to a gallery, the walls of which are lined with boards, it contains twenty-four ſtatues of gilt braſs, repreſenting twenty-four philoſophers, diſciples of Confucius, and at the end of this gallery is a large hall, the refectory of the bonzes After traverſing a ſpacious apartment, the entrance of the temple of *Fo* presents itself, to which there is an ascent by a large stone staircase It is ornamented with vases, full of artificial flowers, and here also are the same kind of musical instruments as those mentioned before. The statue of the god can only be seen but through a piece of black gauze, which forms a curtain before the altar The rest of the pagod consists of several large chambers, neat, but badly disposed, the gardens and pleasure-grounds are laid out on the declivity of the mountain; and a number of delightful grottos are cut out in the rock, which afford an agreeable shelter from the excessive heat of the sun.

Besides the above, there are several other pagods in the isle of Emouy, among which is one called *The Paged of the Ten Thousand Stones*, because it is built on the brow of a mountain where there is said to be a like number of little rocks, under which the bonzes have formed grottos and covered seats.

Strangers are received by these bonzes with great politeness, and may freely enter their temples, but they must not attempt so far to gratify their curiosity as to enter those apartments into which they are not introduced, for the bonzes, who are forbid under pain of severe punishment to have any intercourse with women, but who often keep them in private, might from fear of being discovered, revenge themselves on too impertinent a curiosity Such will ever be the result of the ordinances of any religion which are opposed to reason and nature.

ISLES OF PONG-HOU.

These isles form an archipelago between the port of Emouy and the island of Formosa A Chinese garrison is kept here, with one of those mandarins who are called literati, whose principal employment is to watch the trading vessels which pass from China to Formosa, or from Formosa to China.

These islands being only sand-banks or rocks, the inhabitants are obliged to import every necessary of life; neither shrubs nor bushes are seen upon them, their whole ornament consisting of one solitary tree. The harbour however is good, and sheltered from every wind, and has from twenty to twenty-five feet depth of water; and although it is in an uncultivated and uninhabited island, it is necessary for the preservation of Formosa, which has no port capable of receiving vessels that draw above eight feet of water.

ISLAND OF TAI-OUAN, OR FORMOSA.

This island, which is only thirty leagues from the province of Fo-kien, was not known to the Chinese till the year 1430, nor was it till 1661, in the reign of the late emperor, Kang-hi, that they established themselves on it, and now it is not all under their dominion. The island is divided near the middle by a chain of mountains running from south to north, and that part only which lies on the west side, between 22° 8′ and 25° 20′, belongs to the Chinese; it is a fine country, the air pure and serene, and the soil good, producing grain of every sort, and most of the fruits found in the Indies; but there is a great scarcity of good water.

It is divided into three Hien or subordinate governments, dependent on the capital of the island called Tai-ouan, the governor of which is subject to the viceroy of the province of Fo-kien. The trade of this place is very considerable, and the population is great; the town is handsome, and on the island the emperor keeps a garrison of ten thousand men, commanded by a Tsong-ping or lieutenant-general, two Fu-tsiang or major-generals, and several inferior officers, who are changed once in three years, and sometimes oftener.

The inhabitants of Formosa rear a great number of oxen, which they use for riding, from a want of horses and mules; they accustom them early to this kind of service, and by daily exercise, train them to go well and expeditiously these oxen are furnished with a bridle, saddle and crupper, and a Chinese looks as big and is as proud when mounted in this manner, as if he were carried by the finest Barbary courser

PROVINCE OF TCHE-KIANG.

This province, which was formerly the residence of some of the emperors, is one of the most considerable in the empire, on account of its maritime situation, extent, riches, and the number of its inhabitants It is bounded on the south by Fo-kien, on the north and west by Kiang-nan and Kiang-si, and on the east by the sea The air is pure and healthful, the mountains are well cultivated, and the plains are watered by a number of rivers and canals, broad and deep, kept in good order, and ornamented with bridges at proper situations the springs and lakes with which the province abound, contribute greatly to its fertility. The natives are mild, lively, and very polite to strangers, but are said to be extremely superstitious.

In this province a prodigious quantity of silk-worms are bred, whole plains may be seen covered with dwarf mulberry-trees, purposely checked in their growth, and planted and pruned almost in the same manner as vines, long experience having taught the Chinese, that the leaves of the smallest trees procure the best silk The principal branch therefore of commerce in this province consists in silk stuffs, and those in which gold and silver are intermixed, are the most beautiful and most esteemed in the empire. Of their common pieces, an immense quantity is sent to every part of China, to Japan, the Philippines, and to Europe, and notwithstanding this extensive exportation, a complete suit of silk may be bought as cheap as one of the coarsest woollen cloth in France.

This province is also famous for its hams, and those small gold-fish with which ponds are commonly stocked.

The tallow-tree grows here, and a species of mushrooms, which for their flavour are transported to every province of the empire. They will keep a whole year when dried; when wanted for use, they are soaked in water, which renders them as fresh as they were at first. there are likewise in this province, whole forests of Bam-boo canes, of which the Chinese make mats, boxes, combs, &c.

In Tche-kiang there are eleven cities of the first class, seventy-two of the third, and eighteen fortresses, which in many parts of Europe would be accounted large cities.

HANG-TCHEOU-FOU.

Hang-tcheou-fou, the metropolis of the province, may be considered as one of the richest, best situated and largest cities of the empire. It is four leagues in circumference, exclusive of its suburbs; and the number of its inhabitants are computed to amount to more than a million. It is asserted that there are sixty thousand workmen within its walls, employed in manufacturing silk. a small lake, called Si-hou, washes the bottom of its walls on the western side; its water is pure and limpid, and its banks are almost every where covered with flowers. Halls and open galleries, supported by pillars, and paved with large flag stones, have been erected here on piles, for the convenience of those who are fond of walking; causeways lined with free-stone, traverse the lake in different directions; and the openings, which are left in them at intervals, for the passage of boats are covered by handsome bridges.

In the middle of the lake are two islands, to which the inhabitants generally resort after having amused themselves with rowing in their boats. On these islands a temple and several pleasure-houses have been built for their reception, among which the emperor has a small palace.

The city has a garrison of three thousand Chinese, under the command of the viceroy, and three thousand Tartars, commanded by a general of the same nation. Under its jurisdiction there are seven cities of the second and third class.

KIA-KING-FOU.

The streets of this city are ornamented with piazzas, that shelter passengers from the sun and rain, and canals lined with free stone are cut in every part of it, and on the sides of that to the west of the city, and through which the barks pass, are fifteen towers. The whole country in this district is flat, without so much as one hill, and seven cities of the third class are dependent on it.

HOU-TCHEOU-FOU

This city is situated on a lake, from which it takes its name. The quantity of silk manufactured here is almost incredible, but we may form some idea of it by the tribute paid by a city under its jurisdiction, named Te-tsin-hien, which amounts to more than five hundred thousand *taels* or ounces of silver. Its district contains seven cities, one of which is of the second, and six of the third class, and the country around is exceedingly fertile.

NING PO-FOU.

Ning-po-fou, called by the Europeans Liampo, is an excellent port, on the eastern coast of China, opposite to Japan The city stands on the confluence of two small rivers, which form a canal from thence to the sea, capable of bearing vessels of two hundred tons. Eighteen or twenty leagues from this place is an island called Tcheou-chan, where the English are said to have first landed on their arrival at China, not having been able to find the way to Ning po fou among so many islands as are on this coast

The silks manufactured at Ning-po-fou are much esteemed in foreign countries, especially in Japan, where the Chinese exchange them for copper, gold, and silver. The merchants of Batavia come here annually for the purpose of purchasing this article. This city has four others under its jurisdiction, besides a great number of fortresses

CHAO-HING-FOU.

Chao-hing-fou is situated in an extensive and fertile plain, intersected with canals of clear water, so that persons may travel from every part of the country round to every part of this city by water, for there is no street without a canal The people of this country are said to be the greatest adepts in chicanery of any in China, they are so well versed in the laws, that the governors of the provinces and great mandarins choose their *Siang-cong*, or secretaries, from among them

Half a league from the city is a tomb, which the Chinese say is that of the great *Yu* Near the monument a magnificent edifice has been raised by order of the emperor Chang-hi, who visited it in the twentieth year of his reign, to shew his respect to the memory of that character. This province has under its jurisdiction eight cities of the third class, in most of which they make a wine esteemed throughout the empire.

TAI-TCHEOU-FOU AND KIN-HOA-FOU.

The first of these cities stands on the side of a river in a country surrounded with mountains, and is neither so rich or considerable as those before mentioned, it has however six cities of the third class in its jurisdiction Kin-hoa-fou also stands on the side of a pleasant river, and carries on a considerable trade with many other provinces of the empire, in dried plumbs, rice, hams, and wine. It has been famed for the courage of its inhabitants, who long withstood the power of the Tartars It has eight cities of the third class dependent on it, some situated on the mountains, and some in the open fields

KYU TCHEOU-FOU AND YEN-TCHEOU-FOU.

The first of these cities is the most southern one in the province, bordering on Kyang-se and Fo-kien, its jurisdiction extends over five cities of the third class, but they contain nothing remarkable. Yen-tcheou fou is of still less importance, its jurisdiction extends over six small cities of the third rank. Some copper mines are however found here, and the varnish tree, they also manufacture paper, which is generally esteemed

OUEN-TCHEOU-FOU AND TCHU-TCHEOU-FOU.

The first of these cities stands in a marshy soil, near the sea, its buildings are handsome, and it has a convenient harbour for barks and transports,—the plains around it are fertile, but some of the mountains are frightful. it has five small cities dependent on it Tchu-tcheou-fou is surrounded with vast mountains, its jurisdiction is over ten cities of the third class. Rice here is plenty, owing to the difficulty of transporting of it to other parts; and the pine trees on the mountains grow to an enormous size.

PROVINCE OF HOU-QUANG

This province lies nearly in the centre of the empire; the river Yang-tse-kiang traverses it from west to east, dividing it into two parts. It is celebrated for its fertility so much, that the Chinese call it the store-house of the empire, and it is a common saying among them, that *The province of Kiang si would furnish China with a breakfast, but that of Hou quang alone could supply enough to maintain all the inhabitants of the empire.*

Some princes of the race of Hong-vou formerly resided in this province, but that family was entirely extirpated by the Tartars when they conquered China This country boasts much of its cotton cloths, simples, gold-mines, wax, and paper, the latter of which is made of the bamboo-reed.

The northern part of the province contains eight *fou*, or cities of the first class, and sixty of the second and third. The southern comprehends seven of the first class, and fifty-four of the second and third, exclusive of forts, towns and villages.

VOU-TCHANG-FOU.

Vou-tchang-fou, is the capital of the province, the rendezvous at different times of all the commercial people in China. This city, as well as the rest of the province, suffered greatly during the last wars, but it has recovered so much, that it is now inferior to none of the others, in extent, opulence, or population Every branch of trade is carried on here, and its port, situated on the river Yang-tse-kiang, is always crowded with vessels The beautiful crystal found in its mountains, the plentiful crops of fine tea which it produces, and the prodigious sale of the bamboo-paper made here, contribute to render it famous Its extent is compared to that of Paris, and it embraces in its district one city of the second, and nine of the third class, besides fortified towns and fortresses.

HANG-YANG-FOU, AND NGAN-LO-FOU.

These cities are populous and commercial but they present nothing remarkable, except the first, in which is a very high tower, raised, according to vulgar tradition, in honour of a young woman, whose innocence was declared by a striking miracle the branch of a pomegranate-tree, which she held in her hand, instantly became loaded with fruit. It is situated on the Yang-tse-kyang, and has only one city under its jurisdiction, owing to its commercial advantages, its inhabitants are very rich. Ngan-lo-fou is built on the borders of the river Han, in a vast plain, its commerce with Vou-tchang-fou contributes to the riches of its inhabitants, and it has jurisdiction over two cities of the second, and five of the third class

SIANG-YANG-FOU, YOUEN-YANG-FOU, TE-NGAN-FOU.

The first of these cities stands on the river Han, and shares in most of the advantages of the last city we mentioned, with respect to trade, one part of its territory is mountainous, and abounds with minerals, and gold is said to be found mixed with the sand of its rivers, its district comprehends one city of the second and six of the third class Youen-yang-fou is the most northern city in the province, situated on the Han, and inclosed with mountains, from whence some good tin has been obtained, it has six cities of the third class within its jurisdiction Te-ngan-fou is built on the banks of a river which falls into the Yang-tse-kyang, the country around it is inclosed on the north by mountains, and the south by rivers and canals It has six cities of the third class in its jurisdiction, and is remarkable for a species of white wax, which they say comes from an insect, and from which they make candles.

KIN-TCHEOU-FOU, AND HOANG-TCHEOU-FOU.

Neither of these cities differ much from those last described. The jurisdiction of the former extends over two cities of the second class and eleven of the third; the latter over one of the second and eight of the third. It is built on the Yang-tse-kyang, and as a place of trade is of importance These are all the cities in the northern division of this province.

The southern division contains seven cities of the first class, six of the second and forty-eight of the third; of those of the first class, the principal is

TCHANG-TCHA-FOU.

This city is situated on a large river, which has a communication with an extensive lake, called Tong-ting-hou.

It has under its juriſdiction one city of the ſecond and eleven of the third claſs. The inhabitants of one of theſe cities were the inſtitutors of a grand feſtival, which is celebrated in the fifth month, through all the provinces of the empire, with great pomp and ſplendour The mandarin who governed the city having been drowned, the people, who adored him on account of his virtue and great probity, inſtituted this feſtival in honor of him, and ordered it to be ſolemnized by ſports, feaſts, and combats on the water And this feſtival, which at firſt was peculiar to the city, at length extended over the whole empire

Long, narrow boats, covered with gilding, are prepared for this ſolemnity, which are called *Long-tcheou*, becauſe they repreſent the figure of a dragon; and rewards are beſtowed upon thoſe who are victorious but, as diverſions of this kind have become dangerous, they are forbid by many of the mandarins in their reſpective provinces

YO-TCHEOU-FOU.

This city is built on the banks of the river Yang-tſe-kiang, and may be ranked among the wealthieſt in China It is exceeding populous, and a place of great trade One city of the ſecond claſs, and ſeven of the third, are under its juriſdiction The other cities of the province have nothing remarkable; their names are Pao-king-fou, Heng-tcheou-fou, Tchang-te-fou, Tching-tcheou-fou, and Yong-tcheou-fou.

PROVINCE OF HO-NAN

Every thing that can contribute to render a country delightful is found united in this province, the Chineſe therefore call it Tong-hoa, or *The Middle Flower* It is bounded on the north by Pe-tche-li and Chan-ſi, on the weſt by Shen-ſi, on the ſouth by Hou-quang, and on the eaſt by Chang-tong, and watered by the Hoang-ho, or Yellow River.

The ancient emperors, invited by the mildneſs of the climate and the beauty and fertility of the country, fixed their reſidence here for ſome time The abundance of its fruits, paſtures and corn, the effeminacy of its inhabitants, and the cheapneſs of proviſions, have prevented trade from being ſo flouriſhing here, as in the other provinces of the empire The whole country, excepting towards the weſt, is flat There ariſes a long chain of mountains covered with thick foreſts, and the land is in ſuch a high ſtate of cultivation, that it appears like an immenſe garden.

Beſides the river Hoang-ho, which traverſes this province, it is watered by a great number of ſprings and fountains, it has alſo a valuable lake, which invites to its banks prodigious numbers of workmen, as it is ſuppoſed its water has the property of communicating a luſtre to ſilk, which cannot be imitated Excluſive of forts, caſtles and places of ſtrength, this province contains eight cities of the firſt claſs, and an hundred and two of the ſecond and third. In one of theſe cities named Nan-yang, is a kind of ſerpent, the ſkin of which is marked with ſmall white ſpots, this ſkin the Chineſe phyſicians ſteep in wine, and uſe it afterwards as a remedy againſt the palſy.

CAI-FONG-FOU

Cai-fong-fou is the capital of Ho-nan, it is ſituated at the diſtance of ſix miles from the river Hoang-ho, but the ground is ſo low, that the river is higher than the city. To prevent inundations, ſtrong banks have been raiſed, extending more than thirty leagues. This city was beſieged in 1642 by an army of an hundred thouſand rebels, headed by one Ly-techaung. The commander of the troops ſent to relieve it, formed the deſign of drowning the enemy, by breaking down the large bank of Hoang-ho in this ſtratagem he ſucceeded but the inundation was ſo violent and ſudden, that it is aſſerted that three hundred thouſand inhabitants periſhed on the occaſion.

By the ruins which still subsist it is evident that Cai-fong-fou must then have been three leagues in circumference. It has been rebuilt, but in a style far inferior to its former magnificence. Nothing now distinguishes it from the inferior cities but the extent of its jurisdiction, which comprehends four cities of the second, and thirty of the third class.

KOUEI-TE-FOU.

Kouei-te-fou has under its jurisdiction one city of the second, and six of the third class. It is situated in an extensive and fertile plain between two large rivers, and nothing is wanting to render it opulent but an increase of its inhabitants and trade. The air here is pure, the earth fertile and the fruits excellent, while the inhabitants are remarkably mild, and treat strangers with uncommon hospitality.

TCHANG-TE-FOU.

This is one of the most northern cities of the province. Its district is of small extent, but the soil is rich and fruitful; there are two things here remarkable; the first a fish resembling a crocodile, the fat of which is of so singular a nature, that when once kindled it is scarce possible to extinguish it; the second a mountain in the neighbourhood, so steep and inaccessible that in time of war it affords a place of refuge to the inhabitants, and a safe asylum from the insults and violence of the soldiery. Tchang-te-fou contains in its district one city of the second and six of the third class.

OUEI-KIUN-FOU AND HOAI-KING-FOU.

The territories of these provinces, which are not very extensive, abound with simples and medicinal plants; they have nothing else remarkable, but both these have under their jurisdiction six cities of the third class.

HONAN-FOU.

Honan-fou is situated amidst mountains and between three rivers. The Chinese formerly believed it to be the céntre of the earth, becauſe it was in the middle of their empire. Its juriſdiction is extenſive, comprehending one city of the ſecond and thirteen of the third claſs: one of theſe cities, named Teng-fong-hien, is famous on account of the tower erected by the celebrated *Tcheou-kong* for an obſervatory; there is ſtill to be ſeen in it an inſtrument which he made uſe of to find the ſhadow at noon, for aſtronomical purpoſes. Tcheou-kong lived above a thouſand years before the Chriſtian era, and the Chineſe pretend that he was the inventor of the mariner's compaſs.

NAN-YANG-FOU AND YUNING-FOU.

Theſe cities have under their juriſdiction twenty-two others, of which the former has two of the ſecond and ſix of the third claſs, and the latter, two of the ſecond and twelve of the third. Proviſions are ſo abundant in the firſt, that numerous armies have remained in it without the inhabitants ſcarce perceiving the leaſt ſcarcity, though its diſtrict is ſmall; and the latter is not leſs fruitful. We have nothing elſe particularly worthy of attention concerning them.

PROVINCE OF CHANG-TONG.

This province, which was the birth place of Confucius, is bounded on the weſt by Pe-tcheli and part of Ho-nan, on the ſouth by Kiang-nan, on the eaſt by the ſea, and on the north by the ſame and part of Pe-tcheli. It is divided into ſix diſtricts, containing ſix cities of the firſt claſs and an hundred and fourteen of the ſecond and third. Beſides theſe, there are along the coaſt fifteen or ſixteen forts, ſeveral villages of conſiderable note, on account of their commerce, and a number of ſmall iſlands, the greater part of which have harbours very convenient for the Chineſe junks, which paſs from thence to Corea or Leao-tong.

Besides the grand Imperial Canal which traverses this province, and by which the commodities of the southern parts [illegible] at Pekin, it contains a great many lakes, streams and rivers, which contribute to the [illegible] and fecundity of its plains; still however it has much to fear from drought, as it seldom rains here, and locusts, which at times make great devastation. There is no country in the universe perhaps where game is more plentiful, or where hares, pheasants, partridges and quails are cheaper. For the inhabitants are reckoned the keenest sportsmen in the empire. The lakes produce fish in plenty, and the [illegible] of fruits and grain.

The Imperial Canal adds greatly to the riches of the province. Through this canal, as we have before observed, [illegible] barks from the south of China, which are bound to Pekin, must necessarily pass; their number is considerable, and they transport such quantities of merchandise and provisions of every kind, that the duties collected on this canal alone, amount every year to more than 250,000l sterling. All these barks pass from the Yellow River [illegible] Imperial Canal at Sou-tsien, from thence they go to Tsi-ning, and afterwards to Lin-tsin, where they enter the river Oei. In the course of this navigation are a great number of locks, which the want of [illegible] to carry large barks has rendered necessary. The obstacles which nature opposed to the execution of this magnificent work, the strong and long dikes by which it is contained, its banks decorated and often lined with [illegible], and the ingenious mechanism of its [illegible] all render it an object of admiration to the European [illegible]

[illegible] in the province a [illegible] insect much resembling [illegible] a coarse kind of [illegible] are made, and as these [illegible] very durable, they have an extensive sale throughout China.

TSI-NAN-FOU.

Tſi-nan-fou is the capital of this province, it is ſituated ſouth of the river Tſing ho or Tſi, it is large and populous, and is much reſpected by the Chineſe on account of its having been formerly the reſidence of a long ſeries of kings, whoſe tombs, riſing on the neighbouring mountains, afford a beautiful proſpect. Here a quantity of that inferior ſilk ſtuff we have before mentioned is made.

Tſi-nan has under its juriſdiction four cities of the ſecond and twenty ſix of the third claſs They have nothing remarkable, excepting Yen tching, where a kind of glaſs is made, ſo delicate and brittle, that it cracks if expoſed to the leaſt extra ſharpneſs of the air.

YEN-TCHEOU-FOU.

This is the ſecond city of the province, it is ſituated between the Ta-chin-ho and Hoang ho rivers the air is mild and temperate, which renders it an agreeable place of reſidence The diſtrict of this city is very extenſive, having under its juriſdiction four of the ſecond and twenty-three of the third claſs one of theſe cities, named Tei-ning-tcheou, is little inferior, if any, to the capital, either in extent, number of inhabitants, riches or commerce. Its eligible ſituation for buſineſs upon the banks of the Grand Canal, invites to it a great number of ſtrangers, no leſs celebrated is Kiou-feou, the birth place of *Confucius*, where ſeveral monuments are ſtill to be ſeen, erected in honour of this eminent man A third city, in which we are aſſured that great quantities of gold were formerly collected, and which perhaps gave occaſion to its name of *Kin-kian*, or *The Golden Country*, is likewiſe of ſome note.

TONG-TCHING-FOU.

This city is famous for its riches and trade, being ſituated on the great Canal, with a level country, producing plenty of grain and fruits of all kinds, which procure in exchange whatever the other provinces ſupply. Its juriſdiction extends over three cities of the ſecond and fifteen of the third claſs, among theſe Lin-tcin-tcheou is the moſt remarkable it is ſituated on the great Canal, and is much frequented by veſſels, it may be called a general magazine for every kind of merchandiſe. Among the edifices admired here, is an octagonal tower, divided into eight ſtories the walls of which are covered on the outſide with porcelain, loaded with various figures neatly executed, and within lined with poliſhed marble of different colours, a ſtair-caſe, conſtructed in the wall, conducts to all the ſtories, from which there are paſſages that lead into magnificent galleries of marble, ornamented with gilt baluſtrades, which encompaſs the tower All the cornices and projections are furniſhed with little bells, which, when agitated by the wind form a very agreeable harmony The higheſt ſtory contains an idol of gilt copper, to which the tower is conſecrated Near this tower are ſome other idol temples, the architecture of which is exceedingly beautiful

TSIN-TCHEOU-FOU

This city is inferior neither in extent nor riches to the preceding Its principal branch of commerce is fiſh, which are caught in ſuch abundance on its coaſt that a very conſiderable profit ariſes from the ſale of their ſkins only The juriſdiction of this city extends over one of the ſecond and thirteen of the third claſs

TEN-TCHEOU-FOU, AND LAI-TCHEOU-FOU

Theſe are the two laſt cities of the firſt claſs in this province, they are remarkable for nothing but their ſituation each of them has a convenient harbour, a numerous garriſon and ſeveral armed veſſels to defend the coaſt One city of the second, and seven of the third class depend on the former the jurisdiction of the latter extends over seven, of which two are of the second class.

PROVINCE OF CHAN-SI.

Chan-si is one of the smallest provinces of the empire; it is bounded on the east by Pe-tcheli, on the south by Honan, on the west by Chen-si, and on the north by the great wall. According to Chinese tradition, the first inhabitants fixed their residence in this province. Its climate is healthful and agreeable, and the soil fruitful It furnishes abundance of musk, porphyry, marble, lapis lazuli and jasper of various colours iron mines, salt-pits and crystal are also common here.

The province is full of mountains, some of which are uncultivated, and have a wild and frightful appearance; others are cut into terraces, and from top to bottom covered with corn, on the tops of some are found vast plains, equally fertile with the richest low-lands.

The inhabitants of this province are civil, and in general strong made, but exceedingly ignorant Vines grow here, which produce the best fruit in this part of Asia. The Chinese dry these grapes and sell them in the other provinces The mountains abound with coal, which the inhabitants pound, and form into small cakes by mixing with water, it is not very inflammable, but when once kindled, affords a strong and lasting fire it is used principally for heating the stoves, which are constructed with brick, as in Germany, but here they give them the form of small beds, and sleep on them during the night. This province comprehends five cities of the first class and eighty-five of the second and third within its district.

TAI-YUEN-FOU

This city is the capital of the province: it is ancient, and about three leagues in circumference. It was formerly the residence of the princes of the family of Tai-ming-tchao, but it has lost much of that splendour which it then had: nothing remains of their palaces but heaps of ruins. The only monuments entire are the tombs of these princes, which are seen on a neighbouring mountain.

This burying-place is magnificently ornamented; all the tombs are of marble or cut stone, and have near them triumphal arches, statues of heroes, figures of lions, horses, and different animals. Groves of aged cypresses, planted chequer-wise, preserve an awful and melancholy gloom around these tombs, and make the spectator feel the littleness of human grandeur.

Tai-yuen-fou has under its jurisdiction five cities of the second and twenty of the third class; it has also a small Tartar garrison under an officer called Ho tong-ha. It has manufactories of hard-ware, and stuffs of different kinds, particularly carpets made in imitation of those of Turkey.

PIN-YANG-FOU

This city is not inferior to the capital, either in antiquity, the richness of its soil, or the extent of its jurisdiction, which extends over six cities of the second, and twenty-eight of the third class, besides a number of populous villages.

Near Ngan-y is a lake, the water of which is as salt as that of the sea, and from which a great quantity of salt is made.

LOU-NGAN-FOU.

Lou-ngan-fou has under its jurisdiction only eight cities of the third class; but it is agreeably situated near the source of the river Tso tsang ho; the country around is full of hills, but the land produces all the neceſſaries of life.

FUEN-TCHEOU-FOU.

This is an ancient and commercial city, it is built on the banks of the river Fuen-ho, from whence it has its name; its baths and ſprings, almoſt as hot as boiling water, draw hither a great number of ſtrangers, which adds to its opulence. Its diſtrict is ſmall, having only one city of the ſecond, and ſeven of the third claſs, moſt of which lie between the river Hoang-ho and the Fuen.

TAI-TONG-FOU.

This is a place of ſtrength, built near the great wall. Its ſituation renders it important, becauſe it is the place moſt expoſed to the incurſions of the Tartars, it is therefore ſtrongly fortified, and has a numerous garriſon. The territory of this city abounds with lapis lazuli, and medicinal herbs, ſome of its mountains furniſh a peculiar ſtone of a deep red color, which is [illegible] and uſed for taking impreſſions of ſeals, &c. they furniſh alſo a particular kind of jaſper, called *yu-che*, which is as white and beautiful as agate; marble and porphyry are alſo common, and a conſiderable trade is carried on in them, which are in [illegible]. The juriſdiction of Tai-tong-fou comprehends four cities of the ſecond and ſeven of the third claſs.

PROVINCE OF CHEN-SI

This province is divided into two parts, the eaſtern and the weſtern, and contains eight cities of the firſt claſs, and an hundred and ſix of the ſecond and third. It is bounded on the eaſt by the Hoang-ho, which ſeparates it from Chan-ſi, on the ſouth by Se-tchuen and Hou-quang, on the north by Tartary and the great wall, and on the weſt by the country of the Mogul.

Chen-si had formerly three viceroys, but at present it has only two besides the governors of So-tcheou and Kan-tcheou, which are the strongest places in the country. The province in general is fertile, commercial and rich. It produces little rice, but plentiful crops of wheat and millet; it is, however, subject to long droughts, and sometimes every thing that grows in the fields is destroyed by locusts, which in return the Chinese eat boiled; several wild animals, as bears, tygers, &c. are also found in the woods. This country abounds with drugs, rhubarb, musk, cinnabar, wax, honey, and coals, of the latter it contains inexhaustible veins; it is said also to contain rich gold-mines, which are not allowed to be opened; gold-dust is washed down among the sand of the torrents and rivers, and a number of people obtain their subsistence by collecting it. The natives of this country have the character of being more polite and affable to strangers, and of possessing greater genius, than the Chinese of the other northern provinces.

SI-NGAN-FOU

This is the capital of the province, and, Pe-kin excepted, one of the most beautiful and largest cities in China; its walls are thick, high, and four leagues in circumference; they are flanked with a great number of towers, a bow-shot distant one from the other, and surrounded by a deep ditch. Some of its gates are magnificent and remarkably lofty.

It was for many years the court of the Chinese Emperors, and there is still to be seen a palace where they resided. The rest of the buildings have nothing to distinguish them from those of other cities. The houses are ill constructed, and the furniture inferior to that in the southern provinces; porcelain is very rare, and the varnish is coarse.

The inhabitants are in general more robust, braver, better calculated to endure fatigue, and of greater stature than the people of most of the other provinces. The greater part of the Tartar forces destined for the defence of the northern part of the empire are in garrison here, under a general of their own nation, and they occupy a quarter of the city, separated from the rest by a wall. The mountains in this district are exceedingly pleasant, and furnish a considerable quantity of game, also bats of a singular species: they are as large as domestic fowls, and the Chinese prefer their flesh to that of the most delicate chicken. This country also furnishes the ladies with a white paint, which they use for to soften or rather disfigure their complexions.

Father Le Comte observes, that in 1625 "a large "block of marble was dug up in the neighbourhood of "this city, which had been formerly raised as a monu-"ment: on the upper part it had a cross neatly carved; "and below, an inscription, partly in Chinese, partly in "Syriac characters, the substance of which was, that an "angel had declared, that the Messias was born of a "Virgin in Judea, and that his birth was indicated by a "new star in the heavens, that the kings of the East "observed it, and came to offer presents to this divine "child, that a Christian, named *Olopuen*, appeared in "China in the year 636, and had been favourably re-"ceived by the emperor, who having examined his doc-"trine, acknowledged the truth of it, and published an "edict in its favour."* If this is not a missionary's fabrication, it appears certain, that the Christian religion flourished in China from the year 636 to 782, the year in which this monument was erected. F. Le Comte says, that the emperor then reigning gave orders that it should be carefully preserved in a temple, which is a quarter of a league distant from Si-ngan-fou. If this could be ascer-

* The whole inscription, and the history of its discovery, may be seen in the *China Illustrata* of Kircher.

tained, and the antiquity of the monument and inscription put beyond doubt, it would throw a great additional light on the history of Christianity.

Si-ngan-fou has under its jurisdiction six cities of the second and thirty-one of the third class.

YEN-NGAN-FOU, AND FON-TSIANG-FOU.

The first of these cities is situated in an agreeable plain, and has three cities of the second and sixteen of the third class within its district And some of its mountains are said, by Du Halde, to distil a bituminous liquor, which the inhabitants burn in their lamps A fabulous bird which the Chinese paint on their garments and furniture gave name to this place, which contains nothing remarkable, it has one city of the second and seven of the third class in its jurisdiction.

HAN-TCHONG-FOU.

This is a large and populous city, situated on the river Han, which waters the whole country belonging to its district, in which there are two cities of the second, and fourteen of the third class The mountains and forests serve as bulwarks, and the valleys are fertile and pleasant

There is a highway cut out across the mountains, which conducts to the capital, and is the most remarkable thing in the country. This road was made by the army in the course of a military expedition The number of workmen employed, amounted to more than a hundred thousand, and we know not which to admire most, the difficulty of the labour, or the surprising shortness of time in which it was finished Mountains were levelled, and bridges constructed on arches, which reach from one to another, and when the valleys between appeared too wide, large pillars were erected to support them. These bridges, which form part of the road, are in several places so exceedingly high, that it is impossible to look down from them without terror, four horsemen may ride a-breast upon them. For the ſafety of travellers, they are railed on each ſide, and for whoſe accommodation villages, with inns, have been built at convenient diſtances upon the road.

PING-LEANG-FOU

This is one of the moſt conſiderable cities of the weſtern part of the province, it is ſituated on the river Kin-ho. The air is mild, and the agreeable views which the ſurrounding mountains preſent, added to the ſtreams which water the country, render it a very agreeable reſidence. The diſtrict includes three cities of the ſecond, and ſeven of the third claſs. A valley ſo deep and narrow, as to be almoſt impervious to the light, interſects a part of this country, and a large highway paved with ſquare ſtones runs through it.

KONG-TCHANG-FOU

Kong-tchang-fou is ſurrounded by inacceſſible mountains, and in it is a tomb which the Chineſe pretend to be that of the emperor *Fo-hi*; if this is true, it is the moſt ancient ſepulchral monument known in the world. The juriſdiction of this city extends over three others of the ſecond claſs and ſeven of the third. The country around it is fertile, and from its ſituation on the river *Whey*, it is become a place of conſiderable trade, and of conſequence very populous.

LING-TAO-FOU, AND KIN-YANG-FOU.

Theſe cities preſent nothing remarkable. Two cities of the ſecond claſs and three of the third depend on the former, which is ſituated on a river which falls into the Hoang-ho, the latter has one of the ſecond and four of the third claſs in its diſtrict, and was formerly conſidered as a barrier to the incurſions of the Tartars.

Lan-tcheou, a city of the ſecond claſs depending on the preceding, is ſituated near the great wall, and in the neighbourhood of the principal ports on the western coast, and therefore is classed among the most important cities of the empire it has even been made the capital of the western part of the province, and the seat of government. Its territories are washed by the Yellow river. The trade of this city consists in skins, brought from Tartary, and different kinds of woollen stuffs They likewise manufacture here a coarse kind of stuff of cow's hair, which the inhabitants use for making great-coats to defend themselves from the snow

PROVINCE OF SE-TCHUEN.

Se-tchuen is bounded on the north by Chen-si, on the east by Hou-quang, on the south by Koei-tcheou, and on the west by the kingdom of Thibet and some other neighbouring countries It is divided into ten districts, which, besides a great number of forts and places of strength, include ten cities of the first class and eighty-eight of the second and third. The great river Yang-tse-kiang traverses this province, which is opulent, on account of the abundance of silk it produces, and its mines of iron, tin and lead, which are very valuable Its amber, sugar-canes, loadstone, lapis lazuli, musk and horses are also in great request, as is its rhubarb and the root *fou-lin*, which the Chinese physicians introduce into all their prescriptions, besides these it furnishes a number of other useful productions, which it would be tedious to enumerate. All the salt consumed in this province is got from its mountains, where the inhabitants dig pits, which furnish them with it in abundance.

TCHING-TOU-FOU.

This city, which is the capital of Se-tchuen, was formerly the residence of the emperors, and one of the largest and most beautiful cities in China, but in 1646 it was, with the whole province, ruined and almost destroyed by the civil wars, which preceded the last invasion of the

Tartars. Its temples, bridges, and the ruins of its ancient palaces, are ſtill objects of admiration to ſtrangers, but neither its commerce nor inhabitants have any thing which diſtinguiſhes it from other cities, its ſituation is however exceedingly pleaſant, and well watered It has under its juriſdiction ſix cities of the ſecond claſs and twenty-five of the third.

PAO-NING-FOU, CHUN-KING-FOU and SU-TCHEOU-FOU.

Theſe are very ordinary cities, of which little is mentioned by geographers but the names The firſt is pleaſantly ſituated between two rivers, and comprehends in its diſtrict two cities of the ſecond and eight of the third claſs, the ſecond, two of the ſecond and ſeven of the third claſs, and the third, which is ſituated on the banks of the Yang-tſe-kyang, is a place of ſome trade, having a communication with moſt of the principal towns in the province, and has ten cities of the third claſs in its diſtrict,

TCHONG-KING-FOU

Tchong-king-fou is one of the moſt commercial cities of the province. Its ſituation is at the confluence of two remarkable rivers, one of which, called Hin-cha-kiang, or *golden ſand*, receives in its courſe all the tributary ſtreams from the mountains which riſe on the neighbouring confines of Tartary The other is the Ta-kiang, or Yang-tſe-kiang, the ſource of which is beyond the boundaries of China

Tchong-king-fou is built upon a mountain, and the houſes riſe in the form of an amphitheatre the country is fruitful, the air is wholeſome and temperate, and the rivers are ſtored with fiſh. The city is celebrated for a particular kind of trunks made of canes, interwoven in the manner of baſket work, and painted of divers colours. It has in its diſtrict three cities of the ſecond and eleven of the third claſs.

KOEI-TCHEOU-FOU AND MA-HOU-FOU.

The first of these cities stands on the Yang-tse-kyang, and has a custom house for receiving the duties on goods brought into this province. Its trade renders it rich, but its inhabitants are clownish, particularly those who inhabit the mountainous parts of the district; its jurisdiction extends over one city of the second, and nine of the third class. Ma-hou-fou is situated on the Kin-sha-kyang, and ranks of some importance as a place of trade, though its jurisdiction extends over only one city of the third rank.

LONG-NGAN-FOU, AND TSUN-Y-FOU.

These cities offer nothing remarkable to view; the first was formerly considered important as a place of defence and the key of the province, and as such had the command of several forts; its district includes three cities of the third class. The second lies on the borders of *Quay-fou*, and may, in case of necessity, serve to defend that province on that side; it has two cities of the second and four of the third class in its district.

TONG-TCHUEN-FOU.

This is a fortified place, the inhabitants of which are all soldiers, who have followed the profession of arms from father to son. Besides their pay, they have lands assigned them near the cities they inhabit, and in time of peace they are distributed in the frontier garrisons of the empire. Besides cities of the first class, this province contains also some of the second, which have several important fortresses under their jurisdiction; such are Tong-tcheouan-tcheou, Kia-ting-tcheou, and Ya-tcheou, which commands the frontiers of the province towards Thibet.

PROVINCE OF QUANG-TONG.

This is the most considerable of the southern provinces of China: it is bounded on the north-east by Fo-kien, on the north by Kiang-si, on the west by Quang-si and the kingdom of Tong-king, the rest is washed by the sea.

It is diversified with plains and mountains, and the land is sufficiently fertile to produce two crops of corn yearly. Trade and the fecundity of the soil supply this province with every necessary and luxury of life its products are gold, precious-stones, silk, pearls, eagle-wood, tin, quick-silver, sugar, copper, iron, steel, saltpetre, ebony, and abundance of aromatic woods

Besides a great many of the fruits of Europe, and of those which grow in the Indies, it produces several which are peculiar to itself of which we shall have occasion to speak hereafter The coasts abound with fish, and the oysters, crabs and tortoises are of an immense size

A prodigious number of tame ducks are raised in this province they load a great number of small barks with them and carry them in flocks to feed on the sea-shore, at low water, where they find shrimps, oysters and other kinds of shell fish Small fleets generally go in company, and the ducks mix together on the shore, but when night approaches, each owner by beating on a bason, collects his own flock to his boat without further trouble. The Chinese salt large quantities of their flesh in such a manner that it loses nothing of its original flavour, they also possess the art of salting their eggs by covering them with a coat of clay mixed with salt

The climate of this province is warm, but the air is pure, and the people are robust, healthy, and industrious, and it is asserted, that they possess in an eminent degree the talent of imitation

This province suffered much during the civil wars; but at present it is as flourishing as any in the empire, and, as it is at a great distance from court, its government is important The viceroy of it has also the command of Quang-si, and on that account resides at Chao-king, in order that he may more conveniently issue his orders to either of theſe provinces. There are a number of troops kept in this province, to check the incurſions of robbers and pirates, who, without this precaution, might hurt and interrupt its trade, and for the ſame reaſon, a great number of fortreſſes have been built along the coaſts and in the interior parts of the country.

Quang-tong is divided into ten diſtricts, which contain ten cities of the firſt claſs, and eighty-four of the ſecond and third.

QUEN-TONG OR CAN-TON.

This is the capital of the province, and is a large, populous and wealthy city. It ſtands on the banks of the river Taa, or great river, which, near the city, is wide and ſpacious. The wall of the city is high, and about ſix or ſeven miles in circumference, though not more than one-third of the ground is occupied by buildings, the other parts being appropriated to pleaſure grounds or fiſh ponds. The country is extremely pleaſant, and towards the eaſt hilly, ſo as to command a beautiful proſpect of the city and ſuburbs, the compaſs of which, together, is about ten miles, and its diſtrict extends over one city of the ſecond and ſeventeen of the third claſs.

The buildings of Canton are in general low, conſiſting of one ſtory and a ground floor, which is covered with earth or red tiles, in order to keep it cool; but the houſes of the moſt reſpectable merchants and mandarins are comparatively lofty, and well-built. In different parts of the city and ſuburbs are joſs houſes or temples, in which are placed the images worſhipped by the Chineſe, before whom are placed, at particular ſeaſons, a vaſt variety of ſweetmeats, oranges, great plenty of food ready dreſſed, and alſo incenſe, which is kept perpetually burning.

The ſtreets of Canton are long and narrow, paved with flat ſtones, ornamented at intervals with triumphal arches, which have a pleaſing effect, and much crowded with people. On both ſides are ſhops, appropriated to the ſale of different commodities and a kind of awning is extended from house to house, which prevents the sun's rays from incommoding either inhabitants or passengers. At the end of every street is a barrier, which, with the gates of the city, are shut every evening. In China Street, which is pretty long, and considerably wider than the rest, reside merchants, whose trade, so far as respects China, lackered ware, fans, &c is wholly confined to Europeans. Most of them speak the foreign languages tolerably well, or at least sufficiently intelligible to transact business Besides these merchants, there is a company of twelve or thirteen, called the *Cohong*, who have an exclusive right by appointment from authority to purchase the cargoes from the different ships, and also to supply them with teas, raw silks, &c. in return The establishment of the Cohong, though injurious to private trade, is admirably well adapted for the security of the different companies with which they traffic, because each individual becomes a guarantee for the whole, so that if one fail, the others consider themselves as responsible.

In Canton there are no carriages, all burdens are carried by porters across their shoulders on bamboos, as are also the principal people in sedan chairs, and the ladies always. The streets of Canton may be traversed from morning till evening without seeing a woman, those excepted who are Tartars, and even these but very seldom.

On the wharf of the river, which is commodious and pleasant, stand the factories of the different European nations, viz. the Dutch, French, Swedes, Danes, English, &c In those reside the supercargoes belonging to their respective companies, who are appointed to dispose of the cargoes brought to market, to supply the ships with others from Europe in return; and during their absence, to contract with the merchants for such articles as may be judged necessary for the next fleet. Between the residents of the factories the most perfect cordiality subsists, in each a common and splendid table is kept at the company's expence, and visits are reciprocally exchanged, so that nothing is wanting to make a residence at Canton agreeable to an European, but the pleasure naturally resulting from the society of women.

The side of the river next the city is covered with boats, which form a kind of town or streets, in which live the poorer sort of the Chinese, or rather the descendants of the Tartars. Some of the men come on shore in the morning to their respective employments, and in those sampans, or boats which are not stationary, the women and also the men carry passengers from place to place in the same manner as is done by wherries on the Thames. On this river live many thousand souls who never are permitted to come on shore, whose only habitation is their boat, in which they eat, drink, sleep, carry on many occupations, keep ducks, &c. and occasionally a hog.

The manufactures of Canton are principally carried on in the suburbs, though it has been frequently supposed that they were confined to the city, and this, by some writers, has been given as a reason why Europeans are not permitted to enter within the gates. But this is a mistake; and perhaps the true reason for this very singular restraint is, that the houses in which they keep their women are chiefly within the city.

At Wampoa, a large commodious place for anchorage, and which is about twelve or fourteen miles from Canton, the European vessels lie and unload their cargoes, which are transmitted by lighters to the factories, and by the same conveyance receive their respective freights. Between this place and the city are three hoppo, or custom-houses, at which the boats passing and repassing are obliged to stop, and undergo, with its passengers, an examination, in order to prevent smuggling. The lighters just mentioned, and also the captain's pinnace, are, however, excepted, the former having proper officers on board for the purpose, and the latter being narrowly watched and examined at the landing

The weather at Canton is in summer extremely hot, and in the months of December, January, and February, cold the country is nevertheless pleasant and healthful, abounding with all the necessaries and delicacies of life, which may be procured on terms much cheaper than in Europe. The number of inhabitants has been estimated at one million, and though some calculations have made the number considerably less, Mr Anderson, in his account of the late embassy, supposes it is under-rated.

Four leagues from Canton is the village of Fo-chan, the largest and perhaps most populous in the world, it is called a village on account of its not being inclosed by walls, and not having a particular governor. It carries on a great trade, and contains more houses than Canton itself. It is reckoned to be three leagues in circumference, and to contain a million of inhabitants

At the entrance of the bay of Canton is the celebrated Portuguese port commonly called *Macaa*, situated in lat. 22° 12′. The city is built on a small island, or rather a peninsula, joined to the rest of the island by a small neck, inclosed by a wall. The Portuguese, as we have before observed, obtained this port as a reward for the assistance they gave the Chinese against a celebrated pirate, who infested the neighbouring seas, and had laid siege to the capital of the province

Some travellers have asserted, that this city had no inhabitants but pirates when the Portuguese formed an establishment on it, and that they were only permitted to build huts covered with straw · however this may have been, they fortified the place, and surrounded it with strong walls.

Macao has now a Portuguese governor, and a Chinese mandarin, the palace of the latter is in the middle of the city, and the Portuguese pay a tribute of a hundred thousand ducats per annum for the liberty of choosing their own magistrates, exercising their religion, and living according to their own laws The houses here are built after the European manner, but are very low. The city is defended by three forts, built upon eminences its works are good, and well supplied with proper artillery.

CHAO-TCHEOU-FOU.

Chao-tcheou-fou is the second city in the province of Quang-tong It is situated between two navigable rivers. The surrounding country produces abundance of rice and fruits, the pastures, on which numberless flocks are seen feeding, are also numerous, and the coasts teem with fish; but the air is unhealthful, hence contagious distempers, which generally prevail here from the middle of October to the beginning of December, sweep off a great number of the inhabitants. There is a celebrated monastery of the bonzes at about three miles distance, and nothing can be more delightful than its situation. It stands on the centre of a mountain, called Nan-hoa, from whence there is a charming prospect of a desert, which stretches out into an immense plain, bordered with hills, the tops of which are covered with fruit trees, planted in regular order, and intermixed with groves, the foliage of which is always green. The origin of this monastery is traced back eight or nine hundred years, the bonzes pretend that its founder practised the most edifying austerity but if so, his successors but badly follow his example, for it is asserted, that they abandon themselves to every kind of debauchery, and the people who formerly visited this place on pilgrimage, have complained much of their thefts and robberies, these latter abuses have however been corrected, and devotees may now visit the place in safety. This city has under its jurisdiction six cities of the third clafs, near one of which grows a kind of black reed, of which feveral mufical inftruments are made, that cannot be diftinguifhed from thofe made of real ebony.

NAN-HIONG-FOU AND HOEI-TCHEOU-FOU.

Both of thefe are trading cities, and the firft in particular is much reforted to, it ftands at the foot of a mountain, from whence two large rivers defcend, one of which runs to the North, and the other to the South. The diftrict of this city includes only two others of the third rank. Hoei-tcheou-fou is almoft furrounded with water, and the country abounds with fprings its jurifdiction embraces one city of the fecond, and ten of the third rank.

TCHAO-TCHEOU-FOU AND TCHAO-KING-FOU.

The firft of thefe cities ftands near the mouth of the river Han-kyang, the fea flowing up to its walls. it has a magnificent bridge on the eaft fide, long, and proportionably wide there are eleven cities of the third rank within its diftrict, which is feparated from the province of Fo-kien by high mountains, and which is in general fertile —Tchao-king-fou is fituated on the Ta-ho, and its port is fpacious, being at the confluence of three rivers, one of which flows to Can-ton, between which and this city both fides are covered with large villages Tchao-king has within its jurifdiction one city of the fecond and five of the third clafs.

KAO-TCHEOU-FOU.

The tide flows up to this city, and Chinefe veffels of burthen may fail up to it with conveniency. Its fituation is in a delightful and fertile country, and in its neighbourhood is found a fingular kind of ftone, refembling marble, which reprefents, naturally, rivers, mountains, landfcapes, and trees, thefe ftones are cut into flabs, and made into tables and other curious pieces of furniture, crabs are alſo caught on the coaſts here, which have a great reſemblance to the common ſort, and which are ſaid to have this ſingularity, that when taken from the water, they become petrified without loſing any thing of their natural figure *. Kao-tcheou has in its diſtrict one city of the ſecond and five of the third claſs.

LIEN-TCHEOU-FOU, AND LOUI-TCHEOU-FOU.

Both theſe cities are on the ſea coaſt, and have very convenient harbours. The diſtrict of the former borders on the kingdom of Tong-king, from which it is ſeparated by inacceſſible mountains; it embraces one city of the ſecond claſs and two of the third. The ſecond is ſeparated from the iſland of Hai-nan only by a narrow ſtrait, where there was formerly a pearl fiſhery. The diſtrict of this city is not more extenſive than that of the former, having only three cities of the third claſs, but it abounds with ſmall fiſhing towns on the coaſt.

KIUN-TCHEOU-FOU.

This is the capital of the iſland of Hai-nan, which belongs to this province. This iſland has on the north the province of Quang-ſi; on the ſouth the channel formed between the bank Parcel and the eaſtern coaſt of Cochin-china; on the weſt, the ſame kingdom and part of Tong-king; and on the eaſt, the Chineſe ſea.

Its extent from eaſt to weſt is between ſixty and ſeventy leagues, and from north to ſouth forty-five, being about an hundred and ſixty leagues in circumference.

Kiun-tcheou-fou, its capital, ſtands on a promontory, and ſhips anchor at the bottom of its walls. Two different kinds of mandarins command here, as in the other provinces of China: the firſt are called literati, the ſecond, mandarins of arms, or military officers. Its juriſdiction

* [illegible] Du [illegible]

extends over three cities of the second class and ten of the third. The greater part of the island is under the dominion of the emperor of China, the rest is independent, and inhabited by a free people, who have never yet been subdued Compelled to abandon their plains and fields to the Chinese, they have retreated to the mountains in the centre of the island, where they are sheltered from the insults of their intruders, though they formerly held a correspondence with them Twice a year they exposed, in an appointed place, the gold which they dug from their mines, with their eagle-wood and *calamba*, so much esteemed by the Orientals. They appointed a deputy to visit the frontiers, to examine the cloths and other commodities of the Chinese, whose principal traders repaired to the place of exchange fixed on, and after the Chinese wares were delivered, they put into their hands with the greatest fidelity what they had agreed for By this barter the mandarins made immense profit, but the emperor Kang-hi, informed of the prodigious quantity of gold which passed through their hands, forbade his subjects, under pain of death, to have any communication with these islanders some private emissaries of the neighbouring governors still find the means of having intercourse with them, but the advantages of this clandestine trade is little, in comparison of that which they formerly gained The natives of this island are described as very deformed, small of stature, and of a copper colour both men and women wear their hair thrust through a ring on their forehead, and above they have a small straw hat, from which hang two strings that are tied under the chin. Their dress consists of a piece of dark-blue cotton cloth, which reaches from the girdle to their knees the women have a kind of robe of the same stuff, and mark their faces from the eyes to the chin with blue stripes made with indigo.

Among the animals of this iſland a curious ſpecies of large black apes is found, they have the ſhape and features of a man, and are ſaid to be very fond of women. among the birds there are crows with a white ring round their necks ſtarlings with a ſmall creſcent on their bills, black-birds of a deep blue colour, with yellow ears riſing half an inch, and many other birds, remarkable for their colour or ſong

Beſides mines of gold and lapis lazuli, which enrich the iſland of Hai-nan, it produces in abundance various kinds of curious and valuable wood. The predeceſſor of the preſent emperor cauſed ſome it of to be tranſported to Pe-kin, at an immenſe expence, to adorn an edifice which he intended for a mauſoleum The moſt valuable is called by the natives *hoa-li*, and by the Europeans, roſe or violet-wood, from its ſmell, it is very durable, and of ſingular beauty, it is therefore reſerved for the uſe of the emperor

Hai-nan, on account of its ſituation, riches and extent, deſerves to be ranked among the moſt conſiderable iſlands of Aſia. Not far from thence is another ſmall iſland, commonly called San-cian It is celebrated by the death of St Francis Xavier, whoſe tomb is ſtill to be ſeen on a ſmall hill, at the bottom of which is a plain, covered on one ſide with wood, and on the other ornamented with ſeveral gardens This iſland is not a deſert, as ſome travellers have pretended it contains five villages, the inhabitants of which are poor people, who have nothing to ſubſiſt on but rice and the fiſh which they catch

THE PROVINCE OF QUANG-SI

This province is ſituated between thoſe of Quang-tong, Hou-quang, Koei-tcheou, Yun-nan and the kingdom of Tong-king. it is inferior in extent and commerce to moſt of the other provinces, however, it is ſo abundant in rice, that it ſupplies the province of Quang-tong with a conſiderable portion of its conſumption. The mountains, with which it is covered, eſpecially towards the north, abound with mines of gold, ſilver, copper and tin Some years back the governor of one of the cities of the firſt claſs preſented a memorial to the emperor, in which he propoſed a plan for preventing the inconveniencies dreaded from the working of theſe mines he ſtated, among other things, that the people of the country had offered to open them at their own expence, and to admit no one to work in them without a patent from his mandarin, and four ſureties to anſwer for good behaviour.

The emperor having read this memorial, referred it for examination to the *hou-pou*, or court of finances They approved of the plan, on condition, that, according to what had been practiſed upon ſimilar occaſions, forty per cent ſhould be given to the emperor, and five per cent to the officers and ſoldiers who preſided over the works the emperor afterwards took them wholly to himſelf, and cauſed them to be opened at his own expence

There is a very ſingular tree grows in this province; inſtead of pith it contains a ſoft ſubſtance, which is a kind of meal, and the bread made of it is ſaid to be exceedingly good Paroquets, hedge-hogs, the rhinoceros and a prodigious number of other wild animals, curious birds and uncommon inſects are found in this province, which contains twelve cities of the firſt claſs and eighty of the ſecond and third

QUEI-LING-FOU.

This city, which is the capital, has its name from a flower called *quei*, it grows on a tree reſembling a laurel, and exhales ſo agreeable an odour, that it perfumes the whole country around.

Quei-ling-fou is ſituated on the banks of a river, which flows into the *Ta-ho*, but with ſuch rapidity, and amidſt valleys ſo narrow that it is neither navigable nor of any utility to commerce. This city is large, and partly built after the model of the ancient European fortresses, but it is much inferior to the capitals of most of the other provinces.

There are a number of birds found in the territories belonging to this city, the colours of which are so bright and variegated, that the artists, to add to the lustre of their silks, interweave with them some of their feathers, which have a splendour and beauty that cannot be imitated. Queiling has under its jurisdiction two cities of the second and seven of the third class.

The other cities of the province present nothing remarkable, they have little or no trade, the inhabitants, chiefly Tartars, are a kind of half barbarians, and in general the districts are far from fruitful. Lieou-tcheou-fou, Kin-yuen-fou, Se-nguen-fou and Ping-lo-fou are surrounded with dreary mountains. Ou-tcheou-fou, Sin-tcheou-fou, Nan-ning-fou, Tai-ping-fou, Se-ming-fou, Tchin-ngan-fou, and Se-tchin-fou are rather more pleasantly situated, but none of them claim a more particular description: altogether have thirty other cities of the second class, and forty-one of the third, within their jurisdiction.

PROVINCE OF YUN-NAN

The province of Yun-nan is bounded on the north by Se-tchuen and Thibet, on the west by the kingdoms of Ava and Pegu, on the south by those of Laos and Tong-king, and on the east by the provinces of Quang-si and Kouei-tcheou.

It is reckoned one of the most fertile and opulent in China, its inhabitants are brave, robust, affable and fond of the sciences, its rivers are suited for commerce or pleasure, and its mines of gold, copper and tin, its richness in amber, rubies, sapphires, agates, pearls and precious stones, marble, musk, silk, elephants, horses, gums, medicinal plants and linen have procured it a high reputation. Its commerce is immense, and its riches are said to be inexhaustible

This province has under its jurisdiction twenty-one cities of the first class and fifty-five of the second and third.

YUN-NAN-FOU.

This city, which is the capital of the province, is situated on the borders of a large lake, it was formerly celebrated for its extent and the beauty of its public edifices. Within its walls were magnificent buildings, and without them vast gardens, tombs, triumphal arches and elegant squares were every where seen, but the Tartars, in their different invasions, destroyed all these monuments, and the city at present contains nothing remarkable it is, however, the residence of the governor of the province, as it once was of a Chinese prince, It has a considerable trade in silk, metals, &c and comprehends in its district four cities of the second class and seven of the third

With respect to the other cities of this province, they afford little deserving notice, we shall therefore only enumerate them, they are Ling-ngan-fou, Tali-fou, Tchou-hiung-fou, Tchink-iang-fou, King-tong-fou, Quang-naa-fou, Quang-si-fou, Chun-ning-fou, Ku-tsing-fou, Yao-ngan-fou, Ko-king-fou, Vou-ting-fou, Li-kiang-to-fou, Yuen-kiang-fou, and Mong-hoa-fou Of these the sixth, seventh, ninth, fourteenth and fifteenth have no districts belonging to them all the rest have under their jurisdiction twenty-one cities of the second and sixteen of the third class.

PROVINCE OF KOEI-TCHEOU.

This is one of the smallest provinces in China. It is bounded on the south by Quang-si, on the east by Hou-quang, on the north by Se-tchuen, and on the west by Yun-nan. The whole country is almost a desert, and covered with inaccessible mountains on which account it has been justly called the Siberia of China The people who inhabit a great part of it are mountaineers, unsubdued and accustomed to independence, and are little less ferocious than the savage animals among which they live

The mandarins and governors of this province, are in general disgraced noblemen, whom the emperor does not think proper to discard entirely, on account of their alliances, or the services which they have rendered to the state, he therefore often sends them here with their families, and numerous garrisons are entrusted to their charge, to over-awe the inhabitants of the country, but hitherto these troops have been found insufficient to thoroughly subdue these untractable mountaineers

Frequent attempts have indeed been made to accomplish this object, and new forts have from time to time been erected in their country, but they keep themselves shut up among their mountains, and seldom issue forth, but to destroy the Chinese works, or ravage their lands

Neither silk stuffs nor cotton cloths are manufactured in this province, but it produces a certain herb, nearly resembling European hemp, the cloth made of which is used for summer dresses Mines of gold, silver, quicksilver and copper are found here, of the last metal those small pieces of money which are in common circulation throughout the empire, are made.

Koei-tcheou contains ten cities of the first class, of which Koei-yang is the capital, and thirty-eight of the second and third Koei-yang is said to have been formerly the residence of the ancient kings and the remains of temples and palaces, still to be seen, proclaim its former magnificence, but these monuments are insensibly mouldering and falling to pieces.

The Chinese in this province are more taken up with defending themselves from the incursions of the mountaineers than in preserving remains of antiquity on which they set no value their houses are built of earth and brick, and the greater part of the cities in this province are but heaps of cottages badly disposed the other nine cities are called Se-tcheou, Se nan, Tchin-yuen, Che-tsien, Tong-gin, Ngan-chan, Tou-yun, Ping-yuen, and Ouei-ning.

Some of these are situated on the banks of agreeable rivers, and in fertile valleys, and a great quantity of land might be found which would yield a considerable produce were it improved, but the mountaineers strike a terror into the Chinese, which keeps them in the neighbourhood of their fortresses This province however furnishes the best horses in China, and an immense number of cows and hogs are raised, and some excellent wild poultry, of a most exquisite taste, are every where to be found.

In describing the fifteen provinces of China, we have contented ourselves with pointing out the principal cities which they contain The author of *Yu the Great* and *Confucius* has given the whole number, according to the account *which he says* a learned mandarin caused to be published for the use of government. Although it is impossible to warrant the correctness of this list of the cities and monuments of China, we shall give it a place here.

"There are reckoned to be four thousand four hundred and two walled cities in China, which are divided into two classes—the *civil* and *military*. The civil class containing two thousand and forty-five, and the military two thousand three hundred and fifty-seven. the civil class is again divided into three others, one hundred and seventy-five of the first, which the Chinese call *fou;* two hundred and seventy of the second, which are called *tcheou;* and an hundred and sixty of the third, which are distinguished by the name of *hien.*"

"The military cities are divided into seven classes, there are reckoned to be six hundred and twenty-nine of the first, five hundred and sixty of the second, three hundred and eleven of the third, three hundred of the fourth, one hundred and fifty of the fifth, an hundred of the sixth, and three hundred of the seventh. Soldiers are quartered in some of these cities, and a certain quantity of land assigned them in the neighbourhood for their support. The frontiers and sea coasts are defended by four hundred and thirty nine castles, well fortified, and kept in good order: there are also along the same coasts two thousand nine hundred and twenty towns, many of which are equal in extent and population to several of the walled cities. With regard to towns and villages dispersed throughout the interior parts of the country, we are assured that they are almost innumerable, and that the greater part of them are rich, commercial, and populous."

"Public institutions in China correspond with the extent of the empire. There are one thousand one hundred and forty five royal hospitals, or lodging-places, destined for the use of the mandarins, governors of provinces, officers of the court, couriers, and all those who travel at the expence of the emperor. The towers, triumphal arches, and other monuments, erected in honour of good kings or illustrious heroes, are in number eleven hundred and fifty-nine. The virtues of women, as well as those of the men, are entitled to public honours in China: two hundred and eight monuments are to be seen there, consecrated to the memory of a certain number of females, who, by their modesty, virtue, and attention to the duties of their sex, have merited the esteem and veneration of their fellow citizens. Two hundred and seventy-two celebrated libraries are continually open to the literati and men of genius, and the ſchools or colleges eſtabliſhed by *Confucius*, and thoſe founded in honour of him, are multiplied as much as cities and towns."

GENERAL DESCRIPTION

OF

CHINESE TARTARY.

EXTENT, BOUNDARIES, &c.

CHINESE Tartary is bounded on the north by Siberia, on the east by the gulph of Kamtschatka and the eastern sea, on the south by China, and on the west by the country of the Kalmouks, who are established between the Caspian sea and Casghar. The different tribes which at present inhabit this country were formerly comprehended under the general name of *Mourgal* or *Mogul* Tartars. That they are a warlike and formidable nation is evident from the conquest of Indostan, and the subjection of China under the conduct of the famous Zinghis-kan. After having taken possession of the latter empire, and supported a Tartar emperor there for an hundred years, they were expelled by the Chinese in 1368. The fugitives took different routs: some going towards the eastern sea, where they established themselves between China and the river *Saghalien*; the rest returned westward to their former country, where, intermixing with the Moguls who had remained, they soon resumed their ancient manner of living; those who settled towards the east, found the country almost a desert and without inhabitants, hence they retained the customs which they had imbibed in China: and hence the origin of the difference of these two Mogul nations in language, government, religion and customs. Those of the west still retain their ancient name of Moungal or Mogul Tartars the others are known by the name of Mantchew or Eastern Tartars. Thus, Chinese Tartary may be considered as divided into two parts—the eastern and western, agreeable to which we shall pursue our description.

EASTERN CHINESE TARTARY.

This division of Tartary extends, north to south, from the forty-first to the fifty-fifth degree of north latitude, and east and west, from about the hundred and thirty-seventh degree of longitude, as far as the eastern sea, being bounded north by Siberia, south by the gulph of Lea-tong and Corea, east by the eastern sea, and west by the country of the Moguls

After their expulsion from China in 1368, the Tartars, who came to this part, immediately began to build towns and villages, and to cultivate the earth after the manner of the Chinese, among whom they had lived the greater part of them have, therefore, remained fixed, and are in general more civilized than the rest of the Mogul nation. They were at first governed by particular *Kans*, each independent of the other, but since the *Kan* of *Ningouta* took possession of China, the emperor, who is still one of his descendants, has reduced under his dominion all the other kans of this part of Tartary and governs it immediately by himself, sending governors and officers, as into the other provinces of the empire, at his will It is divided into three grand departments, viz CHEN-YANG, KI-RIN, and TCITCICAR

CHEN-YANG.

Chen-yang comprehends all the ancient Leao-tong, extending to the great wall, which bounds it on the south; but on the east, north and west it is enclosed by a palisade, better calculated to defend the country against robbers than to stop the march of an army: it is constructed only of stakes seven feet high, without any bank of earth, ditch, or the smallest fortification, nor are the gates any better, the guards at which consist only of a few soldiers.

Chen-yang is the capital city of the country: the Mantchew Tartars have adorned it with several public edifices, and provided it with magazines of arms and storehouses. It is considered as the principal place of the nation, and since China has been under the Tartar dominion, the same tribunals have been established here as at Pe-king, excepting that called *Li-pou*: these tribunals are composed of Tartars only, their determination is final, and the Tartar characters and language is used in all their [illegible]. Chen-yang is built on an eminence, and is considered as a double city, one enclosed within the other: the interior contains the emperor's palace, hotels of the principal mandarins, sovereign courts and the different tribunals, the exterior is inhabited by tradesmen, and those whose employments or professions do not oblige them to lodge in the interior: the latter is almost three miles in circumference, and the walls which enclose both are more than nine miles round: these walls were rebuilt in 1631, and repaired several times under the reign of the emperor *Kang-hi*.

Near the gates of the city are two tombs of the first emperors of the reigning family, built in the Chinese manner, and surrounded by a thick wall furnished with battlements, they are entrusted to the care of several Mantchew mandarins.

The rest of the cities of this province are of little consideration, they are for the most part ill built, and without any other defence than a wall, half in ruins, or constructed of earth beat together: an exception must however be made with respect to the city of Fong-hoang-ching, which is populous, and a place of great trade, arising from its situation on the frontiers of Corea. Being near the entrance of that kingdom, the king's messengers, and such of his subjects as are desirous of trading in the empire, must pass it on this account, it is frequented by a great number of Chinese, who are in some manner the factors of the merchants of the other provinces. There are in this country many mountains, some of which abound with metals and wood fit for building the land is in general fertile, producing wheat, millet, leguminous plants and cotton Immense herds of oxen and flocks of sheep are seen feeding in the valleys

KI-RIN

Ki-rin, the second department of Eastern Chinese Tartary, is bounded on the north by the river *Saghalien*, on the east by the sea, on the south by Corea, and on the west by the palisade of the province of Leao-tong. This country is rendered extremely cold by the number of forests with which it is covered. It is thinly inhabited, containing only two or three ill-built cities, surrounded by plain mud walls. Plenty of *gin-seng* grows here, as do most of the fruit trees of Europe, and here the emperor sends those criminals who are condemned to banishment by the laws.

Ki-rin is situated on the river Songari, and is the residence of a Mantchew general, who is invested with all the powers of a viceroy at the distance of forty-five leagues towards the north-east, on the same river, is the city of *Pet-uné*, still less considerable than the preceding having scarcely any inhabitants but Tartar soldiers and Chinese condemned to banishment.

A third city, which may be considered as the cradle of the present imperial family, is called *Ningouta* It is surrounded by a fence of plain stakes driven into the earth, which touch each other, and are twenty feet high without this palisado, there is another of the same kind, a league in circumference, with four gates correſponding to the four cardinal points. This city is the reſidence of a lieutenant-general, who is a Mantchew Tartar, and whoſe juriſdiction extends over the neighbouring country and all the villages of Yupi tſe, with ſome other petty nations that inhabit the banks of the rivers Ouſouri and Saghalien, and along the ſea coaſt.

The Tartars of Yupi-tatſe are of a peaceful diſpoſition, but ſtupid and clowniſh. They ſow nothing but a little tobacco in ſome of the fields ſurrounding their villages. Immenſe foreſts, almoſt impenetrable, cover the reſt of the country, which produce clouds of troubleſome inſects.

The river Ouſouri, on the banks of which theſe people live, ſupplies them with fiſh; they have no other food, and ſcarcely any clothes but what they make of their ſkins, which they dreſs and dye of three or four colours. They cut and join them with ſuch dexterity and neatneſs, that they appear to be ſewed with ſilk, nor can it be perceived until they are ripped, that this thread is only a very ſmall thong cut from a ſkin exceedingly fine: their clothes are ſhaped like thoſe of the Mantchew Tartars, and the women ſuſpend from the bottoms of their long cloaks pieces of money and little bells, the noiſe of which gives notice of their approach; they part their hair into ſeveral treſſes, and let it hang over their ſhoulders: all theſe treſſes are loaded with ſmall mirrors, rings and other toys.

The whole ſummer theſe Tartars are engaged in fiſhing; they generally uſe harpoons for ſtriking large fiſh, and nets for catching the reſt. Their boats are ſmall; and their canoes are made of the bark of trees, ſo well ſewed together, that the water cannot penetrate them. Of one part of their fiſh they make oil, which they burn in their lamps: another ſupplies them with immediate food; and a third they dry in the sun, and reserve for winter when the ice prevents them from fishing.

Dogs are deservedly held in great estimation for their great value and importance in this country: they are yoked to sledges, which they draw and conduct along the ice for hundreds of miles.

Beyond the Yupi-tase Tartars are the Ketcheng-tase Tartars. These inhabit both banks of the river Saghalien-oula, and extend themselves as far as the eastern sea. Their country, which is about four hundred and fifty miles in length, contains only small villages, the greater part of which are situated on the banks of the river. The language of these Tartars is different from that of the Mantchews, and is distinguished by the name of *Fiatta*: it is in all probability the same with that spoken by the other more northerly Tartars who live beyond the mouth of the river Saghalien.

These Tartars do not shave their heads, they wear their hair tied in a knot with a ribband, or inclosed in a bag behind. They appear to be less clownish than the Mantchews, employing much of their time in hunting sables, of the skins of which they are obliged to pay a certain tribute.

TCIT-CI-CAR.

The most northerly of the departments of Eastern Chinese Tartary is that of Tcitcicar. — This is a modern city built by the emperor of China to secure his frontiers against the Muscovites. The country is occupied by different Tartar tribes, the principal of which are the Mantchews, Solons and the Taguris the ancient inhabitants of the country. The two latter tribes submitted to the Mantchews, and implored their assistance against the Muscovites, who had made themselves formidable to the Tartar nations who inhabited the banks of the Saghalien-oula, and the Songari-oula, as well as to those on the little rivers that fall into them.

The city of Tcitcicar is fortified by close palisades and a wall of earth. The space enclosed by the former contains the tribunals and the house of the Tartar general; that between the palisades and the wall is occupied by the soldiers of the Tartar garrison, merchants and tradesmen, the greater part of whom are Chinese drawn here by the hopes of gain, or condemned to exile for their crimes. Their houses are only of earth, but form pretty large streets. The jurisdiction of Tcitcicar extends over the new cities of Merguen and Saghalien-oula-hotun, or *City of the Black River*: the latter is the most populous, rich, and important, on account of its situation. It stands on the southern bank of the river Saghalien, commanding a plain in which several villages have been built, and securing to the Mantchew Tartars the possession of extensive deserts covered with woods, in which a great number of sables are found. The Muscovites would have soon become masters of these valuable forests, if the fort of Yasca, erected higher up on the river Saghalien, had been suffered to remain; but, by the treaty of peace in 1689 between the Russians and Chinese, it was agreed that it should be demolished, that no cause of umbrage or complaint might be left to the Tartar hunters.

This agreement does not, however, prevent the Tartars from keeping strict watch on their territories; and they keep advanced guards constantly posted in proper places, and a number of armed barks on the river Saghalien.

The Tagouris, who are the oldest inhabitants of the country, are tall, strong, and accustomed to labour; they build themselves houses, cultivate their lands, and sow corn, although they are surrounded by Tartars who live under tents, and who are entirely ignorant of agriculture.

The Solon Tartars are robuſt, braver, and more ingenious, than the Tagouris, they are almoſt all hunters; their women mount on horſeback, handle the bow and the javelin, and follow in the chace ſtags and other wild animals. About the beginning of October they take their departure to hunt ſables, clad in ſhort cloſe garments of wolf's ſkin, their heads are covered with caps of the ſame, and their bows are ſuſpended at their backs.

They take with them ſeveral horſes loaded with ſacks of millet, and their long cloaks made of foxes or tygers ſkins, with which they defend themſelves from the cold during the night.

The ſable ſkins of this country are valuable, but the obtaining of them expoſes the hunters to dangers and fatigues almoſt unparalleled. Neither the rigorous cold of winter, which freezes the largeſt rivers, the dread of tygers, which muſt be encountered, nor the death of many of their companions, prevents theſe people from returning every year to this dangerous occupation. The moſt beautiful ſkins are put apart for the emperor, who buys a certain number of them at a fixed price, the reſt are ſold high, even in the country, being immediately bought up by the mandarins and merchants of Tcitcicar.

Pearls are found in ſome of the rivers which diſcharge themſelves into the Saghalien-oula. This fiſhery requires little preparation, as theſe ſmall rivers are generally very ſhallow, the divers plunge to the bottom of the water, and collect whatever oyſters they can, as chance directs, returning to the bank, with their load. This pearl-fiſhery belongs to the emperor, but the pearls are ſmall, and not of a fine water, a kind much more beautiful are found in ſome other rivers of Tartary which flow into the eaſtern ſea. The emperor however ſends every year to this fiſhery a certain number of men choſen from the eight Tartar bands. The three firſt, which are the moſt celebrated and numerous, furnish thirty-three companies, the other five thirty six. Each company has a captain and serjeant, three superior officers command the whole, and a certain number of merchants, well acquainted with the nature of pearls, accompany them. All these companies for their permission to fish must every year pay to the emperor eleven hundred and forty pearls, which is the fixed tribute. The three first companies furnish five hundred and twenty-eight, and the five last, five hundred and sixty-six. These must be pure and without blemish, otherwise they are returned, and others required in their stead. The pearls are examined at the return of these companies and, if they are few in number, the officers are punished as guilty of negligence, and their pay either stopped for a whole year, or they are cashiered.

The Mantchews dispersed throughout Eastern Chinese Tartary have neither temples nor idols: they adore as they express it the *Emperor of Heaven*, to whom they offer sacrifices; but since they have entered China, some of them worship *Fo* and other idols of the Chinese. They are however in general attached to their ancient religion, which they consider as the cause of their actual greatness and the cause of the prosperity of their arms.

Nations who have become conquerors, have in general had the vain ambition of being thought descended from an illustrious origin. Thus when the Mantchew Tartars saw themselves masters of China, they gave themselves a celestial extraction, and placed a god at the head of their race. The following fable concerning their first sovereign, is repeated by them, and also is found in some of their most authentic books.

" On the top of the white mountain towards the rising " of the sun is a celebrated lake, called *Poulkouri*, as well " as that part of the mountain where it is situated. We " have learned by tradition, that the daughter of Hea-

" ven, having defcended on the banks of this lake, tafted " a red fruit, eat fome of it, conceived, and afterwards " brought forth a fon of the fame nature with herfelf. " As this wonderful child was endowed with celeftial gifts, " he fpoke the very moment after his birth, his figure " was wonderful, and every thing in it difplayed majefty " and grandeur When he grew up, he amufed himfelf " fometimes in traverfing the lake in the trunk of a tree, " which was hollowed out in the form of a boat. One " day, having fuffered himfelf to be carried away by the " current, the boat ftopped of itfelf at that place of the " river which ferved as a port to the people on each fide " of it, and as a magazine for their different commodities. " It happened at that time, that tumultuous affemblies " were held every day in the neighbourhood of this place, " for the electing of a fovereign. three chiefs of families " difputed with each another for the honour of command- " ing the reft, each had his partifans almoft equal in num- " ber and ftrength, on which account they could not " agree, neither being willing to yield, and each confi- " dering his party as the moft powerful One of the " company having gone afide to draw water from the " river, beheld with aftonifhment this young ftranger. " After having contemplated him for fome moments, he " haftened back to his companions, to inform them of " what he had feen When he was near enough to be " underftood, *A miracle!* cried he, *a miracle! Let us " ceafe our difputes! Heaven itfelf wifhes to put an end to " them, it hath fent us a king, in the perfon of an extraor- " dinary youth, whom I have juft feen on the river Yes, it " is Heaven itfelf which hath fent him. I judge from " what I have feen For what other purpofe could a young " man of this nature be permitted to land here?* On thefe " words, the whole multitude flocked to the fhore to " enjoy the fpectacle which had been announced to them:

" thoſe who arrived firſt, turning towards the reſt who " followed, cried out, *Nothing is more true, this is really* " *a miraculous child, this is the king whom Heaven ſends* " *us—we have occaſion for no other.*

" Theſe words paſſed ſucceſſively from mouth to mouth, " and every one took a pleaſure in repeating them. As " ſoon as the firſt tranſports of admiration were a little " calmed, two of the chiefs of the company, addreſſing " the ſtranger, ſaid to him, *Amiable young man, illuſtri-* " *ous youth! who art thou? by what fortunate chance* " *have we the happineſs of ſeeing thee among us—I am* " replied the young man, *I am the ſon of the daughter* " *of Heaven, my name is* AISIN-KIORO, *or* KIORO OF " GOLD. *Thus am I named by Heaven itſelf, my ſirname* " *is* POULKOURI-YONGCHONG. *I am ſent to terminate* " *your diſputes, and to cauſe harmony and concord to reign* " *among you.*"

" Scarcely had he done ſpeaking, when tranſports of " joy burſt forth on all ſides with reiterated ſhouts of " applauſe, and the two chiefs who had firſt addreſſed " him, thruſting their fingers between each other, ex- " tended their arms and formed a kind of ſeat, upon " which they placed the illuſtrious youth, and carried " him with reſpect, followed by the whole multitude, " to the place where the three competitors ſtood: *Behold,* " ſaid they, accoſting them, *behold the ſovereign whom* " *Heaven itſelf hath ſent—we have occaſion for no other.* " *Let all contentions among us be now ended, and let every* " *altercation ceaſe.—We conſent,* replied the three candi- " dates, *let this auguſt youth govern us, let him be our* " *king—we henceforth acknowledge him as ſuch.*"

From the period in which the Tartars gained poſſeſſion of the throne of China, their language has been familiar at the court of Pe-kin. Two preſidents, one a Tartar, the other a Chineſe, are at the head of every ſovereign court, and all the public acts issued from these principal tribunals are drawn up in the Tartar and Chinese languages.

This language is considered as much easier to be acquired than that of China, but it would have been in danger of being entirely lost, had not the Tartars taken precautions for its preservation They perceived that it was becoming impoverished by many of its terms being forgotten: the old Tartars gradually died in China, and their children learned with greater facility the language of the conquered country than that of their fathers, because their mothers and servants were in general Chinese

Kang-hi thought his glory interested in perpetuating the language of his nation. He, therefore, in the commencement of his reign, instituted a tribunal composed of literati versed in the Tartar and Chinese idioms, some of whom he ordered to translate books of history and other esteemed works, but the greater number were employed in compiling a *treasure* of the Tartar language this latter work was executed with surprising perseverance and expedition. If any doubt arose, the veterans of the eight Tartar bands were interrogated, was it necessary to make farther researches, persons who had recently arrived from the interior parts of their country were consulted, and rewards were offered to those who should discover any old words or ancient modes of expression proper to be inserted in the *treasure*. These were afterwards used in preference to others, for the purpose of recalling them to the memory of those who had forgot them, or teaching them to the young Tartars who had never had any knowledge of them.

When all these words were collected, they were distributed into several classes the first speaks of the heavens; the second, of time, the third, of the earth, the fourth, of the emperor, government, ceremonies, customs, music, books, war, hunting, man, drinking, eating, silks, cloth, dreſs, labour, workmen, inſtruments, barks, corn, herbs, birds, animals wild and domeſtic, fiſhes, reptiles, &c.

Each of theſe claſſes was divided into chapters and articles, all the words were written in capitals, and under each were found in ſmaller characters the definition, explanation and uſual meaning of the word. Thus a ſtandard of the Tartar language was eſtabliſhed, to which the learner can refer, and of which the Tartars are not a little proud.

WESTERN CHINESE TARTARY.

This vaſt country of the Moguls is bounded on the north by Siberia, on the eaſt by Eaſtern Chineſe Tartary, on the ſouth by the great wall and Leao-tong, and on the weſt by independent Tartary. It was partly from the boſoms of theſe deſerts, that thoſe celebrated conquerors iſſued who made all Aſia tremble, and whoſe exploits fill us with aſtoniſhment. The Mogul nation is ſubdivided into a multitude of others, who all ſpeak the ſame language, generally called the Mogul language: they have, indeed, ſeveral different dialects, but theſe do not prevent them from underſtanding each other. Theſe Tartars have neither towns, villages, nor houſes, they form themſelves only into wandering hordes, and live under plain tents, which they tranſport according as the temperature of the different ſeaſons, or the wants of their flocks require: they paſs the ſummer on the banks of their rivers, and the winter at the bottom of ſome mountain, or little hill, which ſhelters them from the ſharp north wind. Each of theſe tribes has its reſpective limits, and it would be conſidered as an act of hoſtility to encroach on thoſe of their neighbours. They are naturally clowniſh, and dirty in their dreſs, as well as in their tents, where they live amidſt the dung of their flocks, which when dried they burn inſtead of wood. Enemies to labour, they prefer living on the ſpontaneous productions of the earth and the food which their flocks ſupply them with, to being at the trouble of cultivating the ſoil it even appears that they neglect agriculture from pride, for when they were aſked by the miſſionaries why they did not cultivate at leaſt ſome gardens, they replied *the graſs was for beaſts, and beaſts for man*

During the ſummer, they live on the milk which they get from their flocks, uſing without diſtinction that of the cow, mare, ewe, goat, and camel Their ordinary drink is warm water in which a little coarſe tea has been infuſed, with this drink they mix cream, milk, or butter, according to their circumſtances They alſo make a kind of ſpirituous liquor of ſour milk, eſpecially of that of the mare, which they diſtil after having allowed it to ferment Thoſe of better condition, before they diſtil this ſour milk, mix with it ſome of the fleſh of their ſheep which has been alſo left to ferment This liquor is ſtrong and nouriſhing their moſt voluptuous orgies conſiſt in getting drunk with it

The Moguls are free, open and ſincere They pride themſelves chiefly on their dexterity in handling the bow and arrow, mounting on horſeback, and hunting wild beaſts. Polygamy, though permitted among them, is ſeldom indulged in They burn the bodies of their dead, and tranſport the aſhes to eminences, where they inter them, covering the grave with a heap of ſtones, over which they plant a number of ſmall ſtandards. They are unacquainted with the uſe of money, and trade only by barter.

Although the Moguls might appropriate to themſelves the ſpoils of a great number of animals, the ſkins which they uſe for cloathing are generally thoſe of their ſheep. They wear the wool inmoſt, and the ſkin on the outſide.

They are expert at preparing and whitening these ſkins. Some of the better ſort among them uſe the ſkins of ſtags, does, or wild goats for ſpring dreſſes, but whatever care they take to prepare their ſkins, they always exhale a ſtrong and diſagreeable ſmell, hence they are called by the Chineſe *Tſao-ta'ſe*, or *Stinking Tartars*. Their tents almoſt always ſmell of their ſheep, and are endured with difficulty even by thoſe who have been long accuſtomed to them.

Theſe tents are, however, more commodious than the common ones of the Mantchews, which are compoſed of double or ſingle canvas, ſimilar to thoſe of our troops; thoſe of the Moguls are circular, in form of the fruſtum of a cone, and covered with a large piece of white or grey felt. A round hole in the top gives a paſſage to the ſmoke. The fire is made in the middle of the tent, and while the fire laſts, theſe portable huts are very warm, but they ſoon get cold, and in winter the people are in danger of being frozen to death in their beds. They are equally inſupportable during the ſummer, on account of the great heat concentered in them, and of the dampneſs which reſults from the wet and dirt, with which they are ſurrounded, that penetrates them; ſuch, however, is the force of cuſtom and education, that theſe miſerable huts are preferred to the agreeableneſs and convenience of the Chineſe houſes, merely that they may enjoy the pleaſure of changing their habitation every ſeaſon.

The religion of the Mogul Tartars is confined to the worſhip of *Fo*. They have the moſt ſuperſtitious veneration for their *lamas*, who are a ſet of clowniſh, ignorant, and licentious prieſts, who profeſs to have the power of calling down hail or rain: to theſe *lamas* they give the moſt valuable of their effects in return for *prayers*, which they go about reciting from tent to tent. Theſe people wear hanging at their necks a kind of chaplet, over which they ſay their prayers.

All the moguls are governed by *kans*, or particular princes, independent one of the other, but all ſubjected to the authority of the emperor of China, who is conſidered as the grand kan of the Tartars When the Mantchews ſubdued China, they conferred on the moſt powerful of the Mogul princes the titles of *vang*, *petlé*, *peizé* and *cong*, the ſame with our titles of *king*, *duke*, *earl* and *marquis*, each of them had a revenue aſſigned him, but far inferior to the appointments of the Mantchew lords at Pe-kin the emperor ſettled the limits of their territories, and appointed laws, according to which they are at preſent governed theſe tributary kans have not the power of condemning their ſubjects to death, nor of depriving them of their poſſeſſions, theſe two caſes are reſerved for the ſupreme tribunal eſtabliſhed at Pe-kin for the affairs of the Moguls. To this tribunal every individual has the right of appeal from the ſentence of his prince, who is obliged to appear in perſon whenever he is cited

The Mogul nation under the Chineſe government, is divided into four principal tribes, the *Moguls*, properly ſo called—the *Kalkas*, *Ortous*, and the Tartars of *Kokonor*.

THE MOGULS.

According to the map of Chineſe Tartary taken from the memoirs of the Jeſuits, who firſt gave us an account of it, the country of the Moguls extends more than nine hundred miles from eaſt to weſt, and ſix hundred from north to ſouth it is encloſed between the country of the Ortous, the great wall, Eaſtern Tartary and the country of the Kalkas theſe people are divided into forty-nine *ki*, or ſtandards, every ſtandard comprehending an indeterminate number of companies, each conſiſting of one hundred and fifty heads of families, and as theſe families are generally numerous, each company may be reckoned at one thouſand individuals beſides theſe forty-nine standards, there are five others, commanded by officers whom the emperor of China sends thither.

The best cultivated canton of all the Mogul territories is the district of *Cartching*, near the great wall; here the emperor goes every year to enjoy the pleasure of hunting, here he generally passes the summer, and here he has caused several beautiful pleasure-houses to be built, the principal of which is *Gehol*. This prince possesses extensive domains in the country of *Cartching* and along the great wall which belonged to his ancestors, to whose lot they fell in the partition that was made at the time of the conquest of China. The emperor turns these patrimonial possessions to good account by means of farmers which he sends thither, the produce of them being appropriated to the support of his houshold; for he never touches the revenues of the state, which are deposited in the public treasury, for the payment of the troops and officers of the empire. The number of cattle kept on these royal farms is immense; the missionaries have informed us that from accounts furnished by some of the officers belonging to the pastures, they reckoned one hundred and ninety thousand sheep, divided into two hundred and twenty-five flocks, and almost as many oxen and cows, divided into herds, each containing an hundred: the number of stallions kept is still more considerable. These farms, studs and flocks make more impression on the minds of the Tartar and Mogul princes, and render them much more sensible of the grandeur and power of the emperor, than all the magnificence of his court at Pekin.

THE KALKAS.

These Tartars, who are said formerly to have composed a numerous tribe, consisting of more than six hundred thousand families, inhabit to the north of the Mogul Tartars. Their country, which reaches as far as the kingdom of the *Eluths*, is near nine hundred miles in extent from east to west It was in this region, towards the forty-fifth degree of north latitude, that the city of *Karakun*, the seat of the empire of Zinghis-kan, and of that of his successors, was situated

These people live under tents along the banks of the rivers which water their country, the most considerable of which are the Kerlon, Toula, Touy and the Selingue, their banks are well inhabited, and they flow through extensive plains, covered with rich pastures; their waters are wholesome, and abound with excellent fish, particularly trout The Kerlon runs from west to east, and falls into the lake Koulon-nor, the waters of which discharge themselves into the river Saghalien by that of Ergone. The Kerlon is not deep, being in almost every part fordable it does not exceed sixty feet in breadth, but its banks afford the best pastures in Tartary. On the northern side of it are the ruins of a large city, built by the Mogul successors of the famous Coblai-kan, this city appears to have been square, and about two leagues in circumference, its foundations, some pieces of the walls, and two pyramids, half in ruins, still subsist, it was called *Para-hotan*, or *The City of the Tyger*.

The river Toula runs from east to west, and is broader, deeper and more rapid than the Kerlon, its banks are surrounded with woods and beautiful meadows, and the mountains which hang over it on the northern side are covered with forests of aged firs This river, after having received the waters of the Selingue, loses itself in the lake of Pai-cal, the largest in all Tartary. This lake is in the territories of the Muscovites, and even the Selingue does not entirely belong to the Kalkas, for the Russians are masters of the lower part of the river, near which they have built a small city, called Selingeskoi The water of the Touy is pure and wholesome, it waters plains as fertile as the Toula, and after having traversed several very extensive cantons, suddenly loses itself in the bosom of the earth.

The vast desert which the Chinese call *Chamo*, and the Tartars *C[illegible]*, occupies almost all the southern part of the country of the Kalkas. This desert is estimated to be more than three hundred miles in length from east to west, and almost the same in breadth from north to south, and even more towards the western part; it presents nothing but immense plains of sand, interrupted here and there by some little hills, on which are seen a few bushes, but not a single tree. This desert is in general dry, and destitute of pasturage and water of every kind, except a small number of pools in which the rain is collected, and a few bad wells, that are sometimes to be met with. Its situation is very high; the cold here, on that account, is severe, and continues very long. The great quantity of saltpetre with which the sand is impregnated greatly contributes to this temperature, and on digging only a few feet below the surface, the earth may be found frozen in every season of the year.

The neighbouring Tartars, when they traverse these sands, generally make use of camels, because these animals require little food, and can live without water for several days.

In 1688 a war was carried on by the King of the Eleuthes against the Kalkas, which almost destroyed the whole nation. To avoid the pursuit of a superior enemy, they sought the assistance of the Chinese arms, and offered to submit to the empire. Kang-hi undertook their defence, conquered the King of the Eleuthes, and retained the Kalka Tartars under his dominion, after having conferred upon their princes different titles of honour.

The Kalkas have among them one of those grand lamas called [illegible]; he is lodged under a large tent, and shews himself to the public, lying on a kind of altar, where he receives with the greatest indifference the adoration of the Tartar tribes

He salutes no one, not even the princes, but receives homage from them with the dignity of a god. The infatuation of the Tartars, and their stupid veneration for this lama, occasion a prodigious concourse of strangers at Ioen-Pira, where he resides. Bonzes from China, Indostan, Pegu, and many other far more distant countries may be seen there and the great number of tents that are erected around his, form a kind of city, or fair, to which Muscovite merchants sometimes go to traffic

This *hou-toucktou* is however but a lama of the second order, for a lama who resides on the river *Lasa* in Thibet is acknowledged his superior, and is generally considered as the high-priest and supreme chief of the Tartar religion

THE ORTOUS.

The country of the Ortous, who inhabit to the north of the great wall, and to the west of the Moguls properly so called, is three hundred and thirty miles in extent from east to west, and seventy from south to north These people are divided into six standards, comprehending one hundred and sixty six companies, each composed of an hundred and fifty heads of families The Ortous are of a free disposition, extremely lively, and seldom subject to melancholy, on which account they have been called the French of Tartary

The emperor *Kang-hi*, in the course of his expedition against the Eleuthes in 1696, made some stay among the *Ortous*, of whom he gave the following account in a letter which he wrote to the prince, his son, who had remained at Pe-kin, "Hitherto," says he, "I had no "just idea of the Ortous. they are a very polite nation, "and have lost nothing of the ancient manners of the "true Moguls All their princes live in perfect union

"union one with another, and know not the difference "of *mine* and *thine* A robber is never heard of among "them, although they take no precautions to guard their "camels and horses if by chance one of these animals "should stray, the person who finds it takes proper care "of it until he discovers the owner, and restores it to him "without accepting the least gratuity. The Ortous are "intelligent in every thing, especially in the manner of "rearing cattle. The greater part of their horses are "mild and tractable The Tchahar, who live to the "north of the Ortous, are celebrated for breeding them "with care and success, I believe, however, the Ortous "surpass them in that respect, but, notwithstanding this "advantage, they are scarcely so rich as the rest of the "Moguls. They handle the bow very ungracefully, and "in general acquit themselves badly in all exercises of "this kind, but their bows are remarkably strong, and "they hit a mark with wonderful address. The air of "this country is exceedingly wholesome, the waters are "excellent, and the provisions here have an exquisite "taste

TARTARS OF KOKONOR

These Tartars, who are Eleuthes or *Kalmoucks* by nation, and who are at present subjects of the emperor, occupy an extensive country to the west of China and the province of Chen-si, from which they are separated by lofty mountains They take their name from a lake in this country, called in their language *Kokonol*, or *Kokonor*, and which is one of the largest in Tartary They are subject to eight princes, each independent of the other, and all of the race of the kan of the Eleuthes Tartars

These people derive their principal riches from the gold which is found mixed with the sand of their rivers, and above all with that of Altang-kol, or the Golden River, which furnishes in gold dust the principal revenue of the princes of Kokonor, whose vassals during summer are employed in collecting it A man during the four months employed in searching for this gold, may collect, on an average, ten ounces, and even more of it, according to his activity and address The whole process of this labour is very simple the men carry the sand from the bottom of the river, wash it a little, and, retaining what appears to be gold, throw away the rest, that which is retained is afterwards melted in crucibles, and the gold is reckoned to be exceedingly fine, the Tartars however sell it for only six times its weight in silver. Abundance of gold is also found in several other rivers which water the neighbouring states of the grand lama, and great quantities of it are transported to China.

Another principal article of the trade of Kokonor is a kind of napped woollen stuff, called *pou-lou*, manufactured by these Tartars, who have the art of dying it of different colours, long dresses are made of it in the country, and it is generally used at Pe-kin for covering seats The Hoang-ho, or the Yellow River, has its source in this corner of Tartary

Besides the above, the Chinese Empire was extended in Tartary by the conquest of the kingdom of the Eleuthes in 1759, by the arms of the present emperor KIEN-LONG. The whole nation of the Eleuthes, known in Europe and Russia by the name of *Kalmoucks*, may be divided into three branches, all proceeding from the same stem One of these are the Tartars of Kokonor, of whom we have already spoken, but the most westerly and at present the most powerful and numerous, occupy the country contained between the Caspian Sea, Muscovy, Samarcand, and Casghar, which extends eastwards as far as a vast chain of mountains, supposed to be a continuation of Caucasus. Annually during winter these Tartars encamp on the shore of the Caspian Sea, near the village of Astracan, where they carry on a considerable trade The third division inhabits to the east, from the chain of mountains before mentioned, as far as another chain of lofty mountains, the most considerable of which are called Altai many large rivers have their sources in this mountain, the principal of which are the Oby and Irtis The country which these people inhabit is very extensive, bordering on the north with Muscovy, and on the south with the territories of the Usbec Tartars: these are the people whom Kien-long has obliged to submit to the Chinese government

We shall not enter into a detail of the origin, progress, and various events of that war, but content ourselves with mentioning the result of that conquest, and describing the new territory procured by it to the Chinese Empire, as well as the revenue arising from it.

Besides the country which properly formed the kingdom of the Eleuthes, this state possessed several other considerable territories, which have in like manner yielded to the conqueror among this number are Little Boukaria and the cities of Cashgar and Yerguen, with all their dependencies The following information respecting this country is drawn from the letter in which the Chinese general gave an account of his expedition to the emperor

The general informs the emperor, that "besides the principal cities of the Mahometan canton, HASHAR and JERKIM, they had taken seventeen cities, great and small, and sixteen thousand villages and hamlets, and that in all the district of Hashar there were about fifty or sixty thousand families.'

Hashar is situated a little to the south-east of Pe-kin, and distant from *Sou-tcheou*, a city of Chen-si, the westernmost of China, about six thousand *lys*, or eighteen miles It is something more than thirty miles in circumference, but its population is not proportionable to its extent it containing, according to the account taken by the Chinese general, no more than two thousand five hundred families. To the east of Hashar are Ouchei and Aksou, and between Hashar and Aksou, there are three cities and two large villages the number of inhabitants in these cities and villages amount in all to about six thousand families.

Westward from Hashar lies *Antchiten*, between which there are three cities, and two considerable villages, containing together about two thousand two hundred families. Hashar is to the north of Jerkim, and between them lie two cities and two villages, which together contain nearly four thousand four hundred families

When *Kaldan-Tsereng*, the last king of the Eleuthes, reigned over these Mahometans, the tribute which the people of Hashar were obliged to pay him amounted to 67 0 *tenke*, or 2010*l* sterling; this prince received also, by way of tribute for the territories dependent on this city, 40,898 *pathma* of grain, or 1940410 Chinese bushels, 1463 *tcharak* of cotton, or 14630 Chinese pounds, and 365 *tcharak* of saffron, or 3650 pounds

Besides what we have mentioned he received also a tribute from the *Cosacks* and the *Tchokobaches* These two nations were obliged to pay annually the sum of 26000 *tenke*, or 7800l one year to be furnished by the *Cosaks*; the next by the *Tchokobaches* The body of merchants, and those who deal in cattle, provisions, and other things of the same kind, paid a separate tribute of 20.00 *tenke*, or 6000*l* per annum, they were besides obliged to furnish four pieces of tapestry, four pieces of velvet, twenty-six pieces of plush and other stuffs, and the same number of pieces of felt, which the Tartars and Muscovites use for their head-dresses

Besides the usual taxes which the Eleuthes paid in common with others, every ten families among them were obliged to furnish ten ounces of gold those who had gardens or vineyards were obliged to furniſh dried raiſins, to the quantity of a thouſand pounds for every ſeven gardens or vineyards.

Thoſe who properly compoſed the body of merchants paid every year, ſeparately and independent of other tribute, five hundred pounds of red copper, thoſe who carried on trade with *Ouentouſtan* (Indoſtan) or in Muſcovy, had to pay on their return a tenth of their profit With regard to foreign merchants who came to traffic at Haſhar, they paid only a twentieth part of their gain, ſuch was the uſage which the Chineſe general found eſtabliſhed here. It ſeldom, however, happened that all theſe taxes were well paid. The general further informed the emperor that the inhabitants were fewer in number and much poorer than they were in the time of *Kaldan-Tſereng*, and that, owing to the misfortunes of the war, they were become juſt objects of pity He further ſtates the ſoil of this country as far from being rich in good years producing ſeven or eight returns, in common years, only five, and in bad years, three at moſt

OTHER TRIBES SUBJECTED TO THE CHINESE GOVERNMENT

To the preceding ſubjects of the Chineſe Empire we muſt ſtill add, the *Si-fans*, the nation of the *Lo-los*, and the *Miao-tſe* mountaineers.

SI-FANS.

The Si-fans, or Tou-fans, dwell to the weſt of China and the provinces of Chen-ſi and Se-tchuen. Their country is a continued ridge of mountains, encloſed by the rivers *Hoang-ho* on the north, *Ya-long* on the weſt, and *Yang-tſe-kiang* on the eaſt, between the thirtieth and thirty-fifth degrees of north latitude.

The Si-fans are divided into two kinds of people, the one are called by the Chinese *Black Si-fans*, the other *Yellow*—names given them, not from a difference of colour in their persons, but from the different colours of their tents. The black are the most clownish and wretched: living in small bodies, and governed by petty chiefs, depending upon a greater

The Yellow Si-fans are subject to families, the oldest of which becomes a lama, and assumes the yellow dress. These lama-princes have the power of trying causes, and punishing criminals, but their government is by no means burthensome, *and provided that certain honors are paid them, and they receive punctually the dues of the god Fo*, which amount to very little, they molest none of their subjects. The greater part of the Si-fans live in tents; but some of them have houses built of earth and brick. Their habitations are not contiguous, forming at most but small hamlets, consisting of five or six families. They feed a number of flocks, and want none of the necessaries of life. The principal article of their trade is rhubarb, which their country produces in abundance. Their horses are small, but well shaped, lively and robust

These people are of a noble and independent spirit, and it is with reluctance that they acknowledge the superiority of the Chinese government, to which they have been subjected if summoned by the mandarins, they rarely appear, but the government, for political reasons, winks at this contempt, and fearing to use force, endeavours to keep these intractable subjects under by mildness and moderation it would, indeed, be difficult to employ rigorous means, in order to reduce them to obedience, as their wild and frightful mountains, the tops of which are always covered with snow, would afford them places of shelter, from which they could never be driven by force.

The customs of these mountaineers are totally different from those of the Chinese. All their religion consists in

U

their adoration of the god *Fo*, to whom their attachment is great, and their superstitious veneration extends even to his ministers, on whom they have considered it as their duty to confer supreme power, and the government of the nation

Some of their rivers wash down gold mixed with their sands. they form it into vases and small statues, of which they often make offerings to their idol, it even appears that the use of gold is very ancient among them, for Chinese books relate, that under one of the emperors of the dynasty of *Han*, an officer having been sent to them to complain of the ravages committed by some of their chiefs, they endeavoured to appease him by making him a present of a piece of gold plate, which the officer refused, telling the *Si-fans*, that " rice served up in golden dishes was to " him insipid food "

These people have lost much of their ancient splendour At present, they are confined in a wild country, where they have not a single city, but they enjoyed formerly an extensive dominion, and formed a powerful and formidable empire, the chiefs of which often gave great uneasiness to the Chinese emperors They were then in possession of several tracts of land toward the east, which at present make part of the provinces of *Se-tchuen* and *Chen-si*, they even at one period extended their conquests to China, and rendered themselves masters of several cities of the second class, of which they formed four principal governments in the west, they seized upon all the countries which lie beyond the river *Ya-long*, and reach as far as the boundaries of Cachemir, but intestine divisions insensibly weakened this great monarchy, and at length brought it to ruin, according to the Chinese annals about the year 1227 since that time, the *Si-fans* have retired to their native mountains, where, from being a conquering and polished people, they have again sunk in a great degree into their original barbarity

LO-LOS.

The *Lo-los* are dispersed throughout the province of *Yun-nan*, and compose a particular people, distinct from the Chinese They were formerly governed by their own sovereigns, but they submitted to the emperor of China, on condition of having the seals, and enjoying for ever all the honors of Chinese mandarins The emperor on his part stipulated that they should be dependent on the governors of the province in civil affairs, in the same manner as Chinese mandarins of equal rank, that they should receive from him the investure of all their lands, in which, however, they were to exercise no jurisdiction without his consent · the emperor engaging on his part to invest none but the nearest heirs of each family.

The *Lo-los* are in general well made, and enured to labour They have a particular language of their own, and a manner of writing similar to that of the bonzes of Pegu and Ava These *cunning priests* having insinuated themselves into the favour of the richest and most powerful of the *Lo-los*, introduced among them the worship and religious ceremonies of their country; they have even induced them to build large temples, the architecture of which is entirely different from that of the Chinese.

The princes of the *Lo-los* are absolute masters of their subjects, and have the right of punishing them, even by death, without waiting for the answer of the viceroy, and there are no despots more readily obeyed by their slaves, than these lords by their subjects.

These princes have a number of officers attached to their personal service, and they appoint the commanders to all the troops which they have under their inspection; this army, which is a kind of militia, is composed of cavalry and infantry, armed with bows and lances, and sometimes musquets The iron and copper-mines contained in the bowels of their mountains, enable them to make their own armour. These mountains are said also to abound with mines of gold and silver

The dress of the Lo-los consists of plain drawers, a vest of cotton, which hangs down to their knees, and a straw hat, their legs are entirely bare, and they wear only sandals · their princes dress after the Tartar fashion, and generally use silk-stuffs

The women have a long robe, which covers their whole body down to their feet, above which they tie a small cloak that reaches no farther than the girdle In this dress they appear on horseback at marriage ceremonies, or when they pay visits, accompanied by the females in their train, also on horseback, and by their several domestics.

MIAO-TSE MOUNTAINEERS.

Under the name of *Miao-tsé* are comprehended several tribes differing from each other only by some particular customs They are dispersed through the provinces of *Se-tchuen*, *Koei-tcheou*, *Hou-quang*, *Quang-si*, and on the frontiers of the province of *Quang-tong* From their mountains they formerly made incursions into the flat, open country, although the Chinese built castles and fortresses in several places, and furnished them with numerous garrisons for the purpose of restraining them They were for a long time contented with putting a stop to their ravages, without declaring war against them, and when they committed any acts of hostility, they thought it sufficient to drive them back to their mountains, without attempting to force them from their places of retreat.

The Miao-tse lived under the government of princes, who possessed the same authority over them as those of the *Lo-los* have over their subjects they supported a household, and a regular militia, and had under them several petty feudatory lords, who were obliged to levy troops for them whenever they received orders

The usual arms of the *Miao-tse* are bows and half-pikes. Their horses are much esteemed by the Chinese, and sell for an excessive price, on account of the nimbleness and agility with which they climb the mountains. When they chose officers from amongst themselves the candidates were obliged to ride full speed down the steepest declivities, and to clear at one leap wide ditches in which large fires are kindled.

The Miao-tse, who inhabit the province of *Koei-tcheou*, towards *Liping fou*, have houses built of brick, but of only one story, and in the lower part, they keep their horses, oxen, cows, sheep and hogs. These *Miao-tse* are collected into villages, and live in great harmony with one another. They cultivate the earth, make a coarse sort of muslin, and manufacture a kind of carpets, which are good and well woven, and which serve to cover them during the night. The Chinese, who keep up a correspondence with these Miao-tse, purchase the timber of their forests, which they cut down in their mountains, and deliver to the buyer by rolling it into the river that traverses their country. When the purchaser receives it, he makes floats of it and carries it off, after having left the price, which consists of a certain number of cows, oxen and buffaloes. The *Miao-tse* employ the skins of these animals for making breast-plates, which they cover with thin plates of steel or copper these breast-plates are heavy, but exceedingly strong. The ordinary dress of these *Miao-tse* consists of a pair of drawers, and a kind of jacket which covers over their breast.

Those who are dispersed in that part of *Hou-quang* nearest to the provinces of *Quang-tong* and *Quang-si*, though they seemed to acknowledge the jurisdiction of the Chinese madarins, were in reality for a long time independent. They go bare-footed, and by being accustomed to running among their mountains, they climb the steepest rocks, and walk over the roughest ground, without feeling the least inconvenience.

The head-dreſs of their women is very ſingular. They place tranſverſely upon their heads, a ſmall piece of board, of about a foot in length, and five or ſix inches in breadth, over this they ſpread their hair, and fix it to the wood by means of wax. The *Miao-tſe* women conſider this as an elegant head-dreſs, and do not ſeem to perceive the reſtraint to which it ſubjects them, for they cannot lie down unleſs they place ſomething to ſupport their necks; and they are under the neceſſity of turning their heads every moment when they walk, to avoid the buſhes with which their country is covered. The difficulty is ſtill greater when they comb their hair, which is three or four times in a year, on theſe occaſions they are obliged to remain whole hours before a large fire to melt the wax after they have cleaned their hair, they again dreſs it in the ſame manner. This kind of hair bonnet is however uſed only by the young females, for thoſe who are advanced in life pay leſs attention to dreſs, and are contented with only turning their hair up and tying it in a knot on the top of their heads. Thoſe *Miao-tſe* who live towards the middle, and ſouthern part of the province of Koei-tcheou, are ſubject to the mandarins of the province, and make a part of the Chineſe people, whoſe cuſtoms they have in general adopted, a particular head-dreſs, different from the cap commonly worn by the Chineſe, being the only mark of diſtinction which they have preſerved. Others are governed by hereditary mandarins, who are conſidered as naturalized, although Chineſe by extraction, being deſcended from ſubaltern officers of the army of *Hong-vou*, on whom, as a reward for their ſervices, the government of a certain number of villages taken from the Miao-tſe was conferred. Theſe petty princes, or mandarins, judge in the firſt inſtance, the cauſes of their vaſſals, whom they have a right of puniſhing but not capitally. An appeal however may be carried immediately from their trbunal to that of the *Tchi-fou*, or governor of a city of the first class, who may reverse the sentence, or stay the proceedings.

According to the accounts of the Chinese the whole *Miao tse* nation are a restless and barbarous people---men without faith or probity, and above all, notorious plunderers, but Father Regis and the other missionaries who made a map of their country, do not give them the same character --- They on the contrary declare, that they found them an active, laborious and obliging people, and remarkably honest and punctual in restoring whatever effects they had entrusted to their care

These formidable mountaineers, who may be said to have enjoyed liberty and independence for two thousand years, have been at length completely subjected This event must, in the judgement of the Chinese, form one of the most memorable epochs in their history, and the name of KIEN-LONG will no doubt be ranked by them among their most celebrated emperors his active genius, fruitful in resources, and firm and persevering in its plans, brought about this important revolution The most powerful and intractable of the *Miao-tse* had formed on the frontiers of Se-tchuen and Koei-tcheou, two petty states, one of which was called the Greater Kin-tcheouen, the other, the Less—Each of these states was governed by a distinct prince About 1752, the *Miao-tse* having made some devastations in the territories of the empire, an army was sent against them But the general was defeated, and his head cut off His successor, more artful, entered into a treaty with them, and caused rich presents to be distributed among them, with which they retired to their mountains Care was taken to inform the emperor that the *Miao tse* had returned to their duty, had laid down their arms, and acknowledged his authority However, a few years after hostilities commenced again on the part of the *Miao tse*. The emperor, highly incensed, formed a resolution of extinguishing these turbulent subjects, and accordingly sent another army against them, divided into three bodies, each consisting of forty thousand men, ordering the commander in chief, general *Ouer-fou*, to climb their frightful mountains. The enemy, to allure him with the greater confidence, made but a faint resistance in the first defile. But the Chinese general having made his way through it, found himself in a narrow pass, where he had nothing before him but rather steep rocks, the *Miao-tse* then shewed themselves in great force, blocked up every passage, and when the Chinese were almost exhausted by famine, attacked them sword in hand, and did not suffer a single man to escape. It was not known until several years after in what manner they had treated general *Ouer-fou*. The two other generals, who did not support him, were punished, one being strangled, and the other sent into banishment.

The emperor at length appointed *Akou* generalissimo of all his forces. He was a man of great coolness and of unshaken constancy, whom nothing could discourage, and who was not afraid of displeasing the emperor, should the good of the service require him to pursue any plan contrary to his inclination. *Akou* penetrated into the mountains by the same route as his predecessor, but took care to occupy all the neighbouring rocks, and to preserve a retreat. This first display of ability let the *Miao-tse* know what kind of general they had to encounter. *Akou* acted with the greatest caution; he never retreated, each step he advanced was so much ground lost to the enemy. And by continuing resolutely in following the cautious plan of operations which he had laid down, he at length accomplished his design, and subdued these mountaineers, after having driven them into their utmost retreats. One of the Miao-tse princes perished in the course of the war, the other was taken and conducted to Pekin, with his whole family, and the war ceaſed in 1776 *.

The *Miao-tſé*, in defence of their liberty and country, did every thing that could be expected from human valour, their women fought with the moſt obſtinate fury, of which the following anecdote, related of one of theſe female patriots, is a ſufficient proof "Force and ſtratagem had "been employed for two months to get poſſeſſion of a "ſmall fort built on a very high rock, but without ſucceſs. "One morning, at day-break, ſome of the ſoldiers on "guard, being alarmed by a noiſe like that of a perſon "ſtepping with great caution, approached ſoftly, when "they thought they perceived ſomething in motion. Two "or three of the nimbleſt, by the help of cramp-irons "fixed to their ſhoes, ſcrambled up the rock a little way "on that ſide whence the noiſe ſeemed to proceed, when "they diſcovered a woman, who was drawing water. "They immediately ſeized her, and aſked who compoſed "the garriſon that for a long time had made ſuch an ob-"ſtinate reſiſtance in the fort—*I*, ſaid ſhe, *I alone*, *but* "*being in want of water*, *I came hither to fetch ſome*, "*without expecting to meet you* She then diſcovered to "them a ſecret path, by which they were conducted into "the fort where ſhe had remained alone, and of which ſhe "had been the whole defence; ſometimes firing her muſ-"quet, at others tearing off fragments from the rock, "which ſhe rolled down on the ſoldiers who in vain at-"tempted to climb it."

* Thoſe deſirous of fuller information reſpecting this war are referred to the XI Vol of *The General Hiſtory of China*, page 588, and *New Memoirs of China*, Vol. V

GENERAL DESCRIPTION

OF THE STATES

TRIBUTARY TO CHINA.

KINGDOM OF COREA

COREA, called by the Chinese *Kao-li* and by the Mantcheou Tartars *Sol-ho*, is a large peninsula, extended between China and Japan, bounded on the north by Chinese Tartary, on the east by the ocean and isles of Japan, on the south by the ocean, and on the west by the gulph and province of *Leao-tong*. This kingdom is reckoned to be six hundred miles from north to south, and three hundred from east to west. All access to it by sea is dangerous and difficult, from the great number of shoals which surround its coasts. Its least distance from Japan is only twenty-five leagues.

The origin of the Coreans is very obscure: it appears that the country was at first inhabited by different tribes, the principal of which were the *Mé*, *Kéo-kiouli* and the *Hans*: the last subdivided into three hordes—the *Mahan*, *Pin-han*, and *Chin-han*. These inhabitants of Corea at first composed several states, such as that of *Tchaossien*, and that of *Kao-li*: but, in process of time, they became united under the same government, and formed one kingdom called *Kao-li*.

This kingdom is governed by a sovereign, who exercises absolute authority over his subjects, though he himſelf is a vaſſal and tributary of the emperor of China. As ſoon as this prince dies, the emperor deputes to his ſon two mandarins, to confer upon him the title of *koué-vang*, or *king*. When the king of Corea has no immediate heir, or is afraid that the ſucceſſion may occaſion diſturbance after his death, he appoints his heir, and ſolicits the emperor to confirm his nomination. The prince receives on his knees the inveſtiture of his ſtates, and pays the emperor's envoys the ſum of eight hundred taels, beſides diſtributing other cuſtomary preſents. The miniſter of Corea then repairs to Pekin, to proſtrate himſelf before the emperor, and preſent him the tribute; and ſuch is the ſtrictneſs of the Chineſe court, that the princeſs who has eſpouſed the king, cannot aſſume the title of queen until ſhe has received it from the emperor.

The Japaneſe conquered this kingdom about the end of the ſixteenth century; but the Coreans, aſſiſted by the Tartars, who had ſubdued China, drove them again from the country. After the Coreans became tributaries to the Chineſe, and of conſequence to the Tartar government, an attempt was made to compel them to ſhave their heads, and to adopt the Tartar dreſs. This innovation occaſioned a general revolt throughout all Corea, which was at length appeaſed by the prudent care of the reigning family.

We are as yet little acquainted with the interior of this kingdom; but we know that it is divided into eight provinces, containing forty diſtricts, thirty-three cities of the firſt, fifty-eight of the ſecond, and ſeventy of the third claſs. *Kin-ki-tao*, ſituated in the province of *King-ki*, is the capital of the whole kingdom, and the ordinary reſidence of the ſovereign, who is maſter of all the wealth of his ſubjects, which he inherits after their death.

The Coreans are well made, ingenious, brave, and tractable; fond of dancing and muſic, and they apply with ardour and honour, in a particular manner, to the ſciences. Their learned men are diſtinguiſhed by two plumes of feathers in their caps, and are treated with a conſiderable portion of reſpect

The Northern Coreans, who are more robuſt than thoſe of the ſouth, have a taſte for arms, and are good ſoldiers. when in battle they uſe croſs-bows and very long ſabres

The practice of the Coreans, with reſpect to the dead, is, not to inter them until three years after their deceaſe, their affection to their parents ſeems very ſtrong, for they wear mourning for a father or mother three years At the ceremony of interment they place around the tomb the chariot, horſes, and clothes of the deceaſed, and whatever elſe he ſhewed a fondneſs for when alive, all theſe they leave to be taken by thoſe who have aſſiſted at the funeral

Theſe Coreans have borrowed their mode of building, writing, dreſs, religious worſhip, ceremonies, belief of the tranſmigration of ſouls, and the greater part of their cuſtoms, from the Chineſe But their women have more liberty of appearing in public with the other ſex They differ from the Chineſe in their marriage ceremonies very particularly, for in China, fathers and mothers often marry their children without their conſent, and even without their knowledge, in the kingdom of Corea, the parties chooſe for themſelves, and do not regard the inclination of their parents, or ever ſuffer them to throw any obſtacles in the way of their union The buildings of Corea in the country are generally of mud, but in the cities chiefly of brick, the walls of the cities are entirely in the Chineſe mode.

The principal productions of Corea are wheat, rice, and ginſeng gold, ſilver, iron, foſſil ſalt, caſtor, ſable's ſkins, and a yellow varniſh, the ſplendour of which is almoſt equal to gilding the tree from which this gum diſtils has a great reſemblance to the palm tree.

The principal manufacture of Corea is paper, of which China imports every year a considerable quantity. It is made of cotton, is as strong as cloth, and those who write on it make use of a small hair brush or pencil. before it can be written on with pens, it must be washed over with allum water, for without this precaution it will not bear the ink It is with this paper that the tribute due to the emperor is in part paid. The Chinese purchase it for filling up the squares of their sash windows, because, when it is oiled, it resists the wind and rain much better than theirs, it is also used by the Chinese as wrapping paper, their taylors also rub it between their hands until it becomes soft and flexible, and they often employ it in lining clothes, instead of calico.—The Coreans also manufacture small brushes for painting, which are highly esteemed in China.

The sea coasts of Corea abound with a variety of fish, and to the north-east numbers of whales are found, some of which are said to have been seen with the harpoons of the French and Dutch, if so, they must have escaped from the north of Europe

KINGDOM OF TONG-KING.

This kingdom extends between the 17th and 23d degrees of north latitude. It is bounded on the north by the Chinese provinces of Yun-nan and Quang-si, on the east by the provinces of Canton and the sea, on the south by the sea and Cochin-china, and on the west by the country of Laos Tong-king and Cochin-china formerly composed one of the most extensive provinces of China, called *Ngan-nan*, or *The Southern Repose*. It appears that about three hundred years before the Christian æra, these countries were uncultivated, and inhabited by savages, who had neither books nor characters, but in less than a century afterwards they began to assume a new appearance. *Ki-hohang-ti*, emperor of China, having newly conquered them, aſſembled upwards of five hundred thouſand perſons from different parts of his empire, and ſent them into the ſouthern extremities of the provinces of Quang-ſi, Can-ton, Tong-king, and Cochin-china. The arrival of ſo numerous a colony filled this country with Chineſe families, who gradually introduced the characters, government, and religion of the Chineſe.

But the Tonquineſe, about fifty years before the Chriſtian æra, leagued themſelves with the people of Cochin-china, and united their forces to ſhake off the Chineſe yoke. Two Tonquineſe ladies, who were ſiſters, put themſelves at the head of the revolted troops: they poſſeſſed all thoſe charms calculated to inſpire their followers with the ſtrongeſt enthuſiaſm, and all thoſe warlike qualities neceſſary to form the heroine. They ordered the frontier towns and poſts to be fortified, diſciplined a numerous army, and in the moſt endearing manner animated the ſoldiers to defend their country. *Ma-yuen*, the general, who was ſent againſt them with a formidable army, ſtood in need of all his courage and talents. Every ſtep was reſolutely diſputed with him, and he could not advance but by gaining freſh battles. In every action, the two heroines diſplayed equal judgment and bravery; but they at length fell, with their arms in their hands, in a bloody battle, fought near the lake *Si-hu*. The Tonquineſe troops were cut to pieces, and Tong-king was ſubdued. The Chineſe general, to commemorate his victory, cauſed two brazen pillars to be erected on the boundaries that ſeparate *Tong-king* from the province of *Quang-ſi*. They ſtill remain, and have the following inſcription: *When theſe pillars ſhall be deſtroyed, Tong-king will periſh.* The Tonquineſe at preſent conſider this inſcription as a prophecy, and theſe columns as monuments to which the deſtiny of their kingdom is inſeparably attached: they therefore take the greateſt care to preſerve them.

Few countries have been ſubject to more revolutions

than Tong-king sometimes quietly submitting to the Chinese authority, sometimes abandoned to revolt, and ruled by usurpers eagerly bent on destroying one another, sometimes torn by intestine or foreign wars, sometimes humbled, and, at others, giving laws to its neighbours, for several centuries it seems to have been particularly exposed to political convulsions

China, wearied of the wars which she had supported, and harassed by the restless and turbulent disposition of a people so excessively jealous of their liberty, abandoned the project of enslaving the Tonquinese, and consented that it should be governed by its own kings, provided they acknowledged themselves her tributaries This was agreed to, and it is said, that the first tribute which the Tonquinese paid, consisted in three statues of gold, and as many of silver, which they engaged to send every seven years to the emperor

The throne of *Tong-king* was for two hundred and twenty-two years occupied by eight princes of a family called *Ly*, but in 1230, this family becoming extinct, the sovereign authority passed to the family of *T.hin*, which likewise became extinct in 1406 The emperor of China, *Yong-lo* then again reduced *Tong-king* into a Chinese province, and appointed a governor-general and officers for all the departments of war, commerce, justice, &c A map of Tong-king, a list of its inhabitants, and an inventory of the principal effects found in it, were carried to court, and presented to the emperor According to these accounts, the number of inhabitants amounted to three millions one hundred and twenty thousand families There were also found in Tong-king two hundred and thirty-five thousand nine hundred oxen, horses, and elephants, thirteen millions six hundred thousand *tan* of rice (a *tan* weighing an hundred and twenty Chinese pounds), eight thousand six hundred and seventy barks, and two millions five hundred and thirty-nine thousand eight hundred pieces of armour.

That part of *Tong-king* where the emperor had neglected to place strong garrisons, soon gave new proofs of its love of freedom the people again took up arms, and an able officer, named *Lyli*, put himself at the head of the Tonquinese. After a great number of battles, the success of which was various, *Lyli* undertook to persuade the emperor, that one *Tchin-hao* was a branch of the royal family of *Tchin* *Tchin-hao* was proclaimed king, and the Chinese troops were ordered to evacuate Tong-king *Lyli* was now the absolute master of Tong-king, and *Tchin-hao*, who was but the shadow of a king, dying without issue in 1428, the emperor declared *Lyli* hereditary governor, and received his deputies, presents, and a solemn act, by which he acknowledged himself a tributary and vassal of the empire. His son, who succeeded him, obtained the title of king

This family enjoyed the throne until the beginning of the sixteenth century, when an ambitious individual had the boldness to declare himself a descendant from the royal family of *Tchin* the Tonquinese rose in his behalf, the reigning prince was assassinated, and the usurper assumed the sovereign authority Another revolution quickly followed: a grandee, named *Mo-teng-yong*, raised a force, attacked the usurper, and entirely defeated his army, and, in concert with the other grandees of the state, caused Li-ning, the nephew of the assassinated prince, to be proclaimed king.

The new king carried his gratitude for this signal act of friendship too far. he granted *Mo-teng-yong* unlimited and absolute authority in the government of the state. And the minister, elated by this excess of power, conceived the design of becoming sovereign the design conceived in secret was soon openly avowed, he dropped the mask, assumed the title of prince, and took the sovereignty into his own hands The weak king, accompanied by his mother, retired to the western part of Tong-king, and secured himself by fortifications while all the eastern part submitted to the authority of the usurper. The lawful sovereign sent deputies to the court of China: but *Mo-teng-yong* placed spies on the frontiers, by whose activity and intrigues the deputies of *Li-ning* were arrested on the way, and some of them put to death.

In 1537, one of Li-ning's deputies had the good fortune to reach court and the emperor learned from the petition of the prince all the events that had happened in Tong-king, he immediately ordered some of the nobility to repair to the frontiers, and to enquire into the cause of these disturbances, and the present posture of affairs in Tong-king.

Mo-teng-yong also sent deputies to the emperor, and spared no pains to procure protectors at court His address had the success he wished, and he found such powerful friends, that they prevailed on the emperor to refer for examination the proposals he had made, and to treat him with mildness.

The Chinese commissioners arrived at the frontiers of Tong-king in 1540 *Mo-teng-yong* sent to them one of his own sons, accompanied by forty-two principal mandarins, who presented an act by which *Mo-teng-yong* and his son submitted to the authority of the emperor, and declared themselves his faithful subjects. The commissioners made known the rescript of his Majesty, which granted them a free pardon, and the power of retaining the states of which they were in actual possession, on condition of paying a certain tribute every three years. The rescript ordered, that Tong-king should no longer bear the title of a kingdom, but that of an hereditary lordship, dependant on the emperor. The title of hereditary lord of Tong-king was granted to *Mo-teng-yong*, and his son, together with a silver seal, and the same honours were decreed to prince *Li-ning* for those estates which he possessed. *Mo-teng-yong* died in 1542, and was succeeded by his grandson, who obtained a patent as governor and hereditary lord of Tong-king; but, after the death of *Mo-teng-yong*, a dissention arose in the family of *Mo*, his states were divided among several chiefs, who waged such bloody wars, and weakened each other so much, that in 1577 this family entirely lost its power.

The family of *Li* was much more successful. The chief of this family attacked, in 1591, the most powerful lord of *Mo*, defeated him in a battle, retook the capital of Tong-king, and re-entered into those important places which had been usurped from them in 1527. This prince found himself master of the kingdom, paid his tribute to the emperor, presented a statue of gold, and received his patent, as hereditary governor. The lords of *Mo* were now obliged to seek an asylum on the frontiers of the Chinese provinces of Yun-nan, Quang-si and Quan-tong, being reduced to the necessity of giving up all their possessions except the city of Hoa-ping and the territories belonging to it: at the court of the emperor, they however enjoyed the same rank as those of *Ly*.

The family of *Ly* still possesses the throne, and has supported itself with genuine dignity, so much so, that the Court of Ceremonies, in 1665, represented to the emperor *Kang-hi*, that the family of *Ly* was worthy of his favour. In 1683 the emperor *Kang-hi* sent a nobleman to the court of Tong-king, with a diploma, declaring prince *Ly-[illegible]* king: to this diploma the emperor added some lines, written by his own hand, expressive of his approbation of the prince's conduct. In 1725, the emperor *Yong-tching*, son of *Kang-hi*, paid the same compliment to his successor King *L[illegible]-tao*.

Tong-king is divided into eight provinces, each having its own governor and magistrates; but an appeal lies from their sentence to a court consisting of [illegible] hundred counsellors of state This court is appointed to determine finally on appeals from every part of the kingdom, they are a separate body from the thirty-two members of the royal council, who attend the king in all his public audiences Though the monarchy of this country is hereditary in a family, the eldest does not always succeed to the throne, for the king appoints for his successor such of his sons as he thinks proper, subject to the approbation of the emperor of China. The brothers of the prince are confined in the palace, and suffered to go out only four times in a year when they are allowed six days for hunting or walking The military of Tong-king consists of about twenty-two thousand soldiers, twenty thousand of which are stationed on the frontiers, the rest are the king's guard, besides these there are fifty war elephants. On all the rivers of the kingdom, where there is any probability that an enemy might make an invasion, there are kept a number of large gallies and galliots, in which the sailors row standing, with their faces turned towards the prow, where the captain regulates their motions by a small rod which he holds in his hand.

The people of Tong-king, in general, are strong and well made, their disposition free, generous and open, they are lavish in their public expences, and fond of show, especially in feasts, marriages, and funerals.

The Tonquinese are of an olive colour, they blacken their teeth, and suffer their nails and hair to grow, the latter of which they wear as long as possible Such is the absolute authority of the Tonquinese monarch, that, except the citizens of the capital, all the tradesmen, such as joiners, smiths, masons, carpenters, &c who are in general ingenious, are obliged to labour three months every year in the palace, and two months for the mandarins and great lords at these times they are deprived of all the advantages of their labour but mere food thus monarchy and aristocracy discovers the same spirit amongst barbarians as in civilized nations. Marriages are not contracted here without the consent of the governor or judge of the place. A plurality of wives is permitted, but only the most accomplished takes the title of spouse. The law grants a divorce to the men, but denies it to the women: at a separation, the children remain with the husband. The favourite diversions of the Tonquinese are a kind of comedies, which they accompany with abundance of machinery and decorations; and they may be said to excel in the representation of torrents, rivers, seas, tempests, and naval battles.

The learning of the Tonquinese consists principally in the knowledge of a great number of characters, and in the study of the rules and principles of morality, drawn from the writings of Confucius. They apply to letters, because they open the way to honour; and because it is by their means alone that they can ever be promoted to offices of dignity or trust. The literati pass through three degrees, which are those of *sinde*, *doucum* and *tansi*. Before they can attain to the first degree, they must study such parts of the law as belong to notaries, attornies, and counsellors, for eight years. At the end of that period they are examined in the duties of these professions; and if they are found sufficiently capable, they are permitted to assume the title of *sinde*. To obtain that of *doucum*, they must study astrology, music, and poetry, and learn the manufacture of mathematical instruments for five years longer. To obtain the degree of *tansi*, they must employ four years more in learning to read and write the Chinese characters, and in acquiring a knowledge of their laws and customs. The last examination is made in the presence of the king, princes, mandarins of arms, literati, and of all the *tansi*. In the square of the palace stages are erected, in the form of amphitheatres, one for the king and princes, and others for the examiners and candidates; several days are sometimes spent in this ceremony, on the last of which the names of those who have given satisfactory answers to the questions proposed, are put into the hands of sixteen of the chief mandarins, and after the king's consent has been obtained, a robe of violet-coloured silk is put upon them, the emblem of being honoured with the title of *tansi*. To these literati of the first class, pensions are assigned by the state but paid by the people, and from these *tansi*, ambassadors to foreign states are always chosen.

The Tonquinese in their visits and entertainments are very ceremonious The person who pays the visit stops at the gate, and gives the porter certain loose leaves of paper, containing eight or ten pages, in which are written in large characters his name and titles, together with the intention of his visit These leaves are of different sorts and colours, according to the rank and quality of the person to be visited If the master of the house is absent, the paper is left with the porter, and the visit is considered as concluded. A magistrate, when he pays a visit, must be clothed in a robe of ceremony proper to his employment, and those who have some distinction, though they hold no public office, have also particular visiting dresses; and they cannot dispense with the use of them, without transgressing the established rules of civility.

The person visited receives at the door the person who pays the visit they join hands when they accost one another, and, by their gestures alone, shew a thousand marks of politeness The master of the house invites his visitor to enter, by pointing to the door, the person who pays the visit, as soon as seated, again tells the motive which brought him thither the master of the house listens with much gravity, and from time to time inclines his body, according to the rules of politeness. Servants afterwards, clothed in dresses of ceremony, bring a triangular table, upon which are placed cups of tea, together with boxes of betel, pipes and tobacco.

When the visit is ended, the master of the house re-conducts his guest to the middle of the street, where they renew their reverences, bows, elevation of hands, and other compliments: when the stranger is departed, and already advanced a good way, the master of the house sends a footman after him to pay him a fresh compliment; and some time after the visitor, in his turn, sends back another to thank him, which terminates the visit.

It is not only in visits that this troublesome politeness is displayed, but in all their actions which have any relation to society. The Tonquinese, in eating, instead of forks, use small sticks made of ebony or ivory, with the extremities ornamented with gold or silver: they never touch any food with their fingers, and, when at table, they appear to eat in uniform, the motion of their hands and jaw-bones seeming to depend upon some particular rules. They never use napkins, nor are their tables covered with a cloth; they are only surrounded with long embroidered carpets, which hang down to the floor. Every person has a table for himself, unless too great a number of guests obliges two to sit together.

The person who invites to an entertainment, sends, the evening before, to his intended guests, a few leaves of invitation, in which is contained a kind of bill of fare.

On the day appointed for the entertainment, he sends early in the morning a paper like the former, to remind the guests of their invitation, and when the hour of repast approaches, he sends a third paper, with a servant to conduct them, and to acquaint them how impatient he is to see them. When the company are assembled, and are about to sit down to table, the master of the house takes a cup of gold or silver, and, lifting it up with both hands, salutes the person of the greatest rank on account of his employment: he then proceeds to the outer court, where, after having turned himself towards the south, and offered wine to the tutelar spirits who preside over the house, he pours it out in form of a libation. After this ceremony, every one approaches the table deſtined for him, but before they ſit down they waſte above an hour in paying compliments, and the maſter of the houſe has no ſooner done with one, than he begins with another.—When they have occaſion to drink, compliments begin afreſh: they drink a great deal, but ſlowly, and at ſeveral times, and when they begin to grow merry, diſcuſs various topics, and ſometimes play at ſmall games, in which thoſe who loſe are condemned to drink.

Comedies and farces are often repreſented during theſe repaſts, but they are always intermixed with the moſt wretched and frightful muſic. The actors in theſe domeſtic comedies are boys between the age of twelve and fifteen, who, like European ſtrollers, go from province to province, and are every where conſidered as the dregs of the people. They have, however, moſt aſtoniſhing memories, they carry their theatrical apparatus along with them, together with a volume containing their comedies, generally to the amount of forty or fifty, which they preſent, and when a piece is fixed on, they immediately perform it, without any preparation.

About the middle of the entertainment one of the performers goes round to all the tables, and begs of the gueſts, the ſervants of the houſe do the ſame, and carry to their maſters whatever money they receive: a new repaſt is then diſplayed before the company, which is deſtined for their domeſtics.

The end of theſe entertainments is generally ſuited to the beginning. The gueſts praiſe *in detail* the excellence of the diſhes and the politeneſs and generoſity of their hoſt, who, on his part, makes a number of excuſes, and begs pardon, with many low bows, for not having treated them according to their merit.

The Tonquineſe phyſicians pretend that they can diſcover the greater part of diſeaſes by the beating of the pulse alone, which they feel in three parts on each side of the body

For the most part, they use nothing but roots, or simples, in the composition of their medicines but for head-aches, fevers and dysenteries, they commonly prescribe the juice of a certain fruit, which is said to have a wonderful effect in the cure of these disorders

The purple fever, which is so very dangerous in Europe, is said never to be fatal in Tong-king —Grosier gives the following account of their treatment of it They take the pith of a certain reed, dip it in oil, and apply it to the purple spots on the body the flesh then bursts, the corrupted blood is squeezed out, and the cure is finished by rubbing the wounds with a little ginger

Bleeding is not much used in Tong-king this is the last resource of the physicians, who never have recourse to it, until they are well assured of the inefficacy of other remedies

The religion of the Tonquinese is a mixture of the Chinese and other superstitions —Some of them believe in the immortality of the soul, while others confine this to the souls of the just only They worship spirits, with which they imagine the air to be filled, admit the doctrine of transmigration, believe the world to be eternal, and acknowledge one supreme being The literati follow the doctrine of *Confucius*, and conform to the customs of the Chinese in their religious ceremonies There are few cities which have not one temple, at least, raised to *Confucius* The statue of this celebrated philosopher is always seen in the most honourable place, surrounded by those of his ancient disciples, placed around the altar, in attitudes which mark the respect and veneration they formerly had for their master All the magistrates of the city assemble there on the days of new and full moon, and perform a [illegible] ceremonies which [illegible] students on the altar, burning perfumes, and making a number of genuflections.

At both the equinoxes, they offer up ſolemn ſacrifices, at which all the literati are obliged to aſſiſt. The prieſt, who is commonly one of thoſe mandarins called literati, prepares himſelf for this ceremony by faſting and abſtinence: the evening before the ſacrifice is made, he provides the rice and fruits which are to be offered, and diſpoſes in proper order on the tables of the temple every thing that is to be burnt in honour of Confucius, whoſe altar is ornamented with the richeſt ſilk ſtuffs, and his ſtatue is placed on it, with ſeveral ſmall tablets, on which his name is inſcribed in characters of gold. He then pours warm wine into the ears of the animals intended for ſacrifice if they ſhake their heads, they are judged proper, but if they make no motion, they are rejected. Before they are killed, the prieſt bends his body very low, after which he cuts their throats, reſerving their blood and the hair of their ears till the next morning, when the prieſt again repairs to the temple, where he invites the ſpirit of Confucius to come and receive the homage and offerings of the literati, while the reſt of the miniſters light wax candles, and throw perfumes into fires prepared at the door of the temple As ſoon as the prieſt approaches the altar, a maſter of ceremonies cries out, with a loud voice, *Let the blood and hair of the ſlaughtered beaſts be preſented.* The prieſt then raiſes with both hands the veſſel containing the blood and hair, and the maſter of the ceremonies ſays, *Let this blood and hair be buried* At theſe words all the aſſiſtants riſe up, and the prieſt, followed by his miniſters, carries the veſſel, with much gravity and reſpect, to a kind of court which is before the temple, where they inter the blood and hair of the animals. After this ceremony, the fleſh of the victims is uncovered, and the maſter of the ceremonies cries out, *Let the ſpirit of the great* CONFUCIUS *deſcend!* The prieſt immediately lifts up a veſſel filled with ſpirituous liquor, ſome of which he ſprinkles over a human figure made of ſtraw, at the ſame time pronouncing theſe words "*Thy virtues, O Confucius! are great, admirable, and "excellent. If kings govern their ſubjects with equity, it "is only by the aſſiſtance of thy laws and incomparable doc-"trine. We offer up this ſacrifice to thee, and our offering "is pure May thy ſpirit, then, come down among us, and "rejoice us by its preſence.*" When this ſpeech is ended, he then offers a piece of ſilk to the ſpirit of Confucius, and afterwards burns it in a brazen urn, ſaying, with a loud voice, "*Since the formation of men, until this day, who is "he among them, who hath been able to ſurpaſs, or even "equal the perfections of Confucius? O, Confucius! all "that we offer thee is unworthy of thee the taſte and ſmell "of theſe meats have nothing exquiſite, but we offer them "to thee, that thy ſpirit may hear us*" This ſpeech being finiſhed, THE PRIEST DRINKS THE LIQUOR, while one of his miniſters addreſſes this prayer to Confucius "*We "have made theſe offerings to thee with pleaſure; and we "are perſuaded, that thou wilt grant us every kind of good, "favour, and honour*" The prieſt then diſtributes *among the aſſiſtants* the fleſh of the ſacrifices, and thoſe who eat of it believe that Confucius will load them with bleſſings, and preſerve them from every evil The ſacrifice is now terminated by re-conducting the ſpirit of the philoſopher to the place from which it is ſuppoſed to have deſcended

On the firſt day of every new year, the Tonquineſe celebrate a ſolemn feaſt in honour of thoſe who during their lives performed illuſtrious actions, or diſtinguiſhed themſelves by their courage and bravery On this occaſion more than forty thouſand ſoldiers are drawn up in a vaſt plain, to which all the princes and mandarins are ordered to repair, and where the king himſelf attends them After ſacrificing, incenſe is burnt before a number of altars, on which are inscribed the names of the generals and great men in commemoration of whom they are then assembled The king, princes, and all the grandees of the court, afterwards incline themselves before each of the altars, excepting those which contain the names of rebellious generals, against which the king discharges five arrows The whole ceremony concludes with the firing of cannon and musquetry, in order to put to flight all the souls

There are three particular idols to which the Tonquinese render the most superstitious homage—the *Spirit of the Kitchen*, the *Master of Arts*, and the *Lord of the Place where they reside* The *Spirit of the Kitchen* takes its origin from the following tale, preserved by tradition in the country "A woman having separated from her husband "on account of some discontent, married a second time. "This action gave her former husband so much uneasiness, "that he put an end to his days by throwing himself into "a large fire The unfaithful spouse, touched with re-"pentance, went and expiated her fault by throwing "herself likewise into the same fire Her second hus-"band being informed of it, hastened thither also, but "finding his wife reduced to ashes, he was so much affect-"ed with grief, that he rushed into the middle of the same "fire, and was destroyed in an instant" This *spirit* is believed to animate three stones, of which the Tonquinese form their hearth, and these three stones they worship on the first day of every new year.

The idol called *Master of Arts* is the image of one of the literati, whom the people of Tong-king believe to have been the most ingenious, learned, and wise, of mankind. Merchants invoke it before they traffic, fishermen, before they throw their nets, and artists, before they begin any work

The idol called *Lord of the Place where they reside* is as much reverenced as the preceding When any one intends to build a house, he considers that the ground upon which he builds, though it is the property of the king, may have ſome other maſter, who, though dead, preſerves the ſame right as he enjoyed during his life He therefore ſends for a magician, who by beat of drum invites the ſoul of the deceaſed maſter to come and take up its abode under a ſmall hut prepared for it, and where it is preſented with gilt paper, perfumes, and ſmall tables covered with dainties. The object of this ceremony is ſo far to engage the friendſhip of the ancient proprietor as to ſuffer a new tenant to poſſeſs his field

Some of the Tonquineſe are ſo ſuperſtitious, that when they are about to undertake any journey, they inſpect the feet of a chicken others, after they have ſet out, becauſe they have ſneezed once will ſuddenly return, but if they ſneeze twice, they think themſelves obliged to double their pace, and return with the greateſt haſte poſſible.

There are ſome who divide the earth into ten parts, and from time to time pay a degree of adoration to each others divide it into five, one of which is ſuppoſed to be in the middle. They pay their homage to the north dreſſed in black, and uſe black utenſils in their ſacrifices, they clothe themſelves in red when they adore the ſouth, in green, when they ſacrifice to the eaſt, in white, when they invoke the weſt, and in yellow, when they pay their adorations to the middle part

When a Tonquineſe is about to purchaſe a field, undertake a journey, or marry one of his children, he goes and conſults a conjurer, before this conjurer or magician gives an anſwer, he takes a book, but he opens it only half, as if he was afraid of ſuffering profane eyes to ſee what it contains After having aſked the age of the perſon who comes to conſult him, he throws into the air two ſmall pieces of copper, on which are engraven, on one ſide only, certain cabaliſtical figures or characters If they fall with the figures turned towards the earth, it preſages misfortune; but if towards the heavens, the omen is happy.

There are other magicians, who are only conſulted for the cure of diſeaſes. If he announces that the diſeaſe proceeds from ſpirits, they call them wicked genii, and pretend to ſhut them up in earthen vaſes, if it comes from the devil, they invite the old gentleman to a grand feaſt, aſſign him the moſt honourable place, pray to him, and offer him preſents, but if the diſeaſe does not abate, they load him with injuries, and fire muſkets to drive him from the houſe. If it is the god of the ſea who has occaſioned the diſtemper, they repair to the banks of ſome river, where they offer up ſacrifices to appeaſe him, and intreat him to quit the ſick perſon's chamber and return to the waters. Whether the ſick perſon finds himſelf better or not, the magician takes his leave, loaded with gold and preſents

There are in the country of Tong-king a number of mountaineers, who, having ſhaken off the yoke of every nation, and retired to inacceſſible mountains, leading a life reſembling thoſe ferocious wild beaſts which inhabit the ſame rocks with them, form a kind of republic, of which their *prieſt* is the head This chief has deviſed a particular ſyſtem of religion and rites, which have no ſimilarity with thoſe of the Tonquineſe. In the houſes of the prieſts their gods deliver oracles A great noiſe announces their arrival, and theſe mountaineers, who while waiting for them, paſs the time in drinking and dancing, immediately ſend forth loud ſhouts of joy, which are more like howlings than acclamations they cry out, "*Father!* "*art thou already come?*" A voice then anſwers, "*Be of* "*good cheer, my children, eat, drink, and rejoice, it is I who* "*procure you all thoſe advantages you enjoy*" After theſe words, to which they liſten with ſilence, they again return to their drinking. The gods now become thirſty in their turn, and aſk for ſomething to drink; vaſes ornamented with flowers are immediately prepared, which the prieſt receives to carry them to the gods, for he is the only perſon permitted to approach to, or converſe with them.

They have one god who is repreſented with a bald head, and an unlucky countenance, which inſpires horror. This deity never attends aſſemblies with the reſt, to receive the homage of his worſhippers, becauſe he is continually employed in conducting the ſouls of the dead to the other world. Sometimes this god prevents a ſoul from quitting the country, eſpecially if it be that of a young man; in ſuch caſe he plunges it into a lake, where it remains until it is purified; but if his ſoul is not tractable, and reſiſts the will of the god, he falls in a paſſion, tears it to pieces, and throws it into another lake, where it remains without hopes of ever being liberated.

The common opinion of the Paradiſe of theſe mountaineers is, that a great quantity of large trees are found there, which diſtil a kind of gum, with which the ſouls are nouriſhed, together with delicious honey, and fiſh of a prodigious ſize; and that apes are alſo placed there to amuſe the dead; and an eagle ſufficiently large to ſhelter all Paradiſe from the heat of the ſun, by his extended wings.

The whole country of Tong-king enjoys a fertile ſoil, and a healthful and temperate climate. Beſides the rice common to the reſt of India, and which they cultivate in the ſame manner, it produces five other kinds. The firſt a *ſmall rice*, the grain of which is long, thin, and tranſparent; the ſecond is a *long, thick rice*, the grain of which is round; the third is *red rice*, ſo called becauſe its grain is covered with a reddiſh-coloured pellicle. Theſe three kinds of rice require much water, and never grow but in lands frequently overflowed. The *dry rice*, as it is called, from its growing in a dry ſoil, and having no occaſion for any water but what falls from the heavens, is of two kinds, both producing a grain as white as ſnow, and which conſtitute the principal article of the Tonquineſe trade with China. Neither of theſe ſpecies are ever cultivated but on the hills and mountains, where they are ſown in the ſame manner as European wheat, about the end of December or beginning of January, at which time the rainy ſeaſon ends This rice is generally three months on the ground, and is very productive

The Tonquineſe employ a ſpecies of buffaloes in their agriculture, which are very large, and more vigorous than oxen in warm countries, and extricate themſelves with leſs difficulty from the dirt and clay. They have no occaſion for any machines to inundate their fields, a chain of mountains hanging over their plains, from one end of the kingdom to the other, abound with ſprings and rivulets, that in their natural courſe water their grounds

Another important object of cultivation in Tong-king is the ſugar cane, of which the country produces two kinds the one large, growing exceedingly high, with its joints at a great diſtance from each other, it always appears green, and contains abundance of juice The other is ſmaller and ſhorter, when ripe, it is of a yellow colour; it affords leſs liquor than the firſt, but this liquor abounds with more ſugar

The Tonquineſe have but few good fruits; the beſt are pine-apples, oranges, and a ſpecies of red figs, much eſteemed. They have alſo a ſpecies of figs much reſembling thoſe of Provence, both in taſte and figure their figs, inſtead of growing on the branches, ſpring up from the root of the tree, and ſometimes in ſuch abundance that twenty men might eaſily ſatiſfy their hunger with them.

There are ſeveral large trees in Tong-king, the branches of which are covered with flowers, but bear neither leaves nor fruit. There is another kind, the branches of which bend naturally down to the earth, where they take root, and from which other trees ſpring up, and incline in like manner

The Tonquineſe alſo cultivate the mulberry and varniſh trees, cotton, tea, indigo, ſaffron, and pepper, they have few greens, and ſeem to have leſs deſire of procuring them, they neglect the vine, though it is the natural production of their country, but they employ great care in raiſing a plant called *tſai*, which, being put into a ſtate of fermentation, throws up a ſcum of a green colour, of great uſe in dying, giving a beautiful and durable green

Elephants are very common in Tong-king, and many of them are kept for the uſe of the king. Neither lions nor ſheep are ſeen throughout the kingdom, but there are a prodigious number of ſtags, bears, tygers, and apes. Among the birds of this country is a ſpecies of goldfinch, which, for the melody of its ſong is diſtinguiſhed by the name of the *celeſtial bird*, its eyes ſparkle like the moſt brilliant ruby, it has a round and pointed bill, an azure ring round its neck, and a tuft of party-coloured feathers on its head. Its wings, when it is perched, appear variegated with beautiful ſhades of blue, green and yellow. It makes its neſt in cloſe thickets, and breeds twice a year, it conceals itſelf in time of rain, but, as ſoon as the rays of the ſun begin to dart through the clouds it immediately quits its retreat, and, by its warbling, proclaims to the labourers the return of fine weather. This bird is ſaid to be a mortal enemy to the *ho kien*, another ſingular bird, which is found in marſhes. As ſoon as it perceives the *ho-kien*, the feathers of its neck ſtand erect, it extends and agitates its wings, opens its bill, and makes a noiſe like the hiſſing of a ſerpent, its attitude is that of a bird ready to dart on its prey, and its whole body indicates a kind of terror, mixed with fury, but whether it be, that it feels the inferiority of its ſtrength, or whether ſuch is its inſtinct, it only looks at its enemy with a fixed and diſordered eye, without offering an attack.

This country abounds with game of all kinds, ſuch as ſtags, antelopes, wild goats, peacocks, hares, pheaſants, &c. Every perſon is free to hunt, but the diverſion is dangerous, on account of the elephants, rhinoceroſes, tygers, and other voracious animals which inhabit the foreſts. The domeſtic animals raifed here, are horfes, for travelling, buffaloes, for tilling the ground, oxen, hogs, goats, fowls, geefe and ducks.

COCHIN-CHINA.

We have already mentioned, that Cochin-china had a fhare in the early revolutions of Tong-king, that, fubject at firft to the Chinefe government, engaged afterwards in rebellion, and expofed to different ufurpers, thefe two ftates had been compelled to return to their former dependence, after the fuccefsful expedition of general May-ven, about the year 50 of the Chriftian era. The imperial authority, after its re-eftablifhment, fubfifted in Cochin china till the year 263, when a nobleman, named Kulien, undertook to free his country from a foreign yoke He caufed the Chinefe governor to be maffacred, and ufurped the throne, of which he afterwards retained peaceful poffeffion His grandfon Fan-y, during his reign adopted a flave, named Ouen, born at Kouang-nang in Tong-king, whom he caufed to affume the name of Fan-ouen This foreigner, admitted into the royal family, acquired foon, by this adoption and his intrigues, an unlimited power, and after the death of his benefactor, he feized the throne To fignalize the commencement of his reign, and to gain the efteem of his fubjects, he entered Tong-king at the head of an army in the year 347, took poffeffion of Kouang nan, his native country, and ravaged all the territories of Tfin-hoa

The defcendants of this fuccefsful ufurper kept poffeffion of the throne of Cochin-china until 653. But we have little information refpecting the reigns of the different princes we only know, that they were very punctual in paying their tribute to the emperors. The Chinefe hiftory is equally defective with regard to the fucceeding kings, we learn little of Cochin china, till 1179, when the prince who filled the throne turned his arms against Camboya, entered it at the head of an army, and committed great devaſtations. The king of Camboya diſſembled his reſentment, that he might put himſelf into a better ſtate of obtaining revenge. He paſt eighteen years, without any act of hoſtility, but, in 1197, he attacked the king of Cochin-china, made him priſoner, and dethroned him, and, after ravaging his territories, eſtabliſhed a lord of Camboya on the throne, but this change of government did not long ſubſiſt.

The king of Cochin-china having learned in 1280 that the Mogul Tartars were become maſters of China, ſent without delay to the new emperor, deputies loaded with preſents, in order to pay that prince homage. Theſe deputies were honourably received, but the emperor did not content himſelf with tribute, he carried his pretenſions farther, and ſent ſome of the grandees of his court to Cochin-china, to form a tribunal which alone ſhould be entruſted with the government of the kingdom. About two years afterwards, Pouti, the king's ſon, fired with indignation at ſeeing a council of foreigners give laws to his country, refuſed to acknowledge their authority, and prevailed on his father to impriſon the grandees who by order of the emperor compoſed this tribunal.

As ſoon as the emperor was informed of this outrage, he cauſed a fleet to be equipped in the ports of the province of Canton, in which he embarked a number of Tartar and Chineſe troops under the command of Sotou. The fleet arrived at Cochin-china in 1284. Sotou landed his army, marched towards the capital, and made himſelf maſter of it. The king and his ſons, took refuge in the mountains, from whence they diſpatched ſecret orders, to aſſemble large bodies of troops in different places, while they fortified themſelves in a ſmall town, the gates of which were defended by ſome ſtrong works, and batteries of cannon. They then privately put to death the Tartar and Chineſe lords who compoſed the tribunal eſtabliſhed by the emperor, and their whole aim was directed to amuſe Sotou, and to deſtroy his army With this deſign they ſent him rich preſents for himſelf and his troops, and at the ſame time aſſured him, that for the future they would comply with the will of the emperor

Sotou ſuffered himſelf to be deceived by this apparent ſubmiſſion, but, being ſoon after informed by a deſerter, of the maſſacre of the Tartar and Chineſe nobility, of the intrigues of the king and his ſon, and of the march of a formidable army to cut off his retreat, he perceived that he had no time to loſe, he therefore made his troops advance, and laid cloſe ſiege to the fortified tow The attack and defence were equally reſolute, bu the diſadvantage of the ground, and the obſtinate reſiſtance of the beſieged, having occaſioned a great ſlaughter among his troops, Sotou thought it prudent to retire, leſt he ſhould loſe his whole army.

The king of Cochin-china, to gain time, now ſent a deputation to the Emperor of ſome of the grandees of his court, to aſſure him of his reſpectful ſubmiſſion, but the bad ſucceſs of the expedition had ſo chagrined the Chineſe monarch, that he refuſed to admit the ambaſſadors to his preſence, and gave orders to his ſon, to aſſemble an army, and to lead them in perſon againſt the king of Cochin-china. Sotou was commanded at the ſame time to join the prince, and act under his command All theſe preparations ended in a few acts of hoſtility, and ſome ravages committed by the troops of Sotou. the emperor Chi-tſou died before he could revenge himſelf, and the kings of Cochin-china maintained their independence, by paying the uſual tribute, which they ſtill ſend to the emperor

The Mogul Tartars being expelled from China, the new emperor ſent notice to the king of Cochin-china, of his acceſſion to the throne, and, what had until that time been without example, caused sacrifices to be offered up in honour of the spirits of mountains, forests and rivers Itataha, who was then reigning, sent his tribute to the new monarch, from whom he received in return magnificent presents But the friendship between these two courts did not long subsist

About the year 1380 the king of Cochin-china, contrary to the advice, and even orders of the emperor, invaded the territories of Tong-king This war employed the rest of his reign, and continued under those of his successors, for it was not terminated until 1471, when, after a desperate and decisive battle, the king of Tong-king became absolute master of Cochin-china His enemy had exposed himself too much in battle, he was, therefore, taken prisoner, and the whole country was obliged to submit to the conqueror

The Chinese historians speak little of Cochin-china after this revolution, we however know, that it again recovered its independence, and continued afterwards to be governed, as it is at present, by its own kings In 1671 the Tonquinese set on foot an expedition against this country An army of eighty thousand effective men seemed to promise success and an easy conquest, the troops of Cochin-china amounting only to twenty-five thousand. The two armies met and engaged, and the battle continued three days, but, notwithstanding their superiority in number, the Tonquinese lost seventeen thousand men, and the enemy gained a complete victory Since that time, the Tonquinese have remained peaceably within their own boundaries, while Cochin-china has aggrandized herself by subduing the mountaineers, and even the kings of Tsiampa and Camboya, whom she has compelled to become tributaries to her

The people of Cochin-china have a common origin with the Tonquinese, and they differ very little in their manner of living, laws and cuftoms, which they have in a great part borrowed from the Chinefe.

In four iflands fituated near the coafts of this country are found thofe celebrated nefts fo much fought after for feafoning ragouts. To the eaft of thefe ifles, there are five others, that are fmaller, where prodigious numbers of turtles are found, the flefh of which is exceedingly delicate.

The articles of trade in moft efteem, and for which there is readieft fale at Cochin-china, are faltpetre, fulphur, lead, fine cloths, barred or flowered chints. Pearls, amber and coral were formerly in great requeft there, but at prefent the two laft only are faleable; and this is not the cafe, unlefs the beads of coral are round, well polifhed, and of a beautiful red colour. The amber muft be extremely clear, the beads of an equal fize, and not larger than an ordinary nut. The principal exports of Cochin-china are filks, fugar, ebony and Calamba-wood, thofe nefts before mentioned, gold in duft or in bars, which fells for only ten times its weight in filver, and laftly, copper and porcelain, tranfported thither from China and Japan.

European merchants complain of the demands made in this country for entrance, clearance and anchorage. Thefe duties, however, amount to only four per cent. On the arrival of a fhip, nothing can be removed from her until fhe has been infpected, the cuftom-houfe officers unload her, weigh, and count the fmalleft pieces, and take poffeffion of what they find moft valuable, in order to fend it to the king, who keeps what he thinks proper, and returns the value. If the *king* only took this liberty, no great lofs would enfue, but it is faid, that the *grandees* of the court follow his example, while they are not *quite* fo punctual in their payments. The prime articles being thus difpofed of, the ordinary goods fcarce find a purchafer.

This inconvenience, though unavoidable, does not however appear to be without remedy. When the Dutch traded to Cochin-china, from Surat and Coromandel, vessels loaded with cauris, lead and saltpetre, their cargoes were suffered to remain entire, because they had taken the precaution to pay, every year, a certain sum for each vessel that entered. Other nations might have had recourse to the same expedient; but, by attempting to free themselves from a small duty, which it would perhaps have been prudent to pay, they gave a stab to their commerce.

The Japanese coin is the only money current in Cochin-china: it is paid and received by weight. The money of the country is copper, as large as our common counters, of a round figure, with a hole in the middle, by which it may be strung in the same manner as beads.

There is no country where merchants are more liable to be deceived with regard to the value of money; the pieces being unequal in figure and quality, and the difficulty of determining their value, which is regulated only by a few characters that are stampt upon them, is great. Prudence, therefore, requires that they should have honest and skilful people to ascertain the value of these pieces, otherwise they run a risque of becoming dupes to the merchants of Cochin-china, who make a merit of being able to cheat an European.

THIBET.

Thibet is known under different names; the Chinese call it Tsang, the Tartars, Barantola, Bouttan, and Tangut, and both distinguish it also by the name of the kingdom of Lama, because it is in the country of Lasa that the grand lama keeps his court. This vast kingdom is reckoned to be nineteen hundred and twenty miles in extent from east to west, and nineteen hundred and fifty from north to ſouth It is encloſed by the country of Kokonor, the provinces of Se-tchuen and Yun-nan, the kingdom of Ava, the ſtates of the Mogul, Bukaria, and the great deſert of Cobi

We learn nothing certain or diſtinct of the hiſtory of Thibet, till about the year 420, when, we are told, that a prince known by the title of Toufan, ſubdued the provinces of Chen ſi and Se-tchuen, and extended his conqueſts, ſo as to make himſelf maſter of Thibet, where this conqueror and his ſucceſſors reigned for more than a century, without having any communication with China

Long-han, a Toufan, prince and ſovereign of Thibet, about the year 634, ſent ambaſſadors to China Seven years after, the ſame prince eſpouſed the emperor's daughter, and this alliance added ſo much to his power, that he was enabled to ſubjugate all the nations to the weſt of China This power of the Toufan princes ſubſiſted for near two hundred years, but it gradually declined, and was almoſt entirely annihilated about the year 907, towards the end of the dynaſty of Tang. Several ſmall ſtates were then formed in Thibet The prieſts inſenſibly became poſſeſſed of vaſt domains, and the ſuperiors of ſeveral monaſteries, by degrees, rendered themſelves ſo powerful, that they exerciſed an authority almoſt ſovereign within their diſtricts It however is evident, that there was always a prince who had the title of King of Thibet, and under the dynaſty of Song, they were tributary to China.

Thibet continued to decline more and more, until Chi-tſou, firſt emperor of the dynaſty of Yven, divided the country into ſeveral provinces, the principal of which was Ouſſe-hang, the moſt fertile part of Thibet, and that which enjoyed the mildeſt climate. In this province Laſſa, now become the ordinary reſidence of the ſovereign lama, is ſituated There was then in Ouſſe hang a Bonze or prieſt, named Paſſepa. The emperor conferred on him the title of prince, honoured him with a golden ſeal, and permitted him to eſtabliſh tribunals in the country of Ouſſe-hang, and other parts of Thibet. He obtained alſo the titles of tutor to the emperor, doctor of the empire, head of the law, and even that of ouang, which ſignifies king or prince. His ſucceſſors were honoured with the ſame titles, and were, like him, tributary to the emperors of China.

In 1414, about the middle of the reign of Yong-lo, eight other bonzes received the title of ouang, with the ſame prerogatives as thoſe before mentioned. They were ſtyled great doctors, maſters of the law, and zealous propagators of that law; but theſe pompous titles did not exempt them from paying the tribute which had been impoſed on them.

The bonzes of Thibet, about the year 1426, aſſumed the title of grand lamas, and the moſt powerful among them, named Tſong-kepa, made Laſa the place of his reſidence, and was acknowledged chief of all the lamas. His ſucceſſor appointed a tipa or prime miniſter, whom he entruſted with the government of his ſtates, and the next in order was the firſt who took the diſtinguiſhed title of dalai lama, by which he was raiſed far above the reſt; for dalai ſignifies morally and phyſically extended, great, and almoſt without bounds.

The lama princes were not yet however ſole ſovereigns of Thibet. About the beginning of the laſt century, a prince, named Tſang-pa-han, poſſeſſed great part of it, to the weſt of Laſa. His power extended as far as the ſources of the Ganges, and over the country of Sirinagar, watered by the ſame river. Father Andrada, a Jeſuit, who in 1624 was at the court of this prince, aſſures us, that he was a zealous protector of the Chriſtian religion, and that he ſeemed greatly inclined to embrace it. The

Tartar hiſtory of the ſame period corroborates this circumſtance, for it relates, that this prince deſpiſed the lamas, abandoned the law of *Fo*, and ſought every opportunity of deſtroying it. The dalai lama, incenſed at not receiving the homage of Tſang-pa-han, formed a league with the Tartars of Kokonor, whoſe prince, named Kouchi, entered Thibet at the head of a powerful army, attacked Tſang-pa-han, defeated and took him priſoner, and, ſome time after, cauſed him to be put to death. To this Tartar prince the dalai lama was indebted for his ſovereignty over all Thibet, for far from appropriating to himſelf the fruits of his victory, Kouchi declared himſelf a vaſſal of the lama, and received from him the title of han, which he had never before enjoyed This prince, to continue his protection to the lama, and ſecure to him the quiet poſſeſſion of his new conqueſts, eſtabliſhed himſelf, together with his troops, in the neighbourhood of Laſa His ſons had no great inclination for returning to a country that their father had abandoned they therefore followed his example, and remained in Thibet

In 1642 the dalai lama ſent ambaſſadors to Tſong-te, father to the firſt emperor of the preſent dynaſty of the Mantchew Tartars, threw himſelf under his protection, and paid him tribute. Ten years after, the dalai lama himſelf went to Pe-kin, and paid homage to the emperor. He was loaded with honours, received a golden ſeal and magnificent preſents from the emperor, and was confirmed in his title of dalai lama

Kang-hi, being deſirous of honouring the typa or prime miniſter of the dalai lama, declared him a prince in 1693, and granted him a golden ſeal. This miniſter however far from being attached to the intereſts of the emperor, ſecretly betrayed him, and ſeconded the ambitious views of Kaldan, king of the Eleuthes, who was a declared enemy to the Mantchew Tartars He endeavoured to perſuade the grand lama not to go to Pe-kin, to which place the emperor had called him, and when the dalai lama died, he kept that event ſo ſecret, that the emperor was not informed of it for a long time afterwards. Theſe intrigues were at length diſcovered, and in 1705, Latſahan, prince of the Tartars of Kokonor, cauſed this perfidious miniſter to be put to death. The emperor Kang-hi ſent ſome of the grandees of his court to Thibet, to govern it, in conjunction with the Tartar prince, whom he loaded with preſents, and afterwards appointed a new dalai lama.

Tchong-kar, king of the Eleuthes, in 1714, made an irruption into Thibet, and committed the moſt horrid ravages. The Tartar prince, endeavouring to oppoſe this torrent, was killed in combat, and the celebrated pagod of Poutala was almoſt reduced to aſhes. The king of the Eleuthes carried away from this pagod, and from all the others of the country, immenſe riches in gold, ſilver, copper, precious ſtones, ſilk ſtuffs, &c. He put a great number of the lamas to the ſword, and ſent ſeveral of them into Tartary, encloſed in ſacks, thrown acroſs the backs of camels. This prince claimed the ſovereignty of Thibet as his right, and ordered the lamas to renounce all authority over the people, to retire to their monaſteries, and to employ themſelves only in ſaying their prayers.

The lamas immediately fled, and diſperſed themſelves on all ſides. The dalai lama ſought the protection of the emperor Kang-hi, and the princes of Kokonor, whoſe country had been expoſed to the ſame ravages, united with him in ſeeking for relief. The emperor immediately aſſembled a numerous army, commanded by experienced Tartar and Chineſe officers, and placed one of his ſons and a grandſon at their head. This army marched into Kokonor, drove from thence the king of the Eleuthes, and entered

Thibet, while another body of Chinese troops penetrated thither also by the province of *Se-tchuen*

The dalai lama was re-established, the rest of the lamas were put in possession of their pagods and the remainder of the troops of the Eleuthes made their escape through the defiles of the mountains Although tranquillity seemed to be restored in Thibet, the emperor commanded some of the Tartar nobility to remain at Lasa and in Kokonor, to govern in his name, and to watch the motions of Tchong-han. The same plan of conduct was adopted by the emperor Yong tching, the successor of Kang-hi. Some lords of Thibet revolted in 1727, one of whom took the title of governor-general of the country, and caused a Tartar prince of the fourth rank to be put to death But these slight commotions were soon suppressed. Kien-long, the present emperor, raised, in 1739, to the dignity of prince of the second rank a person whom the emperor Yong-tching, his father, had appointed viceroy of Thibet. Peace has been since preserved, and it appears to be now firmly established, as the Thibetians have nothing more to fear from the incursions of the Eleuthes, who, since 1759, have been subjects of the empire

The tribute which the sovereign of Thibet sends to the emperor of China consists of gold or copper statues of the idol *Fo*, perfumes, amber, coral, precious stones, woollen stuffs, and sword blades The emperor it is said also requires from the dalai lama a certain number of vessels, or small pitchers, filled with water from the Ganges. Since the latter end of the reign of Kang-hi, the emperor has always had some of this water in his palace, and he even carries it with him when he travels.

A custom is sanctioned in Thibet, which permits women to have several husbands at one time The degrees of consanguinity between the husbands are no obstacle to these unions, for a woman may marry all the brothers of a family, the children are divided among them, the eldest has the first born, and the younger those born afterwards.

The dalai lama does not reside in the city of Lasa, but on a mountain in the neighbourhood, called Poutala. On this mountain there are a number of pagods, the most sumptuous of which he inhabits He passes great part of his life on a kind of altar, where he sits motionless, in a cross-legged posture, on a large and magnificent cushion, and receives, with the greatest gravity, the adoration, not only of the Thibetians, but also of a prodigious multitude of strangers and pious pilgrims, who undertake long and difficult journies to go and worship him on their bended knees, and to receive his benediction He lays his hand on the head of his adorer who imagines that by this imposition alone, he obtains the remission of all his sins

Next to the Thibetans, the Tartars are the most zealous worshippers of the grand lama, they arrive in crowds at Poutala, from the remotest corners of the country, and even the weakest of the female sex are not terrified by the fatigues that inseparably attend these long journies

This profound veneration, which draws so many people to Lasa, to prostrate themselves at the feet of the grand lama, is founded on the idea of his great power and sanctity They are persuaded, that all the divinity of *Fo* resides in him, that he is omniscient and omnipresent, and that he has neither need of information, nor occasion to ask questions, in order to discover the secret thoughts of men, that he is immortal, and that, when he appears to die, his soul and his divinity only change their place of residence, and transmigrate into another body On these occasions all their endeavours are directed to discover the place where it hath pleased him to be born again, and even some of the Tartar princes themſelves have aſſiſted in this ſearch, but they are obliged to be directed by certain lamas, who alone are acquainted with the ſigns by which the new-born god may be diſcovered, or rather, they only know what child the preceding dalai lama appointed to be his ſucceſſor

Large pagods are common in Thibet, where the moſt diſtinguiſhed of the lamas reſide They aſſume different titles of honour but that of *houtouctou* is one of the moſt venerable, and is never granted but to thoſe who are accounted living *Fos* Theſe *houtouctous* are not always fixed to the ſame place, they have liberty to reſide wherever they pleaſe, and to chuſe for their abode whatever ſpot appears to them moſt agreeable.

The inhabitants of Thibet are not the only people who may attain to the dignity of lama Tartars, and Chineſe, have aſpired to the prieſthood, and repaired to Laſa, in hopes of obtaining it. If they can get themſelves admitted among the diſciples of the grand lama, the number of whom is fixed at two hundred, this admiſſion is the commencement of their promotion, and the firſt ſtep towards dignity and power, for the ſubaltern grand lamas are choſen from among theſe diſciples The *houtouctous*, however, are not acknowledged as ſuch until after having paſſed a certain time in the ſchool of the grand lama When they have done this, they live amidſt ſplendour and opulence, continually ſurrounded by a crowd of adorers, who load them with preſents. The lamas of Thibet are not very magnificent in their dreſs, they wear only a napped kind of woollen ſtuff, called in China poulou, which is uſed for covering ſeats The grand lama was ſeen at Laſa in 1717 clothed in a red dreſs of this ſtuff, having on his head a yellow cap, ornamented with gilding.

Beſides this cap, the lamas have ſeveral bonnets, or tiaras, that are the diſtinguiſhing marks of the different degrees of honour to which they have arrived. The cap which ſtrikes Europeans moſt, has a great reſemblance to a biſhop's mitre: they wear it on horſeback, as well as on foot, but the cloven part of this mitre deſcends directly to the middle of the forehead. The obligations which the office of lama impoſes, are neither few nor trifling, but there is no one among them who engages to diſcharge them all. They divide and ſhare the burden. One takes the charge of obſerving one precept, and another obliges himſelf to practiſe another, and ſo of the reſt, they, however, have certain common prayers, which they chaunt in concert together, and they are all obliged, like prieſts of many other perſuaſions, to engage to renounce the vanities of the world, to live in celibacy, and to have no concern with trade or commerce. The keeping of theſe engagements is quite a different conſideration.

The language ſpoken in Thibet is almoſt the ſame as that of thoſe people called *Si-fans*, the only difference conſiſting in the acceptation of certain words, and ſome few peculiarities of pronunciation.

The phyſicians of Thibet are not deſtitute of ſkill, and ſome of their aſtronomers are acquainted with the motions of the heavenly bodies, and able to calculate eclipſes, but the lamas are in general ſtupid and ignorant. It is rare to find any of them who underſtand their ancient books, or who are able to read them. Prieſts, of all eſtabliſhed religions, are as a body ſubject to the ſame remarks in a greater or leſſer degree, having found a ſubſtitute for virtue, learning and induſtry, in the policy of princes and the credulity and ſuperſtition of the people. Hence, wherever religion has long been eſtabliſhed and ſupported by law, and thus made national, the diſtinguiſhing characteristics of its priests, have been tyranny, voluptuousness, and ignorance, with all their train of concomitant evils There are, indeed, exceptions, but not sufficient to do away the cause of this general remark.

In Thibet there are no fortified towns, or places of defence The cities, in general, are very small And Lasa itself, where the dalai lama keeps his court, is rather a celebrated temple than a city.

COUNTRY OF HA-MI.

Ha-mi is situated to the north-east of China, at the extremity of the great desert, called by the Chinese Chamo, and the Tartars Cobi, and two hundred and seventy miles distant from the most westerly point of the province of Chen-si This country was formerly inhabited by a wandering people, named Iong, who are said to have sent deputies to pay homage to the emperor of China, nine hundred and fifty years before the Christian era, and to have presented some sabres by way of tribute About the end of the dynasty of Tcheou, these people fell under the dominion of the Hiong-nou, who appear to have been the same as the Huns, at that time a formidable nation Under the following dynasties this country experienced various revolutions and vicissitudes, it was sometimes united to the province of Chen-si, and sometimes not only independent of it, but even of the whole empire. The situation of these people, separated by vast deserts from China, must have greatly contributed to facilitate these revolutions. In 610 all the tributary states of the empire having revolted, that of Ha-mi followed their example, but it again submitted to the yoke, under Tai-tsong, second emperor of the dynasty of Tang, who sent one of his generals with an army to reduce it This prince paid particular attention to his new conquest He divided it into three districts, and connected its civil and military government in such a manner with that of the province of Chen-si, that tranquillity prevailed during his reign and several of those that followed. The emperors, prior to the reign of Tai-tsong, imported a considerable quantity of wine into China from Ha-mi; but, *Tai-tsong, having subdued the kingdom of Ha-mi, ordered vine-plants of the species called* [illegible]*, to be removed to China, and planted in his gardens, and got some persons instructed in the manner of making this wine, the use of which proved peculiarly* [illegible] *to him.*

Luxury having weakened the dynasty of Tang, the Mahometans, who had made a rapid progress in the countries situated between Persia, Cobi and the Caspian sea, advanced as far as Ha-mi, and completed its conquest. After this event, this country had princes of its own, but dependent on the Tartars, who successively ruled these immense regions. The *Yuen*, or Tartar emperors, again united the country of *Ha-mi* to the province of Chen-si; and this union subsisted until 1360, at which time the emperor formed it into a kingdom, on condition of its princes doing homage and paying tribute; and in 1404, the king of Ha-mi was honoured with a new title and a golden seal. After a contest of several years for the succession to the throne, this kingdom fell a prey to the king of *Tou-lou-fan*. This yoke soon becoming uneasy, the people of Ha-mi revolted from their new masters, and made conquests from them in their turn. Since this epocha, the country of Ha-mi has been successively exposed to anarchy, or governed by its own princes. The prince who filled the throne in 1696, acknowledged himself a vassal of the empire of China, and sent as tribute to Pe-kin camels, horses and sabres. KANG-HI received his homage with the usual ceremonies, and published a diploma, which established the rank that the king of Ha-mi should hold among the tributary princes, the time when he should come to render homage, the nature of the presents necessary for his tribute, the number of auxiliaries he was bound to furnish in time of war, and the manner of his appointing a successor. All these regulations have subsisted till the present time.

The country of Ha-mi, though surrounded by deserts, is one of the most delightful in the world. The soil produces abundance of grain, fruits, leguminous plants, and pasture of every kind; and the rice which grows here, is particularly esteemed in China, pomegranates, oranges, peaches, raisins and prunes have here a most exquisite taste, but there is no fruit more delicate or more in request than the melons of Ha-mi, which are carried to Pe-kin, for the emperor's table. These melons are much more wholesome than those of Europe, and have this singular property, that they may be kept fresh during great part of the winter.

But the most useful and most esteemed production of the country of Ha-mi, is its dried raisins, which are of two kinds. The first, which are much used in the Chinese medicine, seem to have a perfect resemblance to those known in Europe by the name of Corinthian. The second, which are in much greater request for the table, are smaller and more delicate than those of Provence.

Some of the emperors have caused plants to be transported from Ha-mi to Pe-kin, and planted in the gardens of the palace As these plants have been cultivated with extraordinary care, they have perfectly succeeded, and the raisins produced by them are exceedingly sweet, and have a most exquisite flavour.

Although the country of Ha-mi, the latitude of which is 42° 53′ 20″, lies farther towards the north than several of the provinces of France, we are assured, that its climate is more favourable to the culture of vines, and that its grapes are far superior. At Ha-mi it never rains, and even dew and fogs are ſcarcely ever ſeen the country is watered only by the ſnow which falls in winter, and by the water of this ſnow when melted, which is collected at the bottoms of the mountains, and preſerved with great care.

The method of drying grapes in Ha-mi is more ſimple than that practiſed in the provinces of China The people of Chen-ſi hold them over the ſteam of hot wine, and often boil them a few ſeconds in wine in which a little clarified honey has been diluted In the kingdom of Ha-mi they wait until the grapes are quite ripe, they then expoſe them to the ſcorching rays of the ſun, afterwards pick them, and leave them in that manner until they are quite dry. Theſe grapes become ſhrivelled, without loſing any of their ſubſtance, and without growing flat.

The kingdom of Ha-mi contains a great number of villages and hamlets, but it has, properly, only one city, which is its capital, and has the ſame name as the country.

It is ſurrounded by lofty walls, a mile and a half in circumference, and has two beautiful gates, one fronting the eaſt, and the other the weſt The ſtreets of this city are ſtraight, and well laid out; but the houſes, which contain only a ground-floor, and are for the moſt part conſtructed of earth, make very little ſhew however the ſerenity of the ſky and the goodneſs of its ſituation, in a beautiful plain, watered by a river, and ſurrounded by mountains, which alſo ſhelter it from the north winds, renders it a moſt delightful and agreeable reſidence. On whatever ſide it is approached, gardens are ſeen, which contain every thing that a fertile and cultivated ſoil in the mildeſt climates can produce. The ſurrounding fields are enchanting, but they do not extend far, for on ſeveral ſides they terminate in plains, where a number of beautiful horſes are fed, and a ſpecies of ſheep, which have large flat tails that ſometimes weigh three pounds. The country of Ha-mi appears to be abundant in fossils and valuable minerals the Chinese have, for a long time, procured diamonds and gold from it, and at present, it supplies them with a kind of agate, on which they set a great value. The inhabitants of this small state, are brave, capable of enduring fatigue, very dexterous in all bodily exercises, and make excellent soldiers, but they are fickle and soon irritated, and, when in a passion, are extremely ferocious and sanguinary

ISLES OF LIEOU-KIEOU.

These isles form a powerful and extensive empire, the inhabitants of which are civilized, and ought not to be confounded with other savage nations dispersed throughout the islands of Asia The emperor Kang-hi resolved to send an ambassador to the king of Lieou-kieou, and for this purpose chose one of the great doctors of the empire, named Su-pao-koang. This learned man departed from China in 1719, returned to Pe-kin in 1720, and in the year following, caused a relation of his voyage to be published in two volumes In the first of these, he gives a particular description of the isles of Lieou-kieou; and what he relates appears to be worthy of credit, for he examined, as he himself says, according to the orders of the emperor, whatever he found curious or interesting, respecting the number, situation and productions of these isles, as also the history, religion, manners and customs of the people who inhabit them.

These isles are situated between Corea, Formosa and Japan, and are in number thirty-six. The principal and largest is called Lieou-kieou, the rest have each a particular name The large island extends from north to south almost one hundred and fifty-two miles, and forty-four from east to west. The south-east part of the island, where the court refides, is called Cheouli, and here Kint-ching, the capital city, is fituated. The king's palace, which is reckoned to be twelve miles in circumference, is built on a neighbouring mountain It has four gates, correfponding to the four cardinal points, and that which fronts the weft, forms the grand entry. The view which this palace commands is delightful, it reaches as far as the port of Napa-kiang, at the diftance of four miles, to the city of Kint-ching, and to a great number of other cities, towns, villages, palaces, temples, monafteries, gardens, and pleafure houfes

According to thefe iflanders, the origin of their empire is loft in the remoteft antiquity. They reckon twenty-five fucceffive dynafties, comprehending a period of more than eighteen thoufand years. It is however certain, that the exiftence of the country called Lieou-kieou was not known in China before the year 605 of the Chriftian era. It was in the courfe of that year, that one of the emperors of the dynafty of Soui, having heard of thefe ifles, fent fome Chinefe thither, but their expedition proved fruitlefs, as the want of interpreters prevented them from acquiring that knowledge which was the object of their voyage. They however brought fome of the iflanders with them to Sigan-fou, the capital of the province of Chen-fi, and the ufual refidence of the emperors of the dynafty of Soui An ambaffador from the king of Japan being then at the Chinefe court, he and his attendants immediately knew the ftrangers to be natives of Lieou-kieou, but they fpoke of thefe ifles as of a miferable and wretched country, the inhabitants of which had never been civilized The emperor however learned that from the province of Fo-kien a fhip might reach the largeft of thefe iflands in five days

On this information, he fent fkilful men, accompanied by interpreters, to fummon the prince to do homage and to pay him tribute. This propofal was very ungracioufly received the king of Lieou-kieou fent back the Chinefe, telling them, fternly, that he acknowledged no prince for his fuperior. This anfwer irritated the emperor, who caufed a fleet to be immediately equipped in Fo-kien, in which he embarked ten thoufand men. This fleet fet fail, and arrived in fafety at the port of Nipa-kiang. The army, fpite of every effort made by the natives, landed on the ifland; and the king, who had put himfelf at the head of his troops to oppofe the enemy, having fallen in battle, the Chinefe pillaged, facked and burnt the royal city, made upwards of five thoufand flaves, and returned to China Such is the dreadful confequence of power centering in the hands of one man.

The emperors of the dynafty of Tang, thofe of the fhort dynafties that followed, and thofe of the dynafty of Song, although they were fully informed of every thing refpecting the Lieou-kieou ifles, however made no attempts to render them tributary In 1291, Chi-tfou, emperor of the dynafty of Yven, revived the pretenfions of his predeceffors, and fitted out a fleet to fubdue thefe iflands; but fchemes of conquefts had, from a difafter that befel their army in an expedition againft Japan, became difagreeable to the Chinefe. The fleet therefore went no farther than the ifles of Pong-hou, and the weftern coaft of Formofa, from whence, under divers pretences, it returned to the ports of Fo-kien

In 1372, under the reign of Hong-vou, founder of the dynafty of Ming, thefe iflands however fubmitted voluntarily to the Chinefe government. Hong-vou had fent one of the grandees of his court to the king of Lieou-kieou, to inform him of his acceffion to the throne. This nobleman had received particular inftructions refpecting this commiffion, and he acquitted himfelf with the prudence and addrefs of an able minifter In a private audience, which he had with the king, he exhorted him to declare himself a tributary of the empire, and laid before him the advantages he would derive from this step. His reasoning, supported by the force of his natural eloquence, made so much impression on the mind of the king that he embraced the proposal, and sent immediately to the emperor to demand the investiture of his states.

Hong-vou received his envoys in a magnificent manner, and loaded them with presents. Tsay-tou was solemnly declared a vassal of the empire, and the emperor, after having received his first tribute, consisting of valuable horses, aromatic wood, sulphur, copper, tin, &c. sent him a golden seal, and confirmed the choice he had made of one of his sons for successor. The emperor afterwards sent thirty-six families, chiefly from the province of Fo-kien, to Lieou-kieou. Tsay-tou received them, assigned them lands near the port of Napa-kiang, and appointed certain revenues for their use, and Hong-vou also made them considerable remittances. These families first introduced into Lieou-kieou the language of the Chinese, the use of their characters, and the ceremonies practised in honour of Confucius. On the other hand, the sons of several of the grandees of the court of Tsay-tou were sent to Nan-king, to study Chinese in the imperial college, where they were treated with distinction, and maintained at the emperor's expence.

The isles of Lieou-kieou had neither iron nor porcelain. Hong-vou supplied this want, by causing a great number of utensils and instruments of iron, to be made and sent thither, together with a quantity of porcelain vessels. Commerce, navigation, and the arts soon began to flourish. And these islanders learned to cast bells for their temples, to manufacture paper and the finest stuffs, and to make porcelain, with which they had been supplied before from Japan.

The revolution which placed the Tartars on the imperial throne of China, produced no change in the conduct of the kings of Lieou-kieou Chang-tche, who was then reigning, sent ambassadors to acknowledge Chun-tchi, and received a seal from him, on which were engraven some Tartar characters It was then settled, that the king of Lieou-kieou should pay his tribute only every two years, and that the number of persons in the train of his envoys should not exceed one hundred and fifty

The emperor Kang-hi paid more attention to these isles than any of his predecessors. He caused a superb palace to be erected in honour of Confucius, and a college, where he maintained proper persons to teach the sciences and the Chinese characters. He instituted examinations for the different degrees of the literati, and he ordained, that the king of Lieou-kieou should never send in tribute rose wood, cloves, or any other production which was not really of the growth of the country, but, that he should send a fixed quantity of sulphur, copper, tin, shells, and mother of pearl, which is remarkably plenty in these islands. He permitted, that, besides the usual tribute, he might present him horse-furniture, pistol-cases, and other things of the same kind, which these islanders are said to manufacture with great taste and neatness

It is near a thousand years since the bonzes of China introduced into Lieou-kieou the worship of Fo, and the principal books belonging to their sect This worship is at present the established religion of the country There is likewise in the capital a magnificent temple, erected in honor of another idol borrowed from the Chinese, named Tien-fey, which signifies *celestial queen*, or *lady*

These islanders never make promises or swear before their idols. When they have occasion to do this, they burn perfumes, present fruits, and stand respectfully before some stone, which they call to witness the solemnity of their engagements Numbers of stones are to be seen in the courts of their temples, in most public places, and upon their mountains, which are entirely appropriated to this purpofe. They have alfo among them women confecrated for the worfhip of fpirits, who are fuppofed to have great influence over thefe beings. They are further employed in vifiting the fick, diftributing medicines, and reciting prayers for their recovery.

They refpect the dead as much as the Chinefe, and they are equally ceremonious in wearing mourning, but their funerals are neither fo pompous, nor fo expenfive Their coffins are of an hexagonal or octagonal figure, three or four feet high, and they burn the flefh of the bodies of their dead, preferving only the bones

Families are diftinguifhed in Lieou-kieou by furnames, as in China, but a man and a woman of the fame furname cannot be united in marriage. The king is not permitted to marry but in the three grand families, which always enjoy the higheft offices There is a fourth, of equal diftinction to the three former, but neither the king nor the princes contract any alliances with this family; for it is doubtful, whether it be not fprung from the fame ftem as the royal line.

A plurality of wives is allowed in thefe ifles Young men and young women enjoy the liberty of feeing one another, and converfing together, and their union is always in confequence of their own choice, and not of the conftraint of parents or friends The women are referved, they neither ufe paint, nor wear pendants in their ears, they collect their hair on the top of their heads, in the form of a curl, and fix it in that manner by means of long pins made of gold or filver

Befides the domains which the king poffeffes, he receives the produce of all the fulphur, copper and tin-mines, and falt pits, together with the product of taxes. From thefe revenues he pays the falaries of the mandarins and officers of his court. Thefe falaries are eftimated at a certain number of facks of rice, but are paid in grain, rice, filk, cloth, &c.

There are here, as in China, nine orders of mandarins, who are diſtinguiſhed by the colour of their caps, or by their girdles and cuſhions The greater part of the titles of theſe mandarins are hereditary in their families, *but there are ſome which are only beſtowed upon merit.* In the capital there are tribunals eſtabliſhed for managing the revenue and affairs of the principal iſland, and of all the others dependent on it The latter have agents, who reſide at court. There are alſo particular tribunals for civil and criminal matters, for whatever concerns the families of the grandees and princes, for the affairs of religion, for inſpecting the public granaries, king's revenues, and duties, for commerce, manufactures, civil ceremonies, navigation, public edifices, literature, and war.

The veſſels that are built in this country are highly eſteemed by the people of China and Japan In theſe the natives go to China, Tong-king, Cochin-china, Corea, Nanga-za-ki, Satſuma, the neighbouring iſles, and Formoſa, where they diſpoſe of their different commodities. Beſides thoſe articles of commerce, which their manufactories of ſilk, cotton, paper, arms, copper utenſils, &c. furniſh them, they alſo export mother of pearl, tortoiſe and other ſhells, coral and whet-ſtones, which are in great requeſt both in China and Japan

Three different languages are ſpoken in the iſles of Licou-kicou Letters, accounts, and all the king's orders, are written in Japaneſe characters, and in the language of the country, books of morality, hiſtory, medicine, aſtronomy and aſtrology, are written in Chineſe characters. The diſtribution of the year, and the diviſion of time, are the ſame in Licou-kicou as in China, the people following the calendar of the empire

The edifices, temples, and the king's palace, are built after the Japaneſe manner, but the houſes of the Chineſe, the hotel of their ambaſſador, the imperial college, and the temple of the goddeſs *Tien-fey*, are built after the Chineſe. In many of the temples and public buildings, there are tables of ſtone or marble, on which are engraven Chineſe characters in honour of Chineſe emperors, from Hong-vou to the preſent time. Chineſe inſcriptions are alſo to be ſeen on their triumphal arches and in the king's palace, ſeveral are alſo found in Japaneſe characters, and ſome, but the number is few, in thoſe of India.

The natives of Lieou-kieou are, in general, mild, affable, temperate, active, and laborious, they are equally the enemies of ſlavery, falſehood, and diſhoneſty. The grandees, bonzes and Chineſe eſtabliſhed at Lieou-kieou excepted, few of the inhabitants of theſe iſlands can either write or read. If it happens, that any of the peaſants, artiſts, or ſoldiers can do either, they ſhave their heads, as the bonzes. All others have a kind of tuft on the top of their heads, around which is a circle of very ſhort hair These people are fond of games and diverſions They celebrate, with great pomp and ſplendour, thoſe feſtivals that are inſtituted in honour of their idols, and thoſe which are appointed for the ending and commencement of the year.

Great harmony prevails among different families and individuals, which they preſerve by frequent repaſts, to which they invite one another Suicide is unknown among them, and they are free from most prominent vices and [illegible]

NATURAL HISTORY

OF

C H I N A.

CLIMATE.

CHINA is so extensive, that all its provinces cannot enjoy the same temperature, their climate, and the nature of their soil, are therefore various, according as they are nearer or more remote from the south, severe cold is felt at Pe-kin, while the southern provinces are exposed to excessive heat the air however is in general wholesome, and the people commonly live to a great age

MOUNTAINS, RIVERS AND LAKES.

The principal mountains of China are those in the northern and western parts of the empire. The latter are rendered fruitful by the labour and industry of the Chinese husbandman, but the former are barren, rocky, and incapable of improvement. Those of the provinces of Chen-si, Ho-nan, Quang-tong and Fo-kien, shew few signs of culture, but they are covered with forests of tall, straight trees of every species, fit for building, masts and ship-timber The emperor sometimes procures from these mountains enormous trunks, which he causes to be transported to the distance of more than three hundred leagues, by land and water, to be employed in his palace, or for public works. Other mountains furnish quicksilver, iron, tin, copper, gold and silver. Political foresight has however prevented many of the latter from being opened The chiefs of the early dynasties, aware that artificial riches could not form a solid base for the happiness of states, were afraid of opening these sources of luxury, lest the people should be induced to neglect the natural riches of their soil, by applying to other labours than those of agriculture About the commencement of the fifteenth century, the emperor Tching-tsou caused a mine of precious stones to be shut, which had been opened by a private individual *Useless labours*, said he, *produce sterility, a mine of precious stones does not furnish corn* At present, the Chinese are not so scrupulous, for they carry on a great trade in gold

The Chinese relate several singular and extraordinary phenomena of their mountains, not worth repeating, though their credulity induces them to relate those legendary tales as facts But they admire, above all others, a mountain of Fo-kien, the whole of which they conceit to be a figure of the god *Fo*

The principal lakes of China are the Tong-ting-hou, situated in the province of Hou-quang, and which is more than two hundred and forty miles in circumference, the Tai-hou, part of which extends into Kiang-nan, the Hong-tse, and the Kao-yeou, of the province of Kiang-nan, and the Poyang-hou, formed in Kiang-si by the confluence of four considerable rivers, which, like the sea, is subject to tempests and storms This last mentioned is near three hundred miles in length

Among an infinitude of great and small rivers that water this vast kingdom, there are two particularly celebrated. The first is the Yan-tse-kiang, or Son of the Sea It has its source in the province of Yun-nan, traverses Hou-quang and Kiang-nan, and, after having watered four provinces, through an extent of twelve hundred miles, it falls into the eastern sea, opposite the isle of Tsong-ming This river, at the distance of more than ninety miles from its mouth, is a mile and a half broad. The navigation of it is dangerous, and numbers of vessels are lost in it almost every day It flows with great rapidity, and forms in its course several islands, which are beneficial to the province, on account of the multitude of reeds, from ten to twelve feet in height, which they produce, and which are used for fuel in all the neighbouring cities When this river is swelled by torrents from the mountains, it becomes so impetuous that it overflows and carries away part of these islands, forming others from their wrecks in those places of its bed where it leaves them.

Another great river of China is the Hoang-ho, or Yellow River. The Chinese give it this name, because the clay and sand which it washes down, especially in time of rain, make its water appear of a yellow colour. It rises in the mountains which border the province of Te-tchuen on the west, and, after a course of nearly eighteen hundred miles across Tartary and China, discharges itself into the eastern sea, not far from the mouth of the Yang-tse-kiang It is very broad and rapid, but so shallow, that it is scarcely navigable It often happens, that it overflows its banks, and buries whole villages, and it has been found necessary, in order to confine it, to raise, in several places, long and strong banks, which, however, do not entirely free the cities in its neighbourhood from the dread of its inundations For the same reason, the people of the province of Ho-nan, the land of which is exceedingly low, have taken the precaution to surround most of their cities, at the distance of three furlongs, with strong ramparts of earth faced with turf

The ingenuity which the Chinese display in turning the happy situation of their lakes and rivers to the greatest advantage, is worthy of attention. One of their principal works for the convenience of commerce, is the celebrated canal which reaches from Canton to Pe-kin, and which forms a communication between the southern and northern provinces. This work, called *The Royal Canal*, is eighteen hundred miles in length, and its navigation no where interrupted but by the mountain *Meiung*, where passengers are obliged to travel thirty or forty miles over land. They, however, have no occasion to quit their barks when they are going through the provinces of Quang-si and Hou-quang. In this canal, a number of others terminate, which stretch out into the country, and form a communication between the neighbouring cities, towns and villages. The greater part of these canals have been executed by the industry of the inhabitants, who have spared neither labour nor expence to procure themselves the valuable advantage of having an easy conveyance for their goods into all the provinces of the empire. Near to *Chao-hing* and *Ning-po* there are two canals, the waters of which do not communicate, and which differ ten or twelve feet in their level. To render this place passable for boats, the Chinese have constructed a double glacis of large stones, or rather, two inclined planes, which unite in an acute angle at their upper extremity, and extend on each side to the surface of the water. If the bark is in the lower canal, they push it up the plane of the first glacis, by means of several capstans, until it is raised to the angle, when, by its own weight, it glides down the second glacis, and precipitates itself into the water of the higher canal, with a considerable velocity. It is seldom that any accident happens in this passage, for the Chinese use for the keels of these barks a kind of wood which is exceedingly hard and proper for resisting the violence of such an effort.

MINES, METALS, STONES, EARTHS, CLAYS, &c.

The mountains of China being numerous, and situated under various climates, must contain minerals of every species. There are indeed found there in great abundance, mines of gold, silver, iron, copper, tin, lead, mercury, marble, crystal, cinnabar, lapis lazuli, &c. Gold and silver would be much more common in this empire, was it not for the policy we have already mentioned, which does not permit the mines which contain these metals to be opened. A great part of the gold, therefore, which is to be found in China, is collected in the sand of the rivers and torrents which fall from the mountains, situated on the western boundaries of the provinces of Se-tchuen and Yun-nan, the last of which abounds in silver-mines. The Lo-los, of whom we have already spoken, must procure much gold from their mountains, since it is a custom among them, to inclose a great quantity of plates of gold in the coffins of those people whom they are desirous of honouring. Their gold, however, does not appear beautiful, because it is not thoroughly purified. The Lo-los are little better acquainted with the art of melting silver, which is still blacker, and contains more refuse; but it is as pure and bright as that of any other country, when refined by the Chinese workmen. As the Chinese gold is not coined, it is employed in commerce, and becomes merchandize. It is never used there but in gilding, or for slight ornaments, the emperor being the only person who possesses any quantity of gold plate.

Iron, lead and tin mines are common, and these metals are sold at a low rate throughout the whole empire.

The copper-mines of the provinces of *Yunnan* and *Koei-tchou* have furnished, for a great number of years, all the small coin that is struck in the empire. According to Grosier, the Chinese have a kind of copper which they call *pë-tong*, or *white copper*, so pure and fine, that it approaches near to silver. This copper, he says, is naturally white when taken from the mine, and when it is broken into grains, is found still whiter in the interior part than on the surface. He informs us that a number of experiments have been made at Pe-kin, which sufficiently prove, that this copper does not owe its whiteness to any mixture. Different kinds of works are made of it; but, to soften it and render it less brittle, the workmen are obliged to mix with it a little zinc, or some metal of the same kind. Those who are desirous of preserving its splendour and beautiful colour, add to it a fifth part of silver. This copper is found in the province of Yun-nan. The Japanese bring to China another kind, which is yellow, and sold in ingots. It has a great resemblance to gold, and is used by the Chinese for making different toys. Notwithstanding the assertion of experiments having proved to the contrary, we are inclined to think both these latter are mixtures and not pure copper; if not, there can be little doubt but the change is produced by the influence of some neighbouring mineral, perhaps not yet noticed.

The Chinese have another kind of copper, which they call *tse-lay-tong*, or *copper which comes of itself*. It is nothing else but copper washed down from the tops of the mountains, and which is afterwards found among the pebbles and sand left by the torrents when they become dry.

Quarries and coal-mines are abundant in every province of the empire. Coals are found in great plenty in the mountains of the provinces of Chen-si, Chan-si and Pe-tcheli. Without this supply, fire-wood, which is scarce and very dear, would not be found sufficient for the consumption of the northern provinces.

Lapis lazuli is found in several cantons of the province of Yun-yan, in the whole province of Se-tchuen, and in a district of the province of Chan-si, called Tai-tong-fou; it differs nothing from that imported into Europe. Chan-si furnishes a most beautiful kind of white jasper much resembling agate; it is transparent when polished, and sometimes overcrossed with spots; the Chinese call it *Yu-ch*[illegible].

The most beautiful rock crystal of China is dug from the mountains of Tchang-tcheou-fou, and Tch[illegible]-pou-hien in the province of Fo-kien, situated in latitude 24° 10′. The art[illegible] of the[illegible] are very ingenious in cutting it, and form it into buttons, ſeals, figures of animals, and other trinkets.

Yun-nan furniſhes ſome real rubies, but they are exceedingly ſmall. There is ſold yearly in the capital of this province a number of other precious ſtones; but they are ſaid to be procured from other places, eſpecially from the neighbouring kingdoms of Ava and Laos. It is certain, that there is, at the diſtance of two hundred ſenes or cords from the city of Mohang-leng, the capital of Laos, a mine of precious ſtones, from which rubies are ſaid to be dug that are ſometimes as large as a walnut Emeralds are alſo found there, and it is ſaid, that the king of Laos has one in his poſſeſſion which is equal in ſize to a moderate orange. A rivulet runs acroſs this mine, and detaches ſeveral precious ſtones, which it waſhes down with its current.

Quarries of marble are very common in China, eſpecially in the province of Fo-kien. But the Chineſe artiſts are not ſo well acquainted as Europeans with the art of working it Small pieces of it are however ſometimes found among the merchants, which are poliſhed in a ſuperior manner, ſuch as the ſmall tablets uſed as ornaments in their feſtivals named tien-tſan. They are very elegant, and variegated with different colours, which, though not lively, repreſent, naturally, mountains, rivers, trees and animals These tablets are made from marble procured from the quarries of Taily-fou, and the moſt beautiful pieces are always choſen for that purpoſe.

Among the various ſtones known in China, there are ſome that have obtained the name of ſonorous, and of which the Chineſe make muſical inſtruments. They differ conſiderably from one another in beauty and in the ſtrength and duration of their tone, but what is very ſurpriſing, this difference of tone cannot be diſcovered either by the different degrees of their hardneſs, weight, fineneſs of grain, or any other qualities which might be ſuppoſed to determine it. Some ſtones are found remarkably hard, which are very ſonorous, and others exceedingly ſoft, which have an excellent tone, ſome that are extremely heavy, emit a very ſweet ſound, and others, that are as light as pumice-ſtone, have alſo an agreeable tone These ſtones have different names given them by the Chineſe.

The ſtone called *yu*, is the moſt celebrated, valuable and beautiful of this claſs They are chiefly found in channels made by torrents, and in the rivers which flow at the bottoms of the mountains of Yu-nan, Koei-tcheou, Chen-ſi, Y-ly and Yo-quen They reſemble externally thoſe pebbles which are found in the ſtreams and torrents that ruſh down through the clefts of the mountains The largeſt that the miſſionaries ſaw in the imperial palace, were two feet and a half or three feet in length, and one foot eight or ten inches in breadth, and theſe were conſidered as matchleſs pieces. The yu are alſo found in the earth, in valleys near mines, and in the fiſſures made by torrents in the ſides of the mountains Theſe differ from others becauſe their ſurface is not ſo ſmooth, nor their texture, of ſo fine a grain

Five different properties are remarked in the ſonorous yu, hardneſs, weight, colour, grain and ſound.

Beautiful yu are ſo hard when cut and poliſhed that the beſt tempered ſteel glides upon them without making any impreſſion

The weight of the *yu* is proportionable to its hardneſs. An unpoliſhed block is preſerved in the emperor's palace, two feet ſix inches in length, and ſix inches in breadth, and which to appearance one man could eaſily lift, but four are neceſſary only to move it

The colour moſt eſteemed at preſent in theſe ſtones, is that of whey; thoſe that are next, are bright blue, azure, indigo, citron yellow, orange, logwood-red, pale green, ſea green, deep green, cinder grey, &c. The Chineſe ſet moſt value upon *yu* which is of one colour only, without veins or ſhades, unleſs it be variegated in an agreeable manner with five colours.

The hardeſt and heavieſt has always the fineſt grain. But what kind of *yu* is the moſt ſonorous has never yet been determined The *nieou-yeou-che*, or ox fat ſtone, is the ſecond kind of ſonorous ſtone known in China. It has neither the hardneſs, weight nor ſweet tone of the *yu*, and it is more common, and much leſs eſteemed however, it is very rare to find large pieces of it. That which is in greateſt requeſt, has really the colour of the fat of beef, and is of one ſhade, without clouds or veins. This ſtone is a production of the province of Yun-nan, and is found in the earth near mines, in valleys, or at the bottoms of the mountains. Its exterior coat is rough, and of a dirty colour, between cheſnut and green, below this, there is a ſecond, reſembling curdled milk, after which comes another, tinged with yellow, that becomes deeper as it approaches the centre. The yu emits ſparks when ſtruck with ſteel the *nieou-yeou-che* does not This ſtone ſeems more to reſemble agate, and it perhaps may be an agate of a peculiar kind. None are ſonorous but thoſe which have a beautiful yellow colour, without tranſparent veins, it is however far from being ſo ſonorous as the *yu*.

The third kind is named *hiang-che*, and emits ſo metallic a ſound that it might be taken for a compoſition Some of them are found black, others grey, green, and variegated with white The blackeſt are the moſt ſonorous. It is brought from the lake of Tche-kiang, and appears to be a kind of alabaſter, the colour and nature of which have been changed by the water that has penetrated it

There is a fourth kind reſembling marble in its veins, which are grey, black and dirty white on a milk-white ground. The greater part of theſe ſtones have tranſparent ſpots, which ſhew that a vitrification has commenced. They appear to be ſomething between talc and cryſtal, and it is remarked, that their tone is often interrupted, and of very ſhort duration

The naturalists of Europe have we believe, never yet attempted to discover, whether some of our stones may not have the same properties as the sonorous stones of the extremities of Asia It however appears, that the Romans were formerly acquainted with a sonorous stone of the class of hiang-che "Pliny," says the abbé du Bos *, "when "speaking of curious stones, observes, that the stone "called calcophonas, or brazen sound, is black; and that, "according to the etymology of its name, it sends forth "a sound much resembling that of brass when it is struck. "The passage of Pliny is as follows *Calcophonas nigra* "*est; sed illisa, æris tinnitum reddit* Lib 37 Sect 56"

Some sonorous stones sent into France, roused the curiosity of the chemists there, who thought proper to inquire to what class of stones they may belong, and the late duke de Chaulnes applied with particular attention to this research The following is the result of the experiments which he made on a *king* † in the cabinet of Mr. Bertin

"The Academy of Sciences, Mr. Romé de Lisle, and "several other learned mineralogists, when asked, if they "were acquainted with the black stone of which the Chi-"nese king were made, for answer cited the passage of "Pliny mentioned by Boethius de Bott, Linnæus, and "in the Dictionary of Bomare, and added, what Mr "Anderson remarks in his Natural History of Iceland, "respecting a bluish kind of stone which is very sono-"rous. As the black stone of the Chinese becomes of a "bluish colour when filed, it is probably of the same species "None of the rest who were consulted had ever seen it.

"The Chinese stone has a great resemblance at first "sight to black marble, and, like it, is calcareous, but "marble generally is not sonorous It also externally "resembles touch-stone, which is a kind of basaltes, and

* Vide Reflections on Poetry and Painting

† A musical instrument made of this stone

" the basaltes found near volcanos, but these two stones " are vitrifications

" Its resemblance to black marble induced me to make " some comparative experiments It is not phosphoric; " neither is black marble It has no effect upon a suspended iron bar, and consequently contains no iron in " its metallic state, but when dissolved in acids, to try " whether it contained any particles of that metal, it produced a strong effervescence, which seemed to indicate " it not to be entirely free from them. As black marble " did not present the same phenomenon, the sonorous stone " was examined more attentively by a magnifying glass, " when several small points, resembling pyrites, were " discovered in it, to which this difference was attributed. " When dissolved in nitrous, marine, or vitriolic acids, it " always presents the same phenomena as black marble; " with vitriolic acid it makes a greyish magma, and leaves " behind it a black substance that is not soluble in nitrous " or marine acids, and which, as in black marble, is a real " inflammable bitumen

" Black marble and sonorous stone, when calcined, " become entirely white, and yield a very strong calx; " but it loses its bitumen by the action of fire. Sonorous " stone, however, appears to contain less of the phlogistic " and colouring matter, for a precipitation of it, by " means of fixed alkali, is somewhat whiter, and has " more of a blueish cast than that of black marble. " When tried by volatile alkali, it contains no copper. " Other precipitations of it, by different substances, exhibit " the same appearances "

The duke having proceeded thus far in his analysis, endeavoured to procure some farther information from the stone-cutters. They replied, that blue-coloured marble was very sonorous, and that they had seen large blocks of it which emitted a very strong sound, but the duke having ordered a *king* to be constructed of this kind of stone, it did not poſſeſs that property. By trying the black marble of Flanders, a piece was at length obtained which emitted an agreeable ſound: it was cut into a *king*, which is almoſt as ſonorous as thoſe of China. From theſe obſervations the duke concludes, that the ſtones of which the *king* are formed, are nothing elſe but a black kind of marble, the conſtituent parts of which are the ſame as thoſe of the marble of Europe, but that ſome difference in their organization renders them more or leſs ſonorous.

The duke farther obſerves, that "the Chineſe make "*king* of cryſtal, and that one of this kind is to be ſeen "at St. Bribe, in the cabinet of M. de la Tour, ſecretary "to the king; and that they alſo employ a kind of alabaſtre, ſome pieces of which M. Bertin received from "China, ſhaped like the *king* made of black ſtone, that "were ſaid to be very ſonorous, but they do not appear to "have any ſound at all; laſtly, that the ſtone *yu*, of which "the Chineſe conſtruct their moſt beautiful *king*, is nothing "elſe but a ſpecies of agate."

China abounds with potters earth of various kinds, and of all colours, ſome mixed with gravel, ſome with ſand, and ſome ſingularly formed by nature; the moſt valuable are thoſe uſed in the manufactory of porcelain. The baſis of this article is produced by the mixture of two ſorts of earth, one called *pe-tun-tſe*, and the other *kao-lin*; the latter is intermixed with ſmall ſhining particles, the former purely white, and very fine to the touch. Theſe firſt materials are carried to the manufactories in the ſhape of bricks. The *pe-tun-tſe*, which is ſo fine, is nothing elſe but fragments of rock taken from certain quarries, and reduced to powder. Every kind of ſtone is not fit for this purpoſe. *The colour of that which is good*, ſay the Chineſe, *ought to incline a little towards green*. A large iron club is uſed for breaking theſe pieces of rock; they are afterwards put into mortars, and, by means of levers headed with ſtone and bound round with iron, they are reduced to a very fine powder These levers are put in action either by the labour of men, or by water, in the same manner as the beaters of European paper mills The dust afterwards collected is thrown into a vessel full of water, and stirred with an iron shovel When it has been left to settle for some time, a kind of cream rises on the top, about four inches in thickness, which is skimmed off and poured into another vessel filled with water; the water in the first vessel is repeatedly stirred, and the cream which rises is still collected, until nothing but the coarse dregs, which, by their own weight, precipitate to the bottom, remain: these dregs are then carefully collected, and pounded anew

What was taken from the first vessel is now suffered to remain in the second until it is formed into a kind of crust at the bottom, when the water is poured off, by gently inclining the vessel, that the sediment may not be disturbed, and the paste is thrown into large moulds proper for drying it Before it is entirely hard, it is divided into small square cakes, which are sold by the hundred

The *kao-lin*, which is also used in the composition of porcelain, requires less labour than the *pe-tun-tse*, nature having a greater share in the preparation of it There are large mines of it in the bosoms of certain mountains, the exterior strata of which consists of a kind of red earth. These mines are very deep, and the kao-lin is found in small lumps, that are formed into bricks, after having gone through the same process as the pe-tun-tse It is from the kao-lin that fine porcelain derives all its strength.

The Chinese have discovered, within these few years, a new substance proper to be employed in the composition of porcelain. It is a species of chalk, called *hoa-che*, from which the physicians of China prepare a kind of draught, said to be detersive, aperient, and cooling. The manufacturers of porcelain have thought proper to employ this stone instead of kao-lin. It is called *hoa* because it is glutinous, and has a great resemblance to soap. Porcelain made with hoa-che is very rare, and much dearer than any other. It has an exceeding fine grain, and, with regard to the painting, if it be compared with that of the common porcelain, it appears to surpass it in a very considerable degree.

Hoa-che is seldom used in forming the body of the work, and the artist is sometimes contented with making it into a very fine size, in which the vessel is plunged when dry, in order that it may receive a coat before it is painted and varnished, by which means it acquires a superior degree of beauty.

When hoa-che is taken from the mine, it is washed in rain or river water, to separate it from a kind of yellow earth which adheres to it. It is then pounded, put into a tub filled with water, to dissolve it, and afterwards formed into cakes like kao-lin. We are assured, that hoa-che, when prepared in this manner, without the mixture of any other earth, is alone sufficient to make porcelain. It serves instead of kao-lin, but is much dearer.

FRUITS, LEGUMINOUS PLANTS, &c.

China produces the greater part of the fruits which we have in Europe, and several other kinds peculiar to the country. Apples, pears, prunes, apricots, peaches, quinces, figs, grapes, pomegranates, oranges, walnuts, and chesnuts, are found every where in abundance, but there is no good species of cherries in the country, and in general, excepting grapes and pomegranates, the fruits which they have in common are much inferior to those of Europe. The Chinese have several kinds of olives, but they do not extract oil from them, on what account we know not, whether it be that this fruit in China is not proper for that purpose, or that they are ignorant of the art of making it. When they want to gather their olives, they bore a hole in the trunk of the tree, which, after having put some salt into it, they stop up, and, at the end of a few days, the fruit drops of itself.

Oranges were firſt brought to Europe from China, for which we are indebted to the Portugueſe. Of this fruit the Chineſe have a great number of kinds.

Lemons and citrons are very common: but the Chineſe pay particular attention to the culture of a kind of lemon-tree, the fruit of which is of the ſize of a walnut, round, green, and ſour, and are ſaid to be excellent in ragouts. Theſe trees are often planted in boxes, to ornament courts, halls, and apartments.

. The Chineſe have a very ſmall ſpecies of melons, which are yellow within, and exceedingly ſweet, and which are eaten with the ſkin, as we ſometimes eat apples in Europe. They have alſo another kind, ſtill more eſteemed, which are brought from that part of Tartary called *Hami*. Theſe melons, as we have already obſerved, may be kept freſh for five or ſix months. Great care is taken every year to make a proper proviſion of them for the emperor's table.

The *tſe-tſe* are a ſpecies of fruit peculiar to China, that grow in almoſt all the provinces. There are different kinds of them. Thoſe of the ſouthern parts of the empire are remarkably ſweet; their ſeeds are black and flat, and the pulp is ſlimy and extremely juicy. In Chan-ſi and Chen-ſi the tſe-tſe are larger, firmer, and richer, and much fitter for being kept. The tree which produces this fruit is very beautiful; it is as tall and buſhy as a middling ſized walnut-tree; its leaves in ſpring and ſummer are of a bright green, but in autumn they appear of a beautiful red. The fruit is the ſize of a common apple; in proportion as they ripen, they aſſume an orange-colour; and when they are dried, they are as ſweet and mealy as figs.

Two kinds of fruit with which we are not acquainted, are found in the provinces of Fo-kien, Quang-tong, and Quang-ſi. The firſt, called *li tchi*, of the ſize of a date, has a ſtone, which is long and very hard, and covered with a ſoft juicy pulp, that has an exquiſite taſte. This [illegible] is inclosed with a rough, thin rind, shaped at one end like an egg. We are [illegible], that this fruit is delicious, but it is dangerous when eat to excess, as it is so hot, as to occasion an eruption over the whole body. The Chinese [illegible] to [illegible] the rind, until it becomes black [illegible] like prunes. By these means, it is preserved [illegible], they generally use it in tea, to which it communicates [illegible] in sourness, which they prefer to the [illegible] of sugar. This fruit is carried to Pe-kin for [illegible] of the emperor, inclosed in tin vessels, filled with [illegible] honey and other ingredients, and thus it [illegible] freshness, but loses much of its [illegible]. That [illegible] prince might taste them in the highest [illegible] the trees themselves have been sometimes transported to the capital in boxes, and they have been so well [illegible], that, when they arrived there, the fruit was near its [illegible].

[illegible] other kind of fruit peculiar to the southern provinces, is the [illegible], or *dragon's eye*; it is of a round [illegible], its [illegible] is yellowish [illegible], its pulp is white, but [illegible], and is very agreeably flavoured.

The Chinese distinguish three kinds of apricot trees, the apricot-tree with double flowers, the apricot-tree that produces fruit, and the wild apricot-tree. The apricot-tree with double flowers, is cultivated in gardens, the Chinese divide this tree into four principal classes, which are the [illegible], pale yellow, milk white, and the common, the buds of which at first appear red, but the flowers white [illegible]. There are dwarf apricot-trees with double flowers, which are placed for ornament in apartments, [illegible] flower during winter. The rest are planted [illegible] gardens, and [illegible] very beautiful effect [illegible]. The [illegible] bearing fruit, and [illegible] those of Europe, from the kernels of [illegible] the Chinese extract a good oil, which [illegible] used at table, it is, as least, much superior to the oil produced from walnuts which is burnt in lamps The Chinese peasants warm their stoves with what remains of the stones, and collect the cinders for manuring their land

The barren mountains which lie to the west of Pe-kin, are covered with these trees, and the oil extracted from their kernels, render the peasants as rich as those who live in the low lands Apricots in China, as in Europe, are generally the earliest fruit of summer The Chinese preserve them both dry and liquid, but they always wait until the fruit is quite ripe Besides this, they press out the juice, boil and clarify it, and form it into a kind of lozenges, that may be kept as long as they choose, and which, when dissolved in water, make a cooling and refreshing beverage

China produces abundance of grapes, it is not, therefore from a want of this fruit, that the Chinese make so little use of wine Those who believe that the vine was not known in the Chinese empire until very late, and that it was carried thither from the west, labour under a great mistake, for all the literati assert, that the vine has been known and cultivated in China from the remotest antiquity, and it is certain, that there were vines in Chan-si and Chen-si several centuries before the Christian era, and that a sufficiency of them were cultivated to make abundance of wine Grosier says, that in the large Chinese herbal book it is said that wine made from grapes, was the wine of honour, which several cities presented to the emperors, their governors and viceroys In 1373, the emperor Tai-tsou accepted some of it, for the last time, from Tai-yuen, a city of Chen-si, and forbade any more to be presented, saying, *I drink little wine, and I am unwilling, that what I do drink, should occasion any burden to my people*

The vine has however, like the empire itself, experienced its revolution, it has often been included in the list of profcribed trees and ſhrubs that impeded agriculture, and the extirpation was at times carried ſo far in many provinces, that the remembrance of it was forgotten. With regard to the preſent ſtate of the culture of vines in China, we know from unqueſtionable authority that the emperors Kang-hi, Yong-tching and Kien-long, now on the throne, have cauſed a number of new plants to be introduced from foreign countries, that the three provinces of Honan, Chan-tong and Chanſi, have repaired their former loſſes, that the large cities of Tai-yuen and Ping-yang in Chanſi, are become famous on account of the great quantity of dried grapes that are procured from their environs, and that the province of Pe-tcheli, at all times fruitful in vines, produces ſo many at preſent, that there are fourteen of its diſtricts celebrated for their raiſins, which are preſerved and ſold in Pe-kin at a very moderate price.

As roots and greens are the principal nouriſhment of the people, they ſpare no labour to procure them good. Beſides thoſe kinds common in Europe, they have a great number of others, in a great meaſure unknown to us, at leaſt to the nation at large. Among theſe is a ſpecies of onion, which are not produced from ſeed, as ours are. Towards the cloſe of the ſeaſon, ſome ſmall filaments ſpring from the ends of the leaves, in the middle of which a white onion is formed, like thoſe that grow in the earth. This ſmall onion again ſhoots forth leaves ſimilar to thoſe which ſupport it, and theſe new leaves bear another onion on their points, but in ſuch manner, that the leaves and the onion become ſmaller as they are farther diſtant from the earth.

Rue, ſorrel, cabbage-plants and other greens, when tranſported from India to China, either die or degenerate before the end of two or three years. The Chineſe, however, have real cabbages, but they never grow into a head. They have alſo had parſley for a long time, but it loſes the taſte and beauty which it has in Europe.

Among the pot-herbs which we have not, and for which it is ſaid the Chineſe are to be envied, is a plant called *pe-tſai*. It is much uſed, and bears ſome reſemblance to the Roman beet, but differs from it in its flower, ſeed, taſte and ſize The beſt *pe-tſai* grows in the northern provinces, where the inhabitants leave it to be ſoftened by the hoar-froſts. The quantity ſown and conſumed is very great indeed, and in the months of October and November the bridges of Pe-kin are almoſt blocked up by waggons which continue paſſing from morning till night, loaded with this plant The Chineſe make proviſion of *pe-tſai* for winter, pickling of it, and mixing it with their rice.

The Chineſe cultivate even the bottom of their waters, and the beds of their lakes, ponds and rivulets, produce crops that to us are unknown Their induſtry has found out reſources in a number of aquatic plants, ſeveral of which, as the *pi-tſi*, or water-cheſnut, and the *lien-hoa*, are the greateſt delicacies of a Chineſe table The Government has cauſed this latter plant to be cultivated in all the lakes, marſhes and waſte grounds covered with water, which belong to the ſtate And the emperor has ordered all the canals which ornament his gardens, to be planted with it, and the greater part of the ditches round his palace are full of it The flowers and verdure of this plant cover thoſe two immenſe ſheets of water in the centre of Pe-kin, and which are only ſeparated by a bridge, where every body may paſs, and from which there is an excellent view of the gardens belonging to the imperial palace. The *pi-tſi* grows only in the ſouthern provinces of China, it ſoon dies at Pe-kin, its leaves are as long as thoſe of the bulruſh, but hollow, and formed into a pipe like the top of an onion Its fruit is found in a cover formed by its root, in which it is incloſed, as a cheſnut in its huſk. And when this huſk is broken, the fruit may be extracted, without hurting the plant. It is exceedingly wholeſome, and has a moſt delicate taſte. It is given to ſick people to chew, as it is very cooling for the mouth.

TREES, SHRUBS, AND PLANTS.

China contains almoſt every ſpecies of trees that are known in Europe; but we ſhall only notice particularly thoſe peculiar to the country, or, at leaſt, ſuch as are not to be found in our weſtern climates.

TALLOW-TREE. Among the extraordinary trees, we cannot but diſtinguiſh that which produces tallow. This tree is of the ſize of a cherry-tree; its branches are crooked; its leaves are ſhaped like a heart, and of a bright red colour; it has a ſmooth bark, a ſhort trunk, and a round buſhy top. The fruit is contained in a huſk divided into three ſpherical ſegments, which open when it is ripe, and diſcover three white grains, of the ſize of a ſmall walnut. In each of theſe is a ſtone, and the pulp with which theſe ſtones are covered, has all the properties of tallow, and its colour, ſmell and conſiſtence are exactly the ſame. The Chineſe make candles of it, mixing it only with a little linſeed-oil, to render it ſofter and ſweeter. Did they purify it as tallow is purified in Europe, the candles made from it would not be inferior; but, as this precaution is neglected, they have a more diſagreeable ſmell, produce a thicker ſmoke, and afford a fainter light.

WAX-TREE. The Chineſe procure from certain trees a kind of wax, nearly equal in quality to that made by bees, which they call *pe-la*. This wax is depoſited by ſmall inſects, on two kinds of trees, no other affording them proper nouriſhment. The firſt is ſhort and buſhy, and grows in a dry, ſandy ſoil, called by the Chineſe *kan-la-chu*. The other ſpecies is larger, thrives only in moiſt places, and is named *[illegible]-la-chu*.

The *kan la-chu*, is of a shrubby nature, and easily propagates; walls may be covered, or hedges be formed of it, it equally well endures heat and cold, and thrives, without the least culture, in the barrenest soil.

The small insects that make the *pe-la*, do not naturally frequent these trees, they must be placed upon them but this is not difficult, and, after a tree is once stocked, it always retains them Towards the beginning of winter, small tumours are perceived upon the *kan-la-chu* that have already produced wax, which continually increase, until they become of the size of a small walnut these are so many nests filled with the eggs of insects, called *pe-la-tchong*, or *la-tchong* When the warmth of spring makes the tree shoot forth its blossoms, it also gives life to the insects that cover it Then is the proper time to deposit nests on those trees which have none To do this the Chinese make small bundles of straw, on each of which they put seven or eight nests, they afterwards tie these to the branches, taking care to place the nests immediately on the bark If the shrub is five feet in height, it is capable of supporting one or two nests on each of its boughs After these insects are hatched, they run upon the branches, disperse themselves over the leaves, and perforate the bark, under which they retire, but come forth at the proper season for making their wax

About the middle of June, this wax begins to appear upon the *kan-la-chu* A few filaments, like those of fine soft wool, are perceived rising from the bark, around the body of the insect, by degrees, these filaments form a kind of down, which becomes thicker, and increases in size during the heats of summer This crust covers the insect, and defends it from the heat, rain and ants. The Chinese say, that, if the wax were left too long on the tree, the insects would not make their nest Care must, therefore, be taken to gather it before the first hoar frosts

This wax is white and bright, and preserves its transparency to the depth of an inch. It is carried to court, and there reserved for the use of the emperor, princes and chief mandarins. An ounce of it added to a pound of oil the mixture acquires a consistency, and forms a wax little inferior to that made by bees. The physicians employ it in curing several diseases, and when applied to wounds, it makes the flesh heal in a very short time.

VARNISH-TREE. An opinion long prevailed in Europe, that the celebrated varnish of the Chinese was only a composition, which the Chinese had the art of making. It is now known, that they are indebted to nature and their climate only, for this liquor, which gives so much lustre and beauty to many of their manufactures. It is nothing else than a reddish gum which distils from certain trees called *tsi-chu*. They grow in the provinces of Kiang-si and Se-tchuen, but those which are found in the territories of Kan-tcheou, one of the most southerly cities of Kiang-si, produce the most valuable varnish.

The *tsi-chu*, the bark and leaves of whch resemble the ash, bears neither fruit nor flowers. It is, when full grown, about fifteen feet in height, and the circumference of its trunk, about two feet. The Chinese propagate this tree by cuttings, but they do not procure varnish from it until its trunk is nearly five inches in diameter, a size which it seldom attains in less than seven or eight years. Varnish extracted from a tree smaller, or of less age, has neither the same body or splendour. This liquor distils only in the night time, and during the summer season, for the varnish produced in spring or autumn, is always mixed with a great deal of water, and in winter it does not flow at all.

To obtain the gum, they make several rows of incisions round the trunk, proportioned to the vigour of the tree. The first row is at seven inches from the earth, and the rest at the same distance from each other, to the top of the trunk, and sometimes on the boughs, which are of sufficient strength and size.

Into these incisions, which are made towards evening, they insert a shell, and next morning they collect the varnish that has fallen into them, the following evening they are again inserted; and this operation is continued until the end of summer. A thousand trees yielding, on an average, in one night, near twenty pounds of varnish.

This varnish, for the most part, is not extracted by the proprietors of the trees, but by merchants, who purchase them for the season, at three-pence per foot. These merchants afterwards hire workmen, to attend to them, to whom they give an ounce of silver per month, for their labour and maintenance.

While the varnish distils, it exhales a malignant vapour, the bad effects of which are often severely felt, and can only be prevented by preservatives and great precaution. The merchant who employs these workmen, keeps by him a large vase filled with rape oil, in which a certain quantity of those fleshy filaments found in hog's lard have been boiled. When the workmen are going to fix the shells to the trees, or collect the varnish, they rub their face and hands with this oil, with great care, and after eating, they wash their whole bodies with warm water, in which the bark of the chesnut-tree, fir-wood, crystalized saltpetre, and other drugs, have been boiled. When at work near the trees, they put upon their heads a cloth bag, in which there are two holes, and cover the fore part of their bodies with a kind of apron made of doe-skin, suspended from their necks with strings, and tied round them with a girdle. They also wear boots, and have coverings on their arms, made of the same kind of skin. The labourer who should neglect these precautions would soon be punished for his rashness. The disorder shews itself by tetters, which become of a bright red colour, and spread in a very short time, the body swells, and the skin bursts and appears covered with an universal leprosy The unhappy victim could not long endure the excruciating pains which he feels, was not a speedy remedy found in those preservatives we have before mentioned.

The season of collecting varnish being ended, the merchant having strained it, puts it into small casks, closely stopped. A pound of it costs him about one shilling and eight-pence sterling, and he generally gains cent. per cent. upon it, and sometimes more, according to the distance of the place to which he transports it, besides this he sells the dregs of it to the druggists, who use them for certain purposes in medicine.

Iron wood —This tree rises to the height of a large oak, but it differs both in the size of its trunk and in the shape of its leaves. Its wood is so exceedingly hard and heavy, that it sinks in water, it is said that the anchors of the Chinese ships of war are made of it.

Nan-mou —Travellers describe this tree as the cedar, which it probably is It is one of the tallest in China, its branches shoot up vertically, and grow from the trunk, only at a certain height, and terminate in a bush or tufted top. The Chinese consider its wood as incorruptible.—*When we are desirous*, say they, *of erecting an edifice to last for ever, we must employ only the nan-mou.* Great use, therefore is made of this wood in building the emperor's palaces, where all the pillars, beams, and doors are made of it.

Rose wood —This tree furnishes the most beautiful and valuable wood used by the Chinese artists It is of a very dark colour, striped and variegated with delicate veins, which have the appearance of painting It is employed for making different pieces of furniture, which are in greater request, and cost more, than those that are varnished.

Camphire tree —The tree from which camphire is procured, is also a production of China, and, it is said, that ſome of them are found above an hundred cubits in height, and ſo thick, that twenty perſons cannot encloſe them. The trunks of theſe trees, when old, emit ſparks of fire; but their flame is ſo ſubtle, that no danger is to be apprehended from it.

The method uſed by the Chineſe for obtaining camphire, is as follows —They take branches freſh from the tree, chop them ſmall, and lay them to ſteep in ſpring water for three days and nights After they have been thus ſoaked, they are put into a kettle where they are boiled for a certain time, during which they continually ſtir them with a ſtick of willow —when they perceive that the ſap of theſe ſmall chips adheres to the ſtick, in the form of white froſt, they ſtrain the whole off, throwing away the dregs and refuſe. This liquor is then poured gently into an earthen baſon well varniſhed, in which it is ſuffered to remain during the night, it is then found coagulated, and formed into a ſolid maſs. To purify this firſt preparation, they procure ſome earth from an old wall, which, when pounded and reduced to a very fine powder, they put into the bottom of a copper baſon, over this layer of earth they ſpread a layer of camphire, and continue thus until they have laid four ſtrata. The laſt, which is of fine earth, they cover up with the leaves of the plant *po-ho*, or penny-royal, and over the whole place another baſon, which they join very cloſely to the former, by means of a kind of red earth that cements their brims together. The baſons, thus prepared, are then put over a fire, which is ſo managed as to preſerve the heat equal on all parts. When the baſons have been expoſed to the neceſſary heat, they are taken off and left to cool, after which they are ſeparated, and the ſublimated camphire is found adhering to the cover. This operation is often repeated two or three times, for the purpoſe of having the camphire more pure. The camphire thus collected is then put between two earthen veſſels, the edges of which are ſurrounded with ſeveral bands of wet paper. The veſſels are kept for about an hour over an equal and moderate fire, and when they are cool, the camphire is found in its utmoſt perfection, and ready for uſe.

This method of procuring camphire, may be practiſed in all ſeaſons of the year, which could not be the caſe, were it extracted like other reſinous ſubſtances, that only flow during a certain ſhort ſpace of time. Beſides, by lopping the branches of the camphire tree, leſs hurt is done to it than by making inciſions, which are always injurious.

SIANG.—The *ſiang* grows to the height of a cheſnut tree, and bears a fruit which ſerves, in dying, as a ſubſtitute for the gall-nut; it is incloſed in a double huſk, of the ſize of a cheſnut, which it alſo reſembles in colour. The exterior huſk is that which is uſed properly for dying. Hogs will feed upon this fruit, although it has a diſagreeable taſte. The *ſiang* grows with little culture, to the north of *Pe-kin* and in the province of *Tche-kiang*, and there can be little doubt but it would thrive in the barren and mountainous regions of Europe.

LO-YA-SONG.—This name is given to a kind of pine, found near *Keou-ouai*, beyond the great wall. Its trunk, branches, leaves, and fruit, exactly reſemble thoſe of our common pines, but it is diſtinguiſhed by ſeveral ſingularities: all its leaves fall in autumn, its wood is exceedingly hard, and fit for various purpoſes, but the ſap it contains is poiſonous. Thoſe who are employed in cutting this tree, muſt take great care that no drops ſpurt out on the ſkin, for it raiſes bliſters and pimples which cannot eaſily be cured. If its root, which is of a reddiſh colour, is put into water, it ſoon petrifies; it is then uſed for ſharpening the fineſt and beſt-tempered tools. This petrification changes its figure ſo little, that it cannot be perceived, unleſs examined very cloſely; but its weight is conſiderably augmented.

LUNG-JU-SHU.—The trunk of this tree is equal in thickneſs to a large plumb tree, and divides itſelf into two or three principal branches, which are ſubdivided into others that are much ſmaller. Its bark is of a reddiſh grey colour, and ſpotted like that of hazel The extremities of its branches are knotty, very unequal, and full of pith. The trunk of this tree furniſhes planks which are employed in making of furniture The fruit, which reſembles our cherries before they are ripe, grow from long, green and fibrous pedicles The ſkin of this fruit is very hard, ſpeckled in ſome places with ſmall red ſpots, and containing a greeniſh ſubſtance, which, by maturity, is converted to a kind of jelly. The Chineſe rub their hands with it in winter, to prevent chilblains.

TCHA-KE.—This tre has no bark on its trunk or branches, it grows on the northern coaſts, and if it is thrown into the fire, when green, it burns as readily as the dr eſt wood If made into charcoal, it kindles very eaſily, produces a ſtrong heat, without ſmell or ſmoke, and laſts much longer than any other kind.

TCHU-KOU —This tree is much valued by the Chineſe, as its inner rhind furniſhes them with the greater part of the paper which they conſume. When its branches are broken, the bark peels off in the form of long ribbons. Were we to determine the ſpecies to which this tree belongs, by its leaves, we ſhould claſs it with the wild mulberry-tree, but, by its fruit, it more reſembles the fig tree. This fruit adheres to the branches, without any ſtalk, and, when pulled before its maturity, appears, like the fig, to be full of milk. This tree grows on the mountains, and in a rocky ſoil.

KIN-KOUANG-TSEE, OR SOUR JUJUBE —This is a large tree, the leaves of which are long and ſharp-pointed. Its flowers have a greeniſh tint, and the fruit it produces reſemble large jujubes on accounr of their beautiful yellow colour, they are called *golden jujubes*. This fruit, when dried, retains a fouriſh taſte; and the golden colour changes to a delicate red. The ſtone is hard, and ſhaped like a heart, as well as the kernel which they contain. Theſe ſtones were formerly uſed by the ſuperſtitious votaries of idols, for making chaplets, on which ſeveral figures were engraven. It is ſaid to have been originally brought from Bengal, and that great difficulty was found at firſt to rear it in China, but it is ſo naturalized at preſent, that it riſes to the height of the talleſt fruit-trees. Its wood is hard, and of a very fine grain.

TSE-SONG-YUEN-PE, OR JUNIPER CYPRESS.—This is one of the ſingularities of nature, it partaking of the properties of the juniper and of the cypreſs tree. Its trunk is about half a foot in diameter, and ſhoots out, almoſt where it ſprings from the earth, a great number of branches, which extend on all ſides, and are divided into others that form a top extremely thick and buſhy. Theſe branches are loaded with leaves; ſome reſembling thoſe of the cypreſs, others thoſe of the juniper: the latter are long, narrow, and prickly, and are ranged along the branches in rows of four, five, and ſometimes ſix each; hence, when the branches are viewed lengthwiſe, the leaves appear like ſtars, with four, five, or ſix rays, the leaf neareſt the eye exactly covering that which is next to it, and leaving the intervals between the rows perfectly open. The ſmall branches, or twigs, which are covered with theſe juniper leaves, are generally found below the principal boughs, and the branches that ſhoot out from the upper part of the ſame boughs, bear cypreſs leaves. There are found whole branches which reſemble thoſe of the cypreſs, and there are others, that, in like manner, have an affinity to the juniper alone, there are ſome, alſo, which partake of the nature of both, and, laſtly, there are others, that bear only a few cypreſs leaves, grafted, as it were, on the end of a juniper branch, or a ſmall juniper twig, is ſometimes ſeen ſpringing from a cypreſs bough.

The bark of this tree is very rough and unequal, and of a grayiſh brown colour, inclining to red. Its wood is like that of the juniper; but it is of a reſinous nature. The leaves ſmell like cypreſs, and have ſomething of an aromatic flavour, but ſharp and bitter. This tree bears a ſmall, round green fruit, a little larger than that of the juniper it contains two reddiſh grains, ſhaped like a heart, which are as hard as a grape-ſtone.

BAMBOO.—The *bamboo* is a kind of reed, which grows to the height and ſize of large trees. Its leaves are long, and bend backwards towards the points. The trunk is hollow, and divided at certain ſpaces by knots, but it is very ſtrong, and capable of ſuſtaining an enormous weight. Bamboo-reeds are bored and uſed as pipes to convey water; when ſplit lengthwiſe and divided into thin ſlips, they are woven into mats, trunks, and various other works; paper is alſo made of a certain paſte procured from them, after they have been bruiſed and ſteeped in warer; the *Bamboo* grows in all the provinces of China, but is moſt plenty in the province of *Tche-kiang*, where whole foreſts are found of it.

ACASIA.—The *acaſia* of America is common in China. The Chineſe authors pretend, that the ſeeds extracted from its pods are employed with ſucceſs in medicine.

TEA-PLANT.—Among the aromatic ſhrubs of China, that which furniſhes tea holds the firſt rank. It is not, however, known by this name in the country, but is called *tcha*, and, by corruption in ſome of the maritime provinces, *tha*, from which is derived our word *tea*.

Father le Comte, in his memoirs, has given us a very accurare deſcription of this ſhrub—'Tea,' ſays he, 'grows 'in the valleys, and at the bottoms of the mountains. 'Rocky ground produces the beſt; and that which is 'planted in a light ſoil is next in quality. The worſt is 'found in earth of a yellow colour, but in whatever place 'it is cultivated, care must be taken to expose it to the 'south: it then acquires more vigour, and bears three 'years after it has been planted The root of the shrub 'is like that of the peach tree; and its flowers resemble 'the white wild rose When I entered the province of 'Fokin, I was shewn, for the first time, the tea plant, 'upon the declivity of a little hill It was only about 'five or six feet in height. Several branches joined toge-'ther and separated towards their upper extremities, formed 'a tufted top almost like that of the European myrtle 'The trunk, though to appearance dry, bore branches 'that were covered with beautiful green leaves, narrow 'and tapering towards the points, about an inch and a 'half in length, and indented round the edges The 'oldest, which appeared of a whitish colour below, were 'brittle, hard and bitter The young ones were soft and 'pliable, of a reddish tint, smooth, transparent, and very 'agreeable to the taste, especially after they had been 'chewed for some time As it was then in September, I 'found on them three kinds of fruit On the young and 'tender branches I observed small soft berries, of a green 'colour, filled with very minute yellow grains On the 'rest of the branches the fruit was as large as beans, but 'of different shapes, some were round, and contained a 'pea, others long, and inclosing two, and several were 'triangular, and contained three. The outer rind which 'inclosed this seed was green, smooth, and very thick. 'Under the second, which was white and thinner, was a 'third pellicle, exceedingly fine, that covered a kind of 'nut adhering to the rind by a small fibre, from which it 'derives its nourishment. When this fruit is young, its 'taste is somewhat bitterish, but, two or three days after 'it has been gathered, it lengthens, changes to a yellow 'colour, appears dry and shrivelled like an old filbert, and 'becomes very oily and bitter. I found also upon these 'trees a third kind of old and hard fruit, the black exterior 'rind of which, being half open, discovered within a hard, 'brittle husk, exactly like that of a chesnut; but it was 'so flatted and dried, that after I had broken it, I could 'scarcely discover any vestige of fruit. In some of them I 'found this fruit reduced to powder; and in others, I ob-'served a very small nut, perfectly dry and half covered 'with its first pellicle. Among these fruits were a great 'number called female, which had no germ. Those that 'have a germ, if they are sown, will produce trees; but 'the Chinese generally make use of slips for raising plants. 'That I might be better acquainted with the nature 'of this tree, I had the curiosity to taste the bark of the 'trunk and branches; I also chewed the wood and fibres, 'both of which appeared to have no bitterness, and even 'after a considerable time, I only perceived a taste some-'what like liquorice, but very faint.'

The Chinese distinguish several kinds of tea, but they all may be reduced to the four following; the *Song-lo tcha*, the *Vou-y tcha*, the *Lou-ngan tcha*, and the *Pou-eul tcha*.

The first takes its name from the mountain *Song-lo*, situated in the province of *Kiang-nan*. This mountain is not very extensive, but it is entirely covered with these shrubs, which are also cultivated at the bottoms of the neighbouring mountains. The *Song-lo* is the same which we call *green tea*. It is cultivated almost like vines, and is cropped at a certain height, to prevent it from growing. This shrub must be renewed every four or five years, because, after that period, its leaves harden and become sour. The flower which it bears is white, and shaped like a small rose, composed of five leaves. The *Song-lo tcha* may be kept for several years, and is used, in China, with great success, as a remedy for various distempers.

The Chineſe of the province of *Kiang-nan* are the only people who crop the tea-ſhrub; for every where elſe it is ſuffered to grow to its natural ſize, which ſometimes extends to ten or twelve feet. When the tree is very young, they take care alſo to incline and bend down its branches, that they may collect its leaves afterwards with greater eaſe. This ſhrub grows often on the rugged backs of ſteep mountains, acceſs to which is dangerous, and ſometimes impracticable.

The *Vou-y tcha*, which is known in Europe by the name of *bohea*, and *ſouchong*, grows in the province of Fo-kien, and takes its name alſo from a mountain, called *Vou-y*, ſituated in the diſtrict of *Kien-ning-fou*.

This is the tea moſt eſteemed throughout the empire, as agreeing better with the ſtomach, being in their eſtimation lighter, ſweeter, and more delicate to the taſte than the *Song-lo*.

From theſe two kinds of tea three others are compoſed, the difference of which reſults from the choice of the leaves, and the time when they are gathered. That which contains only the tender leaves of young trees, is called *mao tcha*, or *imperial tea*. This is the moſt delicate, and is that which is tranſported to court for the uſe of the emperor. It is ſeldom ever diſtributed but in preſents; but it may ſometimes be bought on the ſpot where it grows for twenty-pence or two ſhillings the pound.

The ſecond ſort is compoſed of older leaves, and goes under the name of *good Vou-y tcha*. The reſt of the leaves that are ſuffered to remain and grow larger form the third kind, which is ſold to the common people at a very cheap rate.

The flowers of this ſhrub alſo furniſh another kind of tea, but thoſe who are deſirous of procuring it, muſt pay a ſuperior price for it.

The *Lou-ngan tcha*, which is the third kind of tea we have mentioned, grows in the neighbourhood of the city of *Lou-gnan-tcheou*. It differs in nothing from the *Song-lo*, either in the configuration of its leaves, or in the manner of cultivation; but it is neither ſo heating, nor ſo harſh and corroſive—properties which, no doubt, reſult from the difference of the ſoils in which they grow.

The fourth kind is procured from a village named *Pou-eul*, ſituated in the province of *Yun-nan*, on the frontiers of the kingdoms of *Pegu*, *Ava*, *Laos* and *Tong-king*. This village is become conſiderable by its commerce in this article: people reſort to it from all parts; but the entrance of it is forbidden to ſtrangers, who are only permitted to approach the bottoms of the mountains, to receive the quantity of tea which they want. The trees that produce this tea are tall and buſhy, and grow without any cultivation. The leaves are longer and thicker than thoſe of the *Song-lo tcha* and *Vou-y tcha*; and they are rolled up in the ſame manner as tobacco, and formed into maſſes, which are ſold at a dear rate. This tea is much uſed in the provinces of *Yun-nan* and *Koei-tcheou*. It has nothing harſh, but it has not that agreeable taſte and flavour which diſtinguiſh other kinds when infuſed.

The *Kaiel tcha* is chiefly uſed by the Mogul Tartars. It is only the refuſe of the leaves of all the different teas which have been ſuffered to grow hard, mixed indiſcriminately. Theſe people, who feed on raw fleſh, are ſubject to continual indigeſtion, if they give over the uſe of tea; on which account they tranſport great quantities of it from China, and, in exchange, furniſh horſes for the emperor's cavalry.

We muſt not confound with real tea every thing that the Chineſe call *tcha*. What is ſold in the province of *Chang-tong* as tea, is properly but a kind of moſs, which grows on the rocks in the neighbourhood of *Mang-ing-hien*.

A like kind of tea is diſtributed in ſome of the other northern provinces, which is not compoſed of real leaves, although the merchants vend it under the name of *tcha-yu*, *tea-leaves* If this commodity is adulterated even in China, can we flatter ourſelves, that the tea we have in Europe is pure, and without mixture?

When the tea-leaves have been collected, they are exposed to the ſteam of boiling water, after which they are put upon plates of copper, over a fire until they become dry and ſhrivelled, and appear ſuch as we ſee them in Europe.

According to the teſtimony of Kœmpfer, tea is prepared in the ſame manner in the iſles of Japan 'There are to 'be ſeen there,' ſays this traveller, 'public buildings 'erected for the purpoſe of preparing the freſh-gathered 'tea. Every private perſon who has not ſuitable conve- 'niences, or who is unacquainted with the operation, 'may carry his leaves thither as they dry These build- 'ings contain a great number of ſmall ſtoves raiſed about 'three feet high, each of which has a broad plate of iron 'fixed over its mouth. The workmen are ſeated round 'a large table covered with mats, and are employed in 'rolling the tea-leaves which are ſpread out upon them 'When the iron plates are heated to a certain degree 'by the fire, they cover them with a few pounds of freſh- 'gathered leaves, which, being green and full of ſap, 'crackle as ſoon as they touch the plate. The workman 'then ſtirs them with his naked hands, as quickly as poſ- 'ſible, until they become ſo warm that he cannot eaſily 'endure the heat. He then takes off the leaves with a 'ſhovel, and lays them upon mats. The people who are 'employed in mixing them, take a ſmall quantity at a 'time, roll them in their hands always in the ſame direc- 'tion, while others keep continually ſtirring them, in 'order that they may cool ſooner, and preſerve their 'ſhrivelled figure the longer. This proceſs is repeated 'two or three times before the tea is deposited in the 'warehouses. These precautions are necessary to extract 'all the moisture from the leaves.'

The people in the country bestow much less labour on the preparation of their tea They are contented with drying the leaves in earthen vessels, over the fire This operation, being much simpler, is attended with less trouble and expence, and enables them to sell their tea at a much lower price

The Chinese and people of Japan generally keep their tea a year before they use it, because, as they pretend, when quite new, it possesses a narcotic quality which hurts the brain

The Chinese pour warm water over their tea, and leave it to infuse, as we do in Europe, but they drink it in general without sugar

The isles of Japan produce abundance of tea Kœmpfer, in his relation, gives an account of the different seasons in which the people of these islands collect tea The first begins about the middle of the new moon which precedes the vernal equinox. The leaves gathered at this time are called *ficki-tsiaa*, or *tea in powder*, because it is pulverized These young and tender leaves are only three or four days old when they are gathered, and as they are exceedingly dear, they are generally reserved for the great people and princes. This is the imperial tea of the Japanese The labourers employed in collecting it, do not pull the leaves by handfuls, but pick them one by one, and take every precaution that they may not break them. In this manner they gather from four to ten or fifteen pounds a day each person

The second crop is collected in the second Japanese month, about the end of March or beginning of April. At this season some of the leaves are yet in their growth, and others have attained to perfection, they are, however, all gathered indiscriminately, and afterwards picked and ſorted, according to their age and ſize: the youngeſt, which are carefully ſeparated from the reſt, are often ſold for imperial tea. Tea gathered at this ſeaſon is called *Too-tſiaa*, or *Chineſe tea*, becauſe the people of Japan infuſe it, and drink it after the Chineſe manner.

The third and laſt crop of tea is gathered in the third Japaneſe month, that is about our June. The leaves are then very numerous and thick, and have acquired their full growth. This kind of tea, which is called *Ban-tſiaa*, is the coarſeſt of all, and is reſerved for the common people. Some of the Japaneſe collect tea only at two ſeaſons of the year, which correſpond to the ſecond and third, already mentioned; others have only one general gathering, towards the month of June: however, they always form different aſſortments of their leaves.

The moſt celebrated tea of Japan is that which grows near *Ud-ſi*, a ſmall village ſituated cloſe to the ſea, and not far diſtant from *Meaco*. In the diſtrict of this village is a mountain, bearing the ſame name, the climate of which is ſaid to be extremely favourable to the culture of tea; it is incloſed by a hedge, and ſurrounded with wide ditches, to prevent acceſs to it; and the tea ſhrubs that grow on this mountain are planted in regular order, and divided by different avenues and alleys.

The care of this place is entruſted to people who are ordered to guard the leaves from duſt, and to defend them from the inclemency of the weather. The labourers who are appointed to collect the tea, abſtain from every kind of groſs food for ſome weeks before they begin, that their breath and perſpiration may not in the leaſt injure the leaves. They gather them with the moſt ſcrupulous nicety, with very fine gloves on their hands, without which they never touch it. When this choice tea has undergone the proceſs neceſſary for its preparation, it is eſcorted by the ſuperintendant of the mountain and a ſtrong guard, to the emperor's court, and reserved for the uſe of the imperial family alone.

COTTON TREE.—Cotton forms one of the moſt conſiderable branches of the commerce of China, and is cultivated with ſucceſs in the ſouthern provinces. As ſoon as they have reaped their grain, they ſow cotton in the ſame field, after having turned up the earth ſlightly with a rake. When the rain or dew has moiſtened the ground, a ſhrub ſprings up, which riſes to the height of two feet. The flowers appear about the beginning or towards the middle of Auguſt, they are generally yellow; but ſometimes red. To the flower ſucceeds a kind of ſmall button, which increaſes in the form of a pod, till it acquires about the ſize of a walnut. About the fortieth day after the flower has appeared, this pod burſts, divides itſelf into three parts, and diſcovers three or four ſmall cotton balls of a bright white colour, ſomething like thoſe produced by ſilk-worms. Theſe ſmall downy balls adhere to the bottom of the pod, which is half open, and contains ſeeds for the following year. As all theſe ſmall grains are ſtrongly attached to the filaments of the cotton, the Chineſe make uſe of a machine for the purpoſe of ſeparating them. It is compoſed of two cylinders highly poliſhed, one of wood and the other of iron, about a foot in length, and an inch in diameter, placed together like European flatting-mills. With one hand they put the firſt in motion, and the ſecond by the foot, with the other hand they apply the cotton, which is drawn in between them by their motion, and paſſes to the other ſide, while the grains that are left behind quite bare, fall to the ground. The cotton, thus freed from its ſeeds, is carded and ſpun, and afterwards made into cloth.

KOU-CHU.—The ſhrub called *kou-chu* bears a great reſemblance to the fig-tree, both in the form of its branches and leaves. From its root ſeveral ſhoots generally ſpring up, forming a kind of buſh, but ſometimes it consists of only one shoot. The wood is soft and spongy, and covered with bark like that of the fig-tree. Its leaves are deeply indented, and the colour and texture of their fibres are exactly the same as those of the fig-tree, but they are larger, thicker, and much rougher to the touch.

This tree yields a milky juice, which the Chinese use for laying on gold-leaf in gilding. They make incisions in the trunk, into which they insert the edges of a shell, to receive the sap, which they use with a small brush, in delineating the figures they intend for the decoration of their work. They then lay on the gold-leaf, which is so strongly attracted by this liquor, that it never comes off.

TONG-TSAO.—Strangers are generally struck with the beauty of the artificial flowers made by the Chinese, but if the Chinese surpass European artists in these kinds of works, they are indebted for their superiority to the materials they employ. Neither silk, cotton, nor any kind of paper or cloth, is employed in the composition of these flowers. The substance of which their leaves are formed, is the pith of a certain shrub, called by the Chinese *tong-tsao*. It is a kind of cane or bamboo, much resembling the European elder tree, but its pith is whiter, closer, and less spongy.

The *tong-tsao* grows in dark, shady places, and rises to the height of six feet, its leaves resembling those of the nymphæa, or water lily, but are thicker. Its trunk is divided, like the bamboo, by knots, between which are comprehended several pipes, each about a foot and a half long, and which are generally larger towards the root of the plant.

This shrub is cut every year, and it shoots up a new stem the year following. It is transported in barks to *Kiang-nan*, where the [illegible] is extracted, and prepared for the hands of the [illegible]. When taken from the pipes it muſt be preſerved from moiſture, for without this precaution, it would be entirely uſeleſs.

BETEL AND TOBACCO The Chineſe, in imitation of almoſt all other eaſtern nations, uſe the betel-leaf as a ſovereign remedy for thoſe diſorders which attack the breaſt and ſtomach The betel grows like ivy, and twiſts around other trees Its leaves are long and ſharp-pointed, broad towards the ſtalk, and of a pale-green colour. The Chineſe cover them with quicklime, and wrap them around the nut *areca*, which in ſhape greatly reſembles a nutmeg. They chew theſe leaves continually, pretending that they ſtrengthen the gums, comfort the brain, expel bile, nouriſh the glands of the throat, and ſerve as a preſervative againſt the aſthma, a diſeaſe very common in the ſouthern provinces. They carry betel and *areca* in boxes, and preſent it when they meet one another in the ſame manner as ſoldiers and other Europeans, who have habituated themſelves to this filthy cuſtom, do tobacco.

The uſe of tobacco is not ſo extenſive in China as in Europe, but the country produces it in great abundance. The Chineſe do not reduce their tobacco to powder, becauſe they only uſe it for ſmoking. They gather the leaves when they are very ripe, and card them almoſt in the ſame manner as wool. They afterwards put them under a preſs, where they ſqueeze them together like the turf made from the refuſe of the bark in tan yards.

BELVIDERE, OR CHENOPODIUM The belvidere ſprings up about the end of March, its ſhoots riſe to the height of eight or nine inches, in the ſhape of a child's fiſt half ſhut, it afterwards extends itſelf, and ſends forth a number of branches loaded with leaves like thoſe of flax; and as it grows, its branches arrange themſelves naturally in the form of a pyramid, its leaves, yet tender, abound with juice, have a very agreeable taſte; and may be eaten as a ſallad with vinegar, to which the

Chineſe often add a little ginger, being prepared like other leguminous plants, and baked with meat, it gives it an agreeable and pleaſing flavour, when in its full beauty, its leaves become hard and unfit for the table, but nouriſhment is then found in its root, which has ſerved often as a reſource in times of famine and ſcarcity, being reduced to powder and made into bread

The Chineſe Herbal cites an example of four mountaineers, who lived on nothing but the leaves, roots and ſtalks of the belvidere, with which their country abounded, and enjoyed perfect health to a very great age

It alſo adds, that to render this plant ſtrong and flouriſhing fire muſt be ſet to the grounds which are covered with it, as its own aſhes are the beſt manure, and ſupply it with a nouriſhing moiſture.

FLOWERING-TREES.

OU-TONG-CHOU Among the trees which nature ſeems to have deſtined for the ornamenting of gardens, few have greater claims to notice than that which the Chineſe call *Ou-tong-chu* It is of a large ſize, reſembling the ſycamore Its leaves are large, and proceed from a ſtalk about a foot in length, and is ſo buſhy and loaded with ſuch bunches of flowers, that it excludes the rays of the ſun About the month of Auguſt, ſmall cluſters of leaves begin to ſhoot out from the extremities of the branches, which are entirely different from thoſe on the other parts of the tree, being ſmaller, whiter and ſofter, and ſupply the place of flowers. On the edges of theſe leaves grow three or four grains, of the ſize of a pea Theſe grains contain a white ſubſtance, the taſte of which greatly reſembles that of an unripe walnut This is the fruit of the plant, but we have no account of any uſe made of this tree but for ornament

MOLIEN. This is another flowering tree, the branches of which are few in number, very ſlender, full of pith, and covered with a red bark interſperſed with ſmall white ſpots. It bears few leaves but they are large, and very broad at the lower extremity, and adhere to pedicles, which ſeem to incloſe the branch. This tree blows in the month of December, and produces large flowers, formed of ſeven or eight ſharp-pointed oval leaves, from the extremities of which proceed long filaments. Some of the flowers are yellow, others red, and others white. All the leaves fall when the flowers appear, or when they are ready to blow.

LA-MOE This ſhrub reſembles laurel, both in its form and ſize, but its branches are more extenſive, and its leaves are attached, two and two, to ſhort pedicles. The ſize of theſe leaves decreaſes in proportion to their diſtance from the extremities of the branches. Its flowers are produced in winter, they are yellow, and of an agreeable ſmell, reſembling that of roſes.

TCHA-HOA The Chineſe diſtinguiſh four kinds of the tree which they call *tcha-hoa* It bears ſome reſemblance to the Spaniſh laurel It is an evergreen, the leaves grow in alternate rows along each ſide of its branches They are of an oval figure, ſharp pointed, indented on the edges, and of a dark-green colour above, but inclining to yellowiſh below The buds of the *tcha-hoa* are covered with a ſoft, white down, they blow in December, and produce double flowers, ſupported by a calix, of a roſe colour These flowers have no pedicle, and adhere immediately to the branch. The ſecond kind of *tcha-hoa* is very lofty Its leaves are round at the extremity, and its flowers are large and red. The flowers of the two other kinds are whitiſh, and ſmaller

YU-LAN. This tree, the moſt beautiful of any that ornament the Chineſe gardens, riſes to the height of thirty or forty feet. Its trunk, which is ſtraight, and well-proportioned, has very few branches Its leaves are of a beautiful green colour, but few in number they never appear until the flowers are half blown All its branches are crowned with flowers, the fcent of which perfumes the air to a great diftance around they continue in bloffom, however, only a few days The flower, which confifts of five, fix, and eight leaves, difpofed like thofe of a rofe, is fupported by a calix of four leaves, briftly within, and terminating in a point. From the middle of the flower rifes a green, fpongy piftil, furrounded at its bafe by fmall fibres, the tops of which are loaded with ftamina. This flower produces an oblong fruit of a green colour, which reddens towards the end of fummer Its whole fubftance is fibrous, and almoft as hard as wood

The *yu-lan* is divided into feveral fpecies, fuch as double and fingle, the *yu-lan* with white flowers, and that which produces flowers of a peach colour. The flowers of this tree are more beautiful and in greater abundance when it is young, but it then bears no fruit When it is twenty years old, its flowers are fmaller and fewer, but nearly all of them produce fruit The *yu-lan* requires no other care than to be planted in a place fheltered from the north winds, and to be watered in fpring It is raifed in boxes, as the Europeans raife orange-trees When it has fhed its leaves, the Chinefe remove it to the green-houfe, and, by accelerating its vegetation by means of ftoves, procure flowers from it again in the beginning of the year it is then appropriated for ornamenting the interior apartments of the women Some of thefe trees are annually fent by the governors of the fouthern provinces to the emperor

AUTUMNAL HAI-TANG. This beautiful fhrub, originally brought from the rocks which border the fea coaft, has been cultivated in China for more than fourteen centuries, and is as much celebrated in the works of the Chinefe poets, as rofes and lilies are in thofe of ours. Painters and embroiderers ornament almoft all their works with its foliage and flowers. The ftalk of the *hai-tang* is cylindric, and ſhoots forth a number of branches of a purple tint towards their baſes, and full of knots, which are alſo of a purple colour round the edges It throws forth a number of ſhoots, the talleſt of which are about two feet and a half in heighth. Its leaves are much indented, of an oval form towards the ſtalk, pointed at their upper extremities, and full of ſmall prickles, they grow almoſt oppoſite each other on the branches, at the ſame diſtance as the knots. Their colour above is a deep green, that below is much lighter, and almoſt effaced by their fibres, which are large, and of a delicate purple. The flowers grow in bunches at the extremities of the branches Each flower is compoſed of four petals, two great and two ſmall, reſembling in colour the bloom of a peach-tree, and of nearly the ſame figure as the bloſſom of the cherry-tree. The two largeſt are cemented one upon the other, in the form of a purſe. The piſtil is compoſed of bright yellow grains, which ſeparate gradually one from another by the lengthening of the filaments to which they adhere, they then open into little bells, and compoſe a ſmall yellow tuft, ſupported by a ſlender ſtalk, which riſes above the petals The calix, which ſuſtains each of the flowers, is compoſed of two purple-coloured leaves. In proportion as the flowers grow and increaſe in ſize, the two leaves of the calix open, become pale and dry, and drop off. The flowers, ſupported by ſmall ſtalks, ſeparate one from the other, and produce of themſelves other flowers, which riſe up from a new calix

The autumnal *hai-tang* is with difficulty propagated from ſeed. It thrives beſt in a ſandy ſoil, and care muſt be taken to refreſh it only with pure water It cannot endure the ſun in any ſeaſon, it is, therefore, always planted below walls that are expoſed to the north. It generally begins to flower about the end of Auguſt, and after it has produced ſeed, its branches are cut down, it commonly ſhoots forth new ones before the ſpring following; but it is neceſſary to heap up gravel and pieces of brick round its roots, to prevent them from rotting. Great pains are taken to cultivate this tree at Pe-kin, but it does not thrive ſo well there as in the ſouthern provinces. The ſmell of its leaves has an affinity both to the roſe and violet; but it is weaker, and never extends to any great diſtance.

MOU-TAN, or PEONY-SHRUB. This is a wild ſhrub improved by culture, and has been known in China for fourteen hundred years. It is ſometimes called *[illegible]a-ouang*, or the *king of flowers*, and *pe-[illegible]ang-kin* (*an hundred ounces of gold*) in alluſion to the exceſſive price given formerly by ſome of the virtuoſi for certain ſpecies of this plant. A traveller, as is ſaid, having found a peony on a ſhrub in the mountains of Ho-nan, was ſo ſtruck with the novelty, that he tore up ſome of the roots, with the earth adhering to them, carried them home, and planted them in his garden. A bonze, ignorant of the origin of this peony ſhrub, imagined it might be raiſed by grafting. His attempt was attended with ſucceſs, and the peonies he raiſed were more beautiful than thoſe which had been brought from the mountains. This plant ſoon engaged the attention of all the floriſts; and, by careful and continued culture, was brought to greater perfection. An infatuation now became general, and the provinces contended for ſuperiority of ſkill in raiſing it, that they might have the glory of ſending the fineſt to the emperor.

This plant, which is of a ſhrubby nature, ſhoots forth a number of branches, which form a top almoſt as large as that of the fineſt orange-trees that are planted in boxes. Some are grown to eight or ten feet in height, but few are raiſed at preſent to this ſize. The root of the *mou tan* is long and [illegible], of a pale yellow colour, and covered with a greyiſh or reddiſh rind. Its leaves are deeply indented, and of a much darker green above than below. Its flowers, compoſed of numberleſs petals, blow like a roſe, and are ſupported by a calix compoſed of four leaves From the bottoms of the petals ariſe ſeveral ſtamina, which bear on their tops ſmall antheræ, of a beautiful golden colour The fruit bends downward, burſts when they become dry, and ſhed their ſeed.

Pe-gi-hong. This ſhrub is remarkable for the beauty and ſingularity of its flowers, and above all for their duration, which has given riſe to its name, *pé-gé-hong*, or *red of a hundred days*. This beautiful plant, which now holds a diſtinguiſhed rank in the Chineſe gardens, was originally found in the mountains of Fo-kien. Its leaves, ſometimes placed alternately, ſometimes oppoſite one to another, are of an oval form, a little ſharpened towards the points not indented, and their thickneſs ſomewhat between that of the leaves of the phillyrea and plum-tree

The flowers of the *pé gé-hong* blow at Pe-kin about the beginning of July, they grow in bunches at the extremities of the branches, and ſucceed one another in ſuch a manner, that they continue till the end of September, if they are ſheltered from the heat of the ſun. The calix which ſupports them is ſpongy, and ſhaped like a bell, of a pale yellow within, and red on the outſide. It bends over the riſing fruit, and becomes dry when it ripens From this calix ariſe ſix crimſon coloured petals, in the form of feſtoons, which are long, round at top, and ſupported by as many ſlender, whitiſh ſtalks

The trunk of the *pe-gé-hong* is thick, and it appears that the Chineſe floriſts have endeavoured to reduce it to a dwarfiſh ſize—a form for which they ſhew an uncommon fondneſs They prune them in autumn, leaving only a few ſmall branches, in order that they may be loaded with a greater abundance of flowers. The culture of this tree requires little care, nothing is necessary but to place it in a green-house during winter, to expose it to the south on the return of spring, to water it at proper seasons, and to shelter it from the excessive heats of summer

YE-HIANG-HOA. The branches of this shrub are so weak, that they cannot grow upwards, or support themselves, the florists, therefore, prop them with bamboo-reeds, to which small hoops are attached Its leaves are of a deep green colour above, and a pale green below, they are shaped like the head of a lance, and are supported by very long stalks, round which they form two ears. All the property of this tree consists in the exquisite odour exhaled by its flowers, which are of a yellowish green colour —*Their smell is so sweet and agreeable*, according to the account of the missionaries, *that there is no flower existing which can be compared with the delicious* ye-hiang-hoa, but owing to the delicacy of this plant, or to that of its perfume, it has scarcely any smell during the day-time: from this singularity springs its name, *ye hiang-hoa*, or *the flower which smells in the night* The *ye-hiang-hoa* is originally from the southern provinces, and does not thrive at Pe-kin The nicest attention of the most careful florists is scarcely sufficient to make it endure the winter through in a green house, and to preserve it for a few years

LIEN-HOA, OR WATER-LILY This aquatic plant has been known in China from the remotest antiquity. The poets of every dynasty have celebrated the splendour and beauty of its flowers, and its excellent virtues have made the doctors rank it high among medicinal plants Its flowers are formed of several leaves, disposed in such a manner, that they resemble large tulips half open From the middle of the flower rises a conical pistil, that becomes round and ſpongy, it is divided into ſeveral cells, filled with oblong ſeeds, covered with a huſk like the acorn, and compoſed of two white lobes, in the middle of which is the germ. The ſtamina are formed of very delicate filaments, the tops of which are of a violet-colour. The leaves of this plant are round, broad and large, they are thick, fibrous, and indented towards the middle, ſome of them float on the ſurface of the water, to which they ſeem to be cemented, others riſe to different heights, and are ſupported by long ſtems. Its root, which is of the ſize of a man's arm, is very hardy; it is of a pale yellow colour within, and milk-white on the outſide, and is ſometimes twelve or fifteen feet in length. It creeps at the bottom of the water, and attaches itſelf to the mud by filaments The ſtalk which ſupports the flowers and leaves of this plant is full of round holes to its extremity, like thoſe of the root

There are four kinds known in China, the yellow, which is very rare, and ſuppoſed to be the ſame as that of Europe, the red and white roſe coloured, with ſingle flowers, the red and white roſe-coloured, with double flowers, the pale red ſtriped with white, which is ſeldom ſeen, eſpecially with double flowers This plant requires no culture, it is propagated by ſeed, but ſooner by the root. One of its ſingularities is, that it endures much drought, though it grows naturally in water, and that, though a friend to warmth, it thrives and produces the fineſt flowers beyond the great wall, and in the northern provinces. It does not bud before the end of May, but it ſhoots forth very rapidly, and its leaves form a verdure on the ſurface of the water, which is very delightful to the eye, eſpecially when the flowers, in full bloom, unite the variety of their colours

The ſeeds of this plant are eaten in China, they are moſt delicate when they are green, but harder of digeſtion;

they are preserved in many different ways with sugar. The root of this plant is also admitted by the Chinese to their tables in whatever manner it may be prepared, it is equally wholesome Great quantities of it are pickled with salt and vinegar, which they reserve to eat with their rice. When reduced to powder, it makes excellent soup. The leaves are much used for wrapping up fruits, fish, salt provisions, &c When dry, the Chinese mix them with their smoking tobacco, to render it softer and milder.

KIU-HOA, OR PARTHENIUM, so much neglected in Europe, is indebted only to its culture for the distinguished rank it holds among the Chinese flowers The skill of the florists, and their continual care, have brought this plant to such perfection that Europeans scarcely know it The elegance and lightness of its branches, the beautiful indentation of its leaves, the splendour and duration of its flowers seem, indeed, to justify the *flori-mania* of the Chinese for this plant. By their attention to its culture, they have procured more than three hundred species of it, and almost every year produces a new one. A list of the names of all these kinds would be equally tedious and disgusting, we shall only say, in general, that, in its flowers are united all the possible combinations of shapes and colours Its leaves are no less various some of them are thin, others thick, some are very small, and some large and broad, some are indented like those of the oak, while others resemble those of the cherry-tree, some may be seen cut in the form of rins, and others are found serrated on the margin, and tapering towards the points.

HERBS AND MEDICINAL PLANTS.

The simples, and medicinal plants of China, form a rich and extensive branch of its natural history. But as it is not our intention to give a Chinese herbal, we shall only mention a few of the most useful.

RHUBARB. The *tai-hoang*, or *rhubarb*, grows in several provinces of the empire, but the best is that of *Se-tchuen*. The stem of rhubarb resembles a small bamboo, or Chinese cane, it is hollow, and exceedingly brittle, it rises to the height of three or four feet, and is of a dusky violet-colour In the month of March, it shoots forth long, thick leaves, which are very rough to the touch. these leaves are ranged four by four on the same stalk, and form a calix. The flowers of this plant are yellow, and sometimes violet In June it produces a small black seed, and it is pulled in the month of September. The roots of rhubarb reckoned best, are those that are heaviest and most variegated with veins. It is very difficult to dry them, so as to free them from all their moisture. The Chinese, after having cleaned them, cut them in slices an inch or two in thickness, and dry them on stone slabs, under which large fires are kindled They keep continually turning these slices on the warm slabs, but, as this operation is not sufficient to dry them thoroughly, they thread them like beads, and suspend them in a place exposed to the greatest heat of the sun, until they are in a condition to be preserved without danger of spoiling A pound of the best rhubarb in China costs only two pence

HIA-TSAO-TONG-KONG. The shape of this plant is exactly like that of a worm It has the head, eyes, body, different rings which the skin forms upon the back, &c. of that reptile. This resemblance is more particularly striking when the plant is young and fresh, for if it be kept any time, especially when exposed to the air, it becomes blackish, and soon corrupts, on account of the softness of its substance. It is about nine-tenths of an inch in thickness, and of a yellowish colour, it is very rare in China, where it is accounted an exotic, and is seldom to be met with but in the emperor's gardens. It however grows in Thibet, and is also found, though in small quantities, in the province of *Se-tchuen*, which borders on Thibet The properties of this root are almost the same as those attributed to *gin-seng*, except that the frequent use of it does not, like *gin-seng*, occasion bleedings and hemorrhages It strengthens the stomach, and is said to restore and invigorate debilitated constitutions.

SAN-TSI This plant grows without cultivation in the provinces of Koei-tcheou, Yun-nan and Se-tchuen It shoots forth eight stems, which have no branches, that in the middle, which is highest, has three leaves at its extremity, the other seven have only one each From this determinate number of leaves it has its name, *san-tsi*, or *three and seven*. All these stalks proceed from a round root, about four inches in diameter. From this root spring others, which are oblong, smaller, and covered with a rough, hard rind, the interior substance of which is softer, and of a yellowish colour. These little roots are what is generally used in medicine. The middle stem only bears flowers, these are white, they grow from its extremity, in the form of grapes, and blow in the month of July

When the Chinese are desirous of propagating this plant, they cut the root in slices, these they put into the earth about the vernal equinox, and in the space of a month, it shoots forth its stalks, at the end of three years, the plant has acquired its utmost size. The Chinese physicians use the *san-tsi* for wounds and spitting of blood · and consider it as a sovereign specific in the small-pox. Some of the missionaries assert, that they have seen the blackest and most virulent pustules become bright and of a beautiful red, as soon as the patient has swallowed some of this root.

CASSIA-TREE The cassia-tree is found in that part of the province of Yun-nan which borders on the kingdom of Ava. It is very high, and bears long pods on that account, the Chinese have given it the name of *tchang-ko-tse-chu*, *the tree with oblong fruit*. These pods are longer than those seen in Europe.

GIN-SENG. The most esteemed of all the plants of China is *gin-seng*, which the Mantchew Tartars call *or-hota*, *the queen of plants*. The Chinese physicians speak of it with a kind of enthusiasm, and enumerate, without end, the wonderful properties which they ascribe to it. The root of *gin-seng* is white and rough, its stem is smooth and very round, and of a deep-red colour. Its height is various, according to the vigour of the plant. From the extremity of the stalk proceed a number of branches, equally distant one from the other, and, in their growth, never deviate from the same plan. Each branch bears five small leaves full of fibres, the upper parts of which are of a dark green, and the lower of a shining whitish green. All these leaves are finely indented on the margin. A particular stem of this flower produces a small cluster of very round red berries, but not fit for eating. Their stone, which resembles those of other fruits, is very hard, and contains the germ from which the plant is propagated *Gin seng* is easily distinguished by its form, and the colour of its fruit, when it has any, but it often happens that it bears none, though its root may be very old.

This plant decays and springs up every year. The Chinese never sow the seed, because it has never been known to grow. It is probable that the germ of this plant is slow in opening, and that the husk which contains it remains long in the earth before it sends forth any root. some *gin-seng* roots are found which are neither longer nor thicker than the little finger, although they have successively produced more than ten or twelve stems in as many years.

This plant has at all times been the principal riches of Eaſtern Tartary, where it grows. It is found between the thirty-ninth and forty-ſeventh degrees of northern latitude, and between the tenth and twentieth of eaſtern longitude, reckoning from the meridian of Pekin. This extent of country is occupied by a chain of ſteep mountains, covered with almoſt impenetrable foreſts. It is upon the declivities of theſe frightful mountains, and in their foreſts, in the neighbourhood of fiſſures made by floods, below rocks, at the roots of trees, and in the middle of herbs of every ſpecies that this plant is found. It never grows in plains, valleys, or marſhy ground, or in the bottoms of the clefts made by torrents, or in places that are too open. If the foreſt happens to take fire, and to be conſumed, this plant does not again appear for three or four years. It delights in the ſhade, and every where ſeems deſirous of ſheltering itſelf from the rays of the ſun.

No private perſon is allowed to gather *gin ſeng*: it belongs entirely to the emperor, who ſends ten thouſand ſoldiers into Tartary every year to collect it. The following order is obſerved by this army of herbaliſts—After having divided the ground, each troop, compoſed of an hundred men, range themſelves in a line, with certain intervals between every ten. They then advance gradually in the ſame direction, ſearching for the *gin-ſeng* with great care, and in this manner they traverſe, during a fixed number of days, the ſpace aſſigned them. When the term preſcribed is expired, mandarins appointed to preſide over this buſineſs, and who lodge under tents in the neighbourhood, ſend perſons to the different troops, to ſee that their numbers are complete, for it often happens, that ſome of them loſe themſelves, or are devoured by ſavage beaſts.

These herbalists suffer many hardships during this expedition. They carry with them neither tents nor beds, being sufficiently loaded with their provision of millet. During the whole time of their journey, they are exposed to all the inclemencies of the air, and pass the night either in the forests or at the bottom of some rock. The mandarins send them, from time to time, pieces of beef, or other flesh, which they devour, bloody and half raw. In this manner do these ten thousand men pass six months of the year in collecting *gin-seng*.

FOU-LIN This plant must not be confounded with the *tou-fou-lin*, or what is commonly called in Europe *China root*. The latter is very common in China, and is sold at a moderate price, but *fou-lin* is exceedingly dear, and holds a distinguished rank among the medicinal plants which grow in that country.

The Chinese Herbal, describing the *fou-lin*, gives it neither stem, leaves nor flowers; from which we are inclined to think it a kind of mushroom. The best roots of the *fou-lin* were formerly found in Chen-si, but some superior have been since discovered in the province of Yun-nan, which are the only kind now sent to court, where they are sold at a tael the pound This root grows also in the province of Tche-kiang, where it is much cheaper, but it is not so good as that of the province of Yun-nan. A physician has remarked, that the *fou-lin* of Tche-kiang, being soft and spongy, and having less strength and substance than that of Yun-nan, cannot stand the sharp, nitrous air of Pe-kin. on the contrary, the *fou-lin* of the provinces of Yun-nan and Chen-si has few pores, and is very solid and weighty.

The *fou-lin* grows in the neighbourhood of pines, at the distance of about two yards from the largest trees; but, in order to find it, the earth sometimes must be dug up to the depth of six or seven feet. The Chinese pretend that a delicate vapour exhales from the ſpot where this root is incloſed, which does not eſcape the eye of the experienced botaniſt. Good *fou-lin* remains in the earth without rotting, and without being hurt by worms; and the longer it has continued there, its ſubſtance is ſo much the more perfect. *F d'Entrecolles* ſpeaks thus of this root in one of his letters "The Chineſe Herbal," ſays he, "aſſures us, that good *fou-lin* is found in the "earth, on the mountains, or in valleys near which old "pines have been cut down, that it is from the ſubtle "and ſpirituous ſubſtance which flies off from the pines, "and which is diſperſed throughout the ſoil, that it is "formed, and receives its nouriſhment: whence I ap-"prehend that the *fou-lin* may ſpring up in the ſame "manner as ſome kinds of muſhrooms, which do not "adhere to the earth by any viſible root. Perhaps the "*fou-lin* is a ſpecies of *fungus* from the large roots of "pines that have been cut down, the nutritive juices "of which, being kept back, are collected together, and "produce this ſuſtance, which is at firſt ſoft, and more "or leſs ſpongy in proportion to the reſinous quality of "the pine The *fou-lin* which I have had in my hands "appeared to me never to have had any roots by which "it adhered to thoſe of the pine, and no mention is "made of them in any book but if it attaches itſelf "ſtrongly to the roots of the pine, we may conſider it as "a miſletoe peculiar to theſe roots, eſpecially as the "pine often has on its trunk a kind of moſs, united to "it by no fibre, although it derives its nouriſhent from "it."

When the *fou-lin* is to be uſed, it is prepared by ſtripping off its rind, which has no virtue, and by boiling the remaining ſubſtance for a few ſeconds The properties attributed to this root by the Chineſe phyſicians are very numerous. it is mild and temperate in its operation, it contains nothing hurtful, and has no need of any corrective They recommend it in diseases of the liver and breast, for the asthma, dropsy, suppression of urine, for flatulencies, and for dissolving phlegm. They assert that it stops vomitings, prevents convulsions in children, and that, by strengthening the reins, it procures females a safe and easy delivery. As the *fou-lin* grows always in the neighbourhood of pines, it might probably be found in Europe, were proper search made for it.

TI-HOANG The Chinese give this name to the root of the large comfrey the best of which is found in *Honan*, in the neighbourhood of the city Hoai-king The roots of this plant, when dried, are about the size of a finger, but much longer The Chinese physicians ascribe to them many salutary properties, and the use of them has become very common in all the provinces of the empire Rich people take pills of *ti-hoang* every morning, as people in Europe drink tea, coffee and chocolate Some cut it into thin slices, and use it in decoction, or when baked in the steam of boiling water others pound it, and form it into bolules, which they swallow with warm water. Five other kinds of plants, or ingredients, are commonly added to it, which are aromatic, cordial, diuretic, acid and a little soporific, but the *ti-hoang* is always the basis of these pills.

We have now mentioned the most particular of the trees, plants, shrubs, &c that ornament the Chinese gardens, or are used in the *Materia Medica*, these countries are, however, a world of which we are too ignorant, and which some very fortunate event can alone bring us acquainted with.

QUADRUPEDS, BIRDS, BUTTERFLIES AND FISHES.

The mountains and vast forests of China abound with every species of wild animals, such as the rhinoceros, elephants, leopards, tygers, bears, wolves, foxes, buffaloes, camels, horses, wild mules, &c. Beavers, sables and ermines are also found in the northern provinces, but the skins which they furnish are much inferior to those procured from Siberia.

Game is common in China The squares of Pe-kin, in winter, are filled with different heaps of volatile, terrestrial and aquatic animals, hardened by cold and perfectly secure against all corruption. Prodigious quantities of elks, stags, deer, goats, wild boars, hares, rabbits, squirrels and wild rats, geese, ducks, partridges, pheasants and quails are seen there, as are also several kinds of game, not to be found in Europe.

The Chinese horses have neither the strength, beauty, nor swiftness of ours, and the inhabitants of the country have not the art of breaking them properly those in the military service are said to be so timid, that they betake themselves to flight whenever they hear the neighing of the Tartar horses. besides, as they are not shod, their hoofs are soon destroyed, so that, in six years, the best horse becomes unfit for service.

Camels, both wild and domestic, are found in the north east part of China, and the fat found in the bunches of the wild camels, which is named *bunch-oil*, is much used in the Chinese medicine

There are several species of apes in China. A species named *sin-sin*, differ from the rest in their size, being equal to that of an ordinary man They walk with facility on their hind legs, and all their actions have a singular conformity to those of the human species

The most beautiful quadruped of China is a stag, which is about the size of our middle-sized dogs. The princes and mandarins buy them at an excessive price, and keep them as curiosities in their gardens. They have also another ſpecies, of an enormous ſize, which they call the *horſe-ſtag*.

In China is alſo found the *muſk-deer*, or as the Chineſe call it the *hiang-tchang-tſe* This animal is very common, and is met with, not only in the ſouthern provinces, but alſo in thoſe which are to the weſt of Pe-kin, but the fineſt are found in the kingdom of Thibet it has no horns; and the colour of its hair, which is long and rough, approaches near to black or dark brown, under the belly and tail it is white.

The bag which contains its muſk, which is found in the male only, is formed of a very thin membrane covered with a kind of hair exceedingly fine and ſoft, and formed on the belly. The fleſh of the female deer is well-taſted, and is ſerved up at the moſt delicate tables of the Chineſe

The Jeſuits inform us that in the thick foreſts of Tartary, to the north of the great wall, there is found a ſpecies of *flying-fox* They deſcribe his wings as being only thin membranes which extend from one foot to another, and reach to his tail. This animal never flies but by darting himſelf from the top of one tree to another, which is lower he has not the power of raiſing himſelf, and of flying as he mounts A kind of *flying-rat* they ſay, is alſo ſeen near *Keou-ouan* it is larger than a common rat, and has wings like thoſe of the fox already mentioned, it is doubtful whether either of theſe are any thing elſe than different ſpecies of the flying ſquirrels

China has birds of every ſpecies eagles, falcons, pelicans, birds of paradiſe, ſwans, ſtorks and paroquets, which are inferior to thoſe of the Weſt-Indies neither in the variety nor beauty of their plumage, nor in the facility with which they learn to ſpeak

Inſects of almoſt every ſpecies are found in China, and the butterflies or rather moths found on the mountain *Lefeou-chan*, ſituated in the province of *Quang-tong*, are ſo much prized, that they are ſent to court. They are of greater size than those of Europe, their wings are much broader, their colours are variegated in an extraordinary manner, and they have a surprising brightness These butterflies or moths remain motionless on the trees in the day-time, and they suffer themselves to be taken without difficulty In the evening, they begin to flutter about, almost in the same manner as bats, which some of them seem to equal in size, on account of the extent of their wings The Chinese also boast much of the butterflies found on the mountains called *Si-chan*, in the province of *Pe-tche-li* but they are small, and not so much valued as those of the mountain *Lo feou-chan*

The silk insects are different from silk-worms, resemble caterpillars, and are found in great numbers on the trees and in the fields of the province of *Chang-tong* They propagate without any care, and feed indiscriminately upon the leaves of the mulberry, and on those of other trees They do not spin their silk circularly and in the same manner as common silk-worms, which form theirs into balls; they produce it in filaments and long threads, which being carried away by the wind, are caught by the trees and bushes the Chinese collect these threads, and make a kind of stuff of them, called *kien-tcheou*, inferior in lustre to those manufactured of common silk, it might be taken at first sight, for coarse woollen stuff or drugget it is, however, much esteemed in China, and sold there sometimes for more than the richest sattin This stuff is closely woven, it never cuts, lasts very long, washes like linen, and, when manufactured with care, is scarce susceptible of being spotted, even with oil. The insects which produce this singular silk are of two kinds; one larger and blacker than silk-worms, and called *tsouen-kien*, the other smaller, and known by the name of *tiao-kien* The silk of the first species of these worms is of a reddish grey, that of the second is blacker, and the cloth made of them partakes of both these colours.

Ou-pOEY-TSE. This is a name which the Chinese give to a kind of nests made by certain insects upon the leaves and branches of the tree called *yen-fou-tse*. These nests are much used in dying, and the physicians employ them in medicine. Some of these nests were brought to Europe, and put into the hands of the celebrated Mr. Geoffroy, who, after having examined them with the utmost attention, thought he perceived some conformity in them to those excrescences which grow on the leaves of the elm, and which the peasantry call *elm bladders*: he found these nests so sharp and astringent to the taste, that he considered them as far superior to every other species of galls used by the dyers. The Chinese are however satisfied that insects which produce a kind of wax, construct for themselves on the branches and leaves of this tree these little retreats, where they wait for the time of their metamorphosis, or, at least, deposit in safety their eggs, which compose that fine dust with which the *ou-poey-tse* are filled. Some of the *ou-poey-tse* are as large as one's fist; but these are rare, and are generally produced by a worm of extraordinary strength, or which has associated with another, as two silk-worms are sometimes seen shut up in the same ball. The smallest *ou-poey-tse* are about the size of a chesnut, and in form either round or oblong; at first they are of a dark green colour, which afterwards changes to yellow; and the husk, though pretty firm, becomes then very brittle.

The Chinese peasants collect these *ou-poey-tse* before the first hoar-frosts. They take care to kill the worm inclosed in the husks, and for this purpose expose them for some time, to the steam of boiling water. The *ou-poey-tse* are used at Pekin, for giving paper a durable and deep-black colour; in the provinces of Kiang-nan and Tche-kiang, where a great deal of beautiful sattin is made, they are employed for dying the silk before it is put on the loon. The Chineſe literati alſo blacken their beards with them when they become white.

The medicinal properties of the *ou-poey-tſe*, if we can believe the Chineſe phyſicians, are very numerous. They introduce them into the compoſition of many of their remedies. They recommend them as an excellent ſpecific for curing inflammations and ulcers, and for counteracting the effects of poiſon; and they ſay they employ them with ſucceſs in the dropſy, phthiſis, epilepſy, catarrhs, ſickneſs, fluxions of the eyes and ears, and in many other diſorders.

It is impoſſible to give a liſt of the different kinds of fiſh to be found in the lakes, rivers and ſeas of China. The miſſionaries, to whom we are indebted for the greater part of the knowledge we have concerning this empire, have not thrown ſufficient light upon any branch of natural hiſtory. They, however, aſſure us, that they obſerved in China moſt of the different kinds ſeen in Europe; beſides which there is a fiſh called *tcha-kia-yu*, or the fiſh in armour, which the Chineſe highly eſteem. They give it this name, becauſe its body is defended by ſharp ſcales, ranged in ſtraight lines. The fleſh of this fiſh is very white, and it taſtes almoſt like veal. It generally weighs forty pounds. When the weather is fine, they catch another kind of fiſh, ſo extremely white, that it is called the *flour-fiſh*. It is, above all, remarkable for its black eye-balls, which appear as if ſet in two circles of the moſt brilliant ſilver. This fiſh is found in ſuch abundance on the coaſt of the province of *Kiang-nan*, that four hundred pounds weight of them are ſometimes taken at one haul with a net.

The coaſts of the province of Tche-kiang ſwarm with a ſpecies of fiſh which have a great reſemblance to the Newfoundland cod: an incredible quantity of them is conſumed on the ſea coaſt of Fo-kien, beſides what are ſalted on the ſpot, to be tranſported to the interior parts of the country. They are taken from the nets, and ſtowed in the holds of the vessels, between layers of salt, and, notwithstanding the excessive heats, they are thus transported to the remotest provinces of the empire.

The missionaries speak of another kind of fish, the figure of which is as singular as it is frightful and disgusting. The Chinese, they say, call it *hai-seng*; it makes one of their favorite dishes, and there is scarcely any entertainment given at which it is not served up. It is generally seen floating near the sea-coasts of Chang-tong and Fo-kien, where the missionaries at first took it for a lump of inanimate matter, but, having made some of the boys belonging to their vessel catch it, they perceived that this shapeless mass was a living and organized being. It swam about in the tub into which they first threw it, and lived for a long time. The Chinese sailors informed the missionaries, that this fish has four eyes and six feet, but, on examining it with attention, they could only discover two places where it appeared to have sight, for it seemed afraid when any thing approached them. If every thing that enables the hai-seng to move is to be considered as feet, a number of small excrescences, like buttons, dispersed over its body, may be accounted as such. It has no bones, and it dies on being pressed. This fish is easily preserved, when put into salt, and it is transported in that manner, and sold as a delicacy throughout the whole empire. It does not, however, appear to have been much relished by the missionaries.

The Chinese have a salt-water fish which they call *ming-fou-you*, that is literally the *fish with a bright belly*. It has a round head, and a mouth like the beak of a falcon. It has eight legs round its head, but neither scales, tail, nor bones. *The Geography of Moukden* adds, that it has two tufts of a beard, which resemble two bunches of cord, which it uses to attach itself to the bottom of the sea, or to a rock, during a storm, or when the waves are too ſtrong or too much agitated, hence ſprings the name *norré*, which the Mantchew Tartars give it, ſignifying *a moored lark*.

The ſmall fiſh called gold and ſilver fiſh, are kept by the Chineſe for ornament in ſmall ponds in their gardens and courts. In warm countries theſe fiſh multiply faſt, provided care is taken to collect their ſpawn, which floats on the water, and which they almoſt entirely devour. This ſpawn the Chineſe put into a particular veſſel expoſed to the ſun, and preſerve there until vivified by the heat. gold fiſh, however, ſeldom multiply when they are kept in cloſe vaſes, becauſe they are then too much confined. In order to render them fruitful, they muſt be put into reſervoirs of conſiderable depth, in ſome places at leaſt, and which are conſtantly ſupplied with freſh water

At a certain time of the year a prodigious number of barks are ſeen on the great river Yang-tſe-kiang, which go thither to purchaſe the ſpawn of theſe fiſh Towards the month of May the neighbouring inhabitants ſhut up the river in ſeveral places with mats and hurdles, and leave only a ſpace in the middle ſufficient for the paſſage of barks The ſpawn of the fiſh, which the Chineſe can diſtinguiſh at firſt ſight, although a ſtranger could perceive no traces of it in the water, is ſtopped by theſe hurdles The water mixed with ſpawn is then drawn up, and after it has been put into large veſſels, it is ſold to merchants, who tranſport it afterwards to every part of the empire, and diſpoſe of it by meaſure to thoſe who are deſirous of ſtocking their ponds and reſervoirs.

VIEW OF

THE

POPULATION AND GOVERNMENT

OF

C H I N A.

POPULATION.

ONE of those things which have been thought the most incredible by Europeans in accounts of China, is its extensive population, but which does not appear to have been much exaggerated. Father Amiot took great pains to investigate this subject, and fixed the population of China in 1743 at two hundred millions, and though we cannot agree with his reasoning on different statements, it will be impossible to put his account back more than twenty millions, if so much. We possess, however, a more complete enumeration, taken from the accounts of the tribunal of Lands, received in France in 1770. By this enumeration it appears that the population of China in 1761, was as follows:

Province of Pe-tcheli, *including Leao tong*	15,891,792
Kiang-nan, *two divisions* - -	45,922,439
Kiang-si - - -	11,006,640
Fo-kien - -	8,063,671
Tche-kiang - - -	15,429,690
Hou-quang - - -	8,829,320

Ho-nan, *two diviſions* - -	24,413,110
Chang-tong - - -	25,180,734
Chan-ſi - - -	9,768,189
Chen-ſi, *including Kan-ſou* -	14,699,457
Se-tchuen - - -	2,782,976
Quang-tong - - -	6,797,597
Quang-ſi - - -	3,947,414
Yun-nan - - - -	2,078,802
Koei-tcheou - -	3,402,722
Total	198,214,553

This regiſter was accompanied with a comparative ſtatement of the population in the preceding year, 1760, in which the numbers were ſtated at 196,837,977; there was therefore an increaſe of 1,376,576 in the courſe of one year only. But, upwards of thirty years have elapſed ſince the epocha of this numeration, and, as there can be no doubt of the population of China having, for a long time paſt, been progreſſively increaſing, we preſume, that this empire contains at preſent upwards of two hundred and twenty millions of inhabitants. It will, no doubt, be allowed, that there is no empire in the univerſe which contains ſo many people united in the ſame ſociety, and governed by the ſame laws.

SOVEREIGN AUTHORITY

No monarch in Europe poſſeſſes power ſo unlimited as the ſovereign of this numerous nation. All authority is veſted in him alone; he is the undiſputed maſter of the lives of his ſubjects, and thus placed in a ſituation to become the greateſt tyrant in the world.

No ſentence of death pronounced by any of the tribunals can be executed without his conſent. Every verdict in civil affairs is ſubject to the ſame reviſion, and no determination is of any force until it has been confirmed by his [illegible]. On the contrary, whatever ſentence he paſſes is executed without delay His edicts are respected throughout the whole empire as though they proceeded from a divinity, and are immediately published and registered without the least remonstrance This absolute power in the head of the Chinese empire appears to be as ancient as the empire itself, and all the revolutions which have taken place have tended to confirm it.

The emperor alone has the disposal of all the offices of state, who are wholly dependent on his pleasure No employment is however purchased in China, merit, for the most part, raises to place, and rank is attached to place only, thus whatever may be the despotic power of the emperor, the government has an eminent advantage over most of the governments of Europe the offices and honours of which are as saleable as their other mercantile commodities. On this principle, of merit only qualifying for office, the emperor has the right of choosing a successor either among his children, the rest of his family or from among his own subjects, thus Chun, prime minister of the emperor Yao, was chosen by that monarch to succeed him, on account of his superior abilities

Should the successor named by the emperor be wanting in that respectful submission which he conceives is due to him, or manifest some natural weakness of which he was not before suspected, the same hand that raised him towards the throne can remove him from his exalted station In such case another successor is chosen, and the former is entirely forgotten The emperor Kang-hi, one of the latest and best of the Chinese emperors, thus excluded his eldest son from the throne, though he had once nominated him his successor

A prince of the blood is generally esteemed in China; yet the emperor can prevent those from assuming that title who have a natural right to it, but if they are permitted to enjoy their rank, they have neither influence nor power. they possess a revenue proportioned to their dignity, and have a palace, officers and court, but they have less authority than the lowest of the mandarins.

The mandarins, whether of letters, or of arms, compose exactly what are called in Europe the nobility. There are only two ranks in China, the nobility and the people; but the former is not hereditary. These mandarins may in cases of necessity, remonstrate with the emperor, either individually or as a body, upon any action or omission on his part which may be contrary to the interests of the empire. These remonstrances are seldom ill received; but the emperor reserves to himself the right of paying that attention to them which he thinks they deserve.

From this view of the sovereign authority, it is evident that nothing limits its power; but the emperors find, even in this extent of power, the strongest motives for not abusing it. Their private interest, and that of the nation, are inseparably united; and one cannot be consulted without the other. The Chinese consider their monarchy as a large family, of which the emperor, *who ought to govern with paternal affection*, is the head. The prince himself, in his education, imbibes the same principles; and it must be admitted, that no country was ever ruled by more good princes, or ever produced fewer bad.—Such are the fruits of the education they receive, and such is the lesson which this nation holds out to all those who are friends to a monarchical form of government.

China contains about fifteen thousand mandarins of letters, and a still greater number who aspire to that title.

Their influence must be very powerful, since it triumphed over the Tartars, who conquered China, who submitted to the laws and customs, and, what is still more, adopted the character and genius of the people whom they subjected.

MANDARINS OF LETTERS.

To arrive at this degree, it is necessary to pass through several others, such as that of bachelor (*siu* or *tsai*), of licentiate (*kiu-gin*), and of doctor (*tsing-ssee*). The two first, however, are only absolutely necessary; but even those on whom the third is conferred, obtain for a time only the government of a city of the second or third class.

There are eight orders of mandarins in China. The first is that of the *calao*. Their number is not fixed, but wholly depends on the will of the prince. Ministers of state, presidents of the supreme courts, and all the superior officers of the militia, are chosen from among this order, the chief of which is called *cheou-siang*, and is president of the emperor's council.

From the second order of mandarins, called *ta-hiose*, are selected the viceroys and presidents of the supreme councils of the different provinces.

Tchong-chuco, or *school of mandarins*, is the title given to the third order, one of the principal functions of which is to act as secretaries to the emperor.

The mandarins of the fourth order, styled *y-tchuen-tao*, when no particular government is entrusted to them, or when they belong to no fixed tribunal, have to keep in repair the harbours, royal lodging-houses, and barks of which the emperor is proprietor, in their district. The fifth order, *ping-pi-tao*, have the inspection of the troops. The sixth, *tun-tien-hao*, have the care of the highways. The seventh, or *ho-tao*, have the superintendence of the rivers; and the eighth, styled *hai-tao*, that of the sea-coasts. In short, the whole administration of the Chinese empire is entrusted to the mandarins of letters, from among whom are chosen the governors of provinces, of cities of the first, second and third class, and the presidents and members of all the tribunals. The homage which the people pay to every mandarin in office is nearly equal to that paid to the emperor. For as it is the received opinion of the Chinese, that their monarch is the father of the whole empire, so it is their opinion that the governor of a province is the father of that province, and that the mandarin who is governor of a city is also the father of that city

MANDARINS OF ARMS.

The mandarins of arms are never indulged with the smallest share in the government of the state, even the inspection of the troops, as we have before observed, belongs to a class of the mandarins of letters however, to be admitted to the rank of mandarin of arms, it is necessary, as for that of mandarin of letters, to have passed through three degrees Strength of body, agility in performing the different military exercises, and a readiness in comprehending and executing orders, are all that is required, and in these consist the various examinations which candidates are obliged to undergo before they can be admitted to that rank.

The mandarins of arms have tribunals, the members of which are selected from among their chiefs

The principal of these tribunals is fixed at Pe-kin, and is composed of five different classes — The first, named Heou-fou, formed from the mandarins of the rear guard —The second, called Tsa-fou, formed of the mandarins of the left wing — The third, named Yeou-tou, formed of the mandarins of the right wing — The fourth, called Tchong-fou, composed of the mandarins of the advanced main guard —The fifth, called Tsien-tou, consists of the mandarins of the advanced guard

These are subordinate to a supreme tribunal of war, likewise established at Pe-kin, called Iong-tching-fou, the president of which is one of the great lords of the empire, whose authority extends over all the officers and soldiers of the army This president has a mandarin of letters, who is a superintendent of arms, for an assessor He has also for counsellors two inspectors named by the emperor When these four persons have agreed upon any measure, their resolution must be submitted to the revision of another ſupreme court, called *Ping-pou*, and which is entirely of a civil nature And ſuch is the jealouſy occaſioned by military power, that the Ping-pou has under its juriſdiction the whole militia of the empire.

The power of the chief mandarin of arms in the field is equivalent to that of our commanders in chief. Under him he has a certain number of others who act as lieutenant-generals, other mandarins diſcharge the duty of colonels, others that of captains, and laſtly, others that of lieutenants and enſigns

There are reckoned in China between eighteen and twenty thouſand mandarins of war their number conſequently is ſuperior to that of the mandarins of letters, but the importance of the latter makes them conſidered as the principal body of the empire

FORCES, MILITARY DISCIPLINE, ARMS OF THE TROOPS, DIFFERENT KINDS OF FORTIFICATIONS, &c.

The troops of the Chineſe empire amount to more than ſeven hundred thouſand The pay is about two-pence halfpenny, in fine ſilver, and a meaſure of rice, per day The pay of a horſeman is double that of a foot ſoldier The emperor furniſhes a horſe, and the horſeman receives two meaſures of ſmall beans for his daily ſubſiſtence. All arrears of the officers or men are paid every three months, and nothing is left due to the troops beyond that term.

The beſt ſoldiers of this empire are collected from the three northern provinces. Thoſe ſupplied by the reſt are ſeldom called forth. they remain quietly with their families, enjoy their pay, and have ſeldom occaſion to remember that they are ſoldiers, except when ordered to quell an inſurrection, accompany a mandarin governor, or to appear at a review.

At every review their arms are carefully inſpected Thoſe of the cavalry conſiſt of a helmet, a cuiraſs, a lance and large ſabre Foot ſoldiers are armed with a pike and sabre, some with fusees, and others with bows and arrows. If any of these are found in bad condition, or in the least rusted, the neglect is punished by thirty or forty blows with a stick, if the culprit is a Chinese, or with as many lashes, if he is a Tartar.

Besides the superior officers of these troops, whom we have already mentioned, there are twenty-four captains-general, and as many colonels of horse, created by the Tartars, as a kind of inspectors appointed to watch over the conduct of the Chinese officers.

Though there is reason to believe that the use of artillery is very ancient in China, it appears to have been totally lost about the beginning of the last century. Three or four cannons were to be seen at the gates of Nan-kin, but not a single Chinese at that period was to be found who knew how to use them. In 1621, when the city of Macao made a present of three pieces of artillery to the emperor, it was found necessary to send three men also to load and fire them.

The Chinese were then made sensible that artillery might be employed with great success against the Tartars, who, having advanced as far as the bottom of the great wall, had been often dispersed by the three cannons sent from Macao. The mandarins of arms therefore gave it as their opinion, that cannons were the best arms they could use against these barbarians; but the difficulty was in procuring them, the Chinese scarcely knew how to point and fire a great gun, and much less the art of casting them. F. Adam Schaal, a Jesuit missionary, however, rendered them this service. And some time after, Father Verbiest, another Jesuit missionary, undertook, by order of the emperor, to cast a new set, and, it is said, that he raised the Chinese artillery to the number of three hundred and twenty pieces; he also taught them the method of fortifying towns, of constructing fortresses, and of erecting other edifices, according to the rules of modern architecture.

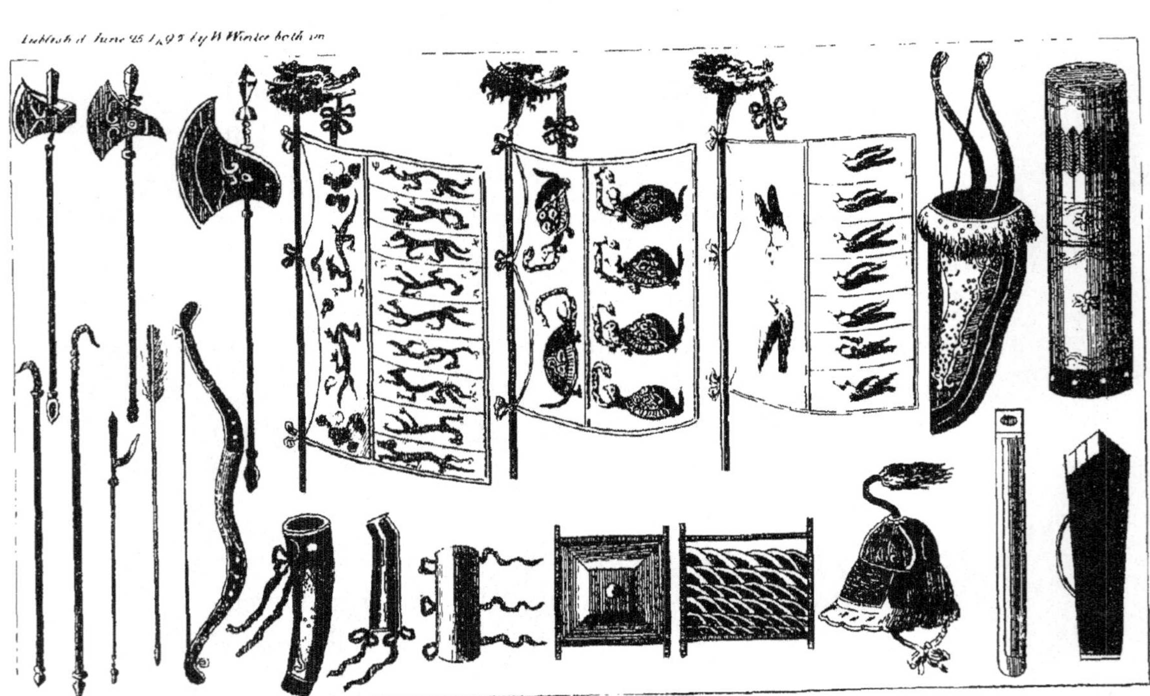

Chinese Standards and Warlike Instruments

The Jesuits sent from Europe to China were not only zealous missionaries, but their zeal was united with talents which procured them admission to the centre of an empire, till then shut against every stranger.

There are reckoned in China more than two thousand places of arms, divided into six different classes, viz. six hundred of the first, five hundred, and upwards, of the second, three hundred of the third, about an equal number of the fourth, an hundred and fifty of the fifth, and three hundred of the last. To these may be added about three thousand towers, or castles, dispersed throughout the whole empire, all of which are defended by garrisons.

The fortresses of China derive their principal strength from their situation, which, in general, is well chosen. They have, besides a rampart, a brick-wall, towers, and a ditch filled with water.

Nature hath fortified a great extent of the frontiers of this empire: the sea borders six of the provinces, but it is so shallow towards the shore, that large vessels cannot approach it: inaccessible mountains cover it on the west, and the remaining part is defended by the great wall.

This stupendous monument of human art and industry exceeds every thing that we read of in ancient history. The pyramids of Egypt are little, when compared with a wall which covers three large provinces, stretches along an extent of fifteen hundred miles, and is of such an enormous thickness, that six horsemen may easily ride abreast upon it. It is flanked with towers, two bow-shots distant one from the other, which add to its strength, and render it much easier to be defended. One third part of the able bodied men of China were employed in constructing this wall, and the workmen were ordered, under pain of death, to place the materials of which it is composed so closely, that the least entrance might not be left for any instrument of iron. This precaution contributed much to the ſolidity of the work, which is ſtill in a great meaſure entire, though built two thouſand years ago. This celebrated wall is not only carried through the low lands and valleys, but alſo over hills, and up the ſteep brows of the higheſt mountains. F. Verbieſt, who had the curioſity to take the altitude of one of thoſe upon which part of it is built, found that it was one thouſand and thirty-ſix feet above the level of the ſpot upon which he ſtood. The execution of this work, therefore, muſt have coſt immenſe labour, ſince it was often neceſſary to tranſport the materials, of which it is conſtructed, through a deſart country, and to convey them to eminences inacceſſible to horſes or carriages. Father Martini, in his Chineſe Atlas, ſays that this wall begins at the Gulph of Leao-tong, and reaches to the mountains near the city of Kin, on the Yellow River, and that, between theſe two places, it meets with no interruption, except to the north of the city of Suen, in the province of Pe-tcheli, where it is intercepted by a ridge of hideous and inacceſſible mountains, to which it is cloſely united, and by the river Hoang-ho, which paſſes through it in its courſe to the ſea. He adds, that for other rivers of inferior ſize arches have been conſtructed, like thoſe of a bridge, through which they find a paſſage. It has no kind of ſupport but what is uſually given to ordinary walls, and it is almoſt of the ſame form, not only where it ſtretches acroſs plains, which are very rare in that country, but even where it is carried over high mountains. An intelligent traveller (Mr. Bell), who, in 1719, accompanied Capt. Ismailoff in his embaſſy to Pekin, tells us, that it is carried acroſs rivers, and over the top of the higheſt hills, without the leaſt interruption, keeping nearly along that circular ridge of barren rocks which incloſes the country, and, after running about twelve hundred miles, ends in impaſſable mountains and ſandy deſarts. According to his account, the foundation consists of large blocks of square stones laid in mortar; but all the rest is constructed of brick The whole is so strong, and well built, that it scarcely needs any repairs, and, in such a dry climate, may remain in the same condition for many ages When carried over steep rocks where no horse can pass, it is about fifteen or twenty feet high, and broad in proportion, but when running through a valley, or crossing a river, you behold a strong wall, about thirty feet high, with square towers at certain intervals, and embrasures at equal distances The top of the wall is flat, and paved with cut stone, and where it rises over a rock or eminence, there is an ascent by easy stone stairs. He adds—"This wall was begun and completely finished "in the short space of five years, and it is reported, the "labourers stood so close for many miles, that they could "hand the materials from one to another This I am the "more inclined to believe, as the rugged rocks among "which it is built must have prevented all use of carriages, "and neither clay for making bricks, nor any kind of "cement, could be found among them"—This barrier, since the re-union of the Tartars and Chinese, is almost become useless.

The Tartars, who perhaps have lost some of their military ardour, form the strongest and bravest part of the Chinese militia Every Tartar born in the ordinary class is enrolled from his cradle, and when of age to carry arms must be ready to take the field on the shortest notice The emperor's son, and every Tartar of distinction must be acquainted with the management of a horse, know how to handle a bow and arrow, and to perform, at least, the elementary evolutions,

SUPERIOR TRIBUNALS.

The principal of these tribunals is the Emperor's Grand Council, composed of all the ministers of state, presidents and assessors of the six sovereign courts, of which we are about to ſpeak, and of thoſe of three other tribunals, which we ſhall alſo have occaſion to mention This council is never aſſembled but on affairs of the greateſt importance, for in ordinary caſes, the Emperor's Private Council is ſubſtituted for it

The ſix other ſuperior tribunals of China are eſtabliſhed, like the preceding, at Pe-kin, under the general denomination of *leou-pou* The firſt is called *li-pou* This tribunal furniſhes mandarins for the different provinces, watches over their conduct, keeps a journal of their tranſactions, and informs the emperor of them, who puniſhes or rewards according to its report

This tribunal is ſubdivided into four others The firſt has the care of ſelecting perſons who, on account of their learning, talents, and morals, are proper for filling the different offices under government. The ſecond has the examining of the conduct of the mandarins The third affixes a ſeal to all public acts, gives to each of the mandarins the ſeals belonging to his dignity and employment, and examines the ſeals of the different diſpatches addreſſed to the court The fourth inquires into the merit and conduct of the grandees of the empire, as well princes of the imperial blood, as others on whom titles merely honorary are conferred The principal object of the Chineſe government in this eſtabliſhment is, that the different departments be properly inſpected, every tranſaction be thoroughly inveſtigated, ſuitable rewards given to the deſerving, and puniſhment inflicted on the guilty adequate to their crimes.

Hou-pou is the name of the ſecond court This tribunal has the ſuperintendence of all the finances of the ſtate It is the guardian of the treaſures and domains of the emperor it keeps an account of his revenues and expences, gives orders for the payment of penſions and ſalaries annexed to certain offices, and for the delivery of rice, pieces of ſilk, and money, which are diſtributed among the great lords, and mandarins of the empire. The coining of money, the management of public magazines, and custom-houses, and the collection of the duties, are all under its inspection, it likewise keeps an exact register of the families that compose this vast empire. This court has to assist it fourteen other inferior courts, which are dispersed throughout the different provinces of China.

The third court, called *Li-pou*, is the court of Ceremonies. Ceremonies form, in part, the basis of the Chinese government It is the duty of this tribunal, therefore, to support, and enforce the observance of them, the arts and sciences are also placed under its inspection, and it takes charge of the repairs of temples, regulates every thing that relates to the annual sacrifices offered up by the emperor, and even to the entertainments which the emperor gives he also consults it when he is about to grant favours, or confer honors This Tribunal also receives, lodges, treats and dismisses ambassadors, and takes care to preserve tranquility among the different religious sects tolerated in the empire. It has four subaltern tribunals to assist it

The Tribunal of Arms, called *Ping pou*, forms the fourth sovereign court It comprehends in its jurisdiction the whole militia, and all the fortresses, arsenals, magazines and storehouses of every kind, it inspects all the manufactories of arms, examines and appoints officers of every rank, and is composed of mandarins of letters only, as are the four tribunals dependent on it.

The fifth superior tribunal, named *Hong-pou*, is the Criminal Bench, or General Court for all the Criminal Affairs of the Empire Fourteen other tribunals are appointed for its assistance, but they are all subordinate, and under its inspection.

The sixth sovereign court, named *Cong-pou*, or the Tribunal of Public Works, has the charge of surveying and keeping in repair the palaces of the emperor, princes and viceroys, the buildings where the tribunals are held, the temples, tombs of the ſovereigns, and all other public monuments. It has, likewiſe, the ſuperintendence of the ſtreets, public highways, bridges, lakes, rivers, barks, and every thing that relates to navigation, and alſo, of the towers deemed neceſſary to maintaining peace and ſafety in the interior parts of the empire. It has four inferior tribunals for aſſiſtants in the diſcharge of its duty. The firſt, for is deſigns and draws plans of public works, the ſecond, has under its direction all the workſhops in the different cities of the empire, the third, ſurveys cauſeways, roads, bridges, canals, rivers, &c. and the fourth, takes care of the emperor's palaces, gardens and orchards, and receives their produce.

The members which compoſe all theſe different inferior tribunals are half Chineſe and half Tartars, and each has two preſidents, one of which is always a Tartar born.

None of theſe tribunals have abſolute power in their own juriſdiction the deciſions of one can have no effect without the concurrence of ſome other tribunal, and ſometimes of ſeveral. Thus the tribunal of War has under its direction the whole troops of the empire, the ſecond is entruſted with the payment of them, and to the ſixth belongs the care of the arms tents ſtores, &c. neceſſary for military operations. Nothing, therefore, that relates to any of theſe can be put in execution without the concurrence of thoſe three tribunals.

Every ſupreme tribunal has alſo its cenſor, an officer merely paſſive, who decides upon nothing, but watches over all. He aſſiſts at all aſſemblies, reviſes all their acts, and makes no mention to the tribunals of any irregularity he has obſerved, but immediately acquaints the emperor. He informs him alſo of the faults committed by the mandarins, either in the public adminiſtration of affairs, or in their private conduct. Theſe cenſors hold their places for life, and this security gives them courage to speak out, when they observe any impropriety or abuse.

Their accusation is sufficient to set on foot an inquiry, which generally leads to a proof, the accused is then discharged from his office, were he even one of the first men in the empire, and the commonest person is afterwards held in as much estimation as he It is, however, something remarkable, that the complaints of these censors are referred to the very tribunals of which the accused are members

These censors form also a tribunal named Tou-che-yven, which has the inspection of the whole empire its members have the power of remonstrating with the emperor, whenever the interest of the public, or that of the prince, renders it necessary Their inspection extends also over all lawyers and military men in public employments, and over every class of citizens In short, they are, strictly speaking, placed between the prince and the mandarins, between the mandarins and the people, between the people and families, between families and individuals, and they unite, generally speaking to the importance of their office the most uncorruptible probity and invincible courage The sovereign may, if he proceeds to rigour, take away their lives, but many of them have patiently suffered death, rather than betray the cause of truth, or wink at abuses · It is not therefore sufficient to get rid of one, in order to gain a point, they must all be treated in the same manner, for the last would tread with the same resolution in the steps of those who had gone before him.

There is still another tribunal, which exists, we believe, no where but in China, it is the tribunal of Princes, and is composed of princes only. Some of the ordinary mandarins indeed belong to it as subalterns, whose business is to draw out cases and other writings necessary for determining any suit The names of the children of the imperial family are inscribed, as soon as they are born, in the registers of this tribunal, and to it are consigned the dignities and titles which the emperor confers upon them. This tribunal is the only court where they can be tried, and, in cases of accusation, it absolves or punishes them, according to its pleasure.

There is another tribunal no less peculiar to China than the two preceding, but better known than either: it is the Tribunal of History, called *Han-lin-yuen*. It is composed of the greatest geniuses and of men of the most profound erudition in the empire; to this tribunal is entrusted the education of the heir apparent to the throne, and the compilation and arranging of the general history of the empire. This last part of their office makes them formidable even to the emperor himself, for his attempts to oppress, or seduce them, would be consigned to history, in spite of all his efforts to the contrary.

From this body are generally chosen the *ca-lao*, or mandarins of the first class, and the presidents of the supreme tribunals.

Civil Laws

The Chinese have taken most of their civil laws from their canonical books of morality, and filial piety is their basis. Some decrees of the emperors, respecting the observance of certain ceremonies, which custom has established, form the rest of the code.

Every mandarin who is a governor of a province or city, is obliged, twice a month, to instruct the people assembled round him, and to recommend to them the observance of the following articles:

I. You must put in practice the duties prescribed by filial piety, and observe that deference which is due from a younger to an elder brother. By these means only can you learn to set a proper value upon those obligations which Nature imposes on all men.

II You muſt always preſerve a reſpectful remembrance of your anceſtors hence will reſult conſtant peace and union in your family

III. Let harmony and concord reign throughout every village. by this, quarrels will be baniſhed, and law-ſuits prevented.

IV Let thoſe who cultivate the earth, and breed ſilk-worms be eſteemed and reſpected, you will then want neither grain for your nouriſhment, nor clothing to cover you

V Let frugality, temperance, modeſty and prudent economy, become the objects of your reflection, and regulate your conduct

VI Let the public ſchools be carefully maintained; and, above all, let youth be inſtructed early in the duties of life, and formed to good morals.

VII. Let every one attend to his own buſineſs, and to the duties of his office they will then be better diſcharged

VIII Let religious ſects be carefully extirpated as ſoon as they ſpring up it might be too late afterwards

IX Let the terror of the penal laws be often held up to the people For rude and untractable minds can be reſtrained by fear only

X. Endeavour to acquire a perfect knowledge of the rules of civility and politeneſs theſe tend to maintain concord

XI Let the education of children, and particularly of younger ſons, be the principal object of your attention.

XII Avoid ſlander, and abſtain from malicious accuſations

XIII Conceal none of thoſe criminals who, on account of their crimes, have been baniſhed from ſociety, and condemned to a wandering life by concealing them, you become their accomplices.

XIV Be punctual in paying the duties and taxes impoſed by the prince. this will free you from the oppreſſion of thoſe who collect them, and from vexatious law-ſuits

XV Be careful to act in concert with the magiſtrates of the diſtrict to which you belong, and to ſecond their efforts in diſcharging the duties of their office by theſe means, they will be enabled to detect the guilty and to prevent robbery and theft

XVI Reſtrain every ſudden emotion of paſſion, and you will avoid many dangers

From the manner in which theſe ordinances are delivered, it is evident that the ſovereigns of China give even to their laws and regulations the form of maxims and precepts Every law in Europe is preceded by a preamble, ſetting forth the reaſon of enacting it, but in China the law invariably precedes the explanation of the motive

Thoſe laws which concern marriage are very extenſive A Chineſe can have only one lawful wife, and it is neceſſary that her rank and age ſhould be nearly equal to his own, but he may have ſeveral concubines, without any formality whatever, except firſt paying to their parents, if they have any, a certain ſum of money, and entering into a written engagement to treat their daughters well

Theſe concubines are totally dependent on the lawful wife, their children are conſidered as hers, they addreſs her as mother, and give this title to her only After her death, they are obliged to wear mourning for three years, and to abſent themſelves from public examinations, but the death of their natural mother ſubjects them to the obſervance of none of theſe regulations.

A widower, or a widow, may enter a ſecond time into the matrimonial ſtate without paying much attention to any of the preceding regulations.

A widow who has children becomes abſolute miſtreſs of herſelf her parents can neither compel her to marry again or to remain in a ſtate of widowhood

Widows do not enjoy the ſame privilege when they have no male children The parents of their firſt huſband can place them in marriage, without their conſent, or knowledge. They are authoriſed by the law to do this, in order that they may indemnify themſelves, for the money they have coſt their former huſbands This ſtrictly ſpeaking is ſelling them however, if they are left with child, this traffic is ſuſpended, and it cannot take place if they bring forth a ſon

To this law there are two exceptions · the firſt when the parents of the widow aſſign her a proper maintenance, and reimburſe thoſe of the deceaſed huſband, the other, when the widow embraces a religious life, and becomes a bonzeſs

Divorces are granted in China, in caſes of adultery, mutual diſlike, incompatibility of tempers and diſpoſitions, indiſcretion, jealouſy, abſolute diſobedience, ſterility, or hereditary and infectious diſeaſes

A huſband cannot ſend away or ſell his wife, until a divorce has been legally obtained If this regulation is not ſtrictly obſerved, the buyer and ſeller become equally culpable

If a wife, acknowledged as lawful, withdraws from her family, the huſband ſues, ſentence is pronounced, and he may ſell the fugitive, who by this ſentence ceaſes to be his wife, and becomes his ſlave.

The law protects alſo the wife who is abandoned by her huſband. If he abſents himſelf for three years, ſhe is at liberty to lay her caſe before the mandarins, who can authoriſe her to take another huſband, but if ſhe anticipates their conſent, ſhe is expoſed to the moſt rigorous puniſhment

If a young woman has been betrothed to a young man, and if presents have been given and received by the parents of the intended husband and wife, that young woman can have no other husband, and if she marries another the law declares such marriage null

If, in the room of a young woman shewn to the female confidant whose business is to make up the match, another be substituted, or if the daughter of a free man marry his slave, or, if any one gives his slave to a free woman and persuades her parents that he is his son or relation the marriage is null and void, and all those who have had any share in carrying on the fraud are severely punished.

Every mandarin of letters is forbid to marry into any family residing in that province or city of which he is governor. The marriage is not valid if he trespasses against this law, and he himself is condemned to be severely bastinadoed

It is unlawful for a Chinese youth to marry while he wears mourning either for a father or mother. If promises have been made prior to the death of his parent, every engagement ceases upon that event, and the man is obliged to give information of it to the parents of his intended bride

Marriage is also suspended when a family experiences any severe misfortune such as a relation being thrown into prison, but this regulation may be set aside, provided he gives his consent

Two brothers cannot espouse two sisters, a widower is not at liberty to marry his son with the daughter of the widow whom he espouses, nor is a man permitted to marry any of his own relations, however distant the degrees of consanguinity may be between them.

Every father of a family is responsible for the conduct of his children and domestics. All faults are imputed to him which it was his duty to prevent

No mother in China has the right of making a will. Adoption is authorised by law, and the adopted child enters into all the rights of a lawful son, assumes the name of the person who has adopted him, wears mourning, if he happens to die, becomes his heir, and has a share of his money and effects, if any are left, as well as the rest of his children a right only is reserved to the father of making a few dispositions in their favour.

Children, whether adopted or not, succeed to the estates of the father, but not to his dignity or titles. the emperor alone can continue or confer these

Custom has rectified among citizens of the higher and middling classes, a law which authorized a father to sell his son, and the sale of children is at present rather tolerated than authorized among people of inferior rank, who are forbid to sell them to comedians, or to those of mean and profligate lives

A son is always a minor during the life of his father, who is absolute master of whatever he has inherited from his ancestors, or acquired by his own industry. A son is liable for the debts contracted by his father, those of gaming excepted.

A father's last will cannot be set aside on account of any error in the form.

Slavery is authorised in China, but the power of the master is entirely confined to what concerns his service. He would be punished with death, were it proved, that he had taken advantage of his power, to debauch the daughter or wife of his slave.

No husbandman can be harassed for the payment of taxes, after he has begun to till the earth; that is from about the middle of spring, to the beginning of harvest.

Such are, in general, the established laws in China, relative to civil affairs. With regard to certain temporary edicts issued by different emperors, it can only be said many of them have discovered wisdom and an attention to the public welfare; and others would certainly never have appeared, in a country where the persons most interested had possessed any share in the government.

PENAL LAWS, AND PROCEDURE IN CRIMINAL MATTERS

The mode of procedure in criminal cases among the Chinese is exceeding slow, and this, as the accused person is kept confinedly in prison during the whole process, is a great evil, to say the least of it, but this slowness becomes often the safeguard of those who are unjustly accused, and time frequently unveils the truth, which must always be unfavourable to the guilty.

Every person accused is examined by five or six tribunals, each of them examines the process, and their inquiries are not only directed against the accused, but also against the accuser and the witnesses.

The Chinese prisons are not dungeons, disgusting with filth and obscurity, like those of many European nations; they are spacious, and have a degree of convenience not generally found in such places.

A mandarin is obliged to inspect them, and to see prisoners properly treated, to send for physicians, and to supply them with remedies at the emperor's expence. In important cases, the mandarins must inform the emperor, who often orders some of the higher mandarins to examine whether he has faithfully discharged his duty.

The difference of the Chinese punishments is regulated by the different degrees of delinquency. Some of them will appear, however, exceedingly severe and rigorous, as no doubt they are.

The slightest of all their punishments is the *bastinado*, used only for chastising those guilty of trivial faults. The criminality of the offender determines the number of blows which he receives, but the lowest number is twenty.

The emperor orders this punishment to be inflicted upon some of his courtiers, but this does not prevent them from being afterwards received into favour.

The baton, or *pan-tsée*, used for this punishment, is a piece of bamboo, a little flatted, broad at the bottom, and polished at the upper extremity. *Every mandarin has authority to use it at pleasure*, when any one forgets to salute him, or when he administers public justice. On such occasions, he sits gravely behind a table, upon which is a bag filled with small sticks, while a number of petty officers stand round him, each furnished with some of these *pan-tsées*, and waiting only for his signal to make use of them. The mandarin takes from the bag one of those sticks which it contains, and throws it into the hall of audience. The culprit is then seized, and stretched out, with his belly towards the ground, his breeches are pulled down to his heels, and an athletic domestic applies five smart blows of his *pan-tsée*, another succeeds, and bestows five more, if the mandarin draws another small baton from the bag, and thus, by gradation, until he is pleased to make no more signals. The offender, who has undergone this chastisement, must then throw himself on his knees before the judge, incline his body three times to the earth, *and thank him for the care which he takes of his education*. It is difficult to conceive how a people not the dupes of the most abject slavery and superstition, can be brought quietly to submit to this arbitrary exertion of power.

The punishment of the wooden collar is also used in China. This wooden collar is composed of two pieces of wood, hollowed out in the middle, which, when put together, leave sufficient room for the neck of an individual. They are laid upon the shoulders of the criminal, and joined together, in such a manner, as to prevent his seeing his feet, or putting his hands to his mouth, he is thus rendered incapable of eating without the aſſiſtance of another, and is obliged to carry his burden night and day. Its weight is from fifty to two hundred pounds, regulated according to the nature of the crime.

For robbery, having broken the peace, diſturbed a family, or being a notorious gambler, the duration of this puniſhment is generally three months. The criminal is not at liberty to take ſhelter in his own houſe: he is ſtationed in ſome public ſquare, at the gate of a city or temple, or of the tribunal in which he was condemned. When the term of his puniſhment is expired, he is taken before the mandarin, who exhorts him in a friendly manner to amend his life, and, after he has received twenty ſound blows, he diſcharges him.

Other crimes, of an inferior nature to homicide, are puniſhed by baniſhment into Tartary, by condemning the guilty to drag the royal barks for three years, or marking the cheeks with a hot iron.

Robbery between relations is more ſeverely puniſhed than when committed on a ſtranger.

If any one gives information againſt his father, mother, grandfather, grandmother, uncle or eldeſt brother, he is condemned to receive an hundred blows of the *pan tſee*, and to be baniſhed for three years, if the accuſation is juſt: if it prove falſe, he is ſtrangled.

Criminal intercourſe between relations of different ſexes is puniſhed in proportion to the degrees of conſanguinity between them.

Deficiency of duty to a father, mother, grandfather or grandmother, is condemned by the law, and puniſhed by an hundred blows of the *pan-tſee*, if abuſive language is uſed, the offender is ſtrangled, if he lifts his hand againſt them, he is beheaded, and if he wounds or maims them, his fleſh is torn from his bones with red-hot pincers, and he is cut into a thouſand pieces.

If a younger brother abuses his elder, he is condemned to receive an hundred blows of the *pan-tsee*. If he strikes him, he is condemned to exile.

The burying place of every family is sacred, unalienable, and cannot be seized. The trees growing upon it cannot, on pain of death, be cut, except when they are decayed, and even then, not until a mandarin has inspected them, and attested their condition. Robbery of these burying places, even of the smallest of their ornaments, is punishable as sacrilege.

The man who in an accidental quarrel happens to kill his adversary, is strangled without remission. A rope, about six or seven feet in length, with a running noose, is thrown over the criminal's head, a couple of domestics belonging to the tribunal pull it in different directions, then on a sudden quit it, a few moments after, they give a second pull, which generally finishes the business.

In certain parts of China, the operation is performed with a kind of bow. The criminal is placed on his knees, the string of the instrument is put round his neck, which being strongly compressed by the elasticity of the bow, he is instantly strangled when the executioner gives it a smart pull towards him.

Beheading is considered by the Chinese as the most disgraceful of all punishments. It is reserved for the most desperate assassins only, or for those crimes equally atrocious as murder.

To be cut in a thousand pieces. This is a punishment we believe unknown but in China. It is destined for state criminals, rebellious subjects, and children who maim their parents. The criminal is tied to a post, the executioner scalps the skin from his head, and pulls it over his eyes, he afterwards tears the flesh from different parts of his body, and never quits this horrid labour until fatigue renders him unable to proceed. He then abandons what remains of the body to the ferocity of the people, who finish what he has left undone.

Much has been written in Europe against the torturing of criminals, either in the *common* or *extraordinary* manner, and the custom is in general happily suppressed, but they are both practised in China, and even the ordinary torture is extremely severe, it is applied to the feet and hands for the feet an instrument is used which consists of three cross pieces of wood, that in the middle is fixed, the two others turn, and are moveable, the feet of the criminal are put into this machine, which squeezes them so close, that the ancle-bones become flat. The torture applied to the hands appears to be less painful, small pieces of wood are placed diagonally between the fingers of the culprit, his fingers are then firmly tied with cords, and he is suffered to remain for a certain time in that painful situation.

The extraordinary torture is horrid, it consists in making small gashes in the body of the criminal, and tearing off his skin in the form of thongs this punishment is used in cases of treason, or when, the criminal's guilt being clearly proved, it is deemed necessary to compel him to discover his accomplices.

No sentence of death is ever put in execution until it has been approved and confirmed by the emperor A copy of the process is laid before him, a number of other copies are also made out, both in the Chinese and Tartar languages, which the emperor submits to the examination of a like number of doctors, either Tartars or Chinese. When the crime is great, and clearly proved, the emperor writes at the bottom of the sentence, "When you receive "this order, let it be executed without delay" When the crime, though punishable by death according to law, is ranked only in the ordinary class, the emperor writes at the bottom of the sentence, "Let the criminal be de-

"tained in prison, and executed in autumn" The emperor never writes an order for any execution until he has prepared himself by fasting.

This monarch, like all other sovereign princes, has the power of pardoning, but he very seldom uses this prerogative there are, however, some exceptions which law or custom direct him to make, they however are not grounded, as in Europe, on some favourable circumstances in the case, but on some relative situation of the culprit, as should he prove the heir of an ancient family, &c.

A jailor who exercises cruelty and oppression towards his prisoners, a subaltern judge who subjects a criminal to any restraints but those authorised by law, a superior judge who assumes a power of adding to the rigour and severity of the law, are all punished, and their slightest punishment always is to be deposed

In crimes where the punishment is not capital, the near relation of an accused person acknowledged to be guilty, is permitted to put himself in his place, and to undergo the punishment inflicted by the law. F. du Halde cites a case of a son, whose father was condemned to be bastinadoed The young man threw his arms around the body of his father, and with tears begged to be punished in his stead. The mandarin, touched by the noble generosity of the youth, pardoned the criminal: so highly respected is filial piety in China

The relations and friends of all persons accused, whatever their crimes may be, are permitted to visit them in prison, and to give them every assistance in their power they are even encouraged to this, instead of being prevented.

INTERNAL POLICE OF THE CITIES.

Every city in China is divided into different divisions. An officer is appointed for each division, who is answerable for every thing that passes contrary to good order, and if he neglects to make proper inquiry into any irregularity*, or to inform the mandarin governor, he is subjected to the same punishment as those who are refractory.

Every father of a family is obliged to answer for the conduct of his children and domestics, because he is vested with every kind of authority over them, short of life or death

Neighbours are obliged to give every help and assistance in their power to one another, in cases of robbery and fire, especially if these accidents happen in the night-time.

Every city is furnished with gates, and all the streets are barricadoed as soon as night commences Centinels are posted at proper intervals, who stop all those who walk abroad in the night-time, and a number of horsemen are generally stationed on the ramparts, who go the rounds for the same purpose Seldom, however, do people of any character expose themselves to the danger of falling into the hands of the police *Night*, say the Chinese magistrates, *is designed for repose, and the day for labour*

Watch is likewise kept in the day-time at every city, to observe those who enter for this purpose a guard is stationed at each gate, passengers are carefully examined, and if they are discovered to be strangers, they are immediately carried before a mandarin, and often detained until the will of the governor is known

The backwardness of the Chinese to admit strangers among them, arises from a supposition, that in process of time, an alteration of manners, customs, and ceremonies, might result from such an intercourse, and give birth to quarrels, party disputes, and sedition, and at length overturn the government.

When, to revenge an insult, a quarrel takes place, each throws aside the stick, or whatever other weapon he may have in his hand, and they decide it with their fists only, but they frequently go before a mandarin, and beg him to settle the dispute for them The magistrate, after having examined into the merits of the case, orders the most culpable to receive a sound bastinading, and sometimes even both of them

None but military people are permitted to wear arms in public, and those only during actual war: at other times they must appear like plain citizens, except when they attend a review, mount guard, or accompany a mandarin Prostitutes are not permitted to remain within the walls of any city, but they may reside in the suburbs, though they must not keep a house of their own. Some individual is expressly authorised to afford them lodging; he must watch over and observe their conduct, and if there arises any noise or quarrel in his house, he alone is responsible, and punished for it

Every city of China, and sometimes even an ordinary town, has an establishment, called by the Chinese *Tang-pou*, where money may be immediately borrowed upon pledges No preliminaries are necessary, the transaction is concealed, and the borrower may remain unknown. If he chooses to tell his name, it is written down, if he does not, no further questions are asked him. Those who belong to these offices take an exact description, when the case requires it, of the figure of the person, that they may be able, in any event, to give an account to the police.

The usual interest of money in China is said to be thirty per cent. which is a proof that coin is very scarce At this rate money may be borrowed at the Tang-pou. Every pledge is marked with a number when left at the office, and the office must be answerable for it, but it is forfeited the very day after the term mentioned in the note of agreement is expired.

Every diversion that tends to promote or encourage idleness, is absolutely forbidden to young people, and almost the whole of their time is devoted to ſtudy. Such a mode of education would no doubt be highly diſguſting to our youth in Europe, but in a country where merit alone conducts to dignity and honour, and where ignorance is neglected and deſpiſed, encouragement overcomes diſguſt, and no application is conſidered as a hardſhip.

GENERAL POLICE

The roads are in general very broad, they are paved in all the ſouthern, and in ſome of the northern provinces. Valleys have been filled up, and paſſages have been cut through rocks and mountains, in order to make highways, and to preſerve them as nearly as poſſible on a level. They are frequently bordered with very lofty trees, and ſometimes with walls eight or ten feet in height, in which openings are left at certain intervals, which give a paſſage into croſs roads. On all the great roads covered ſeats are erected at proper diſtances, where the traveller may ſhelter himſelf from the inclemency of winter, or the heats of ſummer, which are often exceſſive. Temples and pagodas are alſo frequently to be met with, to which admittance is always granted in the day-time, though often refuſed in the night, the mandarins only having the right of reſting in them as long as they think proper.

The inns are ſpacious and ſufficiently numerous on the principal roads, but they are badly ſupplied with proviſions, and paſſengers who have no beds with them muſt ſleep on a plain mat.

The Chineſe government has publiſhed an itinerary of the whole Chineſe empire, which comprehends every road and canal from the city of Pe-kin to the remoteſt extremities of China.

On all the great roads there are towers, on the tops of which watch-boxes are conſtructed for the convenience of centinels, and flag-ſtaffs raiſed in order that they may make certain signals in case of any alarm. These towers, which are square, and generally built of brick, seldom exceed twelve feet in height. They, however, have battlements when they are built upon any of the roads which conduct to court, and they are also provided with very large bells of cast iron They serve also as post-houses, and the soldiers convey the letters on horseback from one to the other, guarded by six other horse soldiers.

Conveyance of every kind is easy in China, and travellers find little difficulty in getting their baggage transported from one place to another. In every city there are numbers of porters associated under a common chief, who regulates their engagements, fixes the price of their labour, receives their hire, and is responsible for every thing they carry. When porters are wanted, he furnishes as many as may be necessary, and gives the same number of tickets to the traveller, who returns one to each porter, when their work is done These tickets they deliver to their chief, who immediately pays them from the money he received in advance.

This establishment is directed by the general police of the empire On all the great roads the traveller finds in every city several offices of this kind, that have a settled correspondence with the next through which he intends to pursue his route Before his departure, he carries to one of these offices a list of those things he wants removed, which is immediately inscribed in a book, and if he has occasion for two, three, or four hundred porters, he immediately obtains them Every thing is weighed by the chief, and the hire is five-pence per hundred weight for one day's carriage An exact register of every article is kept in the office, and the traveller pays the money in advance, after which he has no occasion to give himself any trouble, on his arrival at the next city he finds his baggage at the correſponding office, where it is delivered to him with the moſt ſcrupulous fidelity.

The police alſo regulates the cuſtom-houſes, becauſe every thing is managed on the emperor's account. The officers belonging to theſe cuſtom-houſes are exceedingly civil they have no concern with any claſs of people but merchants, whom they never diſtreſs by rigorous exactions. Travellers are not ſtopt here until their baggage is examined, although the officers are authoriſed to do ſo, nor is the ſmalleſt fee required from them

Duties are paid, either by the piece, or by the load in the former caſe, credit is given to the merchant's book, and no further inquiry is made.

FINANCES

The greater part of the taxes in China are paid in commodities Thoſe who breed ſilk-worms pay their taxes in ſilk, the huſbandmen in grain, and the gardeners in fruits, &c

This mode of impoſing taxes is far from detrimental to the government, as in every province there are in its ſervice numbers of mandarins, officers, ſoldiers, and penſioners of different kinds, who are furniſhed with every neceſſary for food and clothing, ſo that the articles collected as taxes, are nearly all conſumed in thoſe provinces in which they are levied If any thing remains, it is ſold on the account of the emperor, and the amount is depoſited in the imperial treaſury

The taxes paid in money, ariſe principally from the ſale of ſalt, which belongs excluſively to the emperor, from the duties paid by veſſels on entering any of the ports, from the cuſtoms and other impoſts on various branches of manufacture. Theſe excepted, the trader contributes little towards the exigencies of the ſtate, and the mechanic ſtill leſs The weight of the permanent and perſonal taxes therefore falls on the huſbandman

Besides the consumption in each district for discharging the ordinary expences of government, a reserve is made to answer accidental demands A proper statement of taxes paid in the provinces, of what is reserved in the different cities, or contained in the principal treasuries of the empire, is submitted annually to the examination of the grand tribunal of finances, which revises the whole and keeps an account of what is consumed, and of whatever surplus may be left

The emperor's revenue amounts to more than forty-one millions sterling, which might be easily increased by new impositions, but the Chinese emperors seldom exercise this privilege They seem to consider it the principal glory of a prince, to be sparing of the property of his subjects, and to provide for the exigencies of the state, if possible, without having recourse to so disagreeable an expedient.

The annual expences of government are immense; and the emperor directs them as he thinks proper · these expences, however, are regulated in such a manner as never to be augmented but in cases of the utmost necessity Indeed, administration often makes great savings, which serves to increase the general treasure of the empire, and prevents the imposition of new taxes when war becomes unavoidable, or unforeseen calamities desolate the empire.

The current coin of China consists only of one kind; it is denominated a caxee, and is made of copper. It is of a round figure, and about nine-tenths of an inch in diameter, has a small square hole in the middle, and is inscribed with two Chinese words on the one side, and two Tartar words on the other. In some of the provinces it is made of that white copper we have before mentioned.

Silver has no proper figure, its value is regulated by weight only.

The Chinese government does not think that gold or silver money add to the richness of a state. China contains many mines of gold and silver, few, however, are permitted to be opened, but those of iron, copper, tin, and lead are worked, as their productions are judged necessary and useful.

With respect to commerce, the Chinese entertain an opinion that it is useful only so far as it eases them of their superfluities, and procures them necessaries on this account, they consider even that which they carry on at Canton as prejudicial to the interests of the empire "*They take from us,*" say they, "*our silks, teas, and our* "*porcelain the price of these articles is raised through* "*all the provinces, such a trade, therefore, cannot be* "*beneficial. The money brought us by Europeans, and* "*the high-priced baubles which accompany it, are mere* "*superfluities to such a state as ours We have no occasion* "*for more bullion than what may be necessary to answer* "*the exigencies of government, and to supply the relative* "*wants of individuals.*"

The only commerce which the Chinese consider of any advantage, is that which they keep up with Tartary and Russia, as it furnishes them, by barter, with those furs so much used in all the northern provinces

The disputes between the Russians and Chinese, concerning the limits of their respective empires, seem to have first paved the way for that commercial intercourse which has subsisted between them since the peace concluded in 1689 This treaty was signed on the 27th of August of the above year, under the reign of Ivan and Peter Alexiovitz. The chief of the embassy on the part of Russia was Golovin, governor of Siberia. Two Jesuits, *Pereira* and *Gerbillon* (the former a native of Portugal, the latter of France), were deputed by the emperor of China; and the conferences were held in Latin, with a German in the Russian ambassador's train, who was acquainted with that language. By this treaty the Russians lost a large territory, besides the navigation of the river Amoor, called by the Mantchew Tartars, *Saghalien-oula*;

but, in return, they obtained what they had long desired, a regular and permanent trade with the Chinese. The first intercourse between Russia and China commenced in the beginning of the seventeenth century, at which period a small quantity of Chinese merchandize was procured by some Russian merchants from the Kalmouck Tartars. The rapid and profitable sale of these commodities encouraged certain wayvedes of Siberia to attempt a direct and open communication with China. For this purpose several persons were at different times deputed to Pe-kin, and, though they failed of obtaining the grant of a regular commerce, their attempts were, however, attended with some important consequences The general good reception which the agents met with, tempted the Russian merchants to send occasional traders to Pe-kin. By these means, a faint connection was preserved with that metropolis The Chinese learned the advantages arising from the Russian trade, and were soon prepared for its subsequent establishment This commerce, carried on by intervals, was entirely suspended by the hostilities on the river Amoor, but, after the treaty of 1689 (in which both sides swore eternal peace, and prayed, that *the Lord, the Sovereign of All Things, might punish those, by a sudden death, who should first think of rekindling the flames of war)*, the Russians engaged with uncommon alacrity in their favourite branch of traffic. The advantages arising from it were soon found to be so considerable, that Peter I. formed a design of still farther enlarging it. For this purpose, in 1692, he dispatched to Pe-kin *Isbrand Ides*, a native of the dutchy of Holstein, then in his service, who requested, and obtained, that the liberty of trading to China, which, by the late treaty, had been granted to individuals, might be extended to caravans

After this arrangement, caravans went regularly from Russia to Pe-kin, where a caravansary was allotted for their reception, and all their expences, during their continuance in that metropolis, were defrayed by the emperor of China. The right of sending these caravans, and the profits arising from them belonged to the crown of Russia. In the mean time, private merchants continued, as before, to carry on a separate trade with the Chinese, not only at Pe-kin, but also at the head quarters of the Moguls. The camp of these roving Tartars was generally stationed near the confluence of the Orhon and Toula, between the southern frontiers of Siberia and the Mogul desert. A kind of annual fair was held at this spot, by the Russian and Chinese merchants, who brought their respective commodities for sale. This rendezvous soon became a scene of riot and confusion, and repeated complaints of the drunkenness and misconduct of the Russians were transmitted to the Emperor of China. *Kang-hi*, exasperated by these complaints, and by the frequent representations of his subjects, threatened to expel the Russians from his dominions, and to prohibit them from carrying on any commerce, either in China, or in the country of the Moguls. This circumstance occasioned another embassy to Pe-kin in the year 1719. Capt. Ismailof, the ambassador who was deputed to accommodate matters, succeeded in his negociation: he adjusted every difficulty, to the satisfaction of both parties, and, on his departure, Laurence Lange was permitted to remain at Pe-kin, for the purpose of superintending the conduct of the Russians. The residence of this gentleman in that metropolis was, however, but short, for he was soon after compelled to leave China and return. His dismission was owing partly to a sudden caprice of the Chinese, and partly to a misunderstanding between the two courts, respecting some Mogul tribes who bordered upon Siberia. These tribes had thrown themselves under the protection of Russia, and were demanded by the Chinese. Their request was not complied with, and this refusal, added to the disorderly conduct of the Russians, who again began to indulge themſelves in their exceſſes, ſo exaſperated the Chineſe, that an order was iſſued, in 1722, for their expulſion, and all intercourſe between the two nations immediately ceaſed.

Affairs continued in this ſtate till 1727, when a Dalmatian, in the ſervice of Ruſſia, was diſpatched to Pe-kin. Matters were again accommodated by a new treaty, a caravan was allowed to go to Pe-kin every three years, provided it conſiſted of no more than an hundred perſons; and that, during their ſtay, their expences ſhould be no longer defrayed by the emperor of China A permiſſion was at the ſame time obtained by the Ruſſians for building a church within the precincts of their caravanſary; and, for the celebration of divine ſervice, four prieſts were allowed to reſide at Pe-kin. The ſame favour was alſo extended to ſome Ruſſian ſcholars, for the purpoſe of learning the Chineſe language, in order to qualify themſelves for interpreters between the two nations.

This treaty was concluded on the ſpot where Kiatka now ſtands, by Count Raguſinſki, and three Chineſe plenipotentiaries, on the 14th of June 1728 It is the baſis upon which all the ſubſequent tranſactions between Ruſſia and China have been founded.

Since the year 1755, no caravans have been ſent to Pe-kin, Their firſt diſcontinuance was occaſioned by a miſunderſtanding between the two courts of Peterſburgh and Pe-kin, and, though a reconciliation afterwards took place, they have never ſince been re-eſtabliſhed. The preſent Empreſs of Ruſſia, ſenſible that the monopoly of the fur-trade, which was entirely confined to the caravans belonging to the crown, and prohibited to individuals, was prejudicial to commerce, in 1762 wiſely gave up, in favour of her ſubjects, the excluſive privilege which the crown enjoyed, of ſending caravans to Pe-kin; and Kiatka, a place near the Ruſſian frontiers, is now the centre of commerce between the two nations.

This commerce is entirely a trade of barter. The Ruſſians are prohibited to export their own coin, and they find it more advantageous to take goods in exchange, than to receive bullion at the Chineſe ſtandard. The principal commodities which Ruſſia exports to China are furs of different kinds, the moſt valuable of which are thoſe of ſea otters, beavers, foxes, wolves, martens, ſables and ermines. The greater part of theſe ſkins are brought from Siberia and the newly-diſcovered iſlands; but, as they cannot furniſh a ſupply equal to the demand, foreign furs are imported to Peterſburgh, and thence tranſported to Kiatka. England alone furniſhes a large quantity of beavers and other ſkins, chiefly procured from the American ſettlements. According to Mr. Coxe, the number of ſkins exported to Peterſburgh in the year 1777, amounted to twenty-ſeven thouſand three hundred and ſixteen beavers, and ten thouſand ſeven hundred and three otter ſkins. The Ruſſians alſo ſend to China cloth of various kinds, hardware, and live cattle, ſuch as camels, horſes, &c. The commodities procured from China are raw and manufactured ſilk, cotton, porcelain of all ſorts, rhubarb, muſk, &c. The government of Ruſſia has reſerved to itſelf the excluſive privilege of purchaſing rhubarb: it is brought to Kiatka by ſome Bucharian merchants, who have entered into a contract to ſupply the crown with it in exchange for furs. The exportation of the beſt rhubarb is prohibited by the Chineſe, under the ſevereſt penalties: it is, however, procured in ſufficient quantities, ſometimes by clandeſtinely mixing it with inferior roots, and ſometimes by means of a contraband trade. Great part of Europe is ſupplied with this drug from Ruſſia.

INTERIOR ADMINISTRATION.

In this vaſt empire there is kept a regiſter or general enumeration of all the people by families, diſtricts, and provinces, comprehending every individual without regard to age, sex, or rank. Besides this, there is a second, which is partial, containing only the lower classes of people, from sixteen to fifty. This last roll serves to regulate every thing relating to vassalage, to facilitate public surveys, and to assist the operations of the police, &c. By means of these registers, a speedy and certain method is always found of ascertaining the situation of families or individuals in all circumstances, in which government or private persons may be interested. They also enable the government to judge what number of people have perished by inundations, earthquakes, or epidemical distempers, to determine what succours are necessary in years of scarcity, to know the state of agriculture, how far manufactures can be extended, and what number of military people each canton can furnish. The government has also an accurate and minute account of all the lands in each district, of their different degrees of fertility, and what is cultivated in them.

Public magazines and granaries, furnished with every kind of provision necessary for relieving the distresses of the people, in case of public calamities or unforeseen disasters, are erected in the different provinces. Administration are always provided against every event, and as they are acquainted with the minutest expence necessary to be incurred, every thing is done in proper season with dignity, and without embarrassment. Every measure is carried into execution with the consent of the emperor. Memorials are presented to him by the different tribunals, in which they propose plans for promoting the happiness of the people and the welfare of the state, and he receives or rejects them as he thinks proper. These tribunals are entrusted with the execution of those schemes which are approved, they keep an exact account of the money expended, and lay their documents, properly attested, before him. Legal formality is closely adhered to in all tranfactions, and a watchful eye is kept over every department of the ftate

The Chinefe government determines, in the minuteft manner, the drefs for each feafon, and likewife the price of thofe dreffes for every age and condition. The emperor himfelf is not excepted in thefe regulations his dreffes of ceremony are more or lefs fumptuous according to the religious, political, or domeftic ceremonies for which he ufes them. The particular drefs for each clafs is fo accurately defcribed in the fumptuary code, as to diftinguifh, on the firft view, the rank and condition of thofe who wear it.

Of palaces the emperor has a great number Each capital of a province contains one, which is made the refidence of the viceroy There are fome alfo in cities of inferior note, which are appropriated for the ufe of thofe mandarins who enjoy places under government.

Bridges have been multiplied in China in proportion to the number of its canals and rivers they confift of three, five, or feven arches, the centre is from thirty to forty feet wide, and raifed very high, that barks may eafily pafs without lowering their mafts.

The utility of canals muft be great in countries where cultivation is carried to its utmoft extent, as is the cafe in China, and it enjoys the advantage of having a greater number of navigable canals than any other country. Thefe canals are from twenty to thirty yards in breadth, and generally bordered with cut ftone, which has the appearance of flate-coloured marble.

The expence of conftructing and repairing thefe canals is defrayed by government, which thus affords each province the ready means of tranfporting its fuperfluities to another, and of receiving in return a fupply of fuch commodities as it may want

Agriculture is the principal refource of the Chinefe, who confider it as the firft and moft honourable of all profeffions.

The people are allowed to use a portion of the grain of every crop, for the purposes of brewing and distillation, but if the harvest happens to be bad, an order is issued for the suspension of these operations

The Chinese emperors do not confine themselves to the publishing of regulations respecting agriculture, but they encourage it by their own example, of this the celebrated ceremony, in which the emperor tills the earth with his own hands, has been often mentioned, and may be considered as a proof This ceremony is as follows

Spring begins in China always in the month of February, but not regularly on the same day This epocha is determined by the tribunal of Mathematics That of Ceremonies announces it to the emperor by a memorial, in which every thing necessary to be done by the prince on that occasion is mentioned with the most scrupulous minuteness He first names twelve of the most illustrious persons in his court to accompany him, and to hold the plow after he has performed his part of the ceremony. These are always three princes of the blood, and nine presidents of supreme courts The places of those who are too old or infirm to undergo this labour may be supplied by their assessors, but they must always be authorised by the emperor.

This festival is preceded by a sacrifice which the sovereign offers up to the *Chang-ti*, or Supreme Being. The emperor prepares himself by three days fasting, and those who are to attend him submit to the same regulations Others are appointed by the emperor on the evening before the ceremony, to prostrate themselves at the sepulchre of his ancestors, and to acquaint them that on the day following he intends to celebrate a grand sacrifice

The place where the emperor offers up the spring sacrifice, is a small mount, a few furlongs distant from the city, fifty feet in height this elevation is expressly prescribed by the rules of the ceremony, and cannot be dispensed with. The emperor, who sacrifices under the title of sovereign pontiff, invokes the *Chang-ti*, and prays for abundance in favour of his people. He then descends, accompanied by the princes and presidents, who are to put their hands to the plow along with him. The field set apart for this purpose is at a small distance from the mount. Forty labourers are selected to yoke the oxen, and to prepare the seeds which the emperor must sow. These seeds are of five different kinds, and such as are considered as the most useful and necessary, viz. wheat, rice, millet, beans, and another species of millet, called by the Chinese *Cao-leang*. These are brought to the spot in magnificent boxes, carried by persons of the most distinguished rank.

The emperor takes hold of the plow, and turns up several furrows. The princes do the same in succession, and after them the presidents. The sovereign then throws into the earth the five kinds of seed before mentioned, after which four pieces of cotton cloth, proper for making dresses, are distributed to each of the labourers who assisted in yoking the oxen, and who prepared the seeds. The same present is made to forty other persons, more advanced in years, who have been only spectators of the ceremony. This ceremony certainly flatters the minds of the labouring people, and greatly contributes to encourage their industry.

We cannot judge of the Chinese peasantry from those of Europe, especially in what relates to the advantages acquired by education. Free schools are very numerous in every province of China, and many of the villages are not destitute of this advantage. The sons of the poor are there received as readily as those of the rich, and their duties and studies are the same; the attention of the masters is equally divided between them; and from the most obscure sources talents often spring, which afterwards make a conspicuous figure on the grand stage of life. Indeed, nothing is more common in China, than to ſee the ſon of a peaſant, governor of that province in which his father long toiled, in cultivating only a few acres.

The Chineſe have been greatly reproached for their inhumanity in murdering and expoſing their children. And though neither the one nor the other is authoriſed by any law, both, and particularly the latter, are ſanctioned by circumſtances; but theſe melancholy ſcenes are however much leſs frequent than has been reported in Europe.

The crime of murdering children, in China, is moſt commonly owing to the fanaticiſm of idolatry—a fanaticiſm which prevails only among the loweſt of the people, and is in obedience to the oracle of a bonze, to deliver themſelves from the power of magic ſpells, or to diſcharge a vow. Theſe infatuated wretches then precipitate their children into the river, by which they imagine they make an expiatory ſacrifice to the ſpirit of the river.

It frequently happens that the bodies of children which are ſeen floating on the water, have not been thrown into it till after their death; and the ſame likewiſe is the caſe with many of thoſe found in the ſtreets, or lying near the public roads. This has given occaſion to think the crime of murder more common than it is. The poverty of the parents ſuggeſts this ſtep, becauſe their children are then buried at the expence of the police.

With reſpect to thoſe children who are expoſed alive, government employs as much vigilance to have them carried away, as it beſtows care on their education. This certainly is tolerating the cuſtom, and giving people intimation to expoſe their children in the night time, and, no doubt, encourages the practice; but the dictates of humanity ſeem here to be united with thoſe of policy.

Nothing is neglected in China that has any relation to government, and adminiſtration conſiders even the gazette as an eſſential part of the political conſtitution. This gazette is printed daily at Pe-kin, and is circulated throughout every province of the empire. It contains an account of all those objects to which the attention of administration is directed, and administration are remiss in nothing; they enter into the minutest details, grant succour in proper season, reward with liberality, and punish with justice. Nothing is inserted in this gazette which has not been submitted to the emperor, or which has not come immediately from him; and inevitable death would be the consequence to any one who should insert any thing false in this ministerial paper.

No law or sentence is of any force until the emperor's seal is affixed to it. This seal is about eight inches square, of fine jasper, a kind of precious stone highly valued in China. The sovereign only is entitled to have a seal of this substance. Those which he gives to princes are made of gold; those of the viceroys and great mandarins, of silver; and those of inferior mandarins or magistrates must be made of lead or copper; and their size is larger or smaller, according to the rank which they hold as mandarins, or in the tribunals.

The authority of inspectors sent into any of the provinces, is confirmed also by the seal of the emperor. The duty of these deputies is to examine into the conduct of governors, magistrates, and private individuals; and if any of them think it his duty to summon the viceroy before his tribunal—this great man, with all his importance, is obliged to attend. Has a superior behaved ill to an inferior magistrate—the former becomes the prisoner of the inspector; and, until he has cleared himself from every imputation, he is suspended from his office. The viceroy, on the contrary, is permitted to enjoy his, until the inspector's report is made to the emperor, which generally decides his fate.

The emperor himself sometimes thinks proper to discharge the duty of these inspectors in some of the provinces; and *Kang-hi*, one of the most celebrated of the

Chineſe monarchs, gave, in the like circumſtance, a memorable example of ſevere juſtice. Having retired a little way from his attendants, he perceived an old man weeping bitterly. 'What do you weep for?' ſaid the emperor. 'My lord,' replied the old man, who did not know the perſon of his ſovereign, 'I had only one ſon, in whom 'all my hopes were centered, and who might have become 'the ſupport of my family, a Tartar mandarin has torn 'him from me, and carried him away by force. I am 'now deprived of every aſſiſtance, and know not where 'to ſeek relief, for how can a poor feeble old man like 'me obtain juſtice from the governor againſt a power'ful man?'—'Your ſon will be reſtored,' ſaid the emperor, without making himſelf known;—'conduct me to 'the houſe of the mandarin who has been guilty of this 'act of violence.' The old man obeyed, and after having travelled two hours, they arrived at the mandarin's houſe, who little expected ſuch a viſit.

The emperor's retinue arrived almoſt at the ſame time as the prince, and the houſe of the mandarin was ſoon filled and ſurrounded. As he could not deny his guilt, the emperor immediately condemned him to loſe his head; and this ſentence was executed upon the ſpot. The emperor then turning towards the old man, with a grave tone, addreſſed him thus: 'I appoint you to the office 'of the criminal whom I have now put to death; be care'ful to diſcharge the duties of it with more moderation 'than your predeceſſor, and take warning by his crime 'and puniſhment, leſt you yourſelf become an example 'to others.'

The viceroy of a province is diſtinguiſhed by the title of *Tſong-tou*, and poſſeſſes in his diſtrict a power almoſt unlimited. When he goes round the province to diſcharge the duties of his office, his retinue diſplays imperial pomp and magnificence, and he never quits his palace without a guard of an hundred men. He is receiver-general of the taxes collected in his province, which he transmits to the capital after reserving what is necessary for the wants of the province. All law-suits must be brought before his tribunal, and he has the power of condemning criminals to death: but neither his sentence, nor those of the criminal court, can be executed until they have been confirmed and approved by the emperor.

Every *Hien* or bailiwick is under the inspection of a mandarin, whose business is to administer justice, to settle any differences that may arise between individuals, and to inflict punishment on those who are in the wrong. He receives also the tribute which each family pays to the emperor.

Every three years the viceroy sends to court a report of the conduct and behaviour of the mandarins subordinate to him. This report determines their fate; according to its contents, they are either continued or disgraced.

Those of whose conduct he makes an unfavourable report, are punished in proportion to their delinquency, and rewards are bestowed, according to the same rule, on those who have been mentioned in favourable terms.

A singular regulation exists with respect to degraded mandarins in China; every mandarin who is removed to an inferior office, is obliged, at the head of all those precepts or commands which he issues, to mention the number of steps he has lost, as follows: 'I, such a mandarin, degraded 'three, four, or six steps, *according as the case may be*, 'order and command,' &c.

The inspector of a province has a very extensive authority over these inferior mandarins. He can, by his own power, deprive them of their employments, if their offence be great; and he only consults the court in cases where immediate punishment is not necessary.

The father, son, brother, uncle, and grandson, are never admitted together into any of the tribunals at Pekin; and relations in the fourth degree cannot have a seat at the same time in any of the provincial tribunals.

All mandarins, whether Tartars or Chinese, of arms, or of letters, are obliged, every three years, to give in an exact account of the faults they have committed in discharging the duties of their office. This confession is examined at court, if it comes from a mandarin belonging to any of the four first classes; but the confessions of the mandarins in the lower classes, must be laid before the provincial tribunal of the governor. Government also makes private inquiry to discover whether in this confession strict regard has been paid to truth.

These informations are addressed to the Tribunal of Mandarins, and are there carefully examined; the merits and demerits are carefully weighed in the balance of justice, and the names of the examined mandarins are afterwards formed into three classes. The first consisting of those for whom rewards and preferment are intended; the second, of those whose conduct deserves reprehension, and to whom gentle admonition, accompanied with a few oblique hints respecting their future conduct, will be given; and the third of those whom it is intended to suspend for a certain time, or to remove for ever from their employments.

We have already given an account of the war establishments, and military discipline of China. We shall, however, add a few words on that subject as far as it relates to the interference of government. Nothing is neglected by administration that can tend to excite emulation among the troops, or engage them to respect the civil laws.

A great part of the Tartar families are lodged in barracks, erected in the suburbs of Pe-kin, or in the adjacent country, where every common soldier is allowed a separate apartment for the use of his family; and there are houses for the officers, suited to their rank, and even public schools, where the Tartar youth receive a proper education.

The principal military offices are held by Tartars: this precaution is taken to maintain their conquest, independent of the superiority which they have over the Chinese, in point of warlike genius In times of war an exact journal is kept of every military transaction, and those are particularly mentioned, who have given proofs of remarkable courage, or displayed examples of superior skill Promotion is the consequence to those who have signalized themselves, if they survive, if not, the rewards which they have merited are conferred on their widows, children, or brothers Neither the father of a numerous family, an only son, nor the son of an aged widow, is obliged to perform military service, unless the state be in great danger, or in cases of the most urgent necessity Government then advances money to those who enlist, they also receive double pay, the first for themselves, and the second for their family and this they enjoy till their return

That esteem in which military men are held in time of danger, seems, in China, to cease, almost the instant that the danger is over On these occasions government bestows, with a lavish hand, contributions, rewards, and honours of every kind and it extends its favours to the lowest military class. Does a common horse or foot soldier fall in battle, his hat, his boots, or his sabre, is transmitted to his family, to be interred, instead of his body, in the sepulchre of his ancestors. An eulogium, suited to what he has atchieved, is added, to be engraven on the tomb in which these are deposited A full [illegible] share of attention is [illegible] to those who have fallen in defence of their [illegible] their [illegible] honour, their ashes, their [illegible], or their bodies, [illegible] conveyed to their [illegible] the manner in which [illegible] generally serves as a rule [illegible] performed in common [illegible] extended to others [illegible] officer, or the lowest common soldier [illegible] to the [illegible] of a thoufand or fifteen hundred leagues. The latter, as well as the former, is mentioned with honour in the Gazette: his name thus paffes before the eyes of the public, and thence into the General Hiftory of the empire

The degradation, or difmiffion of a fuperior officer in China, can neither fix a ftigma on the character of his fon, nor in the leaft impede his promotion. When the fon is afked by the emperor refpecting his family, he will reply, coolly—*My father was difgraced for a certain offence; my grandfather was beheaded for fuch a crime;* and yet, this acknowledgement is not in the leaft detrimental to the perfon who makes it.

We have already had occafion to mention in this work, the princes of the blood in China, and as Europeans may form very falfe ideas refpecting their fituation, credit and influence in adminiftration, we fhall offer a few additional remarks. All their privileges confift in certain rights of reprefentation, and in being tried by their peers only. They cannot depend upon that diftinction which is conferred by riches, or annexed to place. Every thing in this methodical empire is fubmitted to an examination. The yellow girdle only is what thefe princes inherit by birth, and this right belongs only to thofe who are defcended in a right line from the reigning dynafty. The names of their children, whether girls or boys, the year, month and day of their birth, are infcribed in a large yellow book, particularly appropriated for this purpofe An orange girdle is the diftinguifhing mark of collateral princes; and the names of their children are regiftered in a red book. The emperor alone determines the furnames of princes of the reigning branch

When the princes and princeffes of the laft clafs have attained to the age of fifteen, they prefent a petition to the emperor, requefting permiffion to marry. Princes of the direct line may omit this formula, but if they are defirous of being connected by marriage with any of the

Mogul or Kalka princes, they must first obtain the emperor's consent.

The rank even of the emperor's sons, except of his immediate successor, diminishes one degree every generation. At the seventh, the eldest of these branches only has a title to wear the yellow girdle, the rest find themselves sunk to the rank of plain citizens.

An hereditary sovereignty passes, with all its rights, from one eldest son to another, unless the possessor forfeits his title by being guilty of some crime. In such a case, the emperor appoints to the succession, either one of his younger brothers, or a cousin, but these must be chosen from the same branch, as the lawful branch cannot be deprived of this right, unless all those are condemned who compose it.

The only hereditary authority of the other princes exists among the troops called the Tartar bands, where they enjoy that rank which they derive from their birth. In every thing else, they are on a level with others, at stated periods, they are subjected to a military examination, and they are always promoted or degraded, according to their knowledge and skill. The heir apparent, and the princes, his sons, undergo the same trial, with this only distinction, schools are established for their use only, and their literary and military examinations are made before their own masters. After these examinations, of which an exact register is kept, they are promoted, as opportunity offers, to offices of greater or less importance, according to the genius and abilities which they have displayed.

There are particular titles and degrees of rank which belong to the imperial family only, but the law has prescribed the age at which they may be enjoyed, and the manner in which they must be obtained when claimed by birth right, as the recompence of merit, or when sought for by interest.

The title of prince does not convey to those who enjoy it, a right of sitting in any tribunal: on the other hand, as we have before observed, princes cannot be tried but by a tribunal established entirely for themselves Neither their criminal nor civil affairs can be brought before any other court but the *Tsong-gin-fou*, or Tribunal of Princes. Whoever insults any prince of the imperial family, who is decorated with the yellow girdle, is put to death without remission. But this is not the case if the prince has omitted or neglected to put on his yellow girdle: the affair then becomes a case between citizen and citizen, and the aggressor escapes with a bastinading. A prince is, however, never exposed to this disgrace, even after he has been condemned by his tribunal, for he can commute corporeal punishment for a fine, and sentence of death passed against him, cannot be put in execution until the emperor's consent is obtained.

The privileges of untitled princes are much less extensive. The general police has almost the same authority over them as over every other citizen. it may reprimand and admonish them, and even commit them to prison. If they are brought before its tribunal to be tried, they are treated with the utmost rigour, and no sum of money, however great, can exempt them from punishment.

Thus have we briefly sketched the nature, policy, and administration of the Chinese government, a government which has existed through ages, for the new masters of China made no change they adopted the ancient form, and it still subsists. The Tartar conquerors submitted to the laws and customs of the conquered, and were contented with reforming abuses, which had insensibly crept in, and which a wise government can neither tolerate nor permit. China, therefore, appears to have gained much by a revolution which seemed likely to occasion its ruin.

The Tartars have never yet given any but emperors worthy of governing this immense empire, and emperors who have always governed it by themselves. Whatever faults are discovered, are not, therefore, to be imputed to the Emperors, but to the system of government itself, which we may venture to pronounce radically bad, for such all governments must be that are not in the hands of the people themselves These princes bestow more care and attention on the Chinese than on their natural subjects If a dispute arises between a Chinese and a Tartar, the former must have greatly deviated from the rules of justice, if he is not found to be in the right, even by the tribunals, which are all composed of half Chinese and half Tartars. This policy is easily comprehended, but nevertheless it displays prudence and wisdom. The slightest fault committed by a Tartar mandarin is severely punished, but the punishment of the greatest is often mitigated, if the delinquent be a Chinese It is among the Tartars, in particular, that government endeavours to encourage a taste for arms, keep up discipline, and excite a military spirit. An officer of that nation is sure to be punished if he in the least neglects his duty; however small his offence may be, he is always dismissed. A Chinese officer may be forgiven, but a Tartar is never pardoned.

It will appear evident to the reader, that every person in China who holds a place under government, whether in the civil or military department, always imagines that he sees a sword suspended over his head. He cannot foresee his destiny even when cited before the emperor s tribunal The time, particular circumstances, or the necessity there may be of making an example, sometimes all concur to render his punishment inevitable.

The faults punished with greatest severity are those which wound the interests of the people. they therefore seldom fall a prey to that class of petty tyrants, who, if not narrowly watched, might gradually desolate the empire. Every great mandarin is responsible for the faults committed by his subalterns, he is the inspector who watches over their conduct, and as we may say their surety; he would be punished for their faults, did he neglect to inform himself of them, or to expose them.

The literati are always honoured and esteemed: they enjoy every privilege and distinction annexed to that title; but government checks their pride, and encourages their labours. The severity of their examinations will prevent this class from multiplying too much, it will be less numerous, but more learned and useful.

The Tartar government bestows more care and attention on this class of people, than on any other. No commotion, however small, no insurrection, however slight, remains unpunished, and the mandarin who has occasioned it, or who did not endeavour to prevent it, is treated with still greater severity. In a word, the present government is so rigid towards the great, and so mild and friendly to the people, that it is doubtful if they would not be as much afraid of losing their new masters, as their new masters would be of losing them.

GENERAL VIEW

OF THE

RELIGION OF THE CHINESE.

TO judge properly of the religious ſyſtem of the Chineſe, the ancient and permanent religion of the ſtate muſt not be confounded with popular ſuperſtitions introduced in latter ages The primitive worſhip of the ancient Chineſe has continued invariably the ſame, even to the preſent time This doctrine of the early ages has experienced no change from a long ſucceſſion of years, political revolutions, nor the fantaſtical dreams of philoſophers, it is at preſent the only religion avowed by government, followed by the emperor, grandees, and literati, and authoriſed to be publicly taught We ſhall therefore firſt collect thoſe ſcattered opinions neceſſary to convey an idea of it to our readers, and afterwards give a detail of the modern ſects.

ANCIENT RELIGION OF CHINA

Father Amiot, an able judge of the literature, hiſtory, and ancient monuments of China, gives, in the following words, the reſult of his long and laborious reſearches reſpecting the origin of the Chineſe, and of their primitive religion

"The Chinese are a distinct people, who have preserved "the characteristic marks of their first origin; a people "whose primitive doctrine will be found to agree in its "essential parts with the doctrine of the chosen people, "before Moses, by the command of God himself, had "consigned the explanation of it to the sacred records; "a people whose traditional knowledge, when freed from "whatever the ignorance or superstition of latter ages has "added to it, may be traced back from age to age, "without interruption, even to the renewal of the human "race by the grandson of Noah."

We have indeed every historical probability to support us in believing, that the colony which first peopled China was composed of the immediate descendants of Noah. Full of respect for that distinguished patriarch, whom they considered as their common chief or head, they must have carried along with them the paternal instructions they received from his mouth, his precepts respecting the belief and religious worship which prevailed at that time, and the whole treasure of antediluvian knowledge The traditions of the patriarchs no doubt formed the first religious code of the colonies that departed from the plains of Shinar, and these traces of primitive religion may be found in the oldest books of the most ancient nations. The canonical books of the Chinese every where confirm the idea of a Supreme Being, the Creator and Preserver of all things. They mention him under the names of *Tien*, or *Heaven; Chang-tien*, or *Supreme Heaven; Chang ti*, or *Supreme Lord:* and of *Hoang-chan-ti*, or *Sovereign* and *Supreme Lord* names corresponding to those which we use when we speak of divinity, *God*, the *Lord*, the *Almighty*, the *Most High*. "This Supreme Being," say these books, "is the principle of every thing that exists, "and the Father of all living, he is eternal, immoveable, "and independent, his power knows no bounds, his sight "equally comprehends the past, the present, and the future,

" and penetrates even to the inmost recesses of the heart. " Heaven and earth are under his government all events, " all revolutions are the consequences of his dispensations " and will. He is pure, holy, and impartial, wickedness " offends his sight, but he beholds with an eye of compla- " cency the virtuous actions of men Severe, yet just, he " punishes vice in an exemplary manner, even in princes " and rulers, and often precipitates the guilty, to crown " with honour the man who walks after his own heart, " and whom he hath raised from obscurity Good, mer- " ciful, and full of pity, he forgives on the repentance of " the wicked, and public calamities, and the irregularity " of the seasons, are only salutary warnings, which his fa- " therly goodness gives to men, to induce them to reform " and amend " Such are the character and attributes of the Divinity which are declared in almost every page of the *Chou-king*, and other canonical books.

Do destructive rains, or excessive drought, threaten to destroy the rising crops, and to blast the hopes of the husbandman—is a virtuous emperor attacked by sickness, and is the life of the father of his people in danger—sacrifices are immediately prepared, and solemn vows are addressed to the *Tien*, and often not in vain Has a wicked prince been struck dead by lightning—this punishment is not considered as the effect of chance, it is attributed to the anger of the *Tien*, to his visible justice, and to the power of his avenging arm.

The conduct of the first emperors in times of disaster and public calamity, prove what exalted notions they had formed of the justice and holiness of the Supreme Being. Not contented with putting themselves under the protection of the *Tien*, with offering sacrifices, and addressing prayers to him, they aimed to discover what secret faults they had committed, which might have called down the vengeance of Heaven on their people. They often acknowledged their faults in presence of the whole nation aſſembled, they confeſſed they were ſufficient to excite the indignation of Heaven, and offered themſelves as victims to avert its vengeance from their people.

We ſee, in theſe monuments of remote antiquity, the moſt evident traces of the patriarchal faith, and that the ancient Chineſe worſhipped only one Supreme God, whom they conſidered as a free and intelligent Being, and as an all-powerful, avenging, and rewarding Spirit.

This religious doctrine of the firſt emperors of China has been ſupported and continued under the following reigns to the preſent time.

All thoſe revolutions which ſhake thrones, and change the face of empires, are by the Chineſe conſtantly attributed to the ſupreme direction of the Sovereign Lord of Heaven. *Tcheou-kong* thus expreſſes himſelf in the XIV. chap of the *Chou-king*. "Ye who have been miniſters and officers under "the dynaſty of *Ing*, give ear, and liſten. The *Chang-ti*, "incenſed againſt your dynaſty, deſtroyed it; and, by an "order full of affection for our family, he hath given us "authority to exerciſe ſovereign power in the kingdom of "*Ing* he was deſirous that we might finiſh the work he "had begun. What hath paſſed among the people, "hath ſhewn us, how formidable the Lord of Heaven is. "The king of the dynaſty of *Hya* performed no action "agreeable to his people, for this reaſon, the Lord of "Heaven loaded him with calamities, to inſtruct him, and "make him ſenſible of the error of his ways but this "prince was intractable, he uttered words full of pride, "and gave himſelf up to every kind of debauchery; "Heaven, therefore, ſhewed no farther regard for him: "he was deprived of his kingdom, and puniſhed. *Tchang-"tang*, founder of your dynaſty, was commiſſioned to "execute the orders of Heaven, he deſtroyed the dynaſty "of *Hya*, and, in its ſtead, eſtabliſhed a wiſe king, to "govern the people of the empire. *Tcheou*, the laſt prince "of your dynaſty, neglected the laws of Heaven, he ne-

" ther informed himself of the care which his ancestors " took to preserve their family, nor did he imitate their " zeal and diligence for this reason, the Sovereign Lord " abandoned him, and brought him to punishment. Hea- " ven did not support him, because he deviated from the " paths of equity and justice No kingdom, great or small, " in the four quarters of the world, can be destroyed, unless " such be the will of Heaven."

Vou-vang, in the second year of his reign, was attacked by a malady, which threatened his life, his brother, who tenderly loved him, had recourse to the *Chang-ti*, to beg, that a prince might be spared, whose life was so necessary for the welfare and happiness of his people. He thus addressed him, " Thou, O Lord! didst place him on the throne, " and establish him the father of his people. Wilt thou " then punish us by his loss? If a victim be necessary " to satisfy thy justice, I offer thee my life, I will yield " it up as a voluntary sacrifice, provided thou wilt pre- " serve my brother, my master and my sovereign "

Tchin-vang, when seated on the throne, shewed the same respect for the Lord of the Universe " However high I " may be exalted above the rest of mankind," says he, in the *Chou-king*, " I am, nevertheless, one of the little " subjects of the *Chang-ti*: can I forget to render him " homage?"

The *Chi-king* informs us, what sentiments of gratitude *Chao vang* entertained for the blessings bestowed upon him by the *Chang-ti* — " Rejoice, my people," said he one day to the labourers, " it is now only the end of spring, " and you are about to gather in the fruits of autumn, " your fields, but lately sown, are already loaded with an " abundant crop Let thanks, therefore, be given to the " *Chang-ti*, who enables us so soon to enjoy his benefi- " cent gifts For this reason, I will not wait until the " end of autumn, to present myself before him, and to " thank him for so sudden a fertility "

Bad princes intervened amongst a succession of good emperors, and a *Li-vang* forgot the examples of his pious ancestors, and gave himself up to the caprice of his pride. The *Chi-king* observes, that " the silence of the *Chang-ti* appeared then to be an enigma, and it might have been said, that his Supreme Providence had belied itself, every thing prospered with this wicked prince; the people were intimidated even the censors of the empire applauded his errors —What, then, is there no longer justice in Heaven? Shall the impious enjoy, peaceably, the fruit of their crimes? Attend, and you will soon see, that the *Chang-ti* keeps his arm so long at rest, in order only to strike with redoubled force - for the people, harrassed by oppression, rose up against that tyrant, killed the flatterers who surrounded his throne, and would have sacrificed the prince himself to their fury, had he not escaped by a precipitate flight "

The emperor *Yon-tching*, who succeeded *Kang-hi*, in 1722, furnishes us with a sufficient proof, that the same sentiments respecting the being of a God were held in veneration during his reign The following decree published by him, throughout the whole empire, forms a kind of confession of faith, and a declaration of what he viewed as the religion of his subjects The occasion of its publication is sufficiently expressed in the preamble.

" Some of the principal officers of our provinces have " given a wrong interpretation to the meaning of our " orders, transmitted to them, respecting the means of " preventing the damage occasioned in the country by " destructive insects, and have understood them in a sense " quite different from our intention They have erro- " neously concluded, that, I have fallen into the ridiculous " error of those who believe in the spirits called *couei-chin*, " as if I imagined, that prayers offered up to these pre- " tended beings, could remedy our present afflictions. " My meaning, therefore, is as follows.

"Between the *Tien* or *Supreme Being* and man there "is a relation, a certain and infallible correspondence, "as to what concerns punishments and rewards. When "our plains are desolated, either by inundations, drought "or insects, what is the cause of our calamities? They are "perhaps occasioned by the emperor himself, who devi- "ates from that integrity and justice so necessary for good "government, and thereby lays the *Tien* under the neces- "sity of employing these punishments, to bring him back "to a sense of his duty Perhaps they may be occasioned "by the principal officers of the province, upon which "these misfortunes have fallen, in not consulting the pub- "lic good, and neglecting to take justice as the rule of "their conduct—And may not these calamities be owing "to the governors of cities, who neither act with equity, "nor give the people good examples or suitable instruc- "tion; or because, in certain provinces and districts, they "violate the laws, contemn established customs, and lead "disorderly lives? The heart of man being thus corrupted, "that happy union which ought to subsist between him "and the *Tien*, is interrupted and disturbed, and endless "misfortunes overtake us for, when men come short "of their duty, that beneficent regard which the *Tien* "had for them, becomes changed

"Convinced of the truth of this infallible doctrine, "when I am informed, that some province suffers, either "by long drought, or excessive rains, I search my own "heart carefully, examine my past conduct, and think of "reforming those irregularities which may have crept in- "to my palace Evening and morning, and all the day "long, do I confine myself within the bounds of fear "and respect. I endeavour to give the *Tien* convincing "proofs of my uprightness and piety, in hopes that, by "a regular life, I shall be able to make the *Tien* change "the resolution which he hath formed, of punishing us. "It is in your power, O ye great officers who govern

" provinces! it is in your power to aſſiſt me; it is in " yours, ye people, ſoldiers, and others, of whatever quali- " ty or condition ye be, it is in your power to acquit your- " ſelves alſo of this duty humble yourſelves with fear; " examine your own conduct, ſtrive to attain to perfec- " tion, aid and mutually exhort one another, reform your " manners, endeavour to correct your errors, repent of " your crimes, follow the paths of truth, ſhun thoſe of " error, and be aſſured, that if we, on our parts, per- " fectly diſcharge our duties, the *Tien* will ſuffer himſelf " to be moved by our well-regulated conduct, and will " grant us his peace and protection These injunctions I " cannot too often repeat. To prevent calamities, there " are no means more certain, than to keep a ſtrict watch " over ourſelves, to live in fear, and to ſtrive for perfec- " tion When they tell you to pray, and to invoke ſpirits " what do they mean? It is, at moſt, only to implore " their mediation, to repreſent to the *Tien* the ſincerity " of our reſpect, and the fervour of our deſires. To pre- " tend, therefore, in any manner, that theſe prayers, and " theſe invocations, can remove our calamities, and avert " misfortunes, while we loſe ſight of our duty, neglect to " watch over our own conduct, live not in fear, and have not " our hearts filled with reſpect towards the *Tien*, in order " to move him, is attempting to draw water from the " ſtream, after having ſhut up its ſource; it is omitting " the eſſential part, and attaching ourſelves to that which " is acceſſary only How can you hope, by ſuch a conduct, " to obtain the accompliſhment of your deſires?

" Hear then again, what I think. I am clearly and " fully perſuaded, that there is, between the *Tien* and " man, a reciprocal union, and perfect correſpondence. " It is for your inſtruction, O ye great officers! it is for " you, that I have not diſdained to take up my pen, and " to explain my thoughts in the cleareſt manner I could, " in order that you may conform yourſelves to the ſenti-

" ments which I have expressed. This is the only cause
" of the present instruction "

The present emperor, who succeeded Yon-tching in 1736, holds the same sentiments, and thus this doctrine of the existence and attributes of the Supreme Being, and of the worship and homage due to him, has subsisted in China without change, during a long series of ages. Indeed, if we consult all the monuments and canonical works of this nation, and if we search the ancient part of its annals, we shall not discover the least vestige of idolatry The Chinese history, so minute in its details, and so particular in pointing out every innovation in established customs, makes no mention of any superstitious rite, contradictory to the belief and worship which we have attributed to the ancient Chinese: had there been any such, it would have undoubtedly spoken of them with the same exactness as that with which it relates the establishment of the sect of the *Tao-ssée*, and the introduction of the religion of the idol *Fo*, an idol brought from India in latter ages.

The existence of the Tribunal of Ceremonies, has without doubt greatly contributed to the preservation of the ancient religious doctrine, for to this tribunal is assigned the care of inspecting every thing that relates to religious worship: it is obliged to prevent innovations; to suppress popular superstitions, and to chastise, and brand with some mark of infamy, impious or licentious writers. Their severity never pardons insults offered to the Deity, or to good manners The ancient doctrine of the *Tien* has always found support in this tribunal; and to the constant uniformity of its decrees may be attributed its being at present the established and prevailing religion. The mandarins, who form this tribunal, may sometimes, in secret, and in their houses, give themselves up to superstitious practices, but this personal attachment to particular acts of worship has no influence over their public conduct · when they fit on their benches, they know no other religion but that of the ftate.

The firft facrifices which the Chinefe inftituted in honour of the *Chang-ti*, were offered up to him on a *Tan*, or *Altar*, in the open fields, or on fome mountain.*

Around the *Tan* was raifed a double fence, called *Kiao*, compofed of turf and branches of trees. In the fpace left between the fences, were erected two leffer altars on the right and left, upon which, immediately after the facrifice offered up in honour of the *Tien*, they facrificed alfo to the *Cheng*, that is to fay, to the fuperior fpirits of every rank, and to their virtuous anceftors The fovereign alone, whom they confidered as the high prieft of the empire, facrificed on the *Tan*.

In the early ages, when the empire, confined within narrow boundaries, prefented only a fmall ftate and a rifing population, a fingle mountain was fufficient for the facrifices of the *Chang-ti*. But in procefs of time, the empire being confiderably enlarged, *Hoang-ti* appointed four principal mountains, fituated in the extremities of his ftates, and correfponding with the four quarters of the world, to be ever after places particularly confecrated, and fet apart for the religious worfhip of the whole nation. In the courfe of every year, the prince went fucceffively to offer up facrifice upon each of thefe mountains, and thence took occafion to fhew himfelf to his people, and to inform himfelf of their wants, that he might endeavour to relieve them.

Since the emperors *Yao* and *Chun*, different notions have been entertained refpecting thefe facrifices, We read in the *Chou-king*, and other fragments of the ancient Chinefe hiftory, that *Chun* ordained, 1ft That at the fecond moon, in which the vernal equinox fell, the fovereign fhould repair to the mountain *Tai-chan*, in the

* Tan fignifies a round heap of ftone, or earth.

eastern part of China, and there offer sacrifices on a *Tan* within the fence of the *Kiao*, to beg that Heaven would deign to watch over the seed in the earth, then beginning to spring up. 2dly, That at the fifth moon, in which the summer solstice happened, the sovereign should perform the same ceremonies on the southern mount, and implore Heaven to diffuse warmth through the bowels of the earth, to add vigour to its fostering power, and give effect to its nutritive qualities 3dly, That at the eighth moon, at which time the autumnal equinox fell, sacrifice should be offered on the western mountain to procure an abundant crop, and to prevent insects or destructive vermin, drought, or excessive moisture, winds, and all injuries of the air, from destroying the rising hopes of the labourer And lastly, That at the twelfth moon, after the winter solstice, sacrifice should be offered up on the northern mountain, to thank Heaven for all the blessings received in the course of the year, and to solicit a continuance of them through that which was about to commence.

This custom subsisted a long time after *Hoang-ti* The emperors of the dynasty of *Tcheou* added some other ceremonies, and a fifth mountain, which was supposed to form a centre to the other four Since that time they have been called the *Five Yo*, or mountains of sacrifice

This institution, which subjected the emperor to regular journies, was however found to be attended with certain inconveniencies, to obviate which, a spot was consecrated in the neighourhood of his palace, and substituted for the *Yo* on all occasions, when it was either inconvenient for the sovereign to repair to the mountains of sacrifice. At this place an edifice was erected, which at once represented the *Kiao*, the *Tan* and the *Hall of Ancestors*, and in this the emperor offered the accustomed sacrifice.

The Hall of Anceſtors made part of this edifice, becauſe it was neceſſary for thoſe who offered ſacrifice to the *Chang-ti*, to repair firſt to this hall, and acquaint their anceſtors what they were about to perform. Thither alſo they returned after ſacrificing, to thank them for the protection they had procured from the *Chang-ti*, who had not diſdained to receive the homage of their vows. They then offered up a ſacrifice of thankſgiving, and performed certain ceremonies, to ſhew their reſpect.

This edifice received a different name and a new form under each of the three firſt dynaſties. The *Hya* called it *Chê-chê, the Houſe of Generations and Ages*—or, according to the interpretation of Father Amiot, *a Temple in honour of him, who made generations and ages.* It contained within its circumference five ſeparate halls appropriated for different purpoſes. Theſe halls had neither paintings nor ornaments of any kind; they preſented only four bare walls in which windows were conſtructed for the admiſſion of light. The ſtair-caſe that conducted to the principal entrance conſiſted of nine ſteps.

The *Chang* named this temple *Tchoung-ou*, or the *Renewed Temple.* It was employed for the ſame purpoſes, but it was much richer and better ornamented. The five ſeparate halls were adorned with columns, over which were placed other columns, that ſupported a ſecond roof.

The ſame temple, under the dynaſty of *Tcheou*, received the name of *Ming-tang*, or the *Temple of Light.* The emperors of that family aimed to bring back religious worſhip to its primitive purity, they therefore imitated the ſimplicity of the ancients, and ornamented their temples neither with ſuperb columns, nor ſplendid roofs. The five halls were ſeparated only by plain walls, one of them was the place of ſacrifice, and the other four contained all thoſe things which were neceſſary for ſacrificing. This rude edifice had four gates covered with fine moſs, repreſenting the branches of which the double ſence of the a ccu - *Kau* w re formed. This moss covered also the ridge of the roof, and the whole building was encompassed by a canal, which was filled with water at the time sacrifices were offered up. To this principal temple, a second was added, which they named *Tsing-miao*, or the *Temple of Nortel*. This last was used only for purifications and ceremonies practised in honour of ancestors, the first being entirely consecrated to the worship of the *Chang-ti*.

Pekin contains at present two principal temples, the *Tien-tan* and the *Ti-tan*, in the construction of which, the Chinese have displayed all the elegance and magnificence of their architecture. These two temples are both dedicated to the *Chang-ti*, but under two different titles, in the one he is adored as the *Eternal Spirit*, in the other as *the Spirit that created and preserves the world*. The ceremonies with which modern sacrifices are accompanied, are greatly multiplied, and nothing can equal the splendour and magnificence with which the emperor is surrounded, when he performs this solemn and sacred duty. He alone, in quality of father, and head of the great family of the nation, has a right to offer up sacrifice to the *Chang-ti*, and it is in the name of all the people that he prays and sacrifices. Some time before the day fixed for this important ceremony, the monarch, the grandees of his court, the mandarins, and all those who by their employments are qualified to assist, prepare themselves by retirement, fasting, and continence. During that time the emperor gives no audience, and the tribunals are entirely shut. The mandarins of the Tribunal of Crimes, and every person who has been disgraced, is incapacitated from performing any office in these grand ceremonies. Marriages, funerals, rejoicings, entertainments, and festivals of every kind are then forbidden. On the day appointed for the sacrifice, the emperor appears with all the pomp and magnificence of power. His train is composed of an innumerable crowd, a multitude of princes, lords, and officers, surround him, and his march towards the *Tien-tan* resembles a triumph, the magnificence of every thing in the temple corresponds to that of the sovereign, the vases, and all the utensils employed in sacrificing are of gold, and even the instruments of music are of enormous magnitude, and are never used any where else. If the emperor however never displays more pomp and grandeur than when he walks in procession to the *Tien-tan*, he on the other hand never appears more humbled and dejected than during the time he is sacrificing. By the manner in which he performs his prostrations, rolls in the dust, and speaks of himself to the Chang-ti, it is evident that he assumes this pomp and splendour only for the purpose of declaring, in a sensible and striking manner, the infinite distance which is between the Supreme Being and man.

The ceremony in which the emperor opens and tills the earth with his own hands, we have already noticed, as being an encouragement to agriculture, but we must not imagine this institution to be merely of a political nature, established only for this purpose, it is certain that this ceremony has always been considered and practised as an act of religion. It is expressly said in the *Li-ky*, one of the ancient canonical books, that it is for the *Tsi (sacrifice to Heaven)* that the emperor himself tills the earth in the Kiao of the south, it is to present an offering to him of the grain which has been gathered from it. It is also for the Tsi, that the empress and princesses breed silk-worms in the Kiao of the north, it is in order to make vestments for sacrificing.---If the emperor and princes till the earth, if the empress and princesses breed silk-worms, it is to shew that respect and veneration, which they entertain for the Spirit who rules the universe, it is to honour him according to their ideas in the sublimest of duties.

SECT OF THE TAO-SSE.

The fect of the Tao-ffé was founded by a philofopher named *Lao-kiun*, or *Lao-tfe*, who came into the world 603 years before the Chriftian era. His father was a poor peafant, who from his infancy lived in a rich family as an inferior domeftic; he attained to the age of feventy without having made choice of a wife, but at length united himfelf to a woman of the fame rank, who was then in her fortieth year. The wonderful deftiny of the fon was foretold, according to popular report, by many remarkable circumftances which attended his birth. His mother, who happened to be one day in a retired place, conceived on a fudden, being impreffed by the vivifying virtue of heaven and earth. She carried the fruits of her womb for the fpace of eighty years, but the mafter fhe ferved, enraged at her going with child fo long, drove her from his houfe, and reduced her to the neceffity of wandering about the country. At length, under a plum-tree, fhe brought forth a fon, whofe hair and eye-brows were entirely white. She at firft gave him the name of the tree under which he was born; but perceiving afterwards that the lobes of his ears were uncommonly long, fhe thence took occafion to form a furname, and called him, *Plum-tree-ear Ly-eul*. The people afterwards, ftruck with the whitenefs of his hair, named him the *grey-haired child Lao-tfe*.

We have little account of this philofopher during his infancy; he was appointed librarian to one of the emperors of the dynafty of Tcheou, and afterwards raifed to the rank of an inferior mandarin. His firft employment, which placed him amidft books, infpired him with an ardent defire for ftudy, and to this he entirely gave himfelf up, and acquired by clofe application a profound knowledge of hiftory and of ancient ceremonies. He died at Ou in an advanced age. The principal work he left to his disciples is the book Tao-te, which is a collection of five thousand sentences.

The morality of this philosopher has a resemblance to the doctrines of Epicurus It consists principally in banishing vehement desires, and suppressing those impetuous passions, capable of disturbing the peace and tranquility of the soul He taught that every wise man ought to be employed in endeavouring to live free from grief and pain, and in striving to glide gently down the stream of life, devoid of anxiety and care. In order to arrive at this state of happy repose, he exhorts his followers to banish all thoughts of the past, and to abstain from every vain and useless inquiry into futurity observing that to plan out vast designs, to be harrassed with a solicitous desire of executing them, to give up to the tormenting cares of ambition; to look for riches, and to become a prey to the sordid passion of avarice, is, to live not for one's self, but for posterity and is he not, says he, a fool who sacrifices his repose and mental tranquility, to procure happiness to others, or to enrich a surviving son or nephew? Even when in pursuit of felicity for ourselves, Lao-tse recommended moderation both in the desire, and the exertions to obtain it.

The disciples of this philosopher afterwards changed the doctrine which he had left them. As that passive state, and perfect tranquility of mind to which they endeavoured to attain, was continually disturbed and interrupted by the fear of death, they declared that it was possible to discover a composition from which a drink might be made that would render mankind immortal This foolish idea led them to the study of chemistry, afterwards to search for the philosophers stone, till at length they gave themselves up to all the wild extravagancies of pretended magic.

The desire and hope of avoiding death by the discovery of so valuable a liquor, gained a number of partisans to this new sect, wealthy individuals, especially those of the female sex, shewed the greatest eagerness to be instructed in the doctrine of the diſciples of *Lao-tſe*. Magical practices, the invocation of ſpirits, and the foretelling future events by divination, made rapid progreſs throughout all the provinces of the empire. The credulity of ſome of the emperors gave an air of truth to the error, and the court was ſoon filled with an innumerable crowd of theſe falſe doctors, who were now honoured with the diſtinguiſhed title of *tien-sse*—*celeſtial doctors*. *Vou-ti*, fifth emperor of the dynaſty of the *Han*, ſhewed a paſſionate deſire for the ſtudy of theſe myſteries. Death had deprived him of a favourite miſtreſs, whom he ardently loved, and one of theſe impoſtors, *Tao-ſſee*, found means, by incantations, ſo to work on his imagination as to give him a fancied ſight of the woman whom he ſo tenderly loved, and this fancied apparition attached him more and more to the extravagant notions of the new ſect. Grieved at this infatuation, one of the grandees of the empire, being in the emperor's preſence when the myſterious beverage was brought him, ſuddenly ſeized the cup, and drank up the whole liquor. Enraged at this act, the monarch cauſed him to be arreſted, and gave orders for putting him to death. *Your order is of no avail*, ſaid the courtier, without any emotion, *it is not in your power to deprive me of life, ſince I have now rendered myſelf immortal; however, if I am ſtill ſubject to the power of death, your majeſty owes me much obligation, ſince you muſt thereby be convinced, that this liquor has not that virtue which is attributed to it, and that theſe impoſtors deceive you*. This anſwer ſaved the courtier's life, but it did not reform the monarch. He often drank the liquor of immortality, but his health began to decline, and, after being made ſenſible of his mortality, he died, ſadly deploring his own folly and credulity.

The death of the emperor did not retard the progreſs of the ſect. Temples, conſecrated to ſpirits, reared their heads in every corner of the empire, and two of the moſt celebrated of the *Tao-ſſé* were authoriſed to maintain public worſhip there, after the form which had been appointed for them. They likewiſe diſtributed and ſold to the people ſmall images, upon which were repreſented that immenſe crowd, both of men and ſpirits, with which they had peopled the heavens, and which they named *Sien-gin*—*Immortals*. Theſe were worſhipped as ſo many diſtinct deities, independent of the Supreme Being: in like manner ſeveral of the ancient kings were metamorphoſed into gods, and alſo invoked.

Under the Tang, this ſuperſtition ſtill continued. The founder of that dynaſty erected and conſecrated a magnificent temple to Lao-tſe himſelf, and another emperor of the ſame family cauſed the ſtatue of this philoſopher to be placed with great pomp and ſolemnity in his palace.

The doctors Tao-ſſe increaſed in number, and became more powerful than ever, under the dynaſty of Song. Every fraud and deceit that cunning could ſuggeſt, or ingenuity invent, were employed by theſe impoſtors, to increaſe the reputation of their doctrine, and to inſinuate themſelves into the confidence of princes. On a dark night, they ſuſpended, at one of the gates of the imperial city, a book full of myſtic characters, and magical figures. At break of day, they ſent notice to the emperor of the ſudden appearance of this book, and publicly declared that it had fallen from heaven. The credulous monarch, followed by a numerous train, immediately repaired, on foot, to the ſpot, in order to take poſſeſſion of the precious volume; and, having received it into his hands, in the moſt reſpectful manner, he carried it, as in triumph, to his palace, and ſhut it up in a golden box. The eighth emperor of the ſame dynaſty carried his ſuperſtitious veneration for a celebrated Tao-ſſe ſo far, that he publicly ordered him to be worſhipped under the name of Chang-ti. Until that epoch, the moſt zealous partiſans of Lao-tſe had always reserved this name for the Supreme Being only. This impiety therefore shocked and disgusted the whole sages of the nation

Time, which generally draws aside the veil of illusion and imposture, gave new strength and vigour to this contemptible sect, from age to age it acquired additional influence, the protection of princes, the support of the great, the scenes of admiration, or terror, employed by cunning and deceit to strike the minds of the ignorant people, all concurred to perpetuate and spread it, in spite of the continual opposition made to it by the wiser part of the nation, and the bold remonstrances which were presented to the emperor.

The Tao-sse, at present, offer up three different victims to the spirit which they invoke—a hog, a fowl and a fish The ceremonies which they use in their incantations are various, according to the imagination and address of the person who practises them Some drive a sharp stake into the earth, others trace out fantastical figures on paper, and accompany each stroke of the pencil with grimaces and horrible cries, and others make a hideous and frightful noise with kettles and small drums.

A great number of these Tao-sse in China pretend to be fortune-tellers Although they have never seen the person who consults them, they address him by his name, give a particular account of his whole family, describe the situation of his house, tell him the names and number of his children, and twenty other particularities, which they are cunning enough to learn before-hand, by some means or other, but which astonish the illiterate part of the nation

The chief of the Tao-sse is invested by government with the dignity of grand mandarin, and resides in a town of the province of Kiang-si, where he inhabits a sumptuous palace The superstitious confidence reposed in him attracts an immense concourse of people, who flock thither from every part of the empire, some go to seek a cure for their diseases, others, to consult respecting what may befal them afterwards, and to get an insight into futurity. The Tien-sse distributes small bits of paper, filled with magical characters, to all around him, who depart satisfied, and without regretting either the fatigue or expence which generally attends these pious pilgrimages.

SECT OF THE GOD FOE, OR FO.

This sect, still more pernicious, and much wider diffused throughout China than the preceding, came originally from India. The doctors *Tao sse* had promised to a prince of the *Tcheou*, and brother of the emperor *Ming-ti*, to make him enter into communion with spirits. This credulous and superstitious prince, having heard of a celebrated spirit in India, named *Fo*, by continued importunities prevailed on his brother to send an embassy to this foreign deity. The officer who was charged with this commission set out, accompanied by a train of seventeen persons, and directed his course towards India. When he arrived at the place of his destination, he found only two *Cha-men*, or votaries of *Fo*, whom, not willing to fail in his errand, he carried with him to China. He collected, at the same time, several images of *Fo*, or *Boudha*, painted on fine chintz, with forty-two chapters of the canonical books of the Indians, which he placed, together with the images, upon a white horse. This embassy returned to the imperial city in the eighth year of the reign of *Ming-ti*, and the sixty fifth of the Christian era. Thus was the doctrine and worship of *Foe* first introduced into China, where, in a short time, they made a rapid progress.

We have no certain knowledge of the birth-place of this pretended god; but his followers relate that he was born in one of the kingdoms of India, situated near the line, and that his father was a king. They assure us that his mother, who was named *Mo-yé*, brought him into the world by the left side, and that she expired soon after her delivery, that at the time of her conception, she dreamed that she had swallowed an elephant, and that this strange dream gave birth to the particular veneration which the kings of India have always shewn for a white elephant. " As soon as this extraordinary child " was born," add they, " he had strength enough to " stand erect without assistance, he walked seven steps, " and pointing with one hand to the heavens, and with " the other to the earth, cried out—*In the heavens and* " *on earth there is no one but me who deserves to be ho-* " *noured.*"

At the age of seventeen he espoused three wives, by one of whom he had a son called by the Chinese *Mo-heou-lo* At nineteen he abandoned his home, his wives, and his children, and retired to a vast desert followed by four philosophers, to whose care he committed himself. At the age of thirty, he felt himself all on a sudden filled with the divinity, and he was metamorphosed into *Fo* or *Pagod*, according to the expression of the Indians. No sooner had he become a god, than he thought of establishing his doctrine and proving his celestial mission by performing miracles. The number of his disciples was immense, and his ridiculous errors soon spread through every part of India, and the higher extremities of Asia.

The priests attached to the worship of *Fo* are called *Talapoins* by the Siamese, *Lamas* by the Tartars, *Ho-chang* in China, *Bonzes* in Japan, and it is under the latter appellation that they are generally known by Europeans

One of the principal errors propagated by *Fo* is the doctrine of the metempsychosis, of which he appears to have been the inventor, as he lived at least five hundred years before Pythagoras. This doctrine of the transmigration of souls has given rise to that multitude of idols, which are reverenced in every place where the worship of *Fo* is established. Quadrupeds, birds, reptiles, and the vilest animals had temples, and became objects of public veneration, because the soul of the god in his transmigrations and metamorphoses might have inhabited their bodies.

We shall conclude this subject with the account given by the bonzes of this pretended deity. He had attained to the age of seventy-nine, when he perceived by his feebleness and infirmities, that his borrowed divinity could not prevent him from paying the debt of nature like other men He was unwilling to leave his disciples without revealing to them the whole secret and hidden mysteries of his doctrine. Having, therefore, called them together, he declared, that till that moment he had always thought proper to speak to them in parables, and that for the space of forty years, he had disguised the truth under figurative and metaphorical expressions; but being on the point of bidding them a long farewel, he would disclose his real sentiments, and unveil the whole mystery of his wisdom. *Learn then,* said he, *that there is no other principle of all things, but a vacuum and nothing, from nothing all things have sprung, to nothing they must again return, and there all our hopes end.*

An infinitude of fables were spread by his disciples after his death. They affirmed that their master was still in life, that he had been already born eight thousand times, and that he had appeared successively under the figures of an ape, lion, dragon, elephant, &c. Among his disciples, there was one who had been dearer to him than all the rest, to whom he committed his most secret thoughts, and whom he entrusted with the care of propagaining his doctrine, he is called by the Chinese *Moo-kia-ye*. *He desired him never to attempt to support his tenets by proofs and long reasoning*, and commanded him to put only at the beginning of the books which he published *Thus have I learned.* In one of his works the same *Fo* had made mention of another master still more ancient than himself, whom the Chinese name *O mi-to*, and the Japanese *Amida*. The bonzes assure us that the latter became so eminently holy, that it is at present sufficient only to invoke him in order to obtain immediate pardon for the greatest crimes. the Chinese followers of *Fo*, have therefore almost continually in their mouth these two names, *O-mi to, Fo!*

The last words of the dying *Fo* occasioned much trouble and division among his disciples. Some continued firmly to maintain the original doctrine, while others, embracing a second, formed a sect of atheists. A third party, who were desirous of reuniting the two former, gave rise to the celebrated distinction of the *external* and *internal doctrine*, one of which must naturally precede and dispose the mind for receiving the other. "The "*external doctrine*, say they, "is to the *internal* what "the mould is to an arch which the builder is about "to raise, when the latter is constructed, the former is "knocked down and becomes useless." The case is the same with the two laws, the *external* and *internal*, when we rise to a knowledge of the second, we ought to abandon the first.

We shall not here attempt to examine all the errors contained in this internal doctrine its folly and absurdity will appear sufficiently evident, if we only mention the ideas upon which it is founded. "Nothing is the beginning and end of every thing that exists, from nothing our first parents derived their existence, and to nothing they returned after their death. All beings are the same, their only difference consists in their figure and qualities.

This universal principle is extremely pure, exempt from all change, exceedingly subtle and simple, it remains continually in a state of rest, has neither virtue, power, nor intelligence, besides, its essence consists in being free from action, without knowledge and without desires. To obtain happiness, we must endeavour by continual meditation, and frequent victories over ourselves, to acquire a likeness to this principle, and to obtain that end, we must accustom ourselves to do nothing, will nothing, feel nothing, desire nothing When we have attained to this state of happy insensibility, we have nothing more to do with virtue or vice, punishments or rewards, providence or the immortality of the soul —The whole of holiness consists in ceasing to exist, in being confounded with nothing, the nearer man approaches to the nature of a stone or log, the nearer he is to perfection, in a word, it is in indolence and immobility, in the cessation of all desires, and bodily motion, in the annihilation and suspension of all the faculties both of body and soul, that all virtue and happiness consist The moment that man arrives at this degree of perfection, he has no longer occasion to dread changes, futurity, or transmigrations, because he hath ceased to exist, and is become perfectly like the god *Fo*."

Extravagant and absurd as this philosophy appears, it found partisans in China, and the emperor *Kao-tsong* became so much infatuated with it, that he abdicated the throne, that he might be more at liberty to indulge himself in the practice of this extravagant doctrine, which entirely destroys morality, subverts society, and tends to annihilate that reciprocal relation which unites men together.

The external doctrine is better suited to the comprehension of the vulgar, and has, on that account, gained more followers. The following are the maxims and tenets preached up by the bonzes who profess this doctrine. They admit the distinction between good and evil, and that, after death, rewards will be bestowed on the good, and punishments inflicted on the wicked, in places destined for the souls of each, that the god *Fo* came upon earth to save mankind, and to bring back to the paths of salvation those who have strayed, that it is by him their sins are expiated, and that he alone can procure them a happy regeneration in the life to come They enjoin the strict observance of the five following precepts not to kill any living creature, of whatever nature it may be, not to take away the goods of another, not to pollute themselves by uncleanness, not to lie, and not to drink wine They, above all, recommend the practice of certain acts of mercy, such as, to treat their bonzes well, to build monasteries and temples for them, and to supply them with every thing necessary, in order that they may be able, by the assistance of their prayers, and the penance which they impose, to merit forgiveness, and the remission of all their sins "At "the funeral of your parents, burn," say they, "paper "gilt with gold or silver, dresses and silk stuffs these sub-"stances will be changed into real gold and silver, and "superb vestments, in the other world, and all these riches "will be faithfully transmitted to your fathers. Wo unto "you, if ye do not obey these holy precepts! your souls "will be delivered over, after death, to the severest tor-"ments, and subjected to the most disgusting changes "Ye shall revive in the form of dogs, rats, serpents, horses "and mules, and ye shall be for ever exposed to the most "dismal and wretched transmigrations"

It is difficult to conceive the impression these threats and denunciations respecting futurity, make upon the minds of the credulous Chinese we may, however, form some notion of it by the following relation, taken from F. le Comte's Memoirs. "I remember," says he, "that, "being in the province of *Chan-si*, I was sent for to ad-"minister baptism to a sick man, seventy years of age, "who lived on a small pension, which he received from "the emperor. As soon as I entered his chamber—How

" much. I am obliged to you, my good father," said he; " you are going to deliver me from the greatest misery. " You must know, my good father, that, for a long time, " I have subsisted on the emperor's beneficence The " bonzes, informed of whatever passes in the other world, " have assured me, that, out of gratitude, I shall be obliged " to serve him, and that my soul will pass into one of " his post-horses, to convey his dispatches from court to " the provinces They therefore exhort me to discharge " my duty faithfully, after I shall have taken possession of my " new residence, and neither to stumble, kick, bite or " wound any one.—*Make dispatch*, say they to me, *eat* " *little, and be patient · by such a conduct, you will move the* " *compassion of the gods, who of a good animal, sometimes* " *makes a man of quality, or a great mandarin.* I confess " to you, that this change makes me shudder, and I can- " not think of it without trembling it haunts me all " the night long; and I often imagine, in my sleep, that " I am in the harness, and ready to start on the first smack " of the postilion's whip. I awake all in a sweat, and " half frantic, not knowing whether I am still a man, " or metamorphosed into a horse But, alas! what will " become of me, when my dreams are changed to reality? " Hear, then, worthy father, the resolution I have formed: " I have been told, that those who profess your religion, " are not subjected to these miseries, that those who are " once men, always retain their figure; and that they find " themselves the same in the other world as they were in " this. Receive me, therefore, among you. I well know " it is an arduous task, to observe all the precepts of your " religion, but, were it still more difficult, I am ready " to embrace it; and, let it cost what it may, *I had much* " *rather be a Christian than a beast*"

Although the superstition of the Chinese has multiplied, without end, the number of their idols, it does not appear, that they always entertain a sincere respect for these pretended deities. It often happens, that they are abandoned and neglected, as gods without power, particularly when they are too slow in granting those favours which are requested from them in such cases, the patience of their votaries becomes exhausted, and they carry their offerings somewhere else others, less moderate, treat them with the greatest contempt, kick them about, and load them with abusive language.—*Thou dog of a spirit*, say they, *we lodge thee in a commodious temple, thou art well gilt, and thou receivest abundance of incense, and yet, after all the care we bestow upon thee, thou art ungrateful enough to refuse us even things necessary* They then tie the idol with cords, drag it through the kennels, and bespatter it with filth and nastiness, to punish it for all the perfume which they have uselessly wasted upon it. If, during this scene of folly, these frantic devotees should happen to obtain what they wish for, they carry back the image, with great ceremony, to its niche, after having carefully washed and wiped it they then prostrate themselves before it, and make excuses for treating it with so little respect. *Indeed*, say they, *we were too rash, but, after all, wast not thou in the wrong, to be so obdurate? Why shouldst thou suffer thyself to be beaten, without necessity? Would it have cost thee more to grant our requests with a good grace? But, what is done, is done let us think no more of it We will gild thee again, provided thou wilt forget what is past.*

A ludicrous circumstance happened in the province of *Nan-kin*, at the time F. Le Comte resided there, which is a farther proof of the little respect which the Chinese sometimes entertain of their gods. A man whose only daughter lay dangerously sick, after having, in vain, tried the art of the physicians, resolved to seek the assistance of the gods —Prayers, offerings, alms, sacrifices, all were employed to obtain the wished-for-cure, and the bonzes, who faſtened on the gifts promiſed it, on the faith of their idol, the power of which they much extolled. The girl, however, died, and the father, in the exceſs of his grief, meditated revenge: he reſolved to accuſe the idol with all the ſolemnity of form, and for this purpoſe he laid his complaint, in writing, before the judge of the place. After having repreſented the deceitful conduct of the unjuſt divinity, he affirmed, that exemplary puniſhment ought to be inflicted upon it, for having broken its word. —'If,' ſaid he, 'the *ſpirit* had power to to cure my daughter, it was guilty of a groſs fraud, in taking my money and ſuffering my daughter to die. If it had not power, why did it pretend to it? and by what right does it aſſume the character of a god? Is it for nothing that we adore it, and that all the province offers it ſacrifice? In ſhort, whether it was want of power, or malice in the idol, its temple ſhould be raſed, its miniſters baniſhed with diſgrace, and itſelf puniſhed in its own perſon.'

The judge conſidered the affair as important, and referred it to the governor, who, not liking to have any thing to do with the gods, deſired the viceroy to examine it. The latter, after having heard the bonzes, who appeared much alarmed, called the complainant, and adviſed him to drop his ſuit. 'You are not prudent,' ſaid he, 'to quarrel with theſe kind of *ſpirits*: they are naturally malicious, and, I am afraid, they will ſerve you ſome diſagreeable trick. Believe me, you had much better liſten to the propoſals of accommodation, which the bonzes will make you on their part. They have aſſured me, that the idol, on its part, will hearken to reaſon, provided you do not puſh things to the utmoſt extremity.'

The man perſiſted in his reſolution, and proteſted, that he would rather periſh than relax in his requeſt. 'I am determined, my lord,' ſaid he. 'The idol imagined, that it might commit, with impunity, every kind of in-

'justice, and that no one would dare to attack it; but in 'this it was mistaken, and we shall soon see which of us 'two is the most malicious and obstinate.'

The viceroy, finding he could not prevail on him to yield, ordered preparation to be made for trial; but, at the same time, gave information to the supreme council at *Pe-kin*, before which the affair was carried, and where the parties, some time after, appeared. The idol did not want partisans, and the lawyers, well paid by the bonzes, found its rights incontestable, and spoke with so much warmth in its favour, that the god, in person, could not have pleaded better: but they had to do with a man of much penetration and shrewdness, who had prudently taken the precaution of supporting his proofs by a large sum of money, which he had well employed, in order to make his case clearer to the judges, persuaded that the devil would be very cunning indeed, if he could withstand such a weighty argument. After several pleadings, he completely gained his process; the idol was condemned to perpetual banishment, as useless in the empire; its temple was rased, and the bonzes, who represented its person, were punished in an exemplary manner.

These bonzes are generally men without character, brought up from their infancy in effeminacy, luxury, and idleness, and who, having an aversion to labour, for the most part, devote themselves to that kind of life, merely for the sake of a subsistence. There is no artifice, therefore, which they do not employ to extort presents from the superstitious adorers of *Fo*. The following is borrowed from the *New Memoirs respecting the Present State of China*.

" Two of these bonzes, strolling through the country, " perceived, in the yard of a rich peasant, two or three " large ducks. They immediately prostrated themselves " before the gate, and began to groan and weep bitterly. " The good woman, who saw them from her chamber, im-

"mediately came forth, to inquire into the cause of their "grief 'We know,' said they, 'that the souls of our "fathers have passed into the bodies of these ducks, and "the dread and apprehensions we entertain of your putting "them to death, will infallibly deprive us of our lives.'— "'It is true,' she replied, 'we have resolved to sell them, "but since they are your fathers, I promise you to pre-"serve them.' This was not what the bonzes wanted "'Alas!' said they, 'your husband, perhaps, will not "have so much charity, and you may rest assured, that "we shall die, if any accident befalls them.' After a long "conversation, the good woman was so affected by their "apparent grief, that she entrusted them with the ducks, "in order that, by feeding them for some time it might "alleviate their distress, and afford them consolation. "They received them with respect, after having prostrated "themselves twenty times before them, but, the very "same evening, put their pretended fathers on the spit, "and, together with some of their brotherhood, made a "hearty *meal of them*."

These bonzes are perfectly masters of all the resources of hypocrisy, they embrace every occasion for cringing and fawning, and they affect a meekness and modest civility, which at first deceives, and prepossesses persons in their favour When they cannot obtain gifts by cunning and address, they endeavour to procure them by submitting to the severest penances, and practising the most rigorous austerities They are often seen in the squares, and other public places, exhibiting themselves as frightful spectacles of mortification. Some of them drag, with great pain, along the streets, large chains, thirty feet in length, which are fastened round their necks and legs, and some mangle their bodies, and make them appear all over blood, by slashing their flesh with a hard flint In this situation they stop at the doors of people's houses 'You see,' say they, 'what we suffer, that we may expiate your sins—

'can you be ſo hard-hearted as to refuſe us a ſmall alms?'

One of the moſt extraordinary penances we read of, is that mentioned by Le Comte, of which he himſelf was an eye-witneſs, and which he relates in the following words 'I met, one day, in the middle of a village, a young, 'handſome bonze, whoſe mild and modeſt deportment, 'when he aſked for alms, ſeemed well calculated to enſure 'him ſucceſs. He was ſtanding erect in a kind of nar-'row chair, the inſide of which was ſtuck full of ſharp 'ſpikes, placed very cloſe one to another, in ſuch a man-'ner that he could not enjoy the leaſt reſt, without being 'wounded Two men, hired for the purpoſe, tranſported 'him ſlowly from houſe to houſe, where he begged people 'to have compaſſion upon him. "I have ſhut myſelf up 'in this chair," ſaid he, "for the good of your ſouls, and 'am reſolved never to quit it, until you have purchaſed 'all theſe nails* Each nail is worth five-pence, but 'there is none of them which will not prove a ſource of 'many bleſſings to you and your families If you pur-'chaſe one, you will perform an act of heroic virtue, and 'the alms you beſtow will not be given to the bonzes, to 'whom you may otherwiſe ſhew your charity, but to the 'god *Fo*, in honour of whom we are building a temple."

'I at that time happened to be paſſing by, he ſaw me, 'and paid me the ſame compliment as he did the reſt 'I told him, that he was much in the wrong, to torment 'himſelf ſo uſeleſly in this world, and I adviſed him to 'come forth from his priſon, to go to the temple of the true 'God, in order to be inſtructed in celeſtial truths, and 'to ſubmit to a penance much leſs ſevere, but far more 'ſalutary and effectual He replied mildly, and with great 'coolneſs, that he was much obliged to me for my advice, 'but would be more ſo, if I would purchaſe a dozen of 'his nails, which would aſſuredly procure me a pleaſant 'and ſafe journey "Hold, ſaid he, turning o ene

* Their number exceeded two thouſand.

'side, "take these, on the faith of a bonze, they are 'the best in my chair, because they hurt me more than 'the rest they are, however, all of the same price."

All the bonzes are not so penitent, a great many of them renounce these painful means of procuring alms. To attain to the same end, others commit a thousand abominations in private, and even sometimes murder. 'Some years ago,' says F. Le Comte, 'the governor of a 'city, passing along the highway, with his ordinary train, 'saw a crowd of people assembled together, and being 'desirous to learn the cause of so great a concourse, he 'approached them. He found that the bonzes were ce-'lebrating an extraordinary festival, and that they had 'constructed, on a large theatre, a very high machine, 'at the top of which a young man put forth his head 'above a small ballustrade that ran quite round it. His 'arms and the rest of his body were entirely concealed; 'and he had nothing free but his eyes, which he rolled 'about in a very wild manner. A little lower on the 'theatre appeared an old bonze, who was explaining to 'the people the sacrifice which that pious young man, as 'they called him, had resolved to make of his life, by 'throwing himself into a deep rivulet, which ran along 'by the side of the highway. "He will not die," said he, "because he must be received at the bottom of the wa-"ters by the charitable spirits, which will hasten to give "him the most friendly reception. In short, it will be "the greatest happiness that can befal him: a hundred "other persons offered to supply his place, but his zeal, "piety, and virtues, have justly entitled him to the pre-"ference." The mandarin, after having heard this ha-'rangue, said the young man shewed great courage, but 'expressed his surprise, that he himself did not explain 'the motives of the sacrifice, and the cause of his adopt-'ing such a resolution. "Let him come down," added 'he, "that we may converse a little with him." The 'old bonze, frightened at this order, immediately opposed 'it, and protested that all would be lost, if the victim 'only opened his mouth, and that he could not answer 'for the mischief that might thence arise to the province. "The evil you fear," said the mandarin, "I shall take upon "myself," and at the same time ordered the young man 'to come down: but all the reply he made to these or-'ders, was, by frightful looks, and a wild and irregular 'movement of his eyes, which seemed ready to start out 'of his head. "Behold these looks, and that agitation," 'said the bonze, "and judge of the injury you do him; "he is about to fall a prey to despair, and if you persist, "you will make him expire with grief." The mandarin, 'who continued firm to his purpose, bid his attendants 'mount the theatre, and bring him down by force. They 'immediately obeyed, and found him closely bound and 'gagged. As soon as his cords were loosed, and he was 'in a condition to speak, he cried out, with all his might, "—Ah, my lord! grant me vengeance on these assassins, "who intended to drown me. I am a batchelor, going "to court, to assist at the ordinary examinations. These "bonzes seized me yesterday by force, and this morning, "before break of day, they bound me to that machine, "in such a manner that I could neither move, nor utter "the least complaint, determined to throw me into the "water in the evening, and to perform their abominable "mysteries at the expence of my life." As soon as he 'began to speak, the bonzes betook themselves to flight, 'but the officers of justice, who always make part of a 'governor's train, soon seized some of them. Their chief 'was thrown into the river and drowned, and the rest 'were conducted to prison, and afterwards punished ac-'cording to their deserts.'

A letter of Father *Lo[illegible]*, an Italian Jesuit, fur-nishes us with an anecdote of a different kind, which enables us to form [illegible] of the voluptuous manners of these bonzes, and of the secret profligacy of their lives.—Near the city of *Fou-tcheou*, there was formerly a famous pagoda, inhabited by the most distinguished bonzes of the province. The daughter of a Chinese doctor, who was going to her father's country house, accompanied by two female attendants, had the curiosity to enter this temple, and sent to beg of the bonzes, that they would retire, until she had said her prayers. The principal bonze, desirous of seeing this young female, concealed himself behind the altar. He had no sooner beheld her, than he was smitten with her charms, and he determined to gratify his brutal lust. He ordered some other bonzes, his confidants, to seize the two attendants, and he forced the young woman to submit to his desires, in spite of all her cries and tears.

The father did not long remain ignorant of the cause of his daughter's absence: he knew she had entered the pagoda, and that she had then disappeared; he required, therefore, that she should be restored. The bonzes replied, she had visited their temple, but had departed after having said her prayers. The doctor, who had been educated with sentiments of the utmost contempt for the bonzes, applied to the Tartar general of the province, and demanded justice against the ravishers of his daughter. The bonzes then informed them, in a very mysterious manner, that the god Fo, having become enamoured of the young beauty, had carried her away; and the bonze who had committed the crime, then endeavoured, by a pathetic harangue, to convince the doctor how much honoured he and and his family were by *Fo*, who had judged his daughter worthy of his company and love. But the Tartar general had too much good sense to give credit to these fables: he resolved to search the pagoda; and while he was prying into every corner, and examining all its recesses, he heard some confused cries, which seemed to proceed from the bottom of a rock, he immediately advanced towards the place, and perceived an iron gate, which shut the entrance of a grotto. Having ordered it to be broke open, he descended into a subterraneous apartment, where he found the daughter of the doctor, and above twenty other females, who had been confined in that dismal abode. The general, after having released them, set fire to the four corners of the edifice, and destroyed in the same flames, the temple, altars and gods, together with their infamous ministers.

Notwithstanding that infatuation which, for the most part, induces the vulgar to support popular superstitions, a bonze is generally despised in China. The greater part of these impostors are sprung from the dregs of the people. To recruit and perpetuate their sect, they purchase young children, whom they initiate in all their mysteries, and to whom they reveal every trick and deception which may render their profession profitable; these afterwards succeed them, and carefully transmit their art and knowledge to other young bonzes, whom they educate in the like manner. They are, in general, very ignorant, and the greater part would find themselves much embarrassed, were they required to give an exact account of the true doctrine of their sect.

Though they are not subject to a regular hierarchy, they have their superiors, whom they call *ta-ho-chang*, or grand bonzes. This rank secures particular distinction, and the first place in all religious assemblies at which they may be present. There are bonzes destined only to collecting alms; others, better skilled in the art of speaking, and who have acquired some knowledge of the Chinese literature, are commissioned to visit the literati, and to insinuate themselves into the houses of the great; old men rendered venerable by length of years, and by a composed and grave deportment, are employed to exercise their talents among the female sex; they preside in all their assemblies, which, though not common, are, however, held in ſeveral of the provinces. They are generally compoſed of fifteen, twenty, or thirty ladies, the greater part of whom are of ſome rank in life, or rich widows One of them is elected ſuperior for the ſpace of a year, at her houſe all the aſſemblies are held; and all contribute towards the expence occaſioned by ornamenting their oratory, by the celebration of certain feſtivals, and the aſſiſtance of the bonzes.

When no extraordinary buſineſs is to be tranſacted in theſe aſſemblies, a bonze is called who is almoſt always venerable on account of his age. He enters the chapel where the female devotees are aſſembled, and ſings ſome anthems to the god *Fo* At length, after having, for ſome time, repeated *O-mi-to, Fo!* and been ſtunned with the tinkling noiſe and din of ſeveral ſmall kettles, upon which they beat, they place themſelves at table, and mirth and good repaſt terminate the exerciſes of this noiſy devotion Feſtivals of this kind are, however, only common ceremonies

On days of ſolemnity, they adorn their place of worſhip with ſeveral idols, the bonzes alſo ornament it with a great number of paintings, in which are repreſented, under different forms, the various puniſhments inflicted on the wicked in hell A grand bonze is invited, who repairs thither, attended by his whole train of inferior miniſters. The prayers and feaſting continue ſeven days; and one of the moſt important cares which employ the aſſembly during this time is, to prepare and conſecrate treaſures for the other world. Their manner of proceeding in this myſterious operation is as follows —They begin by conſtructing a ſmall edifice of gilt or painted paper This work is executed according to all the rules of the Chineſe architecture, and is ſupplied with every utenſil, piece of furniture and conveniency that are to be found in the houſes of the great. This little palace is filled with a great number of boxes, painted and varniſhed, in which they depoſit ſmall bits of gilt paper. An hundred of theſe ſmall boxes are deſtined for the purpoſe of redeeming the ſoul of ſome deceaſed perſon, either male or female, from the dreadful puniſhments to which the inexorable king of hell condemns thoſe who have no treaſures to preſent to him. Twenty of theſe boxes are alſo laid in reſerve, to gain over the members who compoſe the tribunal of the terrible prince of darkneſs. The houſe, its furniture, and the riches it contains, are all appropriated each to a particular uſe. The whole is intended to ſerve them as a lodging in the other world, and to enable them to procure an eſtabliſhment there, by the acquiſition of ſome important office. The whole depoſit in theſe ſmall boxes are put under the ſecurity of a paper padlock. The ſmall palace is afterwards ſhut, and the key carefully laid by. When the perſon who has ſupplied the expence neceſſary for the conſtruction of this palace happens to die, the whole is burnt, in great ceremony: with the key of the houſe are burnt thoſe of the ſmall coffers alſo, in order that the ſoul may take out all the treaſures, which are no longer plain paper, but become metamorphoſed into ſolid ingots of pure gold and ſilver.

Men, alſo united by certain acts of devotion, in like manner, hold particular aſſemblies. The beſt known of this kind is that of the *Faſters*, *Tcheng-tchai*: they are under the direction of a ſuperior, who has generally a great number of diſciples, named *tou-ti*, ſubordinate to him. Theſe give their maſter the name of *ſſe-fou*, which ſignifies *father-doctor*. Little induſtry, and ſtill leſs reputation for knowledge or merit, is neceſſary to arrive at this office.—When the chief of theſe *Faſters* is about to hold an aſſembly, all his diſciples are ordered to repair to the place appointed for the purpoſe, and none of them muſt be abſent on any account whatever. A ſeat is placed for the ſuperior at the bottom of the hall, and all the brotherhood, as they enter, proſtrate themſelves at his feet, and after a little file off, in two lines, to the right and left, in which situation they remain. When the assembly is full, each recites his own private prayers, after which, they place themselves at table, to enjoy something more substantial.

These Chinese *Fasters* are not people devoted to abstinence, or who refrain, for a certain space of time, from taking any kind of nourishment.—Their fasting consists only in their renouncing the use of flesh, fish, wine, onions, garlick, and all heating aliments; but they reserve to themselves the liberty of eating as much as they please of other food, and at every hour of the day. It may be easily perceived, that any interdiction of this kind cannot be very mortifying in China, where the people, for the most part, are accustomed to live on herbs and rice only.

Pilgrimages, and places which give rise to them, are not wanting in China, among this sect. On certain mountains in every province there are temples, more or less reverenced, to which prodigious numbers of superstitious votaries repair. Those who are prevented by age, infirmities, or urgent business, from joining these devout caravans, commission some of their friends to bring them a large leaf filled with characters, and stamped by the bonzes in a particular manner. The centre of this leaf is occupied by the image of the god *Fo*. On the vestments of the god, and around his figure, are traced out a multitude of circles, of great use to these fanatics, who, whether male or female, wear, hanging from their necks, or around their arms, a kind of chaplet, composed of an hundred beads, of moderate size, divided by eight much larger: a bead, still bigger, in form of a small gourd, ornaments the top of the chaplet. These beads they roll between their fingers, pronouncing these words, *O-mi-to Fo!* and each of these invocations is accompanied by a genuflection. When they have completed the number of an hundred, equal to that of the beads, they mark, with a red stroke, one of the circles which ſurround the figure of the god *Fo* on the leaf ſtamped by the bonzes This leaf becomes there-fore the regiſter of all the prayers which they have repeated in the courſe of their lives To verify its authenticity, the bonzes are, from time to time, invited to their houſes, where they atteſt the number of circles, marked with red ſtrokes, and imprint their ſeals on the leaf When one of them dies, this valuable memorial is carried at the funeral with the greateſt ſolemnity, and depoſited in a ſmall box, cloſely ſhut, and ſealed this is what they call *lou-in*, or a paſſport for the other world, and it coſts a large ſum of money to have all theſe formalities obſerved, but people ſeldom calculate expence, when they are deſirous of enſuring themſelves ſucceſs in ſo dangerous a journey

The little knowledge which the Chineſe have of the effects that may be produced by nature, contributes much to preſerve their ſuperſtitious credulity, and greatly faci-litates the deceptions of impoſtors. The half-learned fe-males, and almoſt every individual among the lower claſſes, never ſee any unexpected or extraordinary event, without attributing it to the influence of ſome evil genius Every one creates a being of this kind to himſelf, in the folly of his own imagination, one places it in ſome idol, another, in an old oak, a third in a certain lofty mountain, and a fourth, in the body of an enormous dragon, which in-habits the bottom of the ſea there are no ſacrifices ſo abſurd, or whimſical, which they do not invent, to ap-peaſe this malicious demon. Others entertain different notions reſpecting theſe miſchievous ſpirits according to them, they are the ſouls, or rather the purified and aerial ſubſtance of animals, ſuch as foxes, cats, apes, tortoiſes, frogs, &c which, they affirm, have the power of diveſting themſelves of all the groſs and earthly par-ticles which entered into their compoſition when living, that they then become pure eſſences, and take delight in tormenting men and women, in disconcerting their projects, and exposing them to different diseases. For this reason, when they fall sick, they consult no other physicians but the *Taosse*, and, as soon as they arrive, the house resounds with the din and noise which these priests make, in order to banish the malignant spirits that persecute and harass their patients

There are other superstitious practices to which the Chinese are also much addicted, but we should far exceed our bounds, were we to relate the ideas of the Chinese respecting calculating destinies, consulting oracles, the lucky and unlucky situation of houses, the quarter which doors ought to front, and the plan and day proper for constructing the stoves in which they cook their rice. But the object on which they employ the greatest care, is the choice of the ground and situation proper for a burying-place. Some quacks follow no other profession than that of pointing out mountains, hills, and other places which have an aspect favourable for works of that kind When a Chinese is persuaded of the truth of such information, there is no sum which he would not sacrifice in order to obtain a possession of the fortunate spot. The greater part of the Chinese are convinced, that all the happiness and misfortunes of life depend upon it. If this or that person is endowed with a greater share of genius and abilities, if any one rises rapidly to the degree of doctor, if he is promoted to the rank of a superior mandarin, if he is blessed with a numerous progeny, or if he is less subject to severe maladies than others, and if, in his commercial transactions, all his projects succeed, this, according to them, is not to be attributed to his knowledge, activity, or honesty, but because his houses and the burying-places of his ancestors have a happy situation

JEWS AND MAHOMETANS

The discovery of a synagogue in an empire so remote, is a circumstance too [illegible] ing to be omitted. This Jewish colony appeared [illegible] under the dynasty of the *Han*, which began to reign in the [illegible] 206 before Christ. It [illegible] reduced to a small number of [illegible] s, who are esta-blished only at *C[illegible]*, the capital [illegible] the province of *H[illegible]*. As we are indebted to F. *Gozani* Jesuit mis-sionary for the first knowledge of these [illegible] Jews, we [illegible] the account of them in his own [illegible].

'I had a long conversation with them, and they [illegible] d 'me [illegible] inscriptions, some written in Chinese, and [illegible] s 'in Hebrew. I saw also their religious books, and they 'suffered me to enter the most secret place of their sy-'nagogue, to which they can have no access themselves, 'it [illegible] reserved for the chief of the synagogue, whom 'they [illegible] *Chang-[illegible]*, and who never approaches it but '[illegible] most profound respect.

'[illegible] were thirteen tabernacles placed upon tables, 'each of which was surrounded by small curtains. The '*P[illegible]* each was shut up in each of those tabernacles, 'twelve of which represented the twelve tribes of Israel, 'and the thirteenth Moses. The books were written on 'long pieces of parchment, and folded upon rollers. I 'obtained leave from the chief of the synagogue to draw 'the c[illegible] one of these tabernacles, and to unrol 'one of the books, which appeared to me to be written 'in a [illegible] character neat and distinct. One of these 'books had been luckily saved from the great inundation 'of the river *H[illegible]*, which overflowed the city of *[illegible]-fong-fou*, the capital of the province. As the letters of 'this book have been wetted, and on that account are 'almost effaced, the Jews have, at great pains, got twelve 'copies made, which they preserve in the twelve taber-'nacles above-mentioned.

'There are to be ſeen alſo in two other places of the ſynagogue coffers, in which are ſhut up with great care 'ſeveral other little books, containing different diviſions 'of the Pentateuch of Moſes, which they call *Ti-kim*, 'and other parts of their law. They uſe theſe books 'when they pray; they ſhewed me ſome of them, which 'appeared to be written in Hebrew they were partly 'new and partly old, and half torn.

'In the middle of the ſynagogue ſtands a magnificent 'chair, raiſed very high, and ornamented with a beautiful 'embroidered cuſhion. This is the chair of Moſes, in 'which every Sabbath, and on days of great ſolemnity, 'they place the Pentateuch, and read ſome portions of it. 'There alſo may be ſeen a *Fan-ſui-pai*, or painting, on 'which is inſcribed the emperor's name, but they have 'neither ſtatues nor images. This ſynagogue fronts the 'weſt, and when they addreſs their prayers to the Supreme 'Being, they turn towards that quarter, and adore him 'under the name of *Tien*, *Chan-tien*, *Chan-ti*, and '*Tiao-van-voe-tche*, that is to ſay, *Creator of All Things*, 'and laſtly, of *Van-voe-tchu-tcai*, *Governor of the Uni-'verſe*. They informed me, that they had taken theſe 'names from the Chineſe books, and that they uſed them 'to expreſs the Supreme Being and firſt cauſe.

'In going from the ſynagogue, I obſerved a hall, which 'I had the curioſity to enter, but found nothing remark-'able in it, except a great number of cenſers. They told 'me that in this hall they honoured their *Chir[illegible]s*, or 'the great men of their law. The largeſt of theſe cenſers, 'which is intended for the patriarch Abraham, ſtands in 'the middle of the hall, after which come thoſe of Iſaac, 'and of Jacob, and his twelve branches, or the twelve 'tribes of Iſrael; next are thoſe of Moſes, Aaron, Joſhua, 'Eſdras, and ſeveral other illuſtrious perſons, both male 'and female.

'As the titles of the books of the Old Teſtament 'were printed in Hebrew at the end of my Bible, I ſhewed 'them to the *Cham-kiao*, or chief of the ſynagogue, he 'immediately read them, though they were badly printed, 'and informed me that they were the names of their '*Chu-kin*, or Pentateuch. I then took my Bible, and 'the *Chem-kiao* his *Beréſith*, for thus they name the 'book of Geneſis, we compared the deſcendants of Adam, 'until Noah with the age of each, and we found the moſt 'perfect conformity between both. We afterwards ran 'over the names and chronology in Geneſis, Exodus, 'Leviticus, Numbers and Deuteronomy, which compoſe 'the Pentateuch, or five books of Moſes The chief of 'the ſynagogue told me, that they named theſe five books '*Beréſith*, *Veeleſemoth*, *Vaiicra*, *Vaudabber*, and *Haddebarim* Some of theſe they opened, and preſented to me 'to read, but it was to no purpoſe, as I was unacquainted 'with the Hebrew language.

'Having interrogated him reſpecting the titles of the 'other books of the Bible, he replied, that they were in poſſeſſion of ſome of them, but that they wanted a good 'many, and of others they had no knowledge Some of 'the aſſiſtants added, that they had loſt ſeveral books in 'the inundation of the *Hoang-ho*, of which I have ſpoken. 'Their ancient rabbies have mixed ſeveral ridiculous tales 'with the facts recorded in ſcripture, and even in the five 'books of Moſes They told me ſuch a number of extravagant fictions on this ſubject, that I could not forbear laughter [illegible] hence I concluded that they were 'Talmudiſts [illegible] can be determined only by one 'verſed in the ſcriptures, and well acquainted with the 'Hebrew language

'Theſe Jews [illegible] preſerve ſeveral of the ceremonies 'mentioned in the Old Teſtament, such as circumciſion, 'which they [illegible] from the patriarch Abraham, '[illegible] unleavened bread, the paſchal lamb, in com-

'memoration of their departure from Egypt, and of their 'passage through the Red Sea, the sabbath, and other fes- 'tivals prescribed by the ancient law.

'All these Jews, called in China *Tiao-kin-kiao*, com- 'pose at present only a few families, the names of the prin- 'cipal of which are. *Thao*, *Kin*, *Che*, *Cao*, *Theman*, '*Li*, *Ngai*. They form alliances with one another, and 'never mix with the *Hoei-hoei*, or Mahometans

'They have no other synagogue but the one in the 'capital of *Ho-nan*: I perceived in it no altar, nor any 'other furniture, but the chair of Moses, with a censer, 'a long table and large chandeliers, in which were placed 'candles made of tallow. This synagogue resembles 'our European churches, it is divided into three aisles, 'that in the middle is occupied by the table of incense, 'the chair of Moses, the painting, and the tabernacles 'already mentioned, in which are preserved the thirteen 'copies of the Pentateuch These tabernacles are con- 'structed in the form of an arch, and the middle aisle is 'like the choir of the synagogue, the two others are set 'apart as places of prayer, and for the adoration of the 'Supreme Being. Within the building there is a passage 'which runs quite round it'

Father *Gozani* adds, that these Jews, in their inscrip- tions, call their law *Yselals-kiao*, or the law of Israel, also *Ko u-kiao*, or *Ancient Law*, *Tien-kiao*, *the Law of God*, and *Tiao-kin-kiao*, to signify that they abstain from blood. They told him that their ancestors came from a kingdom of the west, called the kingdom of *Judah*, which Joshua conquered, after they had left Egypt, crossed the Red Sea and traversed the desert, and that the number of the Jews who departed from Egypt amounted to sixty *ouan*, that is to say, to six hundred thousand men. They spoke to him of the book of Judges, and of David, Solomon, and Ezekiel, who raised up dry bones, and of Jonas, which proves, that beſides the Pentateuch, they have alſo ſeveral other parts of the ſacred writings.

These Jews neither kindle fire nor cook any victuals on Saturday, but they prepare on Friday whatever may be neceſſary for the day following. When they read the Bible in their ſynagogue, they cover their faces with a tranſparent veil, in remembrance of Moſes, who came down from the mountain with his face covered, and in that manner publiſhed the Decalogue or Law of God.

When F. *Gozani* ſpoke to them of the Meſſias promiſed and announced in the holy ſcriptures, they appeared much ſurpriſed, but when the miſſionary told them that the Meſſias was called *Jeſus*, they replied, that mention was made in their Bible of a holy man named *Jeſus*, who was the ſon of Sirach; but that they were altogether unacquainted with the new *Jeſus*, of whom he ſpoke.

The Mahometans have multiplied much more in China than the Jews. It is above ſix hundred years ſince they firſt entered this empire, in which they have now formed different eſtabliſhments. For a great number of years, they were preſerved only by marriages, and by the alliances which they contracted, but for ſome time paſt, they ſeem to have been more particularly attentive to the propagating their doctrine. The principal means which they employ for this purpoſe, are, to purchaſe, for a ſum of money, a great number of children brought up in idolatry, whom their poor parents, compelled by neceſſity, readily part with. Theſe they circumciſe, and afterwards educate and inſtruct in the principles of their religion. During the time of a terrible famine, which deſolated the province of Chang-tong, they purchaſed more than ten thouſand of theſe children, for whom, when grown up, they procured wives, and built houſes, and even formed whole villages of them. They inſenſibly increaſed, and are now become ſo numerous, that they intirely exclude from thoſe places in which they reſide, every inhabitant who does not believe in their prophet, and frequent a moſque.

We ſhall not here ſpeak of the labours of the European miſſionaries, as what concerns the progreſs of the Chriſtian religion in China, has been already treated of in the General Hiſtory.

VIEW OF THE MANNERS AND CUSTOMS OF THE *CHINESE.*

MARRIAGES

THE manners of the Chinese bear no kind of resemblance to those of any known nation; and what is equally remarkable, they have remained always nearly the same. Every custom formerly practised is still preserved with little variation, whatever they formerly did, they do at present, and exactly in the same manner

Public decency has been always respected in China, because great care and attention have been employed to enforce it. Marriage, recommended and encouraged by all great legislators, is particularly protected in China Whoever seduces the wife of another is put to death, and the same punishment is generally inflicted on the person who debauches a young woman In both these circumstances, the precautions dictated by universal custom tend greatly to support the law, and often render it superfluous

According to the Abbe Grosier, " a Chinese enters into the married state often without ever having seen the woman whom he espouses: he knows nothing of her looks or person, but from the account of some female relation or confidant, who, in such cases, acts the part of match-maker. It is true, that, if they impose upon him, either with respect to her age or figure, he can have recourse to a divorce. Here the law, in its turn, serves to correct the abuses of custom."

"The same matrons who negociate the marriage determine the sum which the intended husband must pay to the parents of the bride, for, in China, a father does not give a dowry to his daughter: but the husband gives a dowry to his wife, or, we may say with more propriety, purchases her of her parents or friends."

"The parents of the bride fix the day for solemnizing the marriage, and they always take care to make choice of one that is lucky; for they consider some as favourable, and others as unfavourable to every great undertaking. During this interval, the two families send presents to each other, and the bridegroom purchases for his intended spouse some jewels, such as rings, pendants or bracelets. Frequent letters pass between the parties, but they are not permitted to see one another."

"When the day appointed for the ceremony arrives, the bride is placed in a chair, or close palankin. Every thing that composes her portion is borne before and behind her by different persons of both sexes, while others surround her, carrying torches and flambeaux, even in the middle of the day. A troop of musicians, with fifes, drums and hautboys, march before her chair, and her family follow it behind. The key of the chair in which she is shut up, is committed to the care of a trusty domestic, to be delivered to the husband only. The husband, richly dressed, waits at his gate for the arrival of the procession. As soon as it approaches, the key is put into his hands, he eagerly opens the chair, and at the first glance learns his fortune. It sometimes happens, that the husband, discontented with his intended spouse, suddenly shuts the chair, and sends her back to her relations. To get rid of her, it only costs him a sum equal to that which he gave to obtain her."

"If the husband is contented, she descends from her chair, and enters the house, followed by the relations of both, where the new-married couple salute the *Tien* four times in the hall, and afterwards the parents of the husband. The bride is then committed into the hands of the women who have been invited to the ceremony, and who, together with her, partake of an entertainment, which continues the whole day: the male part of the guests are treated in the like manner by the husband. The same form prevails among the Chinese at all their grand feasts: the women amuse themselves separately, and the men do the same in another apartment. The pomp increases according to the riches and rank of the parties, and diminishes also in the same proportion."

This account, to which the Abbe adds several ceremonies attendant on the consummation of the nuptials, Mr. Anderson positively contradicts, and observes, that "to give an accurate description of the marriage ceremony in China, is to do little more than to reply to the Abbe Grosier, whose account of the Chinese nuptials, as well as of many other of their customs, is altogether erroneous."

Mr. Anderson says, "the marriage ceremony which I saw at Macao, had little in common with this description, but the palanquin. The bride, seated in that machine, was preceded by music, and ensigns of various colours were borne by men both before and in the rear of the procession, which consisted principally of the relatives of the bride and bridegroom, who escort her to the house of her husband, where a feast is prepared, and the day is passed in mirth and festivity Nor is the evening concluded with those absurd ceremonies with which the Abbe Grosier, and other authors, have ridiculously encumbered the consummation of a Chinese wedding"

It must here be observed, that Mr. Anderson's account extends no farther than the mere procession of the ceremony, and perhaps even this may be in a great measure reconciled by the consideration of the Abbe making his observations at Pe-kin and the other at Macao

We have already noticed that a Chinese is permitted to have only one lawful wife; but that he may purchase several concubines. Every Chinese who is desirous of embracing this privilege, and keeping on good terms with his wife, pretends to be actuated by some good motive, and he is particularly careful to let her know, that if he takes concubines, it is only with a view of procuring her a greater number of women to attend her.

A widower raises sometimes his favourite concubine to the rank of lawful wife He is not then obliged, as in the former case, to examine whether the rank of her whom he espouses approaches near to his own and he is also freed from all preliminary formalities

These concubines are almost all procured from the cities of *Yang-tcheou* and *Sou-tcheou*, where, as we have before observed, they are educated, and taught singing, dancing and music, and every accomplishment suitable to women of quality, or which can render them agreeable and pleasing, and the greater part of them are purchased in other places to be again disposed of

A widow of any rank above the common, seldom enters a second time into the state of marriage when she has children Widows of ordinary rank, who have children, generally avail themselves of the liberty which is granted them, and unite themselves to another husband Grosier observes, that, " those of the poorer sort are not free to follow their own inclination they are sold for the benefit of the parents of the deceased.—As soon as the bargain is concluded, a couple of porters bring a chair, which is guarded by a number of trusty people. The widow is shut up in this chair, and in that manner conducted to the house of her new husband."

He also adds, "that masters, for the most part, are very desirous of promoting marriage among their slaves, whatever *M. de Paw* may say, who, without any foundation, has ventured boldly to assert the contrary. They have even very strong motives to induce them to encourage these marriages: the children produced by them are still their slaves, they become new property to them, and they constitute a fresh tie, which attaches the mothers and fathers more and more to their service."

This assertion of the Abbe's Mr. Anderson, also, boldly contradicts, and declares that "this is a mere fable, as there are no such class of people as slaves in the Chinese empire. They cannot import slaves in their own vessels, which are never employed but in their domestic commerce: and he must be afflicted with the most credulous ignorance, who believes that they import them in foreign bottoms. If, therefore, there are any slaves in China, they must be natives of the country, and among them, it is well known, that there is no class of people who are in that degrading situation."

"Certain classes of criminals are punished with servitude for a stated period, or for life, according to the nature of their offences, and they are employed in the more laborious parts of public works. But if this is slavery, the unhappy convicts, who heave ballast on the Thames, are slaves. There is a custom, indeed, in China, respecting this class of criminals, that does not prevail in England, which is, their being hired for any service they are capable of performing: and this frequently happens, as these convicts may be had at a cheaper rate than ordinary labourers. This regulation, however, has one good effect, that it exonerates government from the expence of maintaining such unhappy persons, without lessening the rigor or disgrace of the punishment. But I re-assert that slavery, by which I mean the power which one man obtains over another, by purchase, or inheritance, as in our West India islands, is not known in China. Indeed, some of the Chinese in the interior parts of the country were, with difficulty, made to comprehend the nature of such a character as a slave; and when I illustrated the matter, by explaining the situation of a negro boy, called Benjamin, whom Sir George Staunton had purchased at Batavia, they expressed the strongest marks of disgust and abhorrence. The conversation to which I allude took place at Jehol, in Tartary; but at Canton, where the communication with Europeans gives the merchants a knowledge of what is passing in our quarter of the globe, poor Benjamin was the cause of some observations on his condition, that astonished me when I heard, and will, I believe, surprise the reader when he peruses, them. The boy being in a shop with me in the suburbs of Canton, some people who had never before seen a black, were very curious in making inquiries concerning him; when the merchant, to whom the warehouse belonged, expressed his surprise, in broken English, that the British nation should suffer a traffic so disgraceful to that humanity which they were so ready to profess. and on my informing him that our parliament intended to abolish it, he surprised me with the following extraordinary answer, which I give in his own words:—"Aye, aye, "black man, in English country, have got one first chop, "good mandarin Willforce, that have done much good "for allau blackie man, much long time allau man "makie chin, chin, hee, because he have got more first "chop tink, than much English merchant men, because "he merchant-man tinkee for catch money, no tinkee

" for poor blackie man Josh, no like so fashion." The meaning of these expressions is as follows "Aye, in " England, the black men have got an advocate and " friend, Mr Wilberforce, who has, for a considerable " time, been doing them service, and all good people, " as well as the blacks, adore the character of a gentle- " man, whose thoughts have been directed to meliorate " the condition of those men · and not like our West- " India planters, or merchants, who, for the love of " gain, would prolong the misery of so large a portion " of his fellow-creatures as the African slaves. But God " does not approve of such a practice '

In this passage Mr Anderson not only denies one, but every species of slavery as existing in China, and herein he not only differs with the Abbe and the general accounts of the missionaries whose opinions we have before given, but with M de Paw, who had before attacked the Abbe on the subject of their marriage M de Paw observes, * " In our days the prepossessions in favor of the people of China have been carried so far as to maintain that neither real nor personal servitude of any kind subsists among them, and this is likewise asserted by the author of the Philosophical and Political History of the European Establishments in the two Indies † But he might with equal reason alledge, that the negroes of St Domingo, who cultivate a few sugar canes, are real republicans "

In another place ‡ he observes, " some are slaves in China from their birth, while others, who were originally free, have been sold either with their own consent, or by force, and their descendants remain in bondage Liberty is so lightly treated, that a man can sell himself

* P[illegible] Dissertations on the Chinese &c

† Vol [illegible]

‡ Dissertation on the Chinese Government.

there at the present day The Chinese are ignorant of that species of slavery known in Greece and Egypt, where one whole nation is condemned to serve another, and which may be called Helotism Yet this fate might have attended the Moguls, had they been subjugated instead of being expelled, but, from causes difficult to be explained, they are again very powerful in China, and they increase daily, as well as the Mahometans The latter have among them a species of slavery less shocking to natural right than all others they rear some of the children exposed on dunghills by the Chinese, and subject them, when grown up, to a very easy yoke"

The account of slavery existing in China, is very generally admitted by all those who have had an opportunity of properly acquainting themselves with the subject, of whom, it must be confessed, none had ever a better than the missionaries, and as their testimony stands in this case admitted by their vigilant and able opponent, we cannot but think it requires a more powerful testimony than any we have yet met with, to induce a European to relinquish the idea that slavery exists in China. Nay we are inclined to rely on the testimony of Grosier, respecting the willingness of masters to promote marriage among them, for M. De Paw agrees with him in saying, that "their descendants remain with their parents in bondage."

The missionaries declare that the Chinese women, even those of the greatest rank, seldom quit their apartment, and the book of *Ceremonies* requires, that there should be two apartments in every house, the exterior for the husband, and the interior for his spouse. They must be separated by a wooden partition, or a wall, and the door must be carefully guarded: the husband is not at liberty to enter the inner apartment, nor must the wife ever quit it without a sufficient cause "A wife," adds this book, "is not mistress of herself, she has nothing at her own "disposal, she can give no orders but within the pre-"cincts of her own apartment, to which all her autho-"rity is confined." Whatever may be the law, or have been the custom in this case, we cannot, however, but think this severity is in a great degree dispensed with, for Mr Anderson observes, in his account of Pe-kin, that "the opinion that the Chinese women are excluded from the view of strangers, has little if any foundation, as among the immense crowd assembled to see the cavalcade of the English embassy, one fourth of the whole at least were women."—He farther informs us, that having taken advantage of the halting of the baggage carts, to step out of the machine in which he was conveyed, and perceiving a number of women in the crowd, he ventured to approach them, and addressed them with the Chinese word *Chou-an* or beautiful. They appeared to be extremely diverted, and gathering round him with an air of great modesty and politeness examined the make and form of his clothes, as well as the texture of the materials of which they were composed—that when he parted from them, he took leave by a gentle shake of the hand, which they tendered him with the most graceful affability, nor adds he, "did the men who were present appear to be at all dissatisfied with my conduct, but on the contrary expressed, as far as I could judge, very great satisfaction at the public attention which I paid to the ladies."

Something of this kind appears to have happened in some of the other cities, but it was not general, and it is possible, that the novelty of the procession may have been the moving cause of this indulgence to the Chinese females on the above occasions.

Mr. Anderson, however, draws from the whole of his observations the following conclusion, "In different parts of that extensive country different customs may prevail; and the power of husbands over their wives may be such as to render them maſters of their liberty, which they may exercise with ſeverity, if circumſtances ſhould at any time ſuggeſt the neceſſity of ſuch a meaſure, or caprice fancy it: but I do not heſitate to aſſert, that women in general, have a reaſonable liberty in China, and that there is the ſame communication and ſocial intercourſe with women, which, in Europe, is conſidered as a predominant charm of ſocial life."

This increaſe of liberty among the Chineſe females, appears to us to be the effect of a change of diſpoſition, rather than a change of laws reſpecting them, for if it originated in an alteration of the latter, the experience would be uniform, which is not the caſe any more than with putting bandages round the feet, which is evidently a partial and declining cuſtom.

EDUCATION OF CHILDREN.

According to the book of Ceremonies, the education of a child ſhould commence at the very moment of its birth, but it may be eaſily conceived that it muſt be then purely phyſical.

At the age of ſix, if it be a male, he is made acquainted with the numbers moſt in uſe, and with the names of the principal parts of the world. At eight he is inſtructed in the rules of politeneſs. The calendar becomes his ſtudy at the age of nine, and at ten he is ſent to a public ſchool, where he learns to read, write, and caſt accompts. From thirteen till fifteen he is taught muſic, and every thing which he ſings conſiſts of moral precepts.

When boys have attained to the age of fifteen, they are taught to handle a bow and arrow, and to mount on horſeback. At twenty they receive the firſt cap, if they are judged to deſerve it, and they are permitted to wear ſilk dreſſes, ornamented with furs, before that period they have no right to wear any thing but cotton.

It is much to be lamented that the Chineſe have no proper alphabet, and their children are above all to be pitied, who must be under the neceſſity of ſtudying ſo many thouſands of characters, each of which has a diſtinct and particular ſignification. The book firſt put into their hands is an abridgement, which points out what a child ought to learn, and the manner in which he ſhould be taught. It is a collection of ſhort ſentences, conſiſting of three or four verſes each, all of which rhyme.

After this elementary treatiſe, they put into their hands the books which contain the doctrines of Confucius and Mencius, the ſenſe and meaning of which is never explained to them, until they know by heart all the characters, a method we conceive very diſguſting. While they are learning theſe letters, they are taught alſo to form them with a pencil. The expedient which they employ for this purpoſe is to furniſh them large leaves of paper on which are written or imprinted with red ink very large characters, and all they are required to do, is, to cover theſe red characters with black ink, and to follow exactly their ſhape and figure; this inſenſibly accuſtoms them to form the different ſtrokes. After this they are made to trace other characters placed under the paper on which they write, but theſe are black, and much ſmaller than the former.

As it is conſidered of great advantage to the Chineſe literati to be able to paint characters well, they on this account take particular pains in forming the hands of young people. A neatneſs in characters is made of the utmoſt conſequence in thoſe examinations, which ſtudents undergo before they are admitted to the firſt degree. A deficiency in this reſpect often occaſions them to be rejected. Of this F. Du Halde gives the following inſtance: "A candidate for degrees, having, contrary to order, "made uſe of an abbreviation in writing the character, "*ma*, which ſignifies *horſe*, had the mortification of ſee-

"ing his composition, though in other respects excellent, "rejected merely on that account, besides being severely "rallied by the mandarin, who told him that a horse "could not walk unless he had all his legs."

When a scholar is become master of a sufficient number of characters, he is permitted to compose. In this exercise a kind of competition is established. Twenty or thirty families, all of the same name, and who consequently have only one hall for the manes of their ancestors, agree to send their children to this hall twice a month in order to compose. Each head of a family in turn gives the subject of this literary contest, and adjudges the prize, a privilege which lays him under the necessity of being at the expence of a dinner, which is given in the hall of competition.

A fine of the value of about ten-pence sterling is imposed on the parent of each scholar, who absents himself from this exercise, but seldom is there occasion for recurring to such an expedient.

Competitions of this kind are, however, private, and have no concern with the rules of public education, but every student is obliged to complete a thesis, or essay, at least twice a year, under the inspection of an inferior mandarin of letters, styled *Hio kouan*, and this practice is general thoughout all the provinces of the empire. The mandarins of letters, likewise, often order these students before them, to examine the progress they have made in their studies, and to excite a spirit of emulation among them, without which it would be impossible for any of them ever to rise to eminence. Even the governors of cities do not think it below their dignity to take this care upon themselves. They order all those students, who live near their residence, to appear at their tribunal once a month. The author of the best composition is honoured with a prize, and the governor treats all the candidates on the day of competition at his own expence.

Europeans can ſcarcely conceive how far the ſovereigns of China have carried their attention, in order to promote and encourage letters In every city and town; and almoſt in every village, there are maſters who keep ſchools for the purpoſe of teaching thoſe ſciences with which the Chineſe are acquainted. Parents poſſeſſed of a certain fortune, provide preceptors for their children at home, who endeavour to form their minds to virtue, to initiate them in the rules of good breeding and the accuſtomed ceremonies, and, when their age admits, to make them acquainted with the laws and hiſtory of their country.

Theſe tutors, for the moſt part, have attained to one or two degrees among the literati. They continue their literary purſuits, and ſubmit to the different examinations; and the pupil frequently finds his preceptor become his viceroy.

Students, who have paſſed the firſt examination, and have been judged capable of undergoing that of the mandarins, have arrived at that point, which terminates the education of infancy, but if they attain to the different degrees without riſing to offices of ſtate, their education continues almoſt as long as their lives

We ſhall ſay very little of the education of the Chineſe females—It is confined to giving them a taſte for ſolitude, and accuſtoming them to modeſty, and even to ſilence If their parents are rich, they are alſo inſtructed in ſuch accompliſhments as may render them agreeable and pleaſing. The duties of women in China, as in other Aſiatic countries, are merely of the paſſive kind

VESTMENTS AND DRESS OF BOTH SEXES.

In cities, the dreſs of the Chineſe is almoſt the ſame among people of both orders, and of either ſex, but certain appendages, or ornaments, diſtinguiſh the rank and dignity of thoſe who wear them, and ſevere chaſtisement would be the consequence to any person who should venture to assume a dress not authorised

The Chinese dress, in general, consists of a vest, which reaches to the ground, one part of which folds over the other, and is fastened by four or five gold or silver buttons, which are placed at a small distance one from another. The sleeves of this garment are wide towards the shoulder, and grow narrower as they approach the wrist, where they terminate in the form of a horse-shoe, covering the hands, and leaving nothing to be seen but the ends of the fingers The Chinese also wear round their middles a large girdle of silk, the ends of which hang down to their knees. From this girdle is suspended a sheath, with a kind of knife, together with those two small sticks which they use at their meals.

Under this robe they wear a pair of drawers suited to the season. In summer they are made of linen; and sometimes covered with another pair, of white taffety: those for winter are of sattin lined with fur, of cotton, or coarse silk, and sometimes of skins, particularly in the northern provinces Their shirts are always wide, but very short, and of different kinds of cloth, according to the season Under his shirt, a Chinese generally wears a silk net, which prevents it from adhering to the skin.

In summer they have their necks always bare, and in winter they wear a collar, made of silk, sable or fox's skin, joined to their robe, which is then trimmed with sheep's skin, or quilted with silk and cotton. That of the mandarins and people of quality is lined throughout with sable brought from Tartary, or with fox's skin, trimmed with sable In spring it is lined with ermine Above their robe, they wear also a kind of surtout, with wide sleeves, but very short, which is lined in the same manner.

We have before observed, that the law has regulated every thing that relates to dress, and even fixed the colours that diſtinguiſh the different conditions. The emperor and princes of the blood alone wear yellow; certain mandarins are permitted to wear ſattin of a red ground, upon days of ceremony, but in general they are clothed in black, blue or violet. The colour to which the common people are confined, is blue or black, and their dreſs is always compoſed of plain cotton cloth. Of the dreſſes of ceremony worn by the Chineſe mandarins, and their ornaments, &c. the annexed plates will furniſh the beſt idea.

The Chineſe ſhave their heads, but they have not been always accuſtomed to do this, they formerly employed great pains in preſerving their hair, but the Tartars, who ſubdued them, compelled them to cut it after their manner. This revolution in dreſs was not effected without bloodſhed, and it was neceſſary to employ force, before they could be induced to imitate the Tartars. It muſt certainly appear ſingular, that the conqueror of China ſhould require this trifling and nonſenſical compliance, when he adopted their laws, their manners, and their conſtitution.

The ſmall portion of hair which the Chineſe preſerve on the tops of their heads, or behind, is all that is allowed by cuſtom, it is generally very long, and they plait it in the form of a tail. In ſummer they wear on their heads a kind of pyramidical cap, lined with ſattin, and covered with ratan, or cane, neatly wrought. To the top they fix a large tuft of red hair, which falling down covers it to the brim.

There is another kind of head-dreſs, which the mandarins and literati only have a right to wear. It is a cap of the ſame form as the preceding, but lined with red ſattin, and covered on the outſide with white. A large tuft of the fineſt red ſilk is fixed over it, which is ſuffered to hang down, or wave with the wind. They, however, generally uſe the common cap when they mount on horſe-

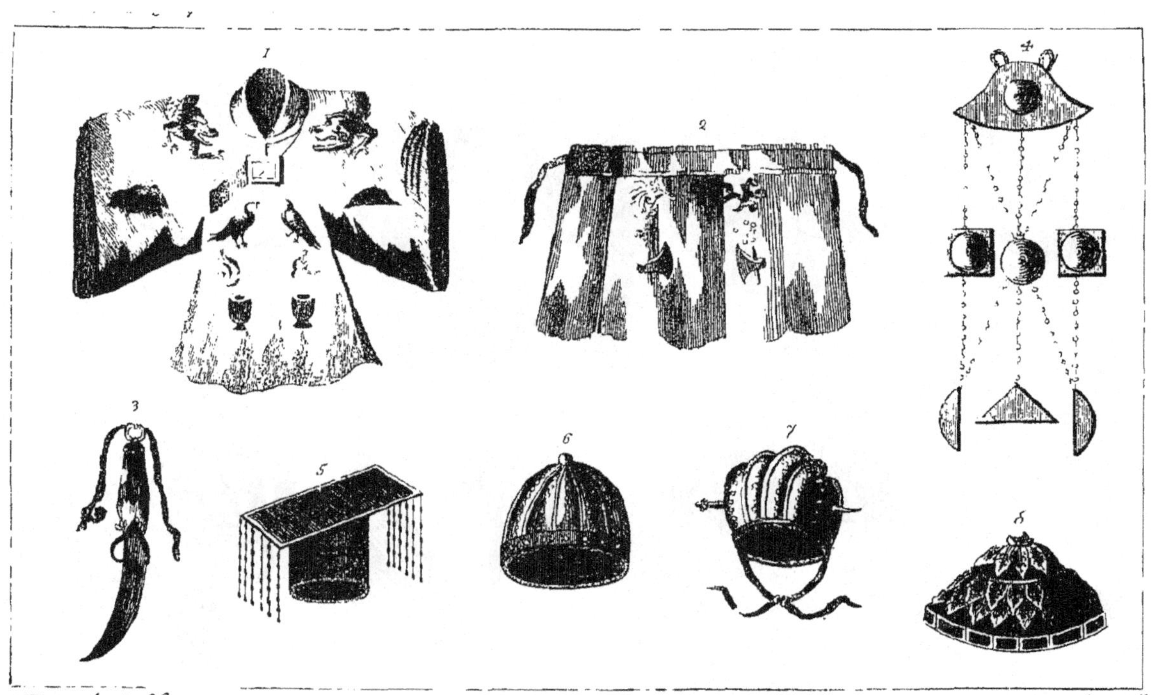

1 Upper dress of Ceremony
2 Under d°.
3 A Dagger

Chinese Dresses of Ceremony.

4 Ornament worn to the Girdle
5 Cap of Ceremony
6.7.8 Other Caps

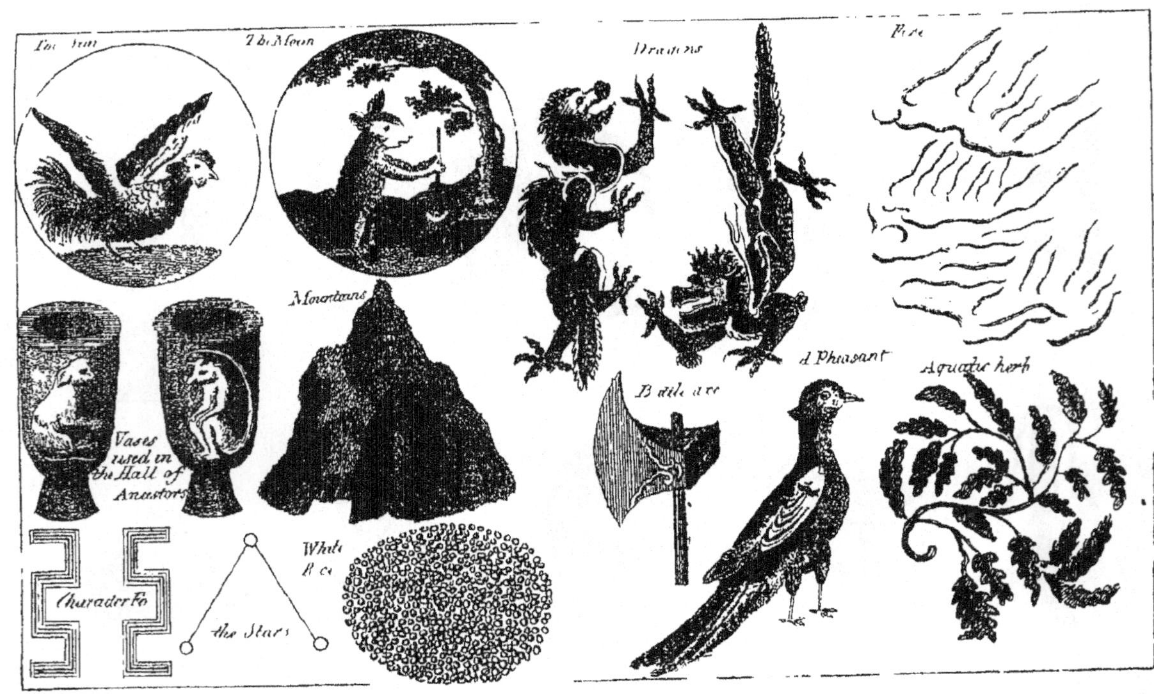

Published June 25 1795 by W. Winterbotham

Ornaments worn on the dresses of the Chinese

back, or during bad weather, because it is better calculated to keep off rain, and to shelter those who wear it from the rays of the sun For winter they have still another cap, which is exceedingly warm it is bordered with sable, ermine or fox's skin, and ornamented with a tuft of silk, like the former.

People of condition when they go abroad wear boots, of sattin, silk or cotton, but always d ed These boots have neither heel nor top, and they are made to fit the foot with the greatest exactness. When they travel on horseback, they have others, made of cow or horse leather, prepared in such a manner, that it is very soft and pliable The boot stockings which they wear in winter, are of quilted stuff, lined with cotton they reach above the top of the boot, and are ornamented with a border of velvet or cloth For summer they have a cooler kind, and in their houses they wear a sort of slippers, made of silk-stuff The common people are contented with a kind of slippers, made of black cotton cloth A Chinese, dressed according to rule, would consider it as great an omission to forget his fan, as it would be to forget his boots

The dress of the Chinese women, in its shape and form, seems to have been dictated by modesty, seconded perhaps by jealousy. Their robes are close at top, and very long. With regard to the colour of their dresses, it is entirely arbitrary, and depends upon choice, but black or violet are generally adopted by those advanced in life

Their general head-dress consists in arranging their hair in several curls, among which are interspersed small tufts of gold or silver flowers

Young ladies wear also a kind of crown or bonnet made of pasteboard covered with fine stuff or silk, the fore-part rises in a point above the forehead, and is covered with pearls, diamonds and other costly ornaments The rest of the head is decorated with flowers, either natural or artificial, among which are interspersed small diamond pins.

Among thofe whimfical and wretched cuftoms from which no nation is wholly free, we muft reckon the means employed by the Chinefe to preferve the feet of their women almoft as fmall as they were when they firft came into the world—This cuftom was formerly general throughout the empire, but appears now to be only very partial, and in the moft unenlightened parts. The means made ufe of are as follows, when a female child is born, the nurfe wraps up its feet, and confines them by a very clofe bandage, and this torture muft be endured until the foot has ceafed to grow On this account, a Chinefe woman fubjected to this cuftom, rather drags herfelf along than walks Some writers have attributed the origin of this practice to jealoufy, while others have confidered it as a political expedient, intended to infpire females with a love of folitude, and to keep them in a continual ftate of dependence; but be its origin what it may, like many other old prejudices, it is evidently growing into difufe.

The drefs of a Tartar lady is fomewhat different from that of a Chinefe The robe of the former is equally long, but the veft which covers it, does not defcend fo low This robe is alfo clofe at the top, and the Tartar ladies wear, befides, upon their breafts, a very large band. Their ufual head-drefs is a hat, ornamented according to the fancy of the wearer.

The drefs of a villager differs from that worn by thofe who live in towns It confifts of a coarfe linen frock, over which is thrown a cotton veft, that defcends to the middle of his thigh He has a pair of large drawers, that rife to his girdle, and reach as far as the ancle, and his flippers, or rather wooden fhoes, terminate at the toe in a fharp point, which is turned backwards.

BUILDINGS AND FURNITURE OF THE CHINESE.

The Chinefe buildings, even public monuments, and the emperor's palaces, ftrike more by their extent than their magnificence. Many of the imperial palaces may be compared to cities, and thofe of the princes, principal mandarins, and people of great fortune are very extenfive. The halls fet apart for receiving vifits are very neat, and provided with feats and other pieces of furniture, but nothing can be perceived in them which marks either magnificence or grandeur. The apartment where they entertain their intimate friends is equally plain and fimple. With regard to thofe fet apart for their women and children, they are inacceffible to every ftranger, were he even the deareft and moft intimate friend of the mafter of the houfe.

The Chinefe gardens are laid out in fuch a manner, as to particularly attract the attention of an European. In thefe gardens are feen groves, ponds, mountains, natural or artificial rocks, and winding alleys, which conduct to different points of view, each of which prefents a new object, &c When the ground is of fufficient extent, part of the garden is formed into a park, in which ftags, does and other wild animals are kept. Fifhes and aquatic birds are alfo bred in ponds and canals made for the purpofe

The Chinefe are fond of every thing gigantic. According to them, the beauty of a column confifts in its fize and height, and that of a hall, in its great extent. all ancient nations were fond of this grotefque architecture.

The Chinefe fhew little defire for ornamenting and embellifhing the interior part of their houfes. they have neither mirrors, tapeftry, nor gilding. They receive no vifits but in a particular hall deftined for that purpofe, in the front part of the houfe, in order to prevent thofe who are admitted into it from having any communication with the inner apartments. Its ornaments confift of large lanterns, made of painted filk, which are fufpended from the ceiling; tables, cabinets, fcreens, chairs, and abundance of vaſes, of porcelain The furniture, in general, is covered with varniſh ſo tranſparent, that the veins of the wood may be ſeen through it, and ſo bright and ſhining, that it ſtrongly reflects different objects, and its ſplendour is not a little heightened by thoſe figures which are painted upon it, in different colours, or done over with gilding.

The Chineſe neither uſe, nor are they acquainted with the art of manufacturing rich tapeſtries like thoſe in Europe. Thoſe uſed by the wealthieſt people, are of white ſattin with birds, flowers, landſcapes, &c. painted upon them. Sometimes they contain alſo, in large characters, a few moral ſentences, which generally compoſe a kind of enigma. The poor are contented with whitening the walls of their apartments, or covering them with that ſort of paper which is brought us from China, and which people of fortune, in Europe, often employ to ornament ſome part of theirs.

PUBLIC AND PRIVATE REJOICINGS.

We have already noticed the manner in which the emperor of China celebrates the vernal feſtival. It is celebrated alſo on the ſame day throughout the reſt of the empire. In the morning, the governor of every city comes forth from his palace, crowned with flowers, and ſeats himſelf in a chair, amidſt the noiſe of different inſtruments, and the acclamations of the people.

A proceſſion is now formed in the following order. A number of perſons bearing flambeaux, &c go firſt, the muſicians follow next, then the governor in the chair ſurrounded with ſeveral litters covered with ſilk carpets, ornamented with the repreſentations of illuſtrious perſons who have encouraged agriculture, or ſome hiſtorical print on the ſame ſubject.

A large figure, made of baked earth, repreſenting a cow with gilt horns, comes next. forty men are ſometimes ſcarcely ſufficient to ſupport it. A child, with one foot naked, and the other ſhod, which repreſents the *Spirit of Labour and Diligence*, follows, and keeps continually beating the image with a rod, to make it advance. Labourers, armed with their implements of huſbandry, march behind, and a number of comedians, and people in maſks, cloſe the rear, whoſe groteſque appearance and attitudes afford much entertainment to the populace.

The proceſſion advances towards the eaſtern gate, to meet the ſpring, and then returns to the governor's palace in the ſame order. After this, the cow is ſtripped of all its ornaments, and a prodigious number of earthen calves are taken from its belly, which are diſtributed among the crowd. The large figure itſelf is broken in pieces, and diſtributed alſo in like manner. The governor then puts an end to the ceremony, by making a ſhort oration in praiſe of agriculture, in which he endeavours to excite his hearers not to neglect ſo uſeful and valuable an art.

During the whole of this proceſſion, the ſtreets through which it paſſes are hung with carpets, lanterns are diſplayed, and the evening is cloſed with a brilliant illumination. A common reader will eaſily diſcern what that leſſon is which the Chineſe government wiſhes to inculcate by the emblematical repreſentations and ceremonious attention to this proceſſion.

The Chineſe have alſo two other feſtivals, which are celebrated with ſtill more pomp and ſplendour than that now deſcribed. One of them is on the commencement of the year, the other is called the *feaſt of lanterns*. During the celebration of the firſt, all affairs, whether private or public, are ſuſpended, the tribunals are ſhut; the poſts are ſtopped, preſents are given and received; the inferior mandarins go to pay their reſpects to their ſuperiors, children to their parents, and ſervants to their maſters, &c. "This," F. Du Halde ſays, "is what the "Chineſe call *taking leave of the old year*." All the family assemble in the evening, and partake of a grand repast. To this no stranger is admitted, but they become more sociable on the day following, and their whole time is employed in plays, diversions and feasting, which is concluded in the evening by illuminations.

The feast of lanterns is fixed for the fifteenth day of the first month but it begins on the evening of the thirteenth, and ends on the sixteenth It is easier to describe this festival than to discover its origin, or the period at which it was at first celebrated. It is universal throughout the empire, and all China is illuminated on the same day, and at the same hour Every city and village, the shores of the sea, and the banks of the rivers, are hung with lanterns, of various shapes and sizes. Some of them are even seen in the courts, and in the windows of the poorest inhabitants. The Abbe Grosier asserts, that rich people sometimes expend eight or nine pounds sterling, for one lantern, and that those which the emperor, viceroys, and great mandarins order to be made, cost sometimes an hundred or an hundred and fifty pounds each.

These lanterns are very large, and some of them are composed of six wooden frames, either painted or neatly gilt, and filled up with fine transparent silk, upon which are painted flowers, animals, and human figures, others are round, and made of a blue, transparent kind of horn. Several lamps, and a great number of wax-candles, are put into these lanterns, to the corners of each are fixed streamers of sattin and silk of different colours, and a curious piece of carved-work is placed over its top

It appears evident that the Chinese are acquainted with our *magic lantern*, which they use in this festival, and which perhaps has been borrowed from them.

F. Du Halde observes, that " they cause shadows " to appear, which represent princes and princesses, sol-

"diers, buffoons, and other characters, the gestures of "which are so conformable to the words of those who "put them in motion, that one is almost induced to "believe that they speak in reality" These seem to be the same as the *Ombres Chinoises*, exhibited at the *Palais Royal* at Versailles, and since at some of our places of summer amusement in London.

The Chinese fire-works, so justly celebrated, are displayed in all their varieties during this festival, and a large one is exhibited in each quarter of the city.

Of the manner in which the Chinese observe their ordinary holidays, Mr. Anderson has given us the following account from his own observation

"In the first place they purchase provisions according to their situation and capacity, which are dressed, and placed before a small idol, fixed on an altar, in some form or other Every Chinese has one of these idols in his habitation, whether it be on the land, or on the water, in a house, or a junk This repast, with bread and fruit, and three small cups of wine, spirits, and vinegar, are, after a threefold obeisance from the people of the house to the idol, carried to the front of their dwelling they there kneel and pray, with great fervour, for several minutes, and, after frequently beating their heads on the ground, they rise, and throw the contents of the three cups to the right and left of them They then take a bundle of small pieces of gilt paper, which they set on fire, and hold over the meat This ceremonial is succeeded by lighting strings of small crackers, which hang from the end of a cane, and are made to crack over the meat. The repast is then placed before the idol or Josh, as it is called, (a term which means a deity) and after a repetition of obeisance, they conclude with a joyous dinner, exhilarated by a plenty of spirits, which are always boiled in pewter or copper vessels before they are taken."

"On the first of March it is usual, according to ancient custom, for dramatic pieces to be performed on stages in the principal streets of the different towns throughout the empire, for the amusement of the poor people, who are not able to purchase those pleasures. This beneficent act continues for a succession of several days, at the expence of the emperor, so that every morning and evening, during this period, the lower classes of his subjects enjoy a favorite pleasure without cost, and bless the hand which bestows it on them."

The Chinese endeavour to render every public ceremony as striking as possible. A viceroy, whenever he quits his palace, does it with a pomp truly regal, indeed far more so than any European monarch; but this splendor is nothing, when compared with that of the emperor when he leaves his palace on any public occasion, or when he goes to sacrifice in the temple of the *Tien*. The whole of the princes of the blood on these occasions attend, as do all the principal mandarins and grandees of the court, in their dresses of ceremony. The procession is wholly regulated by the court of ceremonies, and under their direction; and on any very particular occasion, two thousand of the literati, or mandarins, generally close the procession. Of the appearance of the emperor in his carriage of ceremony, and of the attendant mandarins some idea may be formed by the annexed plate.

PRIVATE DIVERSIONS, ENTERTAINMENTS AND CEREMONIES.

As the Chinese employ most of their time in attendance on their duty as members of society, they bestow very little on amusements. Naturally a grave people, they seldom assume an air of gaiety, but in compliance with

The Emperor of China in his Carriage of Ceremony

Publish'd June 2d 1795 by W. Winterbotham

ſome order, or eſtabliſhed cuſtom. They, however, have actors, and theatrical pieces, both comic and tragic, but they have no public theatres authoriſed by government, and their actors, like thoſe of the Tartar nations, are ſtrollers, who attend the houſes of thoſe who are able to pay them. Dancing, the favourite amuſement of European nations, is little if at all practiſed in China.

Hunting and ſhooting, which the titled tyrants of Europe wiſh to confine excluſively to themſelves, is free to every perſon in China, and if any one is deſirous of enjoying it alone, he cauſes a quantity of game to be ſhut up in a cloſe park. Every farmer is at liberty to prevent the deſtruction of his crops, by killing all thoſe animals which come to ravage his fields, without being in danger of proſecution as a poacher, or ſubjected to impriſonment and fine for ſo doing.

Fiſhing is conſidered by the Chineſe rather as an object of commerce and induſtry than amuſement. In their great fiſheries, they uſe nets, but private people employ a line. They uſe alſo for this purpoſe, in certain provinces, a kind of bird, the plumage of which is grey, its neck and bill are long, and the latter is very ſharp and hooked This bird is trained to catch fiſh, almoſt in the ſame manner as dogs are taught to purſue game

There is another method of fiſhing, which, though very ſimple, is practiſed only by the Chineſe They nail a board, about two feet in breadth, upon the edges of a long, narrow boat, from one end to the other This board, which is covered with a white ſhining varniſh, is placed in ſuch a manner, that it ſlopes almoſt imperceptibly, until it reaches the water it is only uſed on moon-light nights, and is always turned towards the moon, that the reflection of the light may increaſe its brightneſs and ſplendour and deceive the fiſh, which, in ſporting, often miſtake this varniſhed plank for the water, on account of its colour, throw themſelves towards it, and fall into the boat.

The ſoldiers alſo have a method of fiſhing with a bow and arrow, the latter of which is fixed to the bow by a ſtring, both to prevent it from being loſt and to enable them to draw out the fiſh which the arrow has pierced. others make uſe of tridents, to catch large fiſh, which are ſometimes found in the mud

Theſe are almoſt all the amuſements in which the Chineſe indulge themſelves They are entirely ignorant of all games of chance, and though they have muſicians and ſingers, they are far from having *operas*, or any regular ſpectacle deſerving of the notice of an enlightened European

The ceremonies of the Chineſe depend more upon poſitive laws, than on cuſtom Every perſon, from the chiefs of the firſt claſs, to the humbleſt individual in the loweſt, is perfectly acquainted with the titles he muſt give to others, and with thoſe that are due to himſelf, he knows alſo what marks of politeneſs he has reaſon to expect, and thoſe which it his duty to ſhew, the honours he can accept, and thoſe which he ought to pay Thus in China there are no diſputes concerning rank and precedency, two points which, in other countries, have produced quarrels, occaſioned bloodſhed, and propagated enmity, that has been even tranſmitted to ſucceeding generations

A viſit in China is conſidered as an affair of very great ſolemnity, it requires formal preliminaries, with which Europeans are unacquainted, or which they have thought proper to lay aſide. They bear a near reſemblance to thoſe we have noticed among the Tartars, varied only by a few trivial circumſtances, and, therefore, do not call for a particular description. Visits, which are paid by the inhabitants of any city to the governor, are always accompanied with presents, of more or less value.

When a governor has distinguished himself by his zeal, and mildness towards the people, the literati of his district have recourse to the following expedient, in order to acquaint him, that he is universally esteemed. They cause a dress to be made for him, composed of small square pieces of sattin, some red, others blue, green, black, yellow, &c. His birth-day is chosen as a time proper for presenting it, they then carry it with great ceremony, amidst the sound of different musical instruments. On their arrival, they are introduced into the outer hall, their presence is announced, and the magistrate soon after makes his appearance. They then present this vestment, and beg him to put it on. The mandarin at first refuses, and declares he has not merited that honor; but he at length yields to the intreaties of the literati, and the prayers of the people. This chequered garment is considered as the emblem of all the nations that wear different dresses, and by this ceremony they mean to inform the mandarin, that he is worthy of ruling them all.

A visit to a superior must always be paid before dinner, fasting, at least before wine has been tasted, for a mandarin would consider it as a gross insult, did the person who visits him, in the least smell of this liquor. However, if a visit is returned the same day it is received, it may be done after dinner, for this is a mark of attention and respect, which excuses every thing.

No person in China can pay a visit, without previously sending a visiting card, called *Tie-tsée*, to the porter of the person to whom the honour is intended. This card is generally of red paper ornamented with a few gilded flowers, except the person sending or receiving it be in mourning, and then it is black; it is folded up in the form of a ſcreen: the viſitor's name is written on one of the folds, and the ſtile of the card is more or leſs reſpectful, according to the rank and quality of the perſon to whom it is [illegible].

[illegible] ded, if thoſe to whom they are intended be of ſuperior rank to thoſe who propoſe to pay them, but not otherwiſe. By receiving the *Tie-tſee*, or card, the perſon is ſuppoſed to receive the viſit, and the porter is ordered to tell the viſitor, that to put him to as little trouble as poſſible, he is begged not to get out of his chair. After which, either on the ſame or on ſome of the three following days, the perſon viſited returns a *Tie-tſée*, which is either ſimply received, or followed by a real viſit.

Epiſtolary correſpondence, even between private individuals, is always attended with certain eſtabliſhed ceremonies, and these become more complicated if it is with a perſon of rank or diſtinction. Among people of the higher and moderate ranks, ſomething more is required in ſaluting than ſimply bowing or lifting the hat, as in Europe. A common ſalutation conſiſts in joining both hands together before the breaſt, moving them in an affectionate manner, bending the head a little, and reciprocally pronouncing *Tſin-tſin*, a complimentary word, which has almoſt the ſame ſignification as *your humble ſervant.* When a perſon of the lower order meets another of ſuperior rank, it is then neceſſary to join the hands, raiſe them above the forehead, afterwards bring them down to the earth, and bow the whole body.

When two perſons who are acquainted meet after an abſence of any time, they both fall on their knees oppoſite one another, bend their bodies to the earth, then raiſe them up, and repeat the ſame ceremonies two or three times. At an ordinary interview, a common phraſe anſwering to *how d'ye do?* is uſed, and the anſwer is *very well, thanks to your abundant felicity, Cao-lao-ye-hung-fo.*

When the Chinese see a man who is in good health, they say to him *Yung-fo*, that is to say, *prosperity is painted in your looks; you have a happy countenance*

When two mandarins, of equal rank, meet in the street, they never quit their chairs, each joins both hands, moves them downwards, then raises them to the forehead, and this salutation is repeated until they are out of each others sight, but if one of the two be of higher rank than the other, the inferior orders his chair to stop, or if he is on horseback, he dismounts, and makes a profound bow to his superior. In a word, politeness in China is as prevalent even in villages as in cities, and, as it has been established into a law, it is attended with as little sincerity in the one as in the other.

A Chinese, when addressing his superior, speaks neither in the first nor in the second person He will neither say *I*, nor *you*, but if he acknowledges a favour received, he will say, *the service which his lordship has rendered to his little servant, has been very acceptable to him* A son, when speaking to his father, never stiles himself his son, but his grandson, though he is perhaps the oldest of the family, and probably father of a family himself

He will also often make use of his own name, that is to say, of the name given him at that period, for the Chinese have different names, in succession, according with their age and rank The family name is that given at their birth, this is common to all those who are descended from the same grandfather. A month after, the mother and father give what is termed a diminutive name to their son, which is generally that of a flower, animal, &c. This name is changed when the youth has made some progress in his education at a public school, and generally for some flattering appellation, given by the master, which the pupil adds to his family name When he attains to manhood, he requests a new name from his friends, and this he retains during life, unless he rises to ſome dignity He is then honoured with another, ſuited to his talents and office No other is afterwards given him, not even that of his family In this they are the counterparts of the titled ariſtocracy of Europe

The repaſts or entertainments of people of diſtinction are generally ſumptuous, and always accompanied with the moſt ceremonious etiquette, and the ancient emperors eſtabliſhed it as a law, for thoſe who might give entertainments, that they ſhould ſalute each gueſt, ſeparately, every time they drank

The ceremonial of the invitation is not leſs complex than that of the entertainment An invitation is never ſuppoſed to be given with ſincerity, until it has been renewed three or four times in writing A card is ſent on the evening before the entertainment, another, in the morning of the appointed day, and a third, when every thing is prepared, and nothing neceſſary to be done but to ſit down to table Ceremonies are then renewed, which conſume a great deal of time, and conſiſt of apologies, excuſes, acknowledgements, &c much in the Tartar manner, and equally abſurd At theſe entertainments, comedies are often acted, and different exhibitions of ſlight of hand diſplayed The repreſentation commences with the noiſe of drums, covered with buffalo's hide, and the ſound of flutes, fifes, trumpets, and ſome other inſtruments, uſed by the Chineſe only, and which, perhaps, would afford little pleaſure to people of any other country

The Chineſe begin their repaſts, not by eating, but by drinking, the intendant, or *maître-d'hotel*, falling down on one knee invites the gueſts to *take a glaſs* Each then takes hold, with both his hands, of that which is placed for him, raiſes it as high as his forehead, then brings it down below the table, and again lifts it to his mouth the maſter of the houſe preſſes them to drink heartily, and ſets them an example, by ſhewing them all round the bottom of his cup, in order that he may excite each of them to imitate him.

It is while they are drinking, that the dishes on the tables are removed, and others brought in, all of which are in the form of ragouts The Chinese never use knives in their repasts; and two small sharp-pointed sticks, ornamented with ivory or silver, supply the place of forks.

Their boulli, which answers to European soup, is never served up, till towards the middle of the repast, and is accompanied by small loaves, or meat pies, which they take up with their small sticks, steep them in the soup, and eat them, without waiting for any signal, or attending to any ceremony The repast continues, and ceremonies preserve their utmost formality, till the very moment in which tea is introduced: after which the company all rise from table, and retire, either into another hall, or into the garden, where they amuse themselves, and enjoy a short interval of repose between dinner and the dessert.

The dessert, like the entertainment, consists of numerous dishes of sweet-meats, fruits prepared different ways, hams and salted ducks, which have been dried in the sun, together with shell and other kinds of small fish. The same ceremonies are again renewed before the guests take their places at table, and every one sits down to that at which he was before larger cups are then brought, the master of the house invites the company to drink more freely; and he still gives them an example, which is commonly followed

These entertainments begin towards the close of the day, and never end till midnight Each then returns to his own home, carried in a chair, preceded by several domestics, who carry large lanterns of oiled paper, on which the quality, and sometimes the name of their master, are inscribed in large characters Without this attendance no one ever ventures to go abroad, at such an hour, for he would infallibly be stopped by the guard. The day following it is customary to return a card of thanks to the officer of the watch

We have already said, that all their dishes are cooked in the manner of ragouts, but they are all very different in taste, highly seasoned, and much less expensive than ours.

The wines drank at these entertainments have no resemblance to those of Europe, either in taste or quality: they do not procure them from the vine, but from rice of a particular kind The method of preparing this wine is to lay the rice to steep for twenty or thirty days in water, into which ingredients of a different nature are successively thrown, it is afterwards boiled, as soon as it becomes dissolved by the heat it immediately ferments and throws up a vaporous scum, not much unlike that of new wines. A very pure liquor is found under this scum, which is drawn off, and poured into earthen vessels well varnished Of the remaining lees a spirit is made, little inferior in strength to some of ours in Europe it is even sometimes stronger, and much more inflammable The Chinese, or rather the Tartars, use also another kind of wine, made from the flesh of sheep, similar to what we have before noticed when speaking of the Mogul tribes

Such is the food, and such the liquors which the Chinese use at their entertainments, which are given with generous hospitality The Chinese are, however, naturally sober and those in easy circumstances live chiefly on pork, which they eat every day.

The common people, who are the suffering part in every country, live very poorly in China, as well as elsewhere they are satisfied, in times of scarcity, with the flesh of horses and dogs.—That of cats and rats is also sold publicly in the streets

The immense population of China prevents the ease and convenience of the greater number. In such a country, an extensive foreign commerce should be united to the higheſt cultivation —The latter the Chineſe have not neglected, but they are not yet fully ſenſible of the importance of the former, though their mines of gold and ſilver, which are now uſeleſs, might be employed to the utmoſt advantage.

FUNERAL RITES.

The day on which an individual dies in China is always very ſplendid; and many receive more honor and homage at that period than ever they did when alive.

A few moments after a perſon has expired, he is dreſſed out in his richeſt attire, and with every badge of his dignity He is then placed in the coffin which has been purchaſed for him, or which he himſelf provided in his life-time; for one of the moſt anxious cares of a Chineſe is to prepare himſelf a coffin, which ſometimes remains twenty years uſeleſs in the family, though conſidered by the head of it, as the moſt valuable piece of furniture in his poſſeſſion In caſes of poverty, when all other means fail, the ſon often ſells himſelf, *or becomes a ſlave*, to procure his father a coffin

Theſe coffins are formed of ſtrong planks, ſix inches in thickneſs, and often more, and in order that they may better reſiſt the injuries of time, they are daubed over with pitch and bitumen, and afterwards varniſhed.

The cuſtom of opening dead bodies, any more than robbing of burying-grounds, is not practiſed in China. It would be conſidered there as an act of the moſt wanton cruelty, and worthy of the ſevereſt puniſhment. In preparing the body for interment, they firſt ſprinkle, in the bottom of the coffin, a ſmall quantity of lime, on which they lay the corpſe, taking care to place its head on a pillow, and to add a quantity of cotton to keep it more ſteady, and prevent it from ſhaking. The lime and cotton ſerve alſo to receive the moiſture which may iſſue from it

In this manner the body remains expoſed ſeven days, but theſe may be reduced to three, if any ſubſtantial reaſon renders it neceſſary. During this interval, all the relations and friends come and pay their reſpects to the deceaſed, and the neareſt relations remain in the houſe. The coffin is expoſed in the hall of ceremony, which is then hung with white, the colour of Chineſe mourning, but ſome pieces of black, or violet-coloured ſilk, are interſperſed, as well as ſome other ornaments of mourning. Before the coffin is placed upon a table, the image of the deceaſed, or a carved ornament inſcribed with his name, accompanied with flowers, perfumes, and lighted wax candles.

Thoſe who enter the hall, ſalute the coffin, in the ſame manner as if the perſon were ſtill alive, proſtrate themſelves before the table, and knock their foreheads againſt the earth; they afterwards place upon the table ſome perfumes and wax candles, which they have taken care to provide for that purpoſe The intimate friends of the deceaſed, or thoſe who are ſuppoſed to have been ſo, accompany theſe ceremonies with frequent ſighs, and other marks of ſorrow, either real or pretended.

Thoſe who come to pay their reſpects to the dead, are afterwards conducted into another apartment, where they are treated with tea, and ſometimes with dried fruits and ſweetmeats A diſtant relation or ſome intimate friend of the family, on this occaſion performs the part of maſter of the ceremonies, he introduces the viſitors, and in like manner accompanies them to the door when they are about to depart.

The relations and friends of the deceaſed are again informed of the day fixed for performing the funeral rites, and few of them ever fail to attend, according to invitation.

When they arrive at the burying place, the coffin is depoſited in a tomb appropriated for it, not far from which there are tables ranged in different halls, for the purpose of giving a repast to the assistants, which is served up, after the ceremony, with the greatest splendour.

Burying places in China are always situated at a small distance from a city or town, and generally upon some eminence, around which are planted pines and cypresses, a custom which has existed, at the same period, in different nations who never had the least communication with each other.

Some of the Chinese have carried their attachment so far, as to preserve in their houses, for three or four years, the bodies of their deceased fathers. Mourning, as we have before observed, continues in China three years, and during that long interval they abstain from the use of flesh and wine, they can assist at no entertainment of ceremony, nor frequent any public assembly. When they have occasion to go abroad, which is even not permitted them at first, the chair in which they are carried is commonly covered with a white cloth. These are general rules for every Chinese who is in mourning, but those who preserve the bodies of their fathers in their houses, impose on themselves a great many others.

When a Chinese dies in a province in which he was not born, his children formerly claimed a right to transport the body to the burying-place of their ancestors. This right has been converted into an indispensable duty. A son, who should be wanting in this respect, would be disgraced in his family, and his name would never be placed in the hall of ancestors, a place where the different branches of a family meet once a year to pay honor to the memory of their deceased friends, by an offering to their manes.

TRADE OF THE CHINESE, MANNER OF BUYING, SELLING, &c.

The internal commerce of China is immense, but, on the other hand, its foreign trade is much inferior to that of any of the commercial powers of Europe.

The great number of canals and rivers by which China is interſected, tend to facilitate the conveyance of merchandiſe, and its prodigious population ſecures a rapid ſale. It is, beſides, not at all expenſive to commence ſhop-keeper in China: a family poſſeſs often but one crown, and ſometimes leſs, yet with this ſlender ſtock they begin trade; they purchaſe proviſions, which have always a ready ſale; the profits ariſing enable them to deal to a larger extent, and at the end of a few years it is common to ſee a petty ſhop converted into a warehouſe.

In no country is miſtruſt more neceſſary for a merchant, than in China; for a Chineſe trader conſiders it as an eſtabliſhed maxim, that the buyer's intention is to give as little as poſſible, and even nothing, if the vender would conſent, and therefore, by the ſame reaſoning, thinks himſelf authoriſed to draw as much from the other as he poſſibly can.

The beſt attended fairs of Europe afford but a faint picture of that immenſe number of buyers and ſellers, with which the large cities of China are continually crowded, and of whom we may fairly ſay, that the one-half are employed in over-reaching the other. Againſt ſtrangers in particular, the Chineſe merchants exerciſe, without any ſenſe of ſhame, their inſatiable rapacity. Of this F. Du Halde gives a ſtriking example, which might be ſupported by many others. "The captain of an Engliſh veſſel agreed with a Chineſe merchant at *Canton*, "for ſeveral bales of ſilk, to be furniſhed againſt a certain time. When they were ready, the captain went with "his interpreter to examine whether they were ſound "and in good condition. On opening the firſt bale, he "found it according to his wiſh, but all the reſt were "damaged. The captain reſented this treacherous conduct, and reproached the Chineſe merchant in the ſeverest terms for his diſhoneſty. The Chineſe, after having heard him for some time, with great coolness replied, "*blame, sir, your knave of an interpreter; he "assured me that you would not inspect the bales*"

The lower class of people are, above all, very dextrous in counterfeiting and adulterating every thing they sell. Sometimes an European thinks he has bought a capon, and receives nothing but skin, all the rest has been scooped out, and its place so ingeniously filled, that the deception is not easily discovered

The counterfeit hams of the Chinese have been often mentioned. They are made of wood, cut in the form of a ham, and coated over with a certain kind of earth, which is covered with hog's skin, and so curiously painted and prepared, that a knife is necessary to detect the fraud.

The Chinese are not at all fitted for maritime commerce Their vessels seldom go beyond the straits of *Sunda*, their longest voyages towards *Malacca* extend only to *Achen*; towards the straits, as far as *Batavia*, and northward as far as *Japan* Their commerce with this island, considering the articles of exchange which they procure at *Camboya*, or at *Siam*, produces them at least cent per cent.

Their trade with the Manillas is less profitable, their gain being about fifty per cent It is rather more at Batavia, and the Dutch spare no pains to invite the Chinese among them. Chinese traders go also, though but seldom, to *Achon*, *Malacca*, *Thoi*, *Patan* and *Ligor*, belonging to Siam and Cochinchina. From these places they bring gold and tin, but especially objects of luxury for the table, and some other more necessary articles.

One great obstacle to the progress of maritime commerce among the Chinese, is their indifference respecting it, and the bad construction of their vessels This they themselves acknowledge, but to attempt to remove it, according to them, would be derogating from the laws, and subverting the constitution of the empire, and, therefore no doubt, equally ſeditious with an Engliſhman attempting to reſtore the conſtitution of Great Britain to its original ſimplicity.

LITERATURE, ARTS, AND SCIENCES OF THE CHINESE.

LANGUAGE.

IT will not be expected in a work of this kind, that we should enter into criticisms on the Chinese language; it is, however, perhaps of all the languages of the early ages the only one now spoken The following are the observations of the Abbe Grosier respecting it, whose opinion is, that it has never undergone, in its different parts, any material change since the foundation of the empire:

"In the Chinese there are four distinct languages—
"First, the Kou-ouen, or language of the King, and
"other ancient classical books, it is not spoken at pre-
"sent, but the speeches in the Chou-king, and the
"songs of the Chi-king, prove it to have been spoken
"in the early ages. The diction is so laconic, that it is
"almost impossible for those who have little practice
"in reading the Chinese authors to understand it, the
"ideas are so various and so *wrapt up in the words*, as
"one of the missionaries expresses it. Nothing can
"exceed this manner of writing, it unites energy and
"depth of thought, with boldness of metaphor, splen-
"dor of imagery, and harmony of style, but it is dif-
"ficult to learn, and requires a very laborious applica-
"tion to render it familiar.

" Secondly, the Ouen-tchang.—This is the language used in compoſitions where a noble and elevated ſtyle is requiſite. It is never ſpoken, but ſentences and complimentary expreſſions are often borrowed from it. The Ouen-tchang has not the ſame laconic brevity and ſublimity as the Kou-ouen; it is, however, conciſe, natural, and eaſy, and abounds with a variety of grand and beautiful expreſſions; but it is not much adapted to the ambiguities of metaphyſics, or the formal and rugged diction uſed in treating of the abſtract ſciences.

" Thirdly, the Kouan-hoa.—This is the language of the court and of the literati; it is underſtood throughout the whole empire, and pronounced with much gracefulneſs at Pe-kin, and in the province of Kiang-nan, where the court formerly reſided. The Kouan-hoa admits of ſynonimous expreſſions, to moderate the brevity of monoſyllables; of pronouns and relatives for the connecting of phraſes, and perſpicuity of ſtyle; of prepoſitions, adverbs and particles, to ſupply the want of caſes, moods, tenſes and numbers, which have place in other languages.

" Fourthly, Hiang-tan.—This is a kind of provincial dialect, ſpoken by the lower claſſes in China. Every province, city, and almoſt every village, has its own. The ſenſe of the words varies in a great number of places, and they are ſo altered by diverſity of pronunciation, as to be almoſt unintelligible.

" The Chineſe annex great merit to the talent of tracing out characters with taſte; they often prefer them even to the moſt elegant painting, and there are ſome of them who will purchaſe, at an exorbitant rate, a page of old writing, when the characters appear to be well formed.

"The ancient Chinese were as little acquainted with "punctuation as the ancient Greeks and Romans. The "modern Chinese, from a respect for antiquity, never "attend to it in works of an elevated style, nor in any "composition which is to be presented to the Emperor. "However obscure, they are printed without points, "unless they are accompanied with commentaries, and "and intended for the use of students."

POETRY.

A taste for poetry is pretty general in China, and there are few Chinese writers who have not devoted some part of their leisure hours to the muses.

When rules are drawn from nature, they are every where almost the same. The Chinese art of poetry differs therefore very little from that of Horace and Boileau. This is evident from the following precepts laid down in the fragment of a Chinese book, entitled Ming-tchong:

"To make a good poem, the subject must be interest-"ing, and treated in an engaging manner, and genius "supported by a graceful, brilliant, and sublime dic-"tion, must shine throughout the whole. The poet "ought to traverse, with a rapid flight, the exalted re-"gions of philosophy, but without deviating from the "paths of truth, for good taste will only pardon such "digressions as bring him towards his end, and which "exhibit it to him in a more striking point of view. "Disappointment must be the consequence of speaking "otherwise than to the purpose, or without describing "things with that fire, force, and energy, which pre-"sent them to the mind as a picture does to the eyes. "Elevation of thought, continued imagery, softness, "and harmony, form genuine poetry. A poet must "begin with grandeur, paint every thing expressed, "ſoften the ſhades of thoſe which are of leaſt importance, collect all into one point of view, and carry the reader thither with a rapid flight. Poetry ſpeaks the language of the paſſions, of ſentiment, and of reaſon, but when it lends its voice to men, it ought to aſſume the tone proper for the age, rank, ſex, and prejudices of each."

Such are the rules laid down for Chineſe poetry, and we ſhall only add, that they are acquainted with moſt of theſe kinds of poetry which are in uſe among us, as ſtanzas, odes, elegies, idylls, eclogues, epigrams, ſatires, &c. The common people alſo have ballads and ſongs peculiar to themſelves, and ſome of the literati have thought it of importance to turn into verſe for their uſe the moſt celebrated maxims of morality, the duties of the different conditions, and the rules of civility. *If good grain, ſay they, produces only ſtraw, [illegible] the ground by preventing the growth of weed.*

The rules for dramatic compoſition eſtabliſhed in Europe, are not known to the Chineſe. They neither obſerve our unities, nor any thing that can give regularity and probability to the plot. Their dramas do not repreſent a ſingle action, but exhibit the whole life of a hero, and the repreſentation may be ſuppoſed to embrace a period of forty or fifty years.

They make no diſtinction between tragedy and comedy, and therefore have no rules appropriated to each of theſe kinds, ſo different in character and language. Every dramatic piece is divided into ſeveral parts, which are preceded by a kind of prologue or introduction, called *ſie tſé*, the other parts are called *tché*. Each performer when he comes forward, begins by informing the ſpectators of his name, and the character he is going to ſupport. The ſame actor often performs different parts in the ſame piece, and a comedy is ſometimes acted by five persons, though it contains, and successively exhibits, ten or twelve characters

The Chinese tragedies have not what we call a chorus, but they often abound with several pieces for singing. These scraps of poetry are intended to express the violent emotions of the soul, such as those occasioned by anger, joy, love, or grief, a character sings when he is enraged against a villain, when he is animated with vengeance, or when he prepares for death.

The Chinese are not fond of that lively and animated declamation, those expressive gestures, and powerful modulation of the voice which so often contribute to the success of our theatrical representations and public discourses in Europe They think like the savage Illinois, who were persuaded that their missionary had fallen into a passion, because he concluded his sermon with a few pathetic sentences, delivered after the European manner. The Chinese cannot adapt themselves to European action and gestures, which they take for affected grimaces, or transports of fury Grave and composed hearers, they are better pleased with a discourse addressed to their understanding than to their passions

Though China abounds with works of erudition, they are seldom the production of private individuals, these have neither the leisure nor conveniencies requisite for literary pursuits. The first years of the young literati are spent in studying the language, characters, and doctrine of the King, the examinations keep them continually employed. When admitted to the first literary degree, it is still necessary to continue their studies, in order to obtain the second and third. They then obtain employment in the tribunals, or become governors of cities in their own provinces. In this situation their occupations are so various and constant, that it is impossible for them to follow a course of uninterrupted study. The sword of the sovereign is continually suspended over their heads and they have need of all their application, to avoid even slight omissions, which are sufficient to occasion their ruin.

The difficulty of procuring access to libraries is also an inconvenience which the man of genius, unconnected with any literary societies, must experience in China, and the condition of individuals is so liable to change, that it is impossible for any of them to have such a collection of books as are found in the houses of the great and of men of letters in Europe. The great bonzeries are the only resources of the literati: it is there that government, in order to guard against losses, by conflagrations, wars, and revolutions, has ordered the most curious and rare manuscripts to be collected, and there also are deposited copies of every collection and new edition of any work published at the expense of the state. These immense libraries are open to all the literati, but the greater part of the bonzeries which contain them are situated on mountains, at a distance from large cities, and therefore in a great measure cut off from a man of letters.

All the great works, therefore, which have appeared in China have proceeded from the college of the Han-lin. This body, composed of the most celebrated literati, and of the greatest geniuses of the empire, freed from every care, and surrounded with all the literary treasures of the empire, find every convenience and assistance that can facilitate their labour. Employment is assigned to each of them, suited to his taste and talents. They are never subjected to the fettering restraint of time, nor hurried to finish any work which they have undertaken. Interest and self-love unite them closely together, for the glory attending their success is never divided. A reciprocal communication of knowledge, in the fullest and most unreserved manner, is, therefore, a necessary consequence, because every imputation affects the whole body. Hence it happens, that all the works which come from the pencil of the Han-lin bear a character of perfection rarely to be found in those of a private man of letters. To them are the Chinese indebted for all their great historical collections, dictionaries, commentaries, new editions of ancient authors, &c. The emperor generally furnishes for these large works a preface, by his own hand. They are printed at the expense of government, and the whole edition belongs to the emperor, who distributes the copies as presents to the princes of the blood, his ministers, the great, the chiefs of the different tribunals, governors of provinces, and the most celebrated literati of the empire. In 1770 the Han-lin were employed on a new edition of a great work, in which are discussed the most interesting points of history, chronology, geography, jurisprudence, politics, and natural history. This edition was to form a collection of more than an hundred and fifty volumes.

ASTRONOMY.

Much has been said by different writers for and against the knowledge which the Chinese have of astronomy; the advocates on the part of the Chinese have asserted their almost perfect knowledge of the science from the foundation of their empire, in proof of which a chapter from the Chou-king is quoted, where the Emperor Yao instructs two of his mandarins in the science: their opponents have, perhaps, erred as much on the other extreme, and in their attemps to prove the Chinese in a manner ignorant even of the first principles of this science, have been more successful in making assertions than in supporting them by proof. F. Gaubil, who wrote a particular treatise on Chinese astronomy, which he long studied, thus speaks of the Chinese astronomers:

"The Chineſe have been long acquainted with the motion of the ſun, moon, and planets, and even of the fixed ſtars, from weſt to eaſt, though they did not determine the motion of the latter till about four hundred years after the Chriſtian æra. To Saturn, Jupiter, Mars, Venus, and Mercury, they have aſſigned revolutions which approach very near to our's. They have no notion of their different ſituations, when ſtationary and retrograde, and, as in Europe, ſome imagine that the heavens and planets revolve round the earth, and others around the ſun.—By reading their books, we may eaſily perceive that the Chineſe have had a perfect knowledge of the quantity of the ſolar year, that they have alſo known the diurnal motion of the ſun and moon, that they have been able to take the meridian altitude of the former by the ſhadow of a gnomon, and that they have thence made pretty exact calculations to determine the elevation of the pole, and the ſun's declination. It appears that they have had a tolerable knowledge of the right aſcenſion of the ſtars, and of the time when they paſs the meridian, of the reaſon why the ſame ſtars, in the ſame year, riſe and ſet with the ſun, and why they paſs the meridian ſometimes when the ſun riſes, and ſometimes when he ſets. In ſhort, it evidently appears, from peruſing the Chineſe hiſtory, that the Chineſe have always been acquainted with a great many parts of aſtronomy."

The Jeſuit mathematicians contributed much to the enlargement of aſtronomical knowledge in China, for Ricci, Adam Schal, Verbieſt, Couplet, Gerbillon, Regis, d'Entrecolles, Jartoux, Parrenin, and a great many others, were men whoſe talents would have rendered them celebrated, even in Europe. F. Verbieſt found, in the obſervatory at Pe-kin, a certain number of inſtru

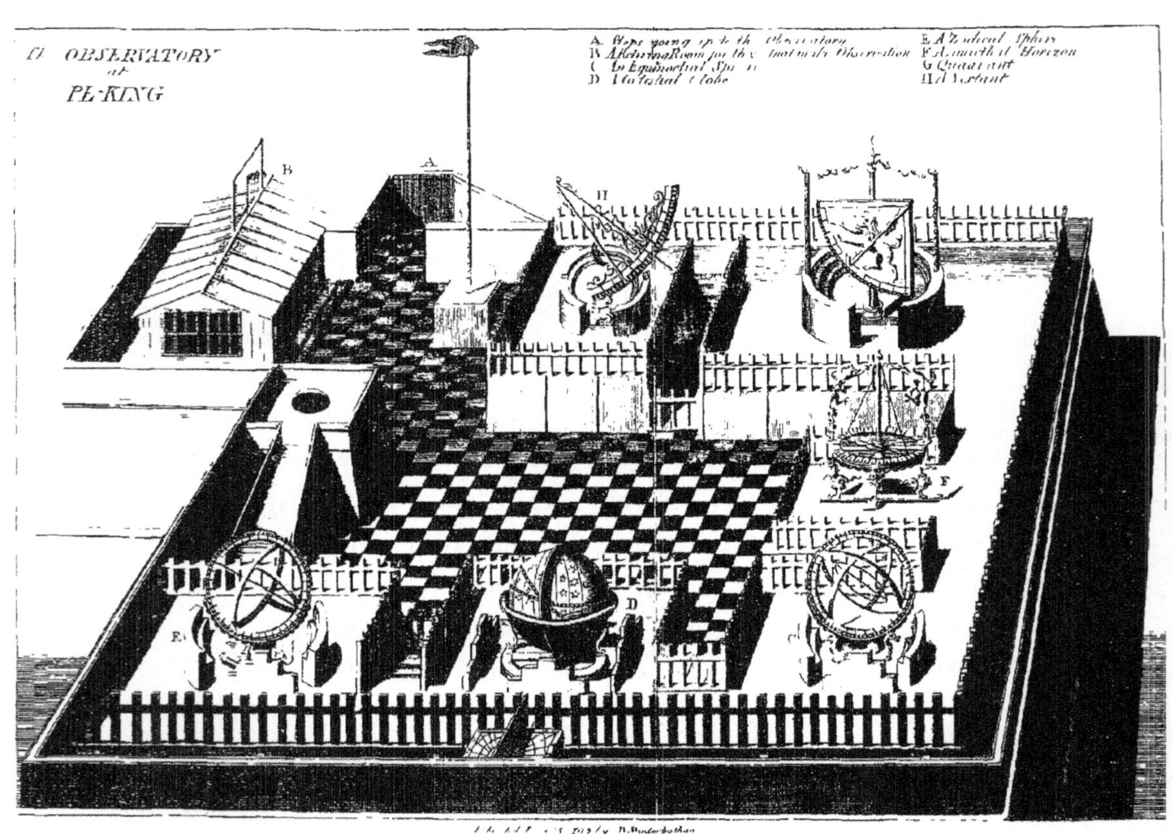
OBSERVATORY
at
PE-KING
A
B
H
D
E
F

ments made of brafs, but, as he judged them improper for aftronomical purpofes, he fubftituted new ones in their room, which ftill remain. F. le Comte has given us, in his Memoirs, an accurate defcription of all thefe machines, correfponding with the annexed plate.

Aftronomy at prefent is cultivated at Pe-kin as it is in the greater part of the capital cities of Europe. A particular tribunal is eftablifhed there, the jurifdiction of which extends to every thing that relates to the obfervation of the celeftial phenomena.

The obfervation of eclipfes is one of the moft important functions of this tribunal. Information muft be given to the emperor of the day and hour of the eclipfe, in what part of the heavens it will happen, its duration, and the number of digits eclipfed. It is neceffary that this intelligence precede the eclipfe by fome months, and it muft be calculated for the longitude and latitude of the capital city of every province. Thefe obfervations, as well as the diagram which reprefents the eclipfe, are preferved by the tribunal of Ceremonies and the Calao, who take care to tranfmit them into all the cities of the empire, in order that it may be obferved according to the form prefcribed.

The ceremonial ufual on fuch occafions is as follows: Some days before the eclipfe, the tribunal of ceremonies caufes to be fixed up, in large characters, in fome public place of Pe-kin, the hour and minute when the eclipfe will commence, the quarter of the heavens in which it will be vifible, the time that the body will remain in the fhade, and the moment in which it will emerge. The mandarins of the different orders have notice to appear in proper drefs, with all the emblems of their dignity, in the court of the tribunal of Aftronomy, and to wait there for the moment in which the phenomenon will take place. Each of them carries in his hand a ſheet of paper, containing a figure of the eclipſe. As ſoon as they perceive that the ſun or moon begins to be darkened, they throw themſelves on their knees, and knock their foreheads againſt the earth. A noiſe of drums and cymbals is immediately heard throughout the whole city. This is the remains of an ancient opinion entertained in China, that by ſuch horrid din they aſſiſted the ſuffering luminary, and prevented it from being devoured by the celeſtial dragon. Although every perſon poſſeſſed of the leaſt knowledge, knows at preſent that eclipſes are only natural events, they continue ſtill to obſerve the ancient ceremonial, in conſequence of that attachment to national cuſtoms which theſe people have always preſerved.

While the mandarins remain proſtrated, others, ſtationed on the obſervatory, examine the beginning, middle, and end of the eclipſe, comparing what they obſerve with the figure and calculations given. They then write down their obſervations, affix their ſeal to them, and tranſmit them to the emperor, who, on his part, has been at no leſs pains to obſerve the eclipſe with accuracy and attention. The ſame ceremonial is eſtabliſhed throughout the whole empire.

The Chineſe have invariably fixed the beginning of the aſtronomical year at the winter ſolſtice, but that of their civil year has varied, according to the will of their emperors, ſome of whom have fixed it at the third, or ſecond moon, after the winter ſolſtice, and others at the ſolſtice itſelf.

The Chineſe year has at all times conſiſted of a certain number of lunations, twelve lunations forming a common, and thirteen the emboliſmic year. They reckon their lunations by the number of days which fall between the moment in which the ſun is in conjunction with the moon, and the moment of the conjunction following; and as in the interval between one conjunction and another, the number of days cannot be constantly equal, they sometimes admit twenty-nine, and sometimes thirty days, to complete their lunations

They divide their days into a greater or smaller number of equal parts, but generally into twelve hours, which are double those used by us. Their day begins and ends at midnight

The Chinese year, divided into lunations, is also divided into four equal parts, or seasons, each of which has three parts, its beginning, its middle, and its end; that is to say, a lunation for each of the three parts. This year is still subdivided into twenty four equal parts, each of which contains fifteen degrees, so that the whole together make up three hundred and sixty degrees.

The intricate and irregular motion of the moon has been long known in China The first day of the new moon they named *cho*, *commencement*, or *beginning*, and the day of full moon *ouang*, signifying to *hope*, or *expect* because the people expected the kindness and protection of certain spirits, which they invoked only at that epocha. To express the age of the moon, besides numbers, they use the words *superior* and *inferior string*, they say, *chang-huen*, *a bow having the string uppermost*, and *hia-huen*, *a bow having the string undermost* thus they distinguish what we call the quarters of the moon. Their method of intercalation has varied, but it has always been admitted, as well as the custom of reckoning twenty-nine or thirty days for one lunation, that which contains only twenty-nine days, they call *a small*, and that of thirty, *a greater lunation*

The Chinese astronomers divide the stars according to the following order they place first the *pe-teou*, or *celestial bushel of the north*, this is what we call the Great

Bear: secondly, the *nan-teou*, or *celestial bushel of the south*, which comprehends the principal stars opposite to the Great Bear, and which together form a figure almost like that of the Great Bear in the north: thirdly, the five planets, *ou-hing*. These five planets are, Saturn, Jupiter, Mars, Venus, and Mercury. Fourthly, twenty-eight constellations, in which are comprehended all the stars of our zodiac, and some of those which lie nearest to it.

PAPER, INK, PRINTING, &c.

The Chinese fix the discovery and first fabrication of that paper which they use at present, about the year 105 before Jesus Christ. Prior to that epocha, they wrote upon cloth, and different kinds of silk stuff. In more early ages, they wrote with a sort of style upon small slips of bamboo, and even upon plates of metal: several of these slips, strung and joined together, formed a volume. At length, under the reign of Ho-ti, a Chinese mandarin invented a kind of paper much more commodious. He took the bark of different trees, hemp, and old pieces of silk stuff, and boiled these substances until they were reduced to a kind of paste, of which he formed paper. Chinese industry improved this discovery, and found out the secret of whitening and smoothing different kinds of paper, and of giving them a beauty and lustre.

Different papers are at present greatly multiplied. The Chinese, for making paper, use the bamboo reed, the cotton shrub, the bark of the *kou chu*, and of the mulberry tree, hemp, the straw of wheat and rice, parchment, the cods of the silk-worm, and several other substances, the greater part of which are unknown in this manufacture in Europe.

Of trees, or shrubs, proper for this purpose, nothing is used but the bark, the bamboo and cotton tree excepted, the woody substance of which is employed, after it has been macerated, and reduced to a thin paste. The greater part of the Chinese paper is very susceptible of moisture, dust easily adheres to it, and worms, insensibly, get into it To prevent the corruption and loss of books, it is therefore necessary to beat them often, and expose them to the sun. Paper made from cotton is not subject to these inconveniences, it is the neatest and most used of any, and may be preserved as long as that of Europe

These kinds of paper are much superior to ours in softness, smoothness, and the extraordinary size of the sheets, it being no difficult matter to obtain, from certain manufactories, sheets thirty or forty feet in length

To strengthen their paper, and prevent it from sinking, the Chinese dip it in alum-water, which generally renders it very brittle, but when it has not undergone this preparation, it may be folded into a thousand shapes, without any danger of its being torn.

The Chinese ink is made from blacking, produced by the smoke of different substances, but principally by that of pines, or of oil burnt in lamps Care is taken to add to it a little musk, or some other perfume, to correct the strong and disagreeable smell which it would otherwise retain The ingredients are mixed, until they acquire the consistence of paste, which is afterwards divided, and put into small wooden moulds. The interior part of these moulds is neatly cut and carved, so that the cake of ink, when taken out, appears ornamented with different figures, such as dragons, birds, trees, and flowers one of its sides is generally marked with some beautiful characters.

The best and most esteemed ink of China is that which is made in the district of Hoei-tcheou, in the province of Kiang-nan Its composition is a secret, which the workmen conceal, not only from strangers, but even from their fellow-citizens The manufacturers of Hoei-tcheou have furnaces of a particular construction for burning pines. The smoke is conveyed, by means of long pipes into small cells, closely shut, the sides of which are covered with leaves of paper The smoke introduced into these cells adheres every where to the walls, and soon condenses At the end of a few days the cells are opened, and the blacking, or soot, is then taken out. The resin, which issues from the burning pines is also collected, by means of small canals, which are level with the ground

The art of printing, so recent in Europe, has long existed in China, but it differs very much from ours. The small number of letters which compose our alphabet permits us to cast a certain number of moveable characters, which, by their arrangement and successive combinations, are sufficient to print the largest works, the types employed in printing the first sheet may furnish characters to print the second But this is not the case in China, where the characters are so prodigiously numerous. The Chinese find it more commodious to engrave upon pieces of wood the whole work which they intend to print Their method of proceeding in this operation is as follows They first employ a writer to transcribe the work The engraver glues each of the leaves of the manuscript upon a piece of plank, made of any hard wood, such as that of the apple or pear tree, and properly prepared, he then traces over, with a graver, the strokes of the writing, carves out the characters in relief, and cuts down the intermediate part of the wood Each page of a book, therefore, requires a separate plank

The beauty of the characters depends evidently on the hand of the copier, and the book is neatly or badly printed accordingly, for the dexterity and precision of the engraver is so great, that he imitates every stroke; it is, therefore, sometimes difficult to distinguish a book which is printed from one simply written

The Chinese, however, are not unacquainted with the use of moveable characters, they have a kind, not cast, but made of wood, and it is with these characters they correct every three months *The State of China*, which is printed at Pe kin. Very small works are also printed sometimes in the same manner

The Chinese do not use a press, as printers in Europe do, their wooden planks and their paper, which is not dipped into alum-water, could not sustain so much pressure They first place the plank level, and then fix it in that position. The printer, who is provided with two brushes, takes that which is hardest, dips it into the ink, and rubs the plank in such a manner, that it may be neither too much nor too little moistened. When a plank has been once prepared, four or five leaves have been thrown off successively without daubing it over every time with fresh ink After a leaf has been adjusted upon the plank, the workman takes a second brush, which is soft, and of an oblong figure, and draws it gently over the paper, pressing it down that it may receive the ink, the degree of pressure is determined by the quantity of ink upon the plank One man with his brush is able in this manner, to throw off almost ten thousand copies in a day.

Ink used for printing is made in a particular manner, it is liquid, and different from that which is formed into oblong sticks, or cakes The leaves are printed upon one side only, because thin and transparent paper, such as the Chinese, would not bear double impresſion, without confounding the characters of the different pages. Each leaf of a book is, on that account double, ſo that the fold ſtands uppermoſt, and the opening is towards the back where it is ſtitched. Hence it happens that the Chineſe books are not cut upon the edges. They are generally bound in grey paſteboard, which is very neat: thoſe who wiſh to have them done in a richer and more elegant manner, get the paſteboard covered with thin ſatin, flowered taffety, and ſometimes with gold and ſilver brocade. The edges are neither gilt nor coloured.

SILKS, GLASS, AND PORCELAIN OF CHINA.

The culture of the mulberry tree, and the manufacturing of ſilk, have been greatly extended in China: this production, indeed, appears to be almoſt inexhauſtible: beſides the immenſe quantity which is annually exported by the greater part of the Aſiatic and European nations, the internal conſumption alone is aſtoniſhing. The emperor, the princes, the mandarins, the literati, women, ſervants of both ſexes, and all who poſſeſs a moderate income, wear no clothes but of taffety, ſatin and other ſilk ſtuffs. None but the lower ſort of people and the very young, uſe dreſſes of cotton cloth which is dyed blue.

The moſt beautiful and valuable ſilk of the whole empire is that which comes from the province of Tche-kiang, which is wrought in the manufactories of Nan-king, by the beſt workmen of China; thence are brought all thoſe ſilk ſtuffs, deſtined for the uſe of the emperor, and thoſe which he diſtributes in preſents to the nobility of the court. The open commerce carried on with Aſia and Europe draws alſo to the manufactories of Canton a great number of excellent workmen who manufacture there ribands, ſtockings, buttons, &c.

The principal silk stuffs manufactured by the Chinese are plain and flowered gauzes, of which they make dresses for summer, damask of all colours, striped and black satins, napped, flowered, striped, clouded, and pinked taffeties, crapes, brocades, plush, different kinds of velvet, and a multitude of other stuffs, the names of which are unknown in Europe.

The Chinese wheels, looms, reels, and all other machines necessary for preparing silk, and for the fabrication of cloth, are very simple in their construction, but contain no improvement worthy of the attention of an European manufacturer.

Porcelain is another object of Chinese industry, and a branch of commerce which employs a vast multitude of workmen. The finest and best is made, as we have before noticed, in a village called King-te-tching, in the province of Kiang-si.

We are indebted to Father d'Entrecolles for a very accurate account of the manner in which porcelain is made, and from his accounts we shall extract the observations we shall make on the subject.

In describing the earths and minerals of China, we have mentioned the pe-tun-tse and the kao-lin, a proper mixture of which produces that fine paste used for making porcelain. To these two principal elements must be added, the oil or varnish from which it derives its splendour and whiteness. This oil, which is extracted from the same kind of stone which produces the pe-tun tse, is of a whitish colour with a mixture of green, it is obtained by the same process used in making the pe-tun-tse, the stone is first washed, and pulverised, it is then thrown into water, and after it has been purified, it throws up, as we have before mentioned, a kind of cream. To an hundred pounds of this cream, is added one pound of che-kao, a mineral something like alum, which is calcined and pounded. This mineral acts as a kind of rennet, and gives a consistence to the oil, which is however carefully preserved in its state of fluidity.

The oil thus prepared is never employed alone, another oil must be mixed with it, which is extracted from lime and fern ashes, to an hundred pounds of which is also added a pound of che-kao When these two oils are mixed, they must be equally thick, and, in order to ascertain this, the workmen dip into each of them some cakes of the pe-tun-tse, and by inspecting their surfaces closely after they are drawn out, thence judge of the thickness of the liquors. With regard to the quantity necessary to be employed, it is usual to mix ten measures of stone oil, with one measure of the oil made from lime and fern ashes.

To enter into a detail of the method of forming the different articles of porcelain would be altogether useless, as they are known in, and are similar to the practice of our own potteries.

After a piece of porcelain has been properly fashioned, it passes into the hands of the painters, who follow no certain plan in their art, nor are they acquainted with any of the rules of drawing, all their knowledge is the effect of practice, assisted by a whimsical imagination. Some of them, however, shew no inconsiderable share of taste in painting flowers, animals, and landscapes, on porcelain, as well as upon the paper of fans, and the silk used for filling up the squares of lanterns. The labour of painting in the manufactories of which we have spoken, is divided among a great number of hands The business of one is entirely confined to tracing out the first coloured circle, which ornaments the brims of the vessel, another designs the flowers, and a third paints them, one delineates waters and mountains, and another, birds and other animals human figures are generally the worst executed.

The Chinese have porcelain painted with colours of every kind, but it is unnecessary for us to attempt a description of the different kinds, as they are all, we believe, well known in Europe When the colour becomes dry, the porcelain is baked, the gold is then laid on, and it is afterwards re-baked, in a particular furnace appropriated for that purpose. The Chinese have tried to paint some vases with their common ink, but this attempt did not succeed. When the porcelain was taken from the furnace, it was found to be quite white. As the particles of this ink have very little body, they were undoubtedly dissipated by the action of the fire, or rather, they had not strength sufficient to penetrate the coat of varnish

The Chinese had formerly the secret of making a singular kind of porcelain they painted upon the sides of the vessel fishes, insects, and other animals, which could not be perceived until it was filled with water This secret is, in a great measure, lost, the following part of the process is, however, preserved the porcelain which the workman intends to paint in this manner, must be extremely thin and delicate When it is dry, the colour is laid on pretty thick, not on the outside, as is generally done, but on the inside The figures painted upon it, for the most part, are fishes, as being more analogous to the water with which the vessel is filled When the colour is thoroughly dry, it is coated over with a kind of size, made from porcelain earth, so that the azure is entirely inclosed between two laminæ of earth. When the size becomes dry, the workman pours some oil into the vessel, and afterwards puts it upon a mould, and applies it to the lathe. As this piece of porcelain has received its consistence and body within, it is made as thin on the outside as possible, without penetrating to the colour, its exterior surface is then dipped in oil, and, when dry, it is baked in a common furnace. The art of making these vases requires the most delicate care, and a dexterity which the Chinese, perhaps, do not at present possess. They have, however, from time to time, made several attempts to revive the secret, but their success has been very imperfect. This kind of porcelain is known by the name of kia-tsing, *pressed azure*.

When the Chinese intend to lay on gold, they pound it, and suffer it to dissolve in the bottom of a porcelain vessel, until they perceive a golden scum floating on the top. It is then left to dry, and when they have occasion to use it, they dilute part of it with a sufficient quantity of gum-water. Three parts of ceruse are mixed with thirty parts of gold, and it is laid on in the same manner as other colours.

Several causes concur to render the beautiful porcelain of China exceedingly dear in Europe; besides the great profit of those who import it, and that gained from them by the Chinese factors, it seldom happens that a baking succeeds completely. It sometimes miscarries entirely, and when the furnace is opened, the porcelain, together with the cases in which it is baked, is found converted into a shapeless mass, as hard as flint. Too strong a fire, or damaged cases, are sufficient to spoil the whole process, and it is the more difficult to regulate the proper degree of heat, as the nature of the weather may change its action in an instant, as well as the quality of the matter upon which it acts, and that of the wood, which produces it. Besides this, the pieces which are transported to Europe, are generally made after new models, and on that account much more difficult to be manufactured. A few faults are sufficient to cause their rejection by the European merchant, in which case they remain in the hands of the Chinese workman, who cannot dispose of them, because they are not fashioned according to the taste of his nation, it is, therefore, necessary, that the porcelain exported by the Europeans should pay for that which has been refused.

The use of glass is very ancient in China, it is related, in the Large Annals, that, "In the beginning of "the third century, the king of Ta-tsin sent the emperor Tai-tsou a magnificent present of glass of all colours, and that some years after, a glass-maker, who "had the art of converting flint into chrystal by means "of fire, taught this secret to some others, by which "those who had come, and those who then came from "the West acquired much glory."—That part of the Annals in which this quotation is to be found, was written in the seventh century but from the little attention which at times seems to have been paid to the art of manufacturing glass, and its being lost and revived at different periods, we have reason to suspect that the Chinese have never set great value upon this branch, and that they have considered glass rather as an object of luxury than utility They greatly admire the workmanship of our European chrystal, but they prefer their own porcelain, which stands hot liquors, and which is much more used and less liable to be broken. A glass-house is still, however, kept up at Pe-kin, at the Emperor's expense, in which a certain number of vases and other works are made, which require so much the more labour and attention, as none of them are blown But this manufactory is considered only as an establishment of pomp, and an appendage of the court, destined merely for the purpose of adding to imperial magnificence This disdainful indifference, shewn by the Chinese for glass manufactures, clearly evinces how different their ideas are at present from those of the Europeans.

MEDICINE.

The ſtudy of medicine among the Chineſe is as ancient as the foundation of their empire. Their phyſicians were never ſkilful anatomiſts, or profound philoſophers, nor will their moſt reſpectable theories bear the ſcrutiny of the practical anatomiſt, indeed, where anatomy is ſhackled by a nonſenſical prejudice which prevents the opening of the human body, it is impoſſible that the practice of medicine or ſurgery can be very perfect.

Vital heat, and radical moiſture, are conſidered by the Chineſe phyſicians as the two natural principles of life, the blood and ſpirits they conſider only as their vehicles. Theſe two principles, according to them, are ſeated in all the principal parts of the body, in which they preſerve life and vigour. The ſeat of radical moiſture they ſuppoſe to be in the heart, lungs, liver, and reins. They place vital heat in the inteſtines, the number of which they make amount to ſix, by means of the ſpirits and blood, the vital heat and radical moiſture are conveyed from theſe different ſeats to the other parts of the body. The Chineſe phyſicians ſuppoſe alſo, ſays F du Halde, "that the body by means of the nerves, muſcles, veins, "and arteries, is like a kind of lute or muſical inſtru"ment, the different parts of which emit various ſounds, "or rather have a temperament proper for each, and "ſuited to their figure, ſituation, and particular uſes, "and that its different pulſes, which reſemble the diffe"rent tones and notes of theſe inſtruments, enable "the practitioner to judge infallibly of their ſituation "and ſtate, in the ſame manner as a cord, more or leſs "tenſe, touched in one place or in another, in a ſtronger "or gentler manner, ſends forth different ſounds, and

" discovers whether it be too much stretched, or too " much relaxed."

In a word, they suppose that between all the parts of the human body, there is a certain influence on the one hand, and a sympathy on the other, and these form the basis of their system of physic They pretend to judge of the state of a patient, and to determine the nature of his disease, by the colour of the face and eyes, by inspecting the tongue, nostrils, and ears, and by the sound of the voice, but it is chiefly upon a knowledge of the pulse that they found their most infallible prognostics. Their theory respecting the pulse is very extensive, and varies according to circumstances. One of the ancient physicians has left a complete treatise upon this subject, which still serves as a guide This work was composed about two hundred years before the Christian era, and it appears certain that the Chinese were acquainted with the circulation of the blood long before any of the nations of Europe.

As before observed, they never use dissection, but it appears that they have long studied living nature with attention and advantage. Living nature may, perhaps, not be impenetrable to an observation of three thousand years. The Egyptians did not permit the opening of dead bodies, and yet it was from their sacred books that Hippocrates derived the greater part of his knowledge. The Chinese physic is, however, almost all quackery. They have the greatest confidence in their simples, which indeed have singular virtues, but it requires no little skill to know them thoroughly, and to be able to administer them seasonably.

Inoculation was practised in China a long time before it was known in Europe, the Chinese, indeed, place less confidence in it than the Europeans, and for this reason, because they are convinced, by numberless inſtances, that it does not prevent a return of the ſmall-pox when it becomes epidemical. The name given to this diſeaſe in China is *tai-tou*, which means, *poiſon of the mother's breaſts*. They diſtinguiſh it into forty different kinds; but experience plainly demonſtrates that it is not dangerous in the warm provinces of China; in the cold it produces little eruption: it is in the temperate that it extends its ravages wideſt. The Chineſe phyſicians, therefore, regulate their mode of treating this diſtemper according to the climate, and to the age and habit of the patient.

MUSIC OF THE CHINESE.

The modern Chineſe entertain the ſame ideas reſpecting their ancient muſic, as thoſe which have been tranſmitted to us concerning that of the Greeks and Egyptians; and they regret their ancient harmony, as we lament the loſs of that which has been ſo much extol'ed by antiquity, and of which ſo many wonderful things have been related. If Egypt had a Hermes, or Mercury Triſmegiſtus, who, by the ſoftneſs and charms of his voice, finiſhed the civilization of men; if Greece had an Amphion, who built cities by his harmony alone; and an Orpheus, who, by the ſound of his lyre, ſuſpended the courſe of rivers, and made the moſt rugged rocks follow him, China boaſts of no leſs miracles performed by her ancient muſicians. We are told of a Lyng-lun, a Kouei, and a Pin-mou-kia, who, by touching their *kin and their ché*, produced ſounds capable of ſoftening the hearts of men, and of taming the moſt ferocious animals.

More than eight centuries before the exiſtence of the ſon of Antiope, and of the famous ſinger of Thrace, it is recorded that the inimitable Kouei ſaid to the emperor Chun, " When I touch the ſtones, which com-

"pose my *king*, and make them send forth a sound, the "animals range themselves around me and leap for "joy."—The ancient music, according to the Chinese writers of every age, "could call down superior spirits "from the ethereal regions, raise up the manes of de-"parted beings, inspire men with a love of virtue, "and lead them to the practice of their duty, &c."—"Are we desirous," say the same authors, "of know-"ing, whether a state be well governed, and whether "the morals of its inhabitants be virtuous or corrupt,—"let us examine what kind of music is esteemed among "them."—This rule was not neglected by Confucius, when he travelled through the different kingdoms into which China was divided in his time, some vestiges of the ancient music even then remained, and his own experience had taught him how much influence harmony has over the passions and movements of the soul. It is, indeed, related, that when he arrived in the kingdom of Tsi, he was entertained with a piece of the music called Chao, that is to say, of that music which Kouei composed by order of Chun "For more than three "months," say the authors of his life, "it was impos-"sible for him to think of any thing else, the most ex-"quisite food, prepared in the most delicate manner, "could neither awaken his taste, nor excite his appe-"tite, &c"

It is not our intention to enter on a dissertation on the ancient music of the Chinese, we shall only observe, that the musical system, so long attributed to the Egyptians and the Greeks, has been discovered in China; and that it is beyond a doubt that it had its origin there, at an epocha much anterior to the times of Hermes, Linus, or Orpheus. We cannot enter into that tedious detail which would be requisite to explain this system, the musical reader may find it in the dissertation of F. Amiot,‡ published by the Abbé Roussier, and which this learned theorist enriched with his own observations.

We shall now speak of the musical instruments of the Chinese. They have always distinguished eight different sounds, and they believe that nature, in order to produce them, formed eight kinds of sonorous bodies. The order in which they distribute these sounds, and the instruments they have constructed to produce them, are as follow: 1st, The sound of skin, produced by drums.* 2dly, The sound of stone, produced by the *king*.† 3dly, That of metal, by bells.‡ 4thly, That of baked earth, by the *hiuen*.§ 5thly, That of silk, by the *kin* and the *che*.‖ 6thly, That of wood, by the *yu* and the *tchou*.¶ 7thly, That of bamboo, by the *koan*, and different flutes.** And, 8thly, That of a gourd, by the *cheng*.††

The first drums were composed of a box made of baked earth, covered at both extremities with the tanned hide of some animal; but, on account of the weight and brittleness of baked earth, wood was soon substituted in its stead. The Chinese have drums of various kinds; the greater part of them are shaped like our barrels, and some are cylindric.

The Chinese are, perhaps, the only nation who have had the ingenuity to apply stones to the purpose of making musical instruments. We have already described the different kinds of sonorous stones which are found in this empire; the instrument constructed of them is called

‡ This dissertation forms the sixth volume of the New Memoirs respecting China.

* Fig. 5, 7, Plate I.
† Fig. 1, 2, 3, ditto.
‡ Fig. 4, 6, ditto.
§ Fig. 8, 9, ditto.
‖ Fig. 9, 10, Plate II.
¶ Fig. 4, 5, 11, ditto.
** Fig. 6, 7, 8, ditto.
†† Fig. 1, 2, 3, ditto.

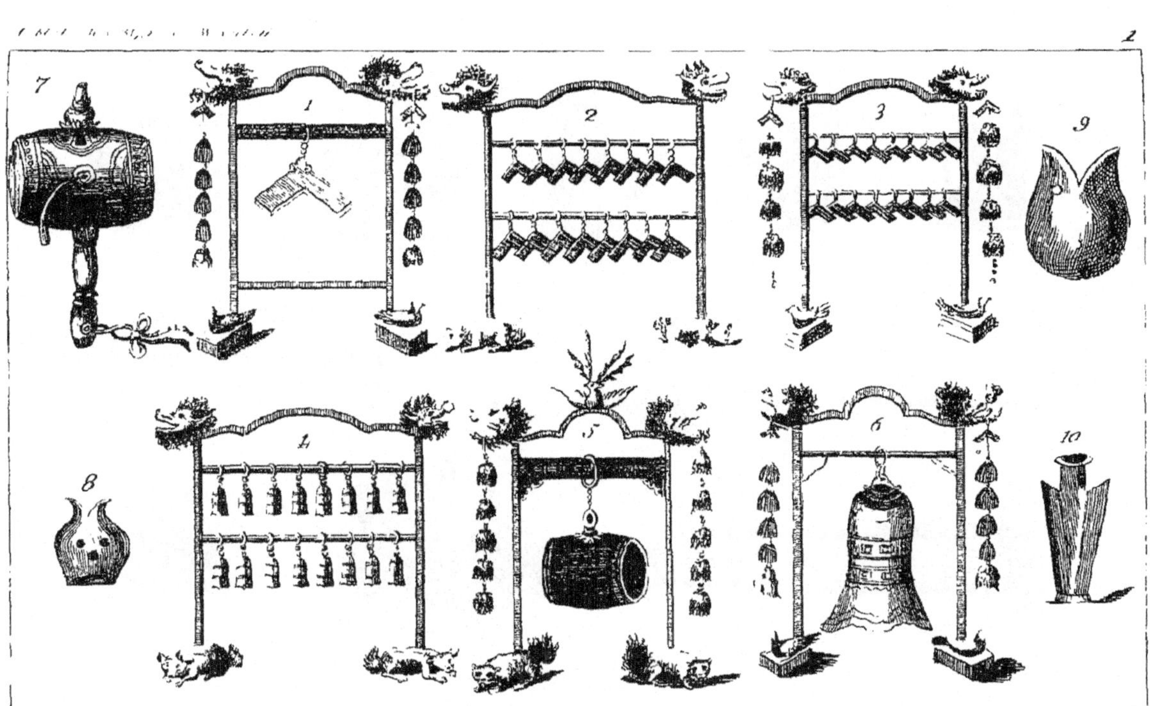

Chinese Musical Instruments

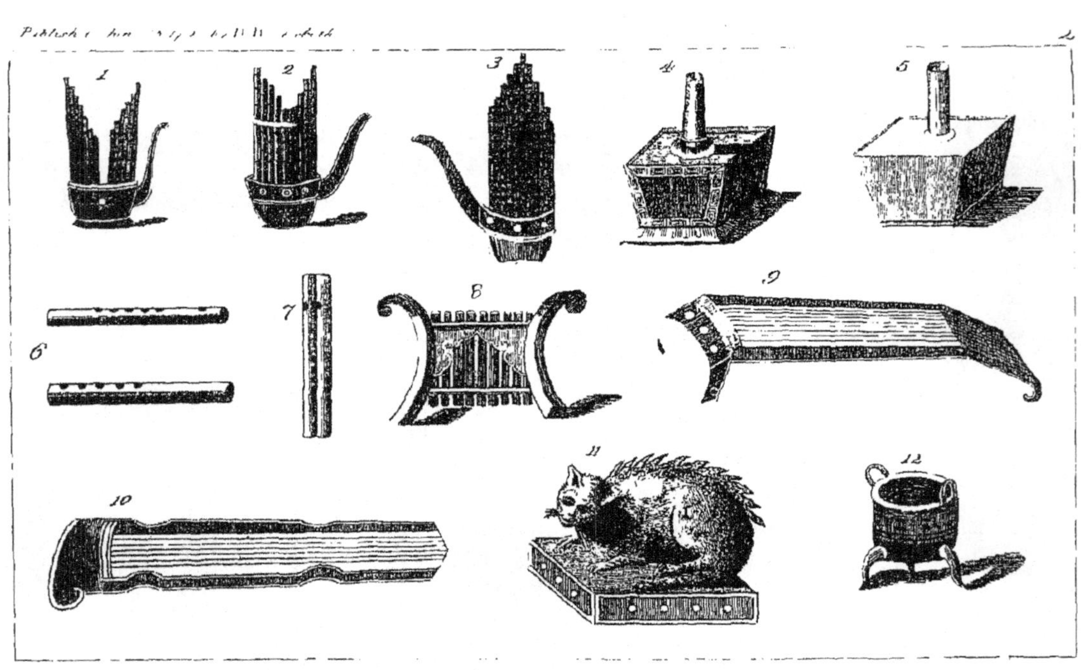

Chinese Musical Instruments

king, and is distinguished into *tse-king*, and *pien-king*. The tse-king consists of only one sonorous stone, which, consequently, produces only one tone. The pien-ting is an assortment of sixteen stones, suspended together, which form all the tones admitted into the musical system of the ancient Chinese. These stones are cut into the form of a carpenter's square, to make their tone flatter, their thickness is diminished, and to render it sharper, something is taken from their length.

The Chinese have always made their bells of a mixture of tin and copper; their shapes are various, those of the ancients were not round, but flatted, and in the lower part resembled a crescent. The Chinese have formed an instrument of sixteen bells, properly assorted, so as to correspond with the sonorous stones, of which the *king* are composed.

The instrument *hiuen*, which is made of baked earth, is highly respected by the Chinese, on account of its antiquity. They distinguish it into two kinds, the great and the small *hiuen*. "The great *hiuen*," says the Dictionary Eulh-ya, "is like a goose's egg, and the small "*hiuen*, like that of a hen; it has six holes for the notes, "and a seventh for the mouth."

The *kin* and the *ché*, which have been known from the remotest antiquity, emit the sound of silk. The *kin* has seven strings, made of silk threads, and is distinguished into three kinds, differing only in size, the great *kin*, the middle *kin*, and the small *kin*. The body of this instrument is formed of the wood of the *toung-mou*, and varnished black; its whole length is about five feet five inches. The *ché*, of which there are five kinds, is furnished with twenty-five strings, and its ordinary length is nine feet. F. Amiot assures us, that we have no instrument in Europe that deserves to be preferred to it.

The inſtruments which emit the ſound of wood, are the *tchou*, the *yu*, and the *tchoung-tou*, the firſt is ſhaped like a ſquare buſhel, and is beat on the inſide with a hammer, the ſecond, which repreſents a tyger ſquatting, is made to ſound by ſcraping its back gently with a rod, the third is a collection of twelve pieces of board tied together, which are uſed for beating time, by holding them in the right hand, and knocking them gently againſt the palm of the left.

The bamboo furniſhes a numerous claſs of inſtruments, compoſed of pipes joined together, or ſeparate, and pierced with more or fewer holes. The principal of all theſe wind inſtruments is the *cheng*, which emits the ſound of a gourd. The neck of the gourd is cut off, and the lower part only is reſerved, to which a cover is fitted, having as many holes as are equal to the number of ſounds required. In each of theſe holes, a pipe is fixed, made of bamboo, and ſhorter or longer, according to the tone it ought to emit. The mouth of the inſtrument is formed of another pipe, ſhaped like the neck of a gooſe, it is fixed to the gourd on one ſide, and ſerves to convey the air to all the pipes it contains. The ancient *cheng* differed in the number of their pipes, thoſe uſed at preſent have only thirteen. this inſtrument appears to have ſome affinity with our organs.

The Chineſe are unacquainted with the uſe of our muſical notes, they have not that diverſity of ſigns which diſtinguiſh the different tones, and the gradual elevation or depreſſion of the voice, nor any thing to point out the various modifications of ſound which produce harmony. They have only a few characters to mark the principal notes, all the airs which they have learned, they repeat merely by rote. the Emperor Kang-hi was therefore greatly aſtoniſhed at the facility with which an European could catch, and remember an air the firſt time he heard it. In 1679, he ſent for Fathers Grimaldi and Pereira to the palace to play ſome tunes upon an organ and a harpſichord, of which they had made him a preſent He appeared much ſatisfied with the European muſic, and afterwards ordered his muſicians to play a Chineſe air; F. Pereira pricked down the whole air while the muſicians were playing it, and when they had done, the miſſionary repeated the air without omitting a ſingle note. The Emperor could not comprehend how a ſtranger could learn a piece of muſic ſo quickly, which had coſt ſo much time and labour to his muſicians, and how it was poſſible, by the help of a few characters, to make himſelf ſo far maſter of it, as not to be in any danger of forgetting it He beſtowed the higheſt praiſes on the European muſic, and admired the means which it furniſhes to facilitate and leſſen the labour of the memory. Some remains of incredulity made him, however, wiſh to have the experiment ſeveral times repeated. He himſelf ſung various airs, which the miſſionary pricked down in proper time, and repeated immediately. "I muſt "confeſs," ſaid the Emperor, "that the European "muſic is incomparable, and that the like of this Fa- "ther (F Pereira) is not to be found in my whole "kingdom"

PAINTING, CIVIL AND NAVAL ARCHITECTURE.

The Chineſe painters have been long ſince decried in Europe; but we are of opinion, that to appreciate their merits juſtly, it would be neceſſary to ſee ſome of their beſt works, and not to judge of them from the fans and ſcreens which are brought us from Canton The Chineſe pretend to have had their Le Brun, their Le Sueur, and their Mignard; and even at preſent they have painters who are held in high eſtimation among them. Their works, however, are never carried from Pe-kin to Canton, because they would not find purchasers among the European merchants, who are fond only of naked figures, of licentious and indecent subjects, and some of the missionaries lamenting the depravity of their taste, assure us, that by the temptation of money, they prevail upon the daubers of Canton to execute pieces for them, the obscenity of which may gratify the taste, and tickle the fancy of an European voluptuary.

It seems, however, to be universally agreed, that the Chinese have no notion of correctness or perspective, and little knowledge of the beautiful proportions of the human body. But those even who refuse them the talent of painting figures well, cannot disallow that they particularly excel in flowers and animals. They execute these subjects with much taste, justness, and freedom, and they pride themselves, above all, in an exactness of representation, which might appear to us trifling and minute.

Painting must make little progress in China, because it is not encouraged by government. It is reckoned among the number of those frivolous arts, which contribute nothing towards the prosperity of the state. The Emperor's cabinets and galleries are filled with European paintings; he employed for a long time the pencils of Castiglione and Attiret, both eminent artists, whom he highly esteemed, and whose works he often inspected; but on account of that notion entertained of the inutility of painting, he rejected an offer made by them of establishing a school for painting, and of instructing pupils in that art.

Painting in fresco was known in China long before the Christian era. It was much in vogue under the Han, who ornamented the walls of their principal temples with it. This kind of painting made fresh progress, and gained more admirers in the fifth and sixth centuries, and it was carried to a degree of perfection ſeldom equalled.

The preſent emperor has in his park an European village, painted in freſco, which produces the moſt agreeable deception. The remaining part of the wall repreſents a landſcape, and little hills, which are ſo happily blended with the diſtant mountains behind, that it is almoſt impoſſible to conceive any compoſition more ingeniouſly imagined, or better executed. This beautiful work is the production of Chineſe painters, and was copied from deſigns ſketched out for them.

Engraving in colours is very ancient among the Chineſe, who diſcovered that method long before it was known in Europe.

The chiſſel of the Chineſe ſculptors is ſeldom employed, becauſe, if we except the idols of their temples, the luxury of ſtatues is not known in this empire. There is not a ſingle ſtatue to be ſeen in the ſquares, public edifices, or palaces of Pe-kin, indeed, the only real ſtatues to be found in China, are thoſe which, for the ſake of ceremonious diſtinction, are uſed to ornament the avenues leading to the tombs of princes, and great men of a certain rank, to which we muſt alſo add thoſe which are placed near the emperor's coffin, and that of his ſons and daughters in the interior part of the vault where their remains are depoſited.

The Chineſe architecture is not the mere effect of cuſtom without any fixed ſyſtem, it has its principles, rules, and proportions. When a pillar is two feet in diameter at the baſe, it muſt be fourteen in height, and by one or other of theſe meaſures that of every part of the building may be determined. This architecture, though it has no relation whatever with that of Europe; though it has borrowed nothing from that of the Greeks, has a certain beauty peculiar to itſelf.

The numberleſs rivers and canals by which China is watered, have rendered it neceſſary to conſtruct a multiplicity of bridges of various ſhapes and forms, the arches of ſome are exceeding lofty and acute, with eaſy ſtairs on each ſide, the ſteps of which are not quite three inches in thickneſs, for the greater facility of aſcending and deſcending others have no arches but are compoſed of large ſtones, placed tranſverſely upon piles, after the manner of planks These ſtones ſometimes are eighteen feet in length ſome of theſe bridges are conſtructed of ſtone, marble, and brick, others of wood, and ſome are formed of a number of barks, joined together by ſtrong iron chains The invention of the latter is very ancient, they are known by the name of *feou-kiao*, *floating bridges*, and ſeveral of them may be ſeen upon the Kiang and Hoang-ho.

The moſt remarkable among the bridges of China is one that is about three leagues from Pe-kin, it is two hundred paces in length, and broad in proportion. Moſt ſtrangers who view it, appear aſtoniſhed at its height, and the apparent inutility of the greater part of its arches, becauſe it is conſtructed upon a very ſmall river. But when this river becomes ſwelled by the ſummer rains, all theſe arches are ſcarcely ſufficient to afford a paſſage to its waters

The naval architecture of the Chineſe appears to have made no progreſs for ſeveral centuries, neither their frequent intercourſe with thoſe Europeans who have viſited their coaſts, nor the ſight of their veſſels, has made them turn their thoughts to change or improve their own. The largeſt are not more than 250 or 300 tons burthen, and they have neither mizen, bow-ſprit, nor top-maſts, but only a main and a fore-maſt, to which is ſometimes added a ſmall top-gallant-maſt, this, however can afford only a feeble aſſiſtance The Chineſe ſupply the place of ſails with mats, made of bamboo, they are ſtrengthened by whole bamboos, equal in length to the breadth of the ſail, and extended acroſs it, at the diſtance of a foot one from another Two pieces of wood are fixed to the top and bottom of the ſail, the upper ſerves as a yard, and the lower, which is about five or ſix inches in thickneſs, keeps the ſail ſtretched, when it is neceſſary to hoiſt or lower it This kind of ſail may be folded and unfolded like the leaves of a ſcreen. The Chineſe veſſels are far from being ſwift ſailers, but they keep their wind well, on account of the ſtiffneſs of their ſails, which do not yield to the breeze; but they ſoon loſe this advantage by the great lee-way they make, owing to their bad conſtruction

The Chineſe do not uſe pitch for caulking the bottoms of their veſſels, but a particular kind of gum, mixed with lime, and this compoſition is ſo excellent, that one or two wells in the hold are ſufficient to keep the veſſel perfectly dry They draw up the water with buckets, for they have not yet adopted the uſe of our pumps. Their anchors are made of a hard and heavy wood, which they call *tié-ly-mou*, or *iron-wood* They pretend, that theſe anchors are far ſuperior to thoſe of iron, becauſe the latter are apt to bend, which never happens to anchors made of *tié-ly-mou*.

The Chineſe make excellent coaſting pilots, but they are bad ſailors in an open ſea It is the ſteerſmen alone who conduct the veſſel, they bring the ſhip's head to that point of the compaſs in which they think they ought to purſue their courſe, and without troubling themſelves about the rolling or motion of the ſhip, they run on as it were at hazard The Chineſe pretend to have been the firſt inventors of the mariner's compaſs, but they ſeem to have little deſire for improving this intereſting diſcovery.

The Chinese have never been exposed to the necessity of fighting naval battles, except on the river Kiang, [illegible] near their own coasts, or in the neighbourhood of the isles of Japan. They have, however, several different kinds of vessels for warlike operations. Those belonging to the port of Canton are much larger than those employed on the coasts of Fo-kien, and the latter are built only of fir, or common deal, whereas the vessels of Canton are entirely constructed of [illegible]. In naval battles they are found to be much stronger, and more useful, but they are heavy, and far inferior to the others in point of sailing — These vessels last long, worms never pierce them, and some of them are armed with cannon.

On the coasts of Fo-kien, the Chinese use a kind of fast-sailing vessel, which is employed in pursuing pirates, and for carrying dispatches. Its sides are strengthened by bands of bamboo nailed over the planks, in order that they may better resist the violence of the waves. These vessels draw from six to seven feet of water, and no weather prevents them from putting to sea.

[illegible] to open the waves. This is a vessel which draws only three or four feet of water, it has a sharp prow, and easily overcomes the resistance of the waves. It is furnished with a helm, a sail, and four oars, and, as they say, *fears neither the wind nor the billows.* It can contain from thirty to fifty soldiers.

[illegible] to run among sand-banks. This is thus named, because it can pass in places where the water is extremely shallow. It is constructed with a flat bottom, and is used for gliding along the coasts of the northern sea, where there is little depth of water, but vessels of this kind are never employed on the southern coasts.

A hawk's-bill vessel. Of all the Chinese vessels this is the swiftest and lightest for sailing, and as its prow and poop are constructed in the same manner, it can advance or retreat with equal facility, without putting about. Its deck is defended, on each side, by a kind of parapet made of bamboo, which shelters the soldiers and rowers from the weapons of the enemy

We shall not extend this account of the Chinese shipping any farther, it may be easily perceived that a whole fleet of such armed barks would not be able to stand an attack from a few of our European ships of war.

NARRATIVE

OF THE

EMBASSY TO CHINA.

AS the object of this work is to furniſh the reader with information reſpecting China, we ſhall ſay little reſpecting the proceedings of the embaſſy in its courſe thither, it may, however, be neceſſary to offer a few introductory remarks.

The diſadvantages under which European countries trade with China are great, and the Britiſh nation, which has felt theſe diſadvantages in a peculiar manner, conceived the idea of attempting their removal. As the exiſtence of the government of Great Britain depends on its commerce, and as from the riſing importance of the United States of America, and the progreſs of civil and religious liberty in Europe, many of the old channels muſt be in a manner ſhut with reſpect to Britiſh manufactures, the Engliſh government acted with the ſtricteſt view to its own intereſt, in planning the embaſſy to China for that purpoſe.

Some intimations were certainly given to the court of London that an ambaſſador would be well received and treated with on a commercial ground, but that ſuch information was ever authoriſed by the court at Pe-kin is somewhat more than doubtful, and from circumstances we are inclined to think that the court of St. James's became in this case, as in many others, the dupe of some artful and interested speculatist.

However, in 1788 the honourable Colonel Cathcart was invested with the character of Minister from this country to the court of China: the Colonel died on his passage, and as ministers with their *accustomed sagacity* had neglected to make any provision for this event, the mission with which he was entrusted may be said to have been buried with him. However, as success might prove highly advantageous to the Board of Controul, and the Court of Directors of the India Company, if to no one else, the character of Ambassador to China was revived in the person of Lord Macartney, a nobleman certainly well qualified for the task. Great expenses were incurred, and many exertions made to render this embassy worthy of the country from which it was sent; but, perhaps, after all that was done, we shall not err in saying, it was better calculated to succeed with a nation of Indians, or with a petty African Prince, than with the government of China; for if the court of Pekin was to be swayed by splendour, much more ought to have been done to have accomplished it than was done;—but supposing the Chinese government to have seriously meditated commercial arrangements, less trick would, perhaps, have succeeded better—be this as it may, the success was what might have been expected, disgrace and contempt—the gentlemen of the embassy had a journey to Pekin, and realized the spirit of a distich written on a certain monarch and his army—"March'd up the hill, and then march'd down "again."

As we shall in the course of our narrative have occasion to mention in particular several of the gentlemen who formed the suite of Earl Macartney, before we proceed it may be proper to present the reader with a general list of their persons and situations:

Sir George Staunton, Bart. Secretary to the Embassy,
Lieut Col. Benson, Commandant of the Ambassador's Guard,
Lieut. H W Parish, of the Royal Artillery,
Lieut. J. Crewe,
Mr. Acheson Maxwell, } Joint Secretaries to the
Mr. Edward Winder, } Ambassador,
Mr. Baring, Assistant Secretary, outward-bound, son of Sir Francis Baring, Bart
Dr. Gillan, Physician and Philosopher to the Embassy;
Dr Scott, Physician and Surgeon to the Embassy,
Mr. Barrow, Comptroller of the Household,
Dr Dinwiddie, Mechanist, Conductor of mathematical and astronomical presents,
Master George Staunton, son of Sir George Staunton, Bart.
Thomas Hickey, Portrait Painter,
Mr. Alexander, Draftsman,
Mr. Huttner, Preceptor to Master Staunton;
Mr. Plumb, Interpreter.

HIS EXCELLENCY'S SERVANTS, &c.

A Steward, and an under do.	A Carpenter and Joiner,
2 Valets de Chambre,	A Saddler,
A Cook,	A Gardener,
2 Couriers,	A Taylor,
A Footman,	A Watchmaker,
A Baker,	A Mathematical Instrument-maker.
A Band of six Musicians,	

BELONGING TO SIR G STAUNTON.

2 Servants, 1 Gardener;

which, with Mr Crewe's Valet de Chambre, formed

the whole of the domeſtic eſtabliſhment, except three natives of China, who were taken from England.

MILITARY ESTABLISHMENT.

20 Men of the Royal Artillery;
10 Ditto 11th Light Dragoons,
20 Ditto drafted from the additional Companies of Infantry, at Chatham.

SHIPS EMPLOYED TO TAKE THE EMBASSY TO CHINA.

The Lion, of 64 guns, Sir Eraſ Gower, Commander,
The Hindoſtan Eaſt Indiaman, Capt. William Mackintoſh, Commander,
The Jackall brig for a tender, manned by officers and men from the Lion.

LIST OF THE OFFICERS ON BOARD THE LION.

Sir Eraſmus Gower, Knight, Commander,
Mr. Cambell, 1ſt Lieutenant,
Mr. Whitman, 2d. ditto,
Mr. Atkins, 3d. ditto,
Mr. Cox, 4th ditto—died at Chuſan,
Mr. Ommaney, acting Lieutenant,
Mr Jackſon, Maſter of the Lion,
Mr Saunders, Maſter's-mate,
Mr. Tippett, ditto;
Mr Simes, ditto,
Mr Lowe, ditto,
Mr Roper, ditto,
Mr. Warren, ditto, ſon of Dr. Warren, promoted to be acting Lieutenant,
Mr Kent,
Mr. Chapman, appointed Gunner, vice Corke, deceaſed,
Right Hon. Lord Mark Kerr, Midſhipman, promoted to be acting Lieutenant,

Hon. Wm Stuart, Midshipman;
Mr Bromely, ditto,
Mr. Swinbourne, do
Mr. Kelly, do.
Mr. Dilkes, do.
Mr. Trollope, do.
Mr. Heywood, do.
Mr Hickey, do.
Mr. Thompson, do.
Mr. Waller, do (died at Wampoa,)
Mr. Beaumont, do (returned home from Angara Point, for the recovery of his health,)
Mr. Snipe, do.
Mr Wools, do.
Mr. Montague, do
Mr. Chambers, do.
Mr. Scott, do
Mr Bridgeman, do
Mr. Perkins, do.
Mr. Sarradine, do.
Mr. Tothill, Purser, (died at Cochin China,)
Mr West, Captain's Clerk,
Mr. Nutt, Surgeon,
Mr Anderson, Chief-mate;
Mr. Cooper, second ditto;
Mr. Thomas, third ditto,
Mr. Humphries, Schoolmaster.

Every necessary arrangement being made, the ambassador and his suite arrived on board the Lion at Spithead, on Friday the 21st of September, 1792, and on Tuesday the 25th, at five o'clock in the afternoon, we took our final departure from that place On the 11th of October we reached Funchal Bay, in the island of Madeira, from whence we again sailed on the 18th, and on the 21st anchored in Santa Cruz Bay, in the island of Teneriffe.

On the 27th we left Santa Cruz, and arrived at the island and town of St Jago on 2d of November, on the 7th we again failed, on the 18th we found ourfelves under the equator, and on the 1ft of December, in the afternoon, we arrived in Rio Janeiro harbour. At this place, mutual compliments and ceremonious attention were paid by the governor and Lord Macartney to each other, and here we remained till the 15th, when we worked down the harbour to fifteen fathom water, and the next day took our leave, and at three o clock in the afternoon, of March the 6th, 1793, came to in Batavia road.

March the 27th, we weighed anchor, and made fail from this place, running between the island of Onrooft and the main

The Jackall brig being given up for loft, Lord Macartney had purchafed a French veffel at Batavia to fupply her place, and gave her the name of the Clarence. The Clarence, however, had only joined us the day before we received intelligence of the Jackall, by a fhip from Oftend to Batavia, and this intelligence was confirmed by the brig joining us on the 23d, to the great joy of the whole embaffy.

On the 29th we loft one of our crew, of the name of Leighton, who had gone afhore to wafh his linen at Sumatra beach, and was found covered with wounds, and murdered by the Malays To the favage difpofition of thefe people, this event gave additional, though melancholy, teftimony The laft rites were paid to the body of the deceafed with the utmoft decency and refpect, and the feelings of the whole fhip s company on the occafion were the beft eulogium on his character and conduct.

Paffing a variety of iflands, without any occurrence worthy of remark, we came to anchor in Pulo Condore

Bay, May 16. Soon after our arrival, a party of gentlemen, accompanied by one of the Chinese interpreters, went on shore. Some of the natives met us on the beach, with whom we proceeded till we came at a small distance to a village of bamboo huts, one of which was the residence of the chief, whose authority extended over the whole island. Like the rest, his habitation was formed of bamboo, raised on four posts, a few feet from the ground. Here we found several natives of Cochin China, who wore no other dress but a piece of linen round their waists, and a black turban on their heads. The chief was habited in a loose black gown, and a pair of black silk trowsers. He was also decorated with a silver cord thrown over his shoulder, from which a small bag of elegant workmanship was suspended. In common with the rest, he wore a turban, but no shoes. He appeared to be the object of very great respect.

Near this palace, if it may be so called, stood the temple. Externally, it resembled the other buildings, but the inside was adorned with various military weapons of Europe, particularly some old fire arms, of which they evidently did not know the use, and seemed to consider them only as objects of veneration. The discharge of a musket against a tree excited the most lively alarm and astonishment. They eagerly examined the place where the ball entered, they even contrived to extract it, and then presented it to each other, with the most visible emotion.

Having entered into a treaty with the chief for a supply of buffaloes, poultry, and fruit, with which he was to furnish us the next day, we were regaled with rice and fish. Finding that cocoa nuts would be acceptable, he immediately ordered some to be procured for us. The dexterity these people shewed in climbing the trees that produced them, is astonishing. On our return to the ship, we observed caves on the beach very ingeniously constructed

Pulo Condore is but thinly peopled The means of subsistence is difficult, and population of course must be influenced thereby. This island is subject to the King of Cochin China

To our utter astonishment, on landing next morning, to receive the stipulated supply of provisions, we found the village deserted, and every moveable carried off. A letter in Chinese characters, left in the hut of the chief, explained the reasons of this sudden and unexpected movement It seems they were apprehensive we meditated hostilities against them, from our ships coming to anchor in their bay, they earnestly implored us to spare their humble dwellings, which they intended to re-occupy on our departure, and dwelt on their poverty, which they perhaps concluded was their best protection, and the strongest argument to allay European rapacity.

Being obliged to set sail without our expected supply, we left Pulo Condore on the 18th, and passing several islands of different forms and magnitudes, we anchored in Turon Bay, in Cochin China, on the evening of the 26th.

Soon after our arrival the Ambassador received a visit from several mandarins, who came in great state They were liberally entertained, but at first seemed averse to take the wines and other liquors which were set before them. This reserve appearing to arise from fear, Lord Macartney set them an example, when they indulged very freely, shewing a particular predilection for cherry and rasberry brandy. These chiefs wore nearly the same kind of dress as we have described at Pulo Condore, except that they had a girdle of silver cordage. Their domeſtics were clad in a fancy dreſs, reſembling Tartan; and their legs and feet were wholly bare.

Intelligence of our arrival having reached the court, in the evening of the 29th the prime miniſter of the King of Cochin China, attended by ſeveral mandarins, came, in his Majeſty's name, to invite the Ambaſſador to dinner. His Excellency obligingly accepted the invitation, but poſtponed the day to the 4th June.

In the interim, he received a preſent from the king, conſiſting of a great number of buffaloes, hogs, fowls, ducks, ſome bags of rice, and ſome jars of ſamptſoo, a Chineſe liquor, reckoned very delicious.

We viſited the town of Fie-Fou, while we lay here. It is nothing but an aſſemblage of wretched bamboo huts; but it has a good market, and were the induſtry of the natives equal to the fertility of the ſoil, this place would be remarkably abundant They ſeem, however, to have little knowledge of agriculture they ſubſiſt, therefore, chiefly on the ſpontaneous produce of the earth, and make their women a principal branch of their trade For a certain conſideration, they are always ready to conſign them to the ſociety of Europeans who touch here, without any apparent ſenſe of impropriety. In one of our excurſions to the ſhore, we ſaw ſix elephants performing a variety of unwieldy feats, for the entertainment of the mandarins who had aſſembled here.

The 4th of June was uſhered in with a ſalute of twenty-one guns, the royal ſtandard of Great Britain, the St George s enſign, and the union, were all diſplayed at their appropriate ſtations Several mandarins waited Lord Macartney's arrival on ſhore, and attended him, under an eſcort of his own troops, to the reſidence of the prime miniſter. A collation was here provided for him, conſiſting of all the dainties the country afforded;

after partaking of which, he returned on board, interchanging mutual civilities with his hosts

Thus far affairs proceeded to the satisfaction of all parties in Cochin China, but the master of the Lion, who had gone in the cutter to take soundings in the bay, having unreflectingly begun to survey the coast, was immediately seized, with seven men who accompanied him, and carried prisoners to the capital

When we first received this disagreeable intelligence, the impression it made is not easily conceived. It was not only the danger to which our countrymen had exposed themselves, that affected the embassy; but as this kingdom is tributary to China, it was feared that a representation of this conduct might make it appear criminal, and have an injurious effect on all our future proceedings, and that the object so much at heart—to inspire confidence, would be changed into suspicion and alarm The good offices of the mandarins were instantly and earnestly solicited, and one of the interpreters was sent on shore to promote an inquiry, and furnish an explanation, and on the 13th, we had the happiness to see the master and his men return in safety, after an absence of six days What they suffered, during this period of suspense, cannot well be described Nothing but a respect for the country to which they belonged, and a regard to the mission on which they were employed, could have saved them from certain death.

This was not the only unpleasant event that befel us here. We lost a respectable gentleman, the purser of the Lion, who died after a few days illness on the 12th, and was interred on shore with all possible solemnity and respect

On June 16, at four in the afternoon, we set sail from Turon Bay, with the weather moderate and fair, and on the 20th, at six P. M saw the land on the north-north-east, at eight the body of the Grand Ladione bore north-north-east

Sir George and Mr. Staunton, with one of Lord Macartney's secretaries, were here charged with letters and business to the commissioners, Mess Brown, Irvine, and Jackson, who had been sent from England to notify the expected embassy, and who were then at Macao. They accordingly set sail in the Jackall brig, accompanied by the Clarence, for that place. Mr Coa and Mr. Niaung, the two natives of China whom we had brought from Europe, accompanied them with the design of proceeding over land to the place of their nativity.

These worthy characters took leave of their friends on board the Lion, with whom they had made so long a voyage, with genuine affection, but they manifested all the impatience natural to those who had been separated for so great a length of time, and at such a distance, from their native land

At half past eight in the morning of the 21st we came to anchor on the north point of the Grand Ladrone island

On Sunday the 23d the Jackall and Clarence returned from Macao Sir George Staunton soon after went on board the Lion, and from what information he had obtained from the commissioners, the most sanguine hopes were entertained that the embassy would be crowned with success.

We now entered the Yellow Sea, when nothing material happened till we arrived at the end of this branch of our voyage We saw many islands in our passage, and met with several Chinese junks and fishing boats

While in the Yellow Sea, Sir Erasmus Gower thought proper to name several rocks on the coast, that had no denomination, after the three principal characters of the embassy.

On Sunday July 21ſt, in the afternoon, the Lion came to an anchor in Jangangfoe Bay, when Lieuts. Campbell and Ommaney, Mr Huttner, and Mr. Plumb, the interpreter, went in the cutter to Mettow, to learn if there was any track by which the Lion could enter the river, or if there was any river on that coaſt, by whoſe navigation ſhe could make a nearer approach to Pe-kin, and if not they were then to concert meaſures with the mandarin of the place for the diſembarkation of the ſame

The next morning the Endeavour brig arrived from Macao and Canton with diſpatches from the commiſſioners

On Tueſday the 23d a mandarin of Chuſan ſent a preſent of twelve fine ſmall bullocks, a number of hogs and a large quantity of fruit, rice, &c.

On the 25th the cutter returned, and Lieut Campbell and his company gave a very pleaſing account of the hoſpitality they experienced from the Chineſe at Mettow, having been not only received with the greateſt civility, but furniſhed with every accommodation and neceſſary It was, however, found abſolutely impracticable to proceed farther with the ſhips, as the whole way to the mouth of the river was a chain of ſhoals, with a bar running acroſs the entrance of it not more than ſix feet deep at high water.

The Jackall and Clarence, therefore, ſailed with Mr. Huttner and Mr Plumb to Mettow, to make arrangements for the landing of the embaſſy, and to fix the time when the Ambaſſador ſhould go on ſhore

On the 2d of Auguſt a preſent of ſixteen bullocks, thirty-two ſheep, ſome hogs, vegetables, tea, ſugar, &c. was ſent on board the Lion. A principal mandarin alſo came on board from one of the junks, and finally ſettled with his Excellency the ſucceeding Monday for the day of his disembarkation, and that the heavy baggage, &c. should be previously removed into the junks. The mandarin, after expressing great surprise at our wooden palace, and the various arrangements and conveniences of it, was hoisted into one of our boats in the accommodation chair, a ceremony with which he appeared to be much pleased

On Monday, at four o'clock in the morning, several junks came along-side the Lion to receive the remainder of the Ambassador's baggage, and his Excellency was now joined by the remainder of his suite from the Hindostan

At eight o'clock orders were given to man ship, previous to his Excellency's disembarkation, which took place almost immediately, when he received three cheers from the seamen, and a salute of nineteen guns from the Lion and Hindostan

At nine o'clock the rest of the suite took their stations on board their different junks, the Ambassador, Sir George Staunton and son, being on board the Clarence brig.

The number of junks occupied by the suite and baggage amounted in all to twenty sail At two o clock in the afternoon we saw the town of Mettow, and at three the junks came to anchor at the mouth of the river, where the Jackall, Clarence, and Endeavour had arrived before us. In the evening the mandarin sent us an acceptable present of dressed meats, and a variety of fruits.

This town, though extensive, has neither the charms of elegance, or the merit of uniformity, it is situated on a swamp, occasioned by the frequent overflowing of the sea, notwithstanding the inhabitants have taken the precaution to make an embankment on the shore.

The houses are built of mud, with bamboo roofs, they are very low, and without either floors or pavements At some distance from the town there are several buildings of a very superior kind, which belong to the mandarins of the place they are constructed of stone and wood, the body of the house being of the former, and the wings and galleries, of the latter, variously painted, they are of a square form, three stories high, and each story has a surrounding range of palisadoes, gilt and fancifully painted The ground floor is fronted with piazzas ornamented in the same manner The wings project on each side the body of the house, and appear to contain a considerable range of apartments

The mandarins here are attended by a great number of guards, infantry and cavalry, who live in tents pitched round the residence of the personage whom they serve.

The immense crowd of spectators who assembled to see the Ambassador land proves Meetow to be a place of prodigious population Many of these people were on horseback and in carriages, and the banks of the river where the junks lay at anchor were entirely covered with them.

The fort in this place consists of a square tower, appearing rather to have been constructed for ornament than public utility, it stands on the margin of the sea, and commands the entrance of the river, but it had not a single piece of ordnance mounted

The river here is about a furlong over, and the colour of the water muddy, its depth is unequal, being in some parts nine feet deep, in others six, and in some parts not more than two

The country round, on both sides of the river, is flat, but the soil is rich and exceedingly fertile.

The whole of the morning of Tuesday the 6th was employed in removing the baggage to the junks, hired for the embassy by Van-Tadge-In, a mandarin of the first class, who had been appointed to conduct the busineſs of the embaſſy, in every thing that related to the reſidence, proviſions, and journey of the ſuite

This perſon was of a pleaſing and open countenance, and his manners were polite and unaffected, the appointment of a man of this deſcription, while it impreſſed us with a favourable opinion of the Chineſe government, ſerved to encourage our hopes of ſucceſs with reſpect to the object of our journey.

At noon the mandarin's boat brought us a quantity of raw beef, bread, apples, pears, ſhaddocks, and oranges the beef was of a very good quality, but the bread was by no means pleaſant to our taſte The ſhape and ſize of the loaves are ſimilar to a middling orange cut in two. They are compoſed of flour and water, and the ſteam of boiling water, to which they are expoſed for a few minutes, is all the baking, if it may be ſo called, which the bread receives. We, therefore, found it neceſſary to cut it in ſlices and toaſt it before we could reconcile it to our plates

In the afternoon of the day we received another ſupply of beef, mutton, pork, whole pigs, and poultry of all ſorts, both roaſt and boiled

The roaſted meat had a very oily taſte, ariſing from ſome preparation that the Chineſe uſe, which gives it a gloſs like that of varniſh The boiled meat, being free from this oily taſte, was far preferable, or, at leaſt, more agreeable to us

We here learned the indifference of the Chineſe concerning their food, and this circumſtance made ſeveral of us very cautious of what we eat, and as to their haſhes and ſtews, many refuſed their allowance, from the apprehenſion of their being compoſed of unwholeſome fleſh

Another circumſtance added to the diſguſt we felt at Chineſe cookery, and furniſhed us with ocular demonſtration of the groſs appetites of the Chineſe people. The pigs on board the Lion being affected with a diſorder which proved fatal to them, ſeveral were thrown overboard, the Chineſe belonging to the junks immediately got out their boats and picked up theſe diſeaſed carcaſes, when having dreſſed a part of them, they appeared to make a very comfortable meal, at the ſame time ridiculing us for our extravagant delicacy.

The junks, or Chineſe veſſels, are built of beach wood and bamboo, with a flat bottom, from thirty to an hundred feet in length, and from about ten to thirty in breadth.

Mr Anderſon gives the following deſcription of that on which he was on board.* "On the firſt deck was a "range of very neat and commodious apartments, "which were clean and decorated with paintings, they "conſiſted of three ſleeping apartments, a dining par-"lour, with a kitchen, and two rooms for ſervants, the "floor is made to lift up, by hatches all along the "junk, to each of which there is a braſs ring beneath "is an hold, or vacant ſpace for containing lumber, and "the quantity of goods that can be ſtowed away in theſe "places is almoſt incredible.

"On the upper or main deck, there is a range of "fourteen or fifteen ſmall chambers, allotted for the "uſe of the men belonging to the junk, and an apart-"ment for the captain or owner of the veſſel.

"In the lower deck the windows are made of wood, "with very ſmall ſquare holes, covered with a ſort of "glazed, tranſparent paper, the ſaſhes are divided into "four parts, and made to take out occaſionally, either "to admit the air for coolneſs, or to ſweeten the apart-"ments. On the outſide there is a coloured curtain,

* Octavo edition of Account of the Embaſſy to China, p. 97.

" that extends from one end of the junk to the other, " which, in very hot weather, is unfurled and fixed up " to shade the apartments from the heat of the sun. " There are also shutters, which slide before the win- " dows, to prevent the effects of cold weather, or any " inclemency of the season.

" There is a gang-way on both sides of the vessel, " about thirty inches broad, by way of passage, without " entering into any of the apartments, and though " many of these vessels carry from two to three hundred " tons, they only draw three feet water, so that they " can be worked with ease and safety in the most shoaly " rivers. Some of these junks have two masts, though, " in general, they have but one, with a very aukward " kind of rudder, but the more elegant vessels of this " kind, which I have just described, are only calculated " for the navigation of a river, as they are not con- " structed with sufficient strength to resist the violent ef- " fects of wind and weather,"

All vessels which navigate the rivers in China have a lamp hoisted to the mast head, as soon as it is dark, to prevent accidents which might otherwise happen from vessels running foul of each other These lamps are made of transparent paper, with characters painted on them, to notify the name of the junk, or the rank of any passengers on board it, and the number of lights are proportioned to the rank of the persons who occupy the junks The same notification is given in the day-time by silken ensigns with painted characters. From the prodigious number of junks which navigate this river, a very pleasing effect is produced by such an assemblage of lights moving along the water.

On the morning of the 7th the Ambassador paid a visit to the principal mandarin of Mettow, to take leave;

and at eleven o clock the whole ſuite proceeded on their voyage

On the 8th we received a large ſupply of tea, ſugar, bread, vegetables of all ſorts, a large quantity of fruit, conſiſting of apples, pears, grapes, and oranges, and a quantity of proviſions of different kinds ready dreſſed, theſe ſupplies were, indeed, at all times furniſhed, in the greateſt abundance We likewiſe received a ſupply of wood and charcoal for culinary uſes

Words can but faintly convey the effect which the novelty and beauty of the ſcene produced on our minds, as we paſſed through a country rich in the charms of nature and of art Cultivation every where around ſeemed to have exhauſted its diligent reſources The fields were enriched with its toils, and preſented a view of various crops, as luxuriant as fancy can conceive, this ſcene was alſo heightened by the abundance of ſheep and the moſt beautiful cattle, which were ſeen grazing in the meadows.

The gardens, on the courſe of the ſtream, appeared alſo delightful, they are equally adapted for pleaſure and utility. and however much Europeans may plume themſelves on their ſuperior knowledge in agriculture, gardening, and ornamental deſign, the Chineſe, in moſt reſpects, would bear away the palm. Their taſte, to our eyes, may be leſs chaſte, but their diligence overcomes difficulties, which in moſt countries would appear inſurmountable

In this delightful voyage, the mandarin's guards marched by day along the banks of the river, and at night pitched their tents oppoſite where the junks lay at anchor Both the fronts of the tents on land, and the junks on the water, were decorated with lamps, which together produced a very pleaſing effect.

The centinels, who kept a regular watch during the night, were furnished with a piece of hollow bamboo, which they strike with a mallet at regular intervals, to signify their vigilance and activity. This custom the soldiers informed us was universally adopted by the Chinese army

At an early hour next morning the gongs gave the signal for sailing These instruments are circular, made of brass, and something resembling the cover of a large culinary vessel, when struck with a large mallet, covered with leather, they produce a sound that may be heard farther than the European trumpet or bell, in the room of which they are substituted

With the usual supply of provisions, for the first time, we received a jar of the country wine, of about three gallons the mouth of this vessel was closed with a large plantain leaf covered with a top of clay, to which was affixed a label, on which were certain Chinese characters. This wine possesses a good body, but the taste is sharp and unpleasant, in its colour it resembles Lisbon

In passing several populous towns, on both sides of the river, the soldiers quartered or resident there, were drawn up on the banks to salute the Ambassador, while crowds of spectators filled every accessible spot of view.

The uniform of a Chinese soldier deserves a description. It consists of black nankeen trowsers, over which a kind of cotton stockings are drawn. Their shoes, which are also made of cotton, are extremely clumsy, broad at the toes, and furnished with immoderately thick soles. From the top of their trowsers is suspended a purse, which contains their money. They have neither shirts nor waistcoats, but only a large black nankeen mantle with loose sleeves, turned up and fringed with red-coloured cloth of the same fabric A broad girdle confines this loose robe, ornamented in front with a kind of plate, said to be a composition of rice A pipe, and bag for tobacco, hangs from this girdle on one side, and a fan on the other These appendages, and a supply of tobacco, are allowed by the Emperor

The Chinese troops were always, when we saw them, drawn up in single ranks, with a great number of colours or standards, made chiefly of green silk, with a red border, and ornamented with golden characters They wear their swords on the left side, with the point forwards, so that, when they draw them they put their hands behind their backs, and unsheath them without being immediately perceived, a manœuvre which they execute with great dexterity, and which is well adapted for the purposes of attack. Under their left arm is slung a bow, and on their backs is hung a quiver, generally containing twelve arrows, others are armed with match locks of a very rusty appearance.

On all occasions when the Chinese troops are called to do military honours, a temporary arch covered with silk is placed at each end of the line, in which the mandarins sit till the person to be saluted appears, when they come forward and make their appearance. Near these arches are three small swivels about two feet and a half in length, which are fixed in the ground with the muzzle pointing to the air. these are discharged as the person to be honoured passes the mandarin at the end of the line. This method of firing salutes the Chinese have adopted to prevent accidents observing, that a loaded gun should never be levelled but at their enemies. In the management of artillery and fire arms, it is not to be expected that Europeans can derive much improvement from the inhabitants of the east, the caution they employ on occasions of rejoicing to prevent accidents from them might give the wisest nations a lesson, for we well know that melancholy, and frequently fatal accidents are occasioned from the want of ſimilar regulations, on our days of public rejoicing.

The ſoldiers have a tuft of hair on the back of their head, which is plaited down the back, and tied at the extremity with a riband. The reſt they ſhave. They cover their heads with ſhallow ſtraw hats, bound under the chin, and decorated with a red plume of camel's hair. According to our ideas, there is little military appearance in the compoſition of a Chineſe ſoldier's dreſs.

In ſailing up the river, we ſaw numbers of ruſtic habitations. chiefly conſtructed of mud, with ſome few of ſtone The country women, with the curioſity natural to their ſex, advanced to ſee the proceſſion. They ſeemed to walk with difficulty, having their feet and ancles bound with a red fillet to confine their growth; and as this practice commences with their infancy, it is aſtoniſhing that they can walk at all. Their front hair is combed back on the crown of the head, clubbed, and decorated with artificial flowers and ſilver pins, the hind hair is then brought up, and ſecured under the club. Except theſe decorations of the head and the bandages on their feet, the dreſs of the Chineſe women differs but little from that of the ſoldiers.

Our progreſs was by no means rapid, but we were every moment attracted by ſome new objects, which prevented our wiſh for greater expedition. In the courſe of one day's ſailing, which could not exceed twenty-four miles, we paſſed ſuch an immenſe number of junks, and ſaw ſuch crowds of people, as would almoſt exceed belief did we attempt calculation Independent of the moving ſcene, the river itſelf, ſpacious and meandering, was a noble object, and the diverſity of its banks, and the views which occaſionally opened over a rich and varied country, would have afforded a ſcope to the moſt glowing pencil.

On the 10th, we for the first time saw the plantations of the tea-tree This plant, which, from being originally an useless luxury, has now become a necessary in so many countries, we have before described, a repetition here would therefore be needless. Plentiful as tea appears to be in this province, it is not within the reach of the lower classes, as the crew of the junks were glad to receive our tea leaves, which they dried, and then boiled, to procure their favourite beverage Tea is universally used in China without sugar, and as the natives, particularly the lower orders, frequently dry and reboil the leaves for some weeks successively, they unite economy with gratification

We this day passed several populous villages, composed of very neat houses built of brick of one story, from every one of which the Ambassador received the same honours which have been already described The crowds of people were beyond all calculation, and impressed on our minds an exalted idea of the immense population of the Chinese empire Nor was the number of junks that appeared on the river less astonishing, being sometimes so numerous, that the water was covered with them

On the morning of the 11th we approached the city Tyen-Sing The banks of the river here presented fields of millet and rice, and the number of spectators that met us, both in vessels and by land, was as great as before. For nearly two miles we observed a range of salt heaps, disposed in columns, and covered with matting, but whether manufactured on the spot, or for what purpose such a prodigious quantity was collected, we were not able to ascertain.

The noise and shouts of an innumerable multitude of people attended our entrance into the city, which is a very populous and extensive place The houses are built of brick, and are in general two stories high, covered with tiles, but the want of regularity offends the eye, and the streets are so uncommonly narrow, that not more than two persons can walk a breast.

Soon after our arrival, the Ambassador, who was received with military honours, went in full form to visit the chief mandarin His palace is in the centre of a garden, it is large and lofty, palisadoed in front, gilt and painted in a very fanciful form Even the external walls are decorated with paintings, and the roof is coated with that bright yellow varnish we have often noticed. Here the ambassador and suite partook of a cold collation, at which all the dainties of the country were collected, particularly confectionary

A play was also performed as a mark of respect and attention to Lord Macartney The theatre is a square building, built principally of wood, and erected in the front of the mandarin's palace. The stage is surrounded with galleries, and the whole was decorated with a profusion of ribands, and silken streamers of various colours The theatrical exhibitions consisted chiefly of representations of imaginary battles, with swords, spears, and lances, in which the performers acquitted themselves with an astonishing activity The scenes were beautifully gilt and painted, and the dresses of the actors were ornamented in conformity to the scenery The exhibition was varied with an agreeable variety of very curious deceptions by slight of hand, theatrical machinery, and that species of agility which we call tumbling, wherein the performers executed their parts with superior address and activity A band of music, consisting of wind instruments, enlivened the scene The novelty of which pleased the eye, rather than delighted the ear. The female characters were performed by eunuchs, for the delicacy of the Chinese would be shocked at the public exhibition of their women.

When the Ambaſſador and attendants returned on board, he was ſaluted by three pieces of ſmall ordnance, ſuch an immenſe number of people accompanied them, in every kind of conveyance capable of floating, that accidents appeared inevitable. We were witneſs to one, where part of the deck of an old junk giving way, from the enormous preſſure of ſpectators, conſigned ſeveral perſons to a watery grave.

A very liberal ſupply of proviſions had been ſent us before we embarked, together with a ſupply of wine ſuperior to that we have before noticed. From the ſuperabundance of our proviſions we entertained the crews who navigated the junks, thus converting the hoſpitality of the country to the benefit of its natives, for which mark of attention they teſtified a due ſenſe of gratitude.

A preſent having been made of three parcels of coloured ſilk by the mandarin Tyen-Sing, to the embaſſy, Mr Maxwell, by the direction of the Ambaſſador, diſtributed them among the ſuite, but it not being poſſible for every one to have an equal ſhare, it was determined, after two pieces were diſtributed to each of the gentlemen, that the remainder ſhould be diſpoſed of by drawing lots, by which means every perſon, whether mechanic, ſervant, muſician, or ſoldier, had an equal chance.

The weather had been exceſſively hot for ſome days, and at an early hour on the morning of the 12th of Auguſt we were viſited by a moſt tremendous ſtorm of thunder, lightning, and rain, which is not unuſual in this climate.

It was found neceſſary, during ſeveral hours in this day, to employ men to tow the junks along. In China, numbers follow this laborious vocation, to which they are called when the wind or tide fails. A rope is fixed to the maſt, and another to the head of the junk. Theſe are of a length proportionable to the breadth of the river, and are fixed, one at each end, to a ſtick of about thirty inches long. This is thrown over the head, and rests on the breast, forming a kind of harness. Every draughtsman is furnished with a similar apparatus, and when all are ready, the leader gives the signal to advance they act in concert, and proceed with a measured step, which is regulated by a kind of musical tone, constantly repeated The fatigue these useful drudges undergo, would appear excessive to any but the Chinese, they wade through marshy banks, and stalk through muddy soil, with a perseverance that claims at once our pity and admiration

Next day, when we received the usual supply of provisions, we set about cooking them ourselves, being perfectly disgusted with Chinese filthiness in regard to their victuals. With respect to rice, however, they deserve the praise of cleanliness. They wash it well in cold water, and drain it through a sieve, then throw it into boiling water, and when pulpy, take it out with a ladle, and put it into another clean vessel, where it is suffered to remain till it becomes quite white and dry. In this form it is used for bread Indeed, boiled rice, and sometimes millet, with vegetables, fried in oil, constitute the usual food of the lower class They eat regularly every four hours of the day, and seldom vary their humble repast Their tables are about a foot high, on them a large vessel of rice is placed, and each person, sitting on the floor, helps himself into a small bason The vegetables are taken up with a couple of chop-sticks, and eaten with the rice. On particular days of rejoicing or sacrifice, a more genial diet is used, but seldom on any other occasion. The usual beverage is a weak infusion of tea

Amid the new and extraordinary things which in such rapid succession caught the view, perhaps the number of the inhabitants that every where presented themselves, was the moſt wonderful. It may be thought to border on the marvellous, but it is a certain fact that we could not paſs fewer than four thouſand junks in the courſe of this day.

On the 14th the weather was extremely hot and ſultry, and the muſquitos ſo troubleſome, as to prove a very painful interruption to our repoſe.

We continued to paſs extenſive fields of millet and rice, and the country maintained its character for fertility, cultivation, and abundance, though in ſeveral parts it aſſumed a more varied and irregular appearance than we had yet ſeen.

In the forenoon we paſſed a large town called Cho-tung-poa, pleaſantly ſituated on the banks of the river. The houſes are of brick, but moſtly only one ſtory in height; walls are erected in the front of them, over which we diſcovered a great number of women viewing the junks as they paſſed. The ſpectators, whom curioſity had led to the banks of the river, were, as uſual, in prodigious numbers.

Soon after leaving Cho-tung-poa, we came to a fork of the river, over the lateral branch of which there were two bridges of two arches, conſtructed with the appearance of much architectural ability. At a ſmall diſtance we ſaw the ruins of another bridge of one arch, originally built of hewn ſtone, which bore the appearance of European maſonry. At a ſmall diſtance, on a gentle eminence, ſtood the palace of the mandarin, built of ſtone, two ſtories high, in a pleaſing ſtyle of architecture, with a flight of ſteps aſcending to the door.

At ſix o'clock in the evening we came to anchor near the ſhore, and in a ſhort time after the grand mandarin of Tyen-ſing, eſcorted by a numerous train of attendants, came to pay his reſpects to the Ambaſſador; a troop of men preceded him, who were employed in ſhouting aloud as they came on, in order to notify his approach. This party was followed by two men carrying large ſilk umbrellas, with pendent curtains of the ſame materials, to ſhelter the palankin from the rays of the ſun; then followed a large band of ſtandard-bearers, who were ſucceeded by foot ſoldiers. The mandarin in his palankin appeared next, and a large eſcort of cavalry cloſed the proceſſion.

The mandarin of Tyen-ſing remained with Lord Macartney about an hour; and, on his return, the proceſſion was rendered more brilliant by a great number of people bearing lamps and torches.

On the 15th, the heat ſtill continued to be extreme, but the country ſtill preſented an equally fertile appearance, and the large fields of corn which we paſſed, appeared to be in crop and cultivation equal to any which are the boaſt of England. We this day paſſed a large plantation of tea, where there was a vaſt number of boxes ranged in order, for the purpoſe of packing the tea.

The banks of the river became more and more diverſified; and the alternate view of extenſive meadows, luxuriant fields, and beautiful gardens, did not ſuffer the gratification of the eye, or the mind, to be for a moment ſuſpended.

In the evening we walked along the ſhore; the corn was almoſt ripe, agriculture appeared in its moſt pleaſing form, and copious plenty ſeemed to vie with the immenſe population of this aſtoniſhing empire.

As we continued on our voyage, the villages became more numerous and populous, until we arrived at the city of Tong-tchew on the 16th of Auguſt in the afternoon, and here our voyage ended.

Soon after our arrival, the conducting mandarin, accompanied by Lord Macartney and Sir George Staunton, went on ſhore to inſpect the place which the Chineſe had prepared for the landing the preſents and baggage. It contained about the ſpace of an acre, fenced in with matting and furniſhed with long ſheds made of uprights of wood, covered with matting, in order to prevent the packages from being injured by damp The ground was entirely covered with mats, and the place well guarded on all ſides by mandarins and ſoldiers

A building, termed a temple, was allotted for the reſidence of the embaſſy, and the whole ſuite, of every deſcription, received an invitation from the grand mandarin to partake of a public breakfaſt, which was to be provided here on the next morning, and during the ſtay of the embaſſy at this place, notice was therefore given to each junk, and orders iſſued for diſembarking Accordingly, Lord Macartney and Sir George Staunton ſet out in two palankins, which had been ſent for them, and were eſcorted to the temple by a party of Chineſe ſoldiers The breakfaſt was compoſed of various ſtews, made diſhes, meat of all kinds, eggs, tea, wines, fruit, and confectionary

Every exertion was made to land the baggage, and preſents, with ſpeed and ſafety, and for this purpoſe a number of Chineſe porters were ordered to each junk, and ſuch emulation was diſplayed in this ſervice, that moſt of it was ſafely lodged in the depot before night. Two Chineſe officers inſpected every caſe and package at the gate of the incloſure, of which they appeared to take a written account, and paſted marks correſpondent with their minutes on every ſeparate article, for not a ſingle box was ſuffered to paſs, till it had undergone this ceremony

The temple appropriated for the reſidence of the embaſſy, was, in fact, the habitation of a timber merchant, and hired by the Chineſe government for this purpoſe it ſtands about a mile diſtant from the city, it is a neat, low building, of one story high, and consists of several courts, which were severally occupied by the soldiers, servants, Ambassador, and suite The soldiers court was next the entrance, beyond this was the servants quarter, opposite to which is a square building of one room, consecrated to religious worship In the middle of this stands an altar, supporting three porcelain statues as large as life, and on each side are candlesticks, containing candles, which are lighted regularly whenever any person is paying his devotion, and regularly at morn and eve Before the images stands a pot full of dust, into which a number of long matches are thrust, which are likewise lighted during the celebration of worship The devotees having finished, the candles and the matches are extinguished, and an attendant on the altar strikes a bell thrice with a mallet. All persons present then kneel before the images, inclining their heads three times, with their hands clasped, which they lift over their heads as they rise Such is the simple ceremony of the daily worship of the Chinese, invariably observed from the humblest to the highest, from the peasant to the emperor This worship obtains the appellation of Chin-chin-josh, or the service of God

The court adjoining this domestic chapel was occupied by the Chinese as a kitchen, from thence there is a circular entrance to that part of the building which was particularly assigned to the Ambassador and his suite

It surrounds a spacious court, which was used as a dining apartment on the occasion, on one side there was a platform, raised on two steps, with a beautiful roof, supported by four gilt pillars, and an awning was stretched over the whole court to protect it from the heat of the sun. Lamps, consisting of frames of box-wood, covered with transparent silk and flowered gauze of various colours, added much to the pleasing effect of the illumination,

The dinner ſerved up for the Ambaſſador and his company, conſiſted of about one hundred different diſhes, dreſſed according to the faſhion of the country: they conſiſted principally of ſtews, ſerved up in ſmall baſons, without either table-cloths, or knives and forks.

During the time of dinner, a great number of Chineſe crowded round the table, and not only expreſſed their ſurpriſe by peculiar actions and geſtures, but ſeemed highly diverted with the diſplay of European manners.

A guard of Britiſh ſoldiers attended the Ambaſſador's apartments; but as we were removed from public view, theſe centinels were placed at the outer gate, and the entrance of the inner court, that they might attract the notice of the Chineſe, and give conſequence to the diplomatic miſſion, in the opinion of the people of the country: a circumſtance on which the ſucceſs of the embaſſy was ſuppoſed in a great meaſure to depend, and which ſpeaks pretty plainly the erroneous ſentiments imbibed reſpecting the perſons we had to treat with.

In the ſeveral apartments appropriated to the uſe of the embaſſy, Chineſe ſervants were diſtributed, to ſupply thoſe who were diſpoſed to call for drink, with hot and cold tea, cold and hot water, ice water, &c.

The city of Tong-tchew is about ſix miles in circumference, almoſt ſquare, ſurrounded by a wall thirty feet high, and ſix broad, to which an external ditch is added, in the moſt acceſſible ſpots. It has three gates, each well fortified, and may, altogether, be conſidered as a ſtrong place.

The houſes are almoſt univerſally of wood, one ſtory high, with exterior decorations in the Chineſe ſtile, but moſt of them are deſtitute of furniture. The ſhop is the principal room; before this are high pillars, ſupporting an awning covered with painting and gilding, and decorated with ſtreamers, which indicate the commodities to be fold, and fometimes a wooden figure is fuper-added, to direct to the fpot

In the form and fize of the houfes and fhops there is very little variety, the fame plan prevails throughout the city in almoft every refpect The ftreets, indeed, are of different breadths, but all of them have a pavement on each fide for the accommodation of the foot paffengers.

As a fubftitute for glafs, a thin glazed paper is ufed; but fome of the palaces of the higher claffes are furnifhed with filk to admit the light

Tong-tchew feems to carry on a very extenfive trade; an immenfe number of junks refort to it, and the population is computed at nearly half a million

The fhortnefs of our ftay, and our ignorance of the language, rendered it impoffible to obtain any correct idea of the nature of the municipal government

The curiofity of the people was fo very troublefome during our excurfion round the city, that we were frequently obliged to feek an afylum in the fhops till the gazing multitude had difperfed

The fecond day after our arrival, the ordnance and ftores were examined, and a trial made of the guns in the prefence of the Ambaffador, which were found to anfwer perfectly well, after which his Excellency and the reft of the fuite dined as on the preceding day.

In the evening his Excellency was vifited by the chief mandarin, accompanied by Van-Tadge-In A band of mufic performed during his ftay, with which the vifitors feemed vaftly pleafed.

We had hitherto efcaped without a death, or any ferious illnefs in the embaffy, fince we entered China, but this evening we loft Mr. Eades, one of the mechanics, by a violent flux, with which he had been fome time afflicted. To imprefs the natives with a favourable idea of the folemnity of our funerals, Lord Macartney directed that the deceafed fhould be interred with military ho-

hours Colonel Benfon therefore gave orders for the troops to appear with their fide arms, except thofe who were appointed to fire over the grave In China, coffins are kept ready made, Mr Plumb was therefore requefted to order one, they are chiefly of the fame fize for all grown perfons, are ftrong and very heavy, in fhape fomewhat like a flat-bottomed boat, and the lid is fecured with a cord inftead of nails. Having procured one of thefe receptacles of mortality, we placed the corpfe in it with all poffible decency, and as, by fome ftrange accident, there was no clergyman attached to the embaffy, Mr Anderfon, an attendant on his Lordfhip, was called on to officiate on this mournful occafion

At nine o clock the order of the proceffion was formed as follows

A detachment of the royal artillery, with arms reverfed.

The coffin carried on men s fhoulders.

Two fifes playing a funeral dirge

The perfons appointed to officiate at the grave.

The fervants, mechanics, &c. two and two

The troops, which clofed the whole, excepting feveral of the gentlemen belonging to the embaffy, who accompanied it

The proceffion being thus previoufly marfhalled, proceeded flowly to the burying-ground, at about a quarter of a mile's diftance from the Ambaffador's refidence, where permiffion for interment had been granted, with a liberality far fuperior to what would be experienced in Great Britain by a follower of Confucius or Fo.

An immenfe concourfe of fpectators were allured by the novelty of the fcene to accompany us. Perhaps the moft fplendid exhibition in any European city would not have procured a larger affembly. The body was committed to the ground with due folemnity, and the proceffion returned in the fame order as it went.

We obſerved that the graves were very ſhallow, having no greater depth than what is juſt neceſſary to cover the coffin, and that the Chineſe have memorials of marble and ſtone as with us, charged with inſcriptions, and ſome of the monuments here exhibited traces of no ordinary ſculpture This receptacle of duſt was of very conſiderable extent, but without walls Except in the vicinity of large towns, there are no public burial grounds in the country, the deceaſed repoſe in the premiſes where they lived

Several mandarins this day paid a viſit to the Ambaſſador, and notified that the day following was appointed for the embaſſy's departure to Pe-kin Theſe viſits we conſidered as a favourable omen of our ultimate ſucceſs

At a very early hour, on the morning of the 21ſt of Auguſt, the ſignal was given by beat of drum, to prepare for our departure The ſoldiers were firſt marched off, and then the ſervants, for both of whom covered waggons had been provided. The gentlemen of the ſuite followed in light carts, but the Ambaſſador, Sir George Staunton, and the interpreter, had each a palankin carried by four men. In point of equipage and appearance, this proceſſion was mean, indeed, it ſunk the diplomatic dignity of the nation, and mortified thoſe who compoſed the embaſſy, for the carts which carried the ſoldiers and ſervants, were wretched paſt deſcription.

After leaving Tong-tchew, we entered a fine champaign country, through which we travelled on a road of uncommon breadth and beauty. A foot pavement, about ſix yards wide, occupied the centre, and on each ſide ſeveral carriages had room to run a-breaſt Roads of a ſimilar deſcription conduct to the capital from the principal towns of the empire, and theſe are kept in perfect repair by labourers regularly disposed, and constantly employed.

We reached the town of Kiang-Fou by seven in the morning, and as it was, probably, a matter of general notoriety when we were to enter Pe-kin, the concourse of people who filled every accessible spot of view, and even crowded on us, exceeded what we had hitherto seen of Chinese population. To our mortification we here observed, that our appearance excited rather more ridicule than respect; and bursts of laughter accompanied every transient sight of us from our contemptible vehicles.

Such was the appearance of an embassy which quitted England with the view of prepossessing the Chinese with exalted sentiments of the grandeur and opulence of the British nation, and for the purpose of obtaining those political distinctions and commercial privileges which no other European nation could boast.

We stopped nearly an hour at Kiang Fou, and received some refreshments of meats, tea, and fruits, of which the suite in the inferior department partook in the open yard, and those of the upper in miserable rooms adjoining.

Van-Tadge-In likewise ordered some joau, an unpleasant Chinese wine, to be distributed to the attendants of the embassy. This he did from the benevolent motive of enabling them to resist the calls of appetite, till another opportunity offered of gratifying them, which at what distance could not be ascertained. When summoned to prepare for our departure, a scene of confusion ensued, not calculated to impress the numerous beholders with a very favourable opinion of English manners, nor to wipe off the unfavourable impression already made; indeed, it was with difficulty that the mandarins could assign the whole to their respective vehicles. Of the face of the country between this town and Pe-kin, it is impossible to speak. Myriads of people intercepted our view.

We paſſed beneath ſeveral beautiful triumphal arches on entering the ſuburbs of the metropolis, where the magnificence diſplayed, ſerved only for a contraſt to the meanneſs of our appearance, and of courſe added to our mortification and regret

At two in the afternoon we reached the gates of the imperial city of Pe-kin Ordnance and troops are ſtationed at every gate, and though the olive branch of peace bleſſes Pe-kin with almoſt a perpetual ſhade, the arts of defence and of prudent caution are neither neglected nor unknown As we have before deſcribed this city, we ſhall here only make ſuch obſervations as have not before occurred

On the moſt moderate computation, from the ſouth gate to the eaſt gate is a ſpace of ten miles. This was our route through Pe-kin, and every ſtep preſented ſome new object to arreſt our attention The ſtreets are ſpacious, clean, and commodious, well paved, and well regulated An exact police is kept up, and as every public functionary, from the higheſt to the loweſt, is attentive to the diſcharge of his duty, order, neatneſs, and activity, are every where perceptible Large bodies of ſcavengers are employed in ſeparate diſtricts in removing every ſpecies of filth, and another claſs of men ſprinkle the ſtreets, to prevent the duſt from incommoding paſſengers, or injuring the gaudy wares and elegant manufactures which every ſhop preſents for ſale

In the capital, as indeed in almoſt every town in China, the pride of architectural elegance and embelliſhment ſeems to be chiefly diſplayed in the ſhops The tradeſmen wiſely lay out the greateſt expenſe in that apartment which brings them in the moſt profit, hence the ſhops in general are magnificent, while their domeſtic accommodations are neither numerous nor great

In Pe-kin, many thousands derive their livelihood from the exercise of their business in the streets These itinerant tradesmen, according to the nature of their business, either carry baskets over their shoulders, or a kind of pack Street barbers are very numerous, they carry with them the implements of their trade, being a chair, a small stove, and a water bason Their customers sit down in the street, where the operation is performed. A pair of large steel tweezers, snapped with force, gives the signal that the barber is at hand, and in a country where it is impossible that any person can entirely shave himself, if he complies with the established mode, this must be a lucrative trade.

Street auctioneers, apparently possessed of all the low eloquence and the vociferous exertions of that craft, present themselves frequently on a kind of platform

The principal streets being of enormous length, are subdivided by arched gateways, under each of which the name of the partial street is written in gilt characters These arches continually appearing, serve as central objects for the eye to repose on

The women here frequently present themselves from the galleries in front of their houses, and amid the immense concourse that were assembled to view our procession, perhaps there were more women in proportion than we should have seen in any principal town of Europe. They possess delicate features, the effects of which they heighten by cosmetics They also apply vermilion to the middle of their lips, marking along the middle a stripe of the deepest die. Their eyes are small, but very expressive, and their brilliance is contrasted by a peak of black velvet or silk, set with stones, which depends from the forehead to the insertion of the nose Their feet appear to be of the natural size, and are free from those bandages we have before mentioned In fact, the women seem to enjoy as much liberty in this place as is consistent with the delicacy of the sex, nor is jealousy, as far as we could judge, a predominant passion among the men, at least in this part of the empire.

In our way through the city, we met a funeral procession The coffin was covered by a rich canopy, with silk curtains, highly ornamented, and hung with escutcheons It was placed on a large bier, and had a great number of men to support it, who advanced with a slow and solemn step A band of music followed, playing a kind of dirge, and after them came the friends and relations of the deceased, in dresses of black and white

Passing the eastern suburbs, we again entered a rich and beautiful country, and soon arrived at Yeumen-man-yeumen, one of the Emperor s palaces, distant about five miles from the city Here we found rather a scanty and indifferent refreshment, but being much fatigued with the extreme heat, and the various impediments we had met with from the concourse of people in our way, the idea of rest was our most acceptable gratification.

This palace is low, both in situation and building. We entered it by a common stone gateway, guarded by soldiers, beyond this is a kind of parade, in the centre of which is a small lodge for the accommodation of the mandarins in waiting. The body of the palace is divided into two square courts, equally destitute of elegance and convenience, the windows of the apartments are formed of lattice, covered with glazed and painted paper, and throughout the whole range there was no other furniture than a few ordinary tables and chairs. Not a bed or bedstead was any where to be seen, the Chinese having nothing of this kind, instead of bedsteads they use a large wooden bench, raised about two feet from the ground, and bottomed with bamboos or wicker work. On one of these several persons may spread their mattreſſes, it was therefore fortunate for us that we had brought our hammocks and cots with us.

Every thing about this reſidence evinced that it had been long deſerted or neglected, and, indeed, a more unpromiſing ſituation for a royal reſidence could no where be found. The ſituation is naturally ſwampy; it is ſurrounded by an high wall, and two ponds of ſtagnant water communicated their mephitic odours to every apartment. Some ſmall graſs fields, indeed, belong to the palace; but theſe too were an exception to the general cultivated appearance of the country. In ſhort, centipedes, ſcorpions, and muſquetos, infeſted every part of this palace, and for ſuch inhabitants it was ſolely adapted.

Yet, diſagreeable as the internal ſtate of our reſidence was, we were cut off from all external communication. Soldiers and mandarins guarded every avenue, and the embaſſy could be conſidered in no other light than as priſoners of ſtate, receiving, like them, a daily allowance from the government which oppreſſes them.

The Ambaſſador's apartments were guarded night and day by Britiſh centinels, and to keep up ſome appearance of dignity, of which, indeed, we appeared to have but little, Lord Macartney required that a table ſhould be, in future, furniſhed for himſelf, Sir George, and Mr. Staunton, diſtinct from the other gentlemen of his ſuite. This requiſition was readily complied with; from this time therefore he dined in his own apartment, while the upper ranks of thoſe who attended on the embaſſy, had a table prepared for them in one of the courts, and beneath the ſhade of a tree, which ſeemed to participate in the general wretchedneſs of the place. Even the preſents were ſo careleſsly depoſited, and ſo much expoſed to the ſun, that there was reaſon for apprehending that ſome of them would receive conſiderable injury from their unfavourable ſituation; a temporary ſhed was therefore immediately erected, to which they were speedily removed.

The Ambassador being very much dissatisfied, and having justly conceived a disgust at his treatment and situation, made a serious requisition for a residence more suited to the character which he sustained, and better calculated for the convenience and accommodation of the embassy To obtain this object, Mr. Plumb, the interpreter, made several visits to Pe-kin, and at last succeeded in his application little occurred worthy of a recital during the remainder of our stay in this uncomfortable and wretched abode, in which we continued till the twenty-sixth day of this month, which was appointed for the Ambassador's departure for Pe-kin.

During this interval several unpleasant altercations took place between the members of the embassy and the soldiers on guard the former could ill brook the disgraceful restraints laid on them by confinement within the walls of their prison, and the latter pertinaciously opposed every attempt at greater liberty Col Benson in particular was so mortified at being denied the liberty of passing the walls of the palace, that he made a resolute attempt to gratify his inclinations, which produced a very unpleasant affray The Colonel, however, was not only forced to abandon his design, but was also threatened with very severe and illiberal treatment from the Chinese who were on duty at the gates. These fracas were not unfrequent, and perhaps were productive of future ill consequences to the interests of the mission. Conciliatory measures by means of negotiation would certainly have been preferable and far more prudent than menaces, which could not be carried into effect, and altercations with those, who in the punctual discharge of the duty imposed on them, were rather objects of respect than of enmity and opposition It must, however, be acknowledged that it was a very humiliating circumstance to be made prisoners when upon a mission, that by the laws of European nations possesses almost universal privileges.

So much pleasure did every person attached to the embassy feel, at the prospect of leaving this wretched place, that every necessary preparation was made for the purpose in the shortest possible space of time Some of the presents and the more delicate articles of art or manufacture, as chandeliers, mathematical apparatus, clocks, time pieces, &c were left here, lest they should be injured by frequent removal

The business of our setting off was as usual a scene of confusion, but by eleven o clock, to our great satisfaction, the procession set out on its return to Pe kin, but with the same wretched beggarly accommodations as it came, we arrived however, without any accident, at the north-gate of Pe-kin about one in the afternoon This was the counter-gate to what we had entered in our former procession through Pe-kin, and presented new views of streets and buildings A pagoda attracted our notice in our progress, being the first we had found an opportunity of observing It stands in the centre of a beautiful garden, adjoining to a mandarin's palace, is square, built of stone, and gradually diminishes from the bottom till it terminates in a spire It rises to the height of seven stories, and has a gallery near the top, encompassed by a rail with a projecting canopy, from which hung a curtain of red silk

As it is probable our return was unexpected, we passed with facility through the streets, and soon arrived at a princely palace belonging to the Viceroy of Canton, who, it seems, was a state prisoner here for some misconduct in office This palace consists of twelve large and six smaller courts it is built of a grey-coloured brick, of most excellent workmanship, but, except two detached edifices, which were occupied by Lord Macartney and the secretary to the embaſſy, the palace was only one ſtory high, though this was of unuſual elevation. Every thing without and within convinced us we now lodged in a palace, the embelliſhments were in the firſt ſtyle of Chineſe taſte, and in regard to the beauty of colours and the brilliant effect of houſe painting, no nation can enter into competition with this. The gloſſy effect of japan is every where perceptible, without the intervention of varniſh, for we were convinced, that the beauty produced aroſe from ſome ingredients in the original compoſition.

The apartments were very ſpacious, and hung with the moſt elegant paper, enriched with gilding Lord Macartney's reſidence was ſingularly ſuperb, and moreover had an elegant private theatre belonging to it, and, in a word, all ranks and deſcriptions were accommodated in a ſtile that gave ſatisfaction, and deſerved acknowledgment Here, however, the furniture was neither valuable nor in any quantity Chairs and tables, a few platforms, covered with bamboo matting and carpets, were the only moveables in a palace whoſe decorations, both external and internal, would not have diſgraced the reſidence of the Emperor himſelf

In ſeveral of the courts there are artificial rocks and ruins, which, though not very congenial to their ſituation, are formed with conſiderable ſkill, and are in themſelves very happy imitations of thoſe objects they were deſigned to repreſent To theſe may be added the triumphal arches, which ariſe, with all their fanciful devices, in various parts of the building, giving it a novel but pleaſing appearance

Under the floor, in each of the principal apartments, is a ſtove, with a circular tube, which conveys warm air to every part of the room above. We ſaw no chimnies in this country, and underſtood that ſtoves ſupplied with charcoal were the univerſal cuſtom.

The ſupplies for the table were in the beſt ſtile of Chineſe living, but conſiſting more of ſtews and haſhes than ſolid joints In this reſpect, however, we had no reaſon to complain, but the ſame ſuſpicious vigilance was employed to keep us within the limits of our reſidence as ever, and on no pretence could we paſs the gates, or even ſcale the walls, every acceſſible part being conſtantly guarded by an active military force.

We were told, that the palace in which we were confined was built by the Viceroy of Canton, at the expenſe of one hundred thouſand pounds, the fruits of his exactions while in that office, and that theſe exactions were chiefly made on the Engliſh

Though we wiſhed that our continuance in this place might be of no long duration, as it was impoſſible to make any progreſs in the grand object of our miſſion till we had an interview with the Emperor, yet every arrangement was made to add to the dignity of the embaſſy, or promote its convenience Having ſettled this buſineſs, we waited with anxious expectation the return of a mandarin, who had been diſpatched to learn his Imperial Majeſty's pleaſure, whether we ſhould proceed to Tartary, where he was then reſident, or wait till the period of his uſual return to Pe-kin

Among the mandarins who paid their reſpects to the Ambaſſador, on his taking up his reſidence here, there were ſeveral natives of France, formerly of the order of Jeſuits, who being prohibited from the promulgation of their religious tenets, had aſſumed the dreſs and manners of the Chineſe, and who had, on account of their learning, been promoted to civil rank among them. Theſe, who were well acquainted with the intereſts of the country, in which they were now naturaliſed, gave Lord Macartney hopes of a favourable iffue to the important embaffy he conducted.

On the morning of the 28th of Auguft, the conducting mandarin acquainted the Ambaffador, that it was his Imperial Majefty's pleafure to receive him in Tartary.

A new arrangement immediately took place, and the following gentlemen belonging to the embaffy were felected to accompany his Excellency into Tartary

Sir George Staunton,	Mr Winder,
Mr Staunton,	Dr. Gillan.
Lieut. Col Benfon,	Mr Plumb,
Capt. Mackintofh,	Mr. Baring, and
Lieut. Parifh,	Mr Huttner.
Lieut. Crewe,	

Mr. Maxwell was left at Pekin, with three fervants, to fettle the houfehold of the Ambaffador, as, whatever had yet been the cafe, it was now determined, that on his return from Tartary his eftablifhment and appearance fhould be, as far as poffible, fuited to the dignity of the character he fuftained.

Dr Scott was alfo left, to take care of the fick, for feveral of the foldiers and fervants were, at this time, afflicted with the bloody flux

Mr Hickey and Mr Alexander were to prepare the portraits of the King and Queen of Great Britain, which, with the ftate canopy, were to ornament the prefence chamber of the Ambaffador

Dr. Dinwiddie and Mr Barrow were left to regulate and arrange the prefents which had hitherto remained at the palace of Yeumen-manyeumen, and to prepare them for prefentation to the Emperor on the Ambaffador's return

The guards, muficians, and fervants, received orders to hold themfelves in readinefs, with only indifpenfable neceffaries, and even the gentlemen of the fuite were to be as little incumbered as possible They were to carry with them only the uniform of the embassy and a common suit of cloaths the musicians and servants were to be dressed out in a suit of state liveries, which, on being unpacked, furnished evident proof, that this was not their first appearance in public, from several of their dresses bearing the names of their former wearers, and from some circumstances we discovered that they had been made up for the servants of M de la Luzerne, late French ambassador at London But whether they were of diplomatic origin, or derived their existence from the theatre or Monmouth-street, is of little importance to the reader With these habiliments, such as they were, every man fitted himself out in the best manner he could, at least with coats and waistcoats, for with respect to breeches, there were only six pairs in the package, and not a single hat accompanied them Such, indeed, was the grotesque figure they made, when thus dressed out, that had the party appeared as ridiculous to the Chinese as they did to each other, they might reasonably have supposed, that we rather wished to acquire money by the exhibition, than to add dignity to an embassy of the nature of that in which we were engaged

The Ambassador and Sir George Staunton agreed to travel in an old chaise belonging to the latter, which, on being unpacked, certainly had none of that gaudy appearance which distinguishes the works of art in China, and some of the Chinese did not hesitate to express their disapprobation of its external appearance, which was, indeed, contemptible

When the chaise was put in order for the journey, a difficulty arose, for which, as it had not been foreseen, no provision was made, this was to get a couple of postilions at length, however, a corporal of infantry, who had once been in this situation, offered his service, and a light-horſeman was ordered to aſſiſt him in conducting the carriage

A man who has learned two trades is frequently uſeful to himſelf and to others this humble corporal was the only man who could have headed the Ambaſſador, and conducted him on his way. He and his aſſiſtant were permitted to exerciſe the horſes in the chaiſe for a ſhort time through the ſtreets of Pe-kin, under a guard of mandarins and ſoldiers, and ſuch crowds aſſembled to ſee this extraordinary ſpectacle, that authority was abſolutely neceſſary to reſtrain the impertinent treſpaſſes of curioſity

Such of the ſuite as preferred riding on horſeback were to be accommodated on giving in their names, and carts were to be provided for thoſe who preferred thoſe kind of vehicles to the ſaddle

On the morning of the 31ſt of Auguſt, ſuch of the preſents and baggage as were intended to be forwarded to Tartary, being ſent off, ſome on mules, others in carts, and ſome borne by men A number of horſes were brought, from which the riders having made a ſelection, very early on the morning of September the ſecond we began our march, but meeting with frequent interruption, it was ſome time before we could paſs the city gate This, however, being effected, we ſoon drove through the ſuburbs, and entered a rich and beautiful country by a road of great width, but without any central pavement. After travelling about ſix miles, we reached the village of Chin-giho, where we were allowed our morning refreſhments In our route we paſſed a great number of populous villages, and took up our firſt night's lodging at one of the Emperor's palaces, named Nan-ſhighee

Our benevolent conductor, Van-Tadge-In, ſeemed to redouble his activity as we approached the imperial presence. We were now furnished every day with the best accommodations, and received an allowance of samt-choo, and a kind of wine, which the Chinese call jooaw, the former is a spirit distilled from rice and millet, and may deserve the appellation of Chinese gin.

From Pe-kin to Jehol, the Emperor's Tartar residence, the distance is one hundred and sixty miles, which was divided into seven days journies, that we might have the advantage of sleeping in an imperial residence every night. This flattering mark of distinction is the highest, it seems, that can be paid, and is never conferred even on the first mandarins The palace where we passed the first night had but little to demand attention, either in its external appearance or its internal decorations, it was environed by a spacious garden, but to this we were denied access

The journey of this day we computed at above twenty-five miles, which may be considered as a tolerable progress, when it is known that the same horses were to take us the whole journey, and the same men were to carry the baggage all the way, and what delayed us still more, the whole of our provisions were ordered and dressed at the several places through which we passed on the road, and conveyed in covered trays, on men's shoulders, to every stage of our journey, for our refreshment there.

We resumed our journey at four next morning, and having passed a populous village called Can-tim, took our refreshment at the town of Wheazon, a place of some consequence. From thence we proceeded through dusty roads, beneath a burning sun, till we reached the palace of Chan-chin, where we halted for the night. This is a spacious structure, covering a great extent of ground, containing ten or twelve courts, and adorned with gardens and plantations. The surrounding country is inclosed, and in point of fertility equalled any we had seen It fed immense herds of cattle, which are small, but very fat.

As we proceeded on our journey the next morning, the distant country assumed a mountainous aspect, fertility sensibly diminished, and the villages became more thin; at one of these, called Cua-bu-cow, we breakfasted in a farm yard About noon we saw the city of Caung chum-fou.

We met nothing worth remark in this day's march, except about two hundred camels and dromedaries, carrying wood and charcoal, entirely under the direction of one man

The palace of Caung-chum-fou received us at an early hour in the afternoon, after a most fatiguing and disagreeable journey. This palace appeared to be little different from those we had before occupied, and the treatment which the Ambassador and his attendants received, corresponded in every respect with what they had undergone before, in their journey to and from Pe-kin. It is almost unnecessary to say, that however unfavourable appearances might be, most of us gladly accepted of whatever was prepared for our refreshment; and it will be doubted by none, that we received with great satisfaction the message of our conductor, that informed us we might retire to the different apartments allotted for our repose

Early the next morning we were summoned together, and soon after departed

The roads were now become very indifferent, and the country displayed a mountainous appearance. At a small distance from Waung-chau-yeng, where we had arrived at about nine o'clock, we passed a prodigious arch, which stretches across a valley, uniting two hills, the farther of which is crowned with a fort, whose ramparts extend to a very considerable distance. Beneath this fort is a stone arch-way conducting down the hill, so steep as to render travelling dangerous. In a romantic valley, at the bottom, appears the town of Waung-chaa-yeng; it is irregularly built, about a mile in length, and displays a considerable share of commerce and opulence. At the extremity of this town, a temporary triumphal arch, ornamented with silken streamers, was erected in honour of the embassy, and the Ambassador was complimented with a band of music, and received a salute from some guns while he passed between a double line of soldiers, extending from the arch to the great wall, who displayed a martial appearance and military parade beyond what we had hitherto observed in China. They were regularly drawn up in companies, and each regiment was distinguished by a different dress; they all wore a kind of coat of mail, and had their head and shoulders covered with steel helmets; their arms were matchlocks, sabres, spears, lances, and bows and arrows, together with some weapons of which we knew not the appropriate name. Almost every division varied in its arms as well as its dress. The number of divisions on each side of the road were seventeen, consisting of about eighty men each.

We now approached one of the wonders of the world, the wall that separates China from Tartary, the most stupendous work ever produced by man. In the vicinity are cantonments for an army of considerable magnitude, at the extremity of which is a massy gateway of stone, defended by three iron doors, which guard the pass between countries formerly distinct. This wall we have already described, when speaking of the forts and places of defence in the Chinese empire, and to that description we refer the reader.

Man, and all his works are doomed to decay. Time has already discovered its influence on this celebrated monument of labour, and as it is now no longer neceſſary for ſecurity or defence, ſince the nations on both ſides acknowledge one ſovereign, no attention is paid to its preſervation, and it is more than than probable, that future travellers in ſome remote age, for it will exiſt for ages ſtill, may deſcribe its ruins, and pauſe while they contemplate the inſtability of ſublunary grandeur. In ſome places fragments have already tumbled down, and in others menace to incumber the plains they once defended.

Having now paſſed the wall, the country aſſumed a new aſpect, even the climate appeared to be changed. Inſtead of high cultivation, the abodes of wealth, and the buſtle of commerce, nothing preſented itſelf but barren waſte, where art has not yet diſplayed her magic powers.

The traveller, however, is amply compenſated by the variety of natural objects which preſent themſelves to his view, and the lover of picturesque beauty finds, amidſt all the increaſing inconveniencies of his journey, a ſource of entertainment which makes him forget all the difficulties he from time to time encounters

About ſeven miles from the great wall, we arrived at the foot of a very high mountain, which the carts could not aſcend without an additional number of horſes. The paſſage through this mountain is an additional proof, if ſuch be wanting, of the genius and indefatigable ſpirit of the Chineſe people, in works that relate to public utility. This road, thirty feet in breadth, is cut through a ſolid rock, and what appeared to us more extraordinary, to leſſen its declivity, it is ſunk ſo much, that it is not leſs than one hundred feet from the top of the mountain to the ſurface of the road; yet ſtill the aſcent is tremendous, and at the beginning has a very fearful appearance, while on the other ſide the way ſlopes down with a gentle declivity between two large mountains towards a beautiful valley.

After paſſing this mountain, at about a mile and a half diſtance, we arrived at the palace of Chaung-ſhanuve, ſituated on a ſmall elevation, it is of large dimenſions, and ſurrounded by an high wall, being the reſidence of a conſiderable number of the Emperor's women, many of whom we diſcovered peeping over the partition which ſeparated their apartments from the part of the palace aſſigned to the accommodation of the embaſſy. Though we were not permitted, as may well be ſuppoſed, to viſit theſe ladies, the eunuchs who were their guardians came to viſit us. There were ſeveral mandarins among them, to whom was conſigned the care and conduct of this female community. This palace is ſurrounded with very extenſive gardens and pleaſure grounds, but from the particular ſervice to which they are applied, it would have been an idle riſk of danger, to have made any attempt to ſee them.

We left Chaung-ſhanuve at ſix o'clock next morning, the road takes the character of the country, which was every where broken and mountainous yet ſterile as it now appeared, this evidently did not proceed from any want of activity in the natives Every ſpot capable of cultivation was covered with corn, and in one place we ſaw ſeveral patches of tillage where the declivity ſeemed to be wholly inacceſſible. This excited our admiration, but judge our ſurprize when we obſerved a peaſant labouring on one of them, where we at firſt could not conceive how he was capable of ſtanding

A more minute examination informed us, that this peaſant had a rope faſtened round his middle, which was ſecured at the top of the mountain, and by which this hardy cultivator lets himſelf down to any part of the precipice where a few yards of ground give him encouragement to plant his vegetables or sow his corn · and in this manner he had decorated the mountain with those little cultivated spots that hung about it. Near the bottom, on an hillock, he had erected a wooden hut, surrounded with a small piece of ground, planted with a few necessary vegetables, where he supported, by his hazardous industry, a wife and family The whole of these cultivated spots, which did not appear to amount to more than half an acre, offered from their situation, at such hazardous distances from each other, a very curious example of the natural industry of the people.

We have before noticed, and we again repeat, that the wise policy of the Chinese government is in nothing more perceptible than in its receiving the greatest part of the taxes imposed, in the produce of the country. This serves as a spur to the exertions of both body and mind. The landlord also is paid his rent in the produce of his farms, and the farmer again pays his labourers by an allotment of small portions of land, from whence industry, with a little occasional encouragement, may derive a comfortable subsistence The only real wealth of nations is agriculture, which is here perfectly understood. A regular chain is established between all ranks for its encouragement, and the artificial and unnatural medium of money, the source of wretchedness and of crimes, is only employed as the cement, not as the materials of the building.

Before noon we arrived at the palace of Callachottueng, where we spent the remainder of the day. This palace stands between two lofty hills, it appears of more modern erection, but is built in stile and form, resembling those we had already passed, the apartments are, however, better fitted up.

At this place the Ambassador gave orders to practise the procession and ceremonies with which we were to appear before the imperial court. His Excellency was pleased to approve of the rehearsal, which was under the direction of Colonel Benson, and during which, the band played the favourite march, known by the appellation of the Duke of York's.

On the next morning, being the 7th of September, we continued our route over a hilly country, where the air was piercingly cold. We passed several well-peopled villages, but neither the cultivation of the country, nor its population, will bear any comparison with that on the other side of the Chinese wall.

Early in the afternoon we reached the palace of Callacnotreshangsu, much fatigued by the badness of the roads; this palace, in extent and form, is equal to any we had lately seen, but we found it tenanted only by squirrels, which bounded round the courts and haunted the apartments.

At six o'clock next morning we continued our route, and arrived at one of the Emperor's pagodas in about two hours; here we found an abundant supply of provisions, but we made only a stay sufficient to enable us to arrange our dress and equipage.

After travelling for about an hour, we came to the village of Quarangcho, within a mile of Jehol, the imperial residence. Here we were marshalled, and proceeded amid an immense concourse of spectators, with all the parade that circumstances would allow. The soldiers of the royal artillery led the way, commanded by Lieutenant Parish, the light horse and infantry succeeded, commanded by Lieutenant Crewe, then followed the Ambassador's servants, two and two, two couriers, mechanics, two and two, musicians, two and two, the gentlemen of the suite, two and two, Sir George Staunton in a palankin, the Ambassador and

Mr Staunton closed the cavalcade in the post-chaise, behind which stood a black boy in a turban

The military, for their numbers, made a respectable shew, and the gentlemen of the suite, it may be reasonably supposed, were not forgetful of their dignity, indeed, it is but doing them justice to say, they strove to support it by every external display in their power, but the generality were a motley group, without even the advantage or a tolerable uniformity in any part of their dress or appearance The whole certainly was not calculated to convey any extraordinary ideas of the splendor or power of the country from which we came, but the contrary. The Chinese might, indeed, possibly be amused with the novelty of the scene, but it was utterly impossible that they should be impressed with its grandeur

Proceeding with a slow pace, in this state we reached Jehol about ten in the morning, and drew up before the palace provided for the reception of the embassy. The British military formed a line for the Ambassador as he passed, but not a mandarin was in waiting to receive him, and we took possession of the palace without the welcome of an address This, indeed, was a mortal blow to all our hopes and expectations, for it had been given out, that the Grand Choulaa would meet the Ambassador, and escort him to Jehol, and after our arrival, we were kept for some hours in anxious expectation of receiving this honour, the troops holding themselves in readiness to fall into a line, and the servants and mechanics ranged in order before the Ambassador s door, but at last dinner being served up, put an end to our expectations of seeing him for the day.

The palace we now inhabited is situated on the declivity of a hill. We entered it by a wooden gateway, which conducts to a large court, each side of this court has a long gallery, ſupported by wooden pillars, and roofed with black gloſſy tiles; that on the left was converted into a kitchen, the others ſerved for the ſoldiers to exerciſe in. At the upper end was another gallery of more elegance, from which a door opens into a farther court, the principal apartments of which were appropriated for the uſe of the Ambaſſador and Sir George Staunton, the reſt for the military gentlemen attached to them; a third court was occupied by the gentlemen of the ſuite, the muſicians, ſervants, and mechanics. The whole fabric is ſurrounded by a high wall; but owing to the declivity of the ſituation, the view was not wholly confined.

Such was our ſituation at Jehol; we had plenty within our walls, but no one had liberty of egreſs.

On the day after our arrival, ſeveral mandarins viſited the Ambaſſador; nothing, however, was ſaid on the ſubject of the miſſion, but on the ſecond day he received a viſit from a mandarin, with a very numerous retinue, who remained nearly an hour in conference with his Excellency and Sir George Staunton. During his ſtay, his attendants amuſed themſelves in examining the dreſs of the Engliſh ſervants, and on rubbing the lace on their cloaths with a ſtone, to aſcertain its quality, they ſhook their heads and ſmiled, when they found it leſs valuable than brilliant.

What paſſed at this conference, could not be generally known, but from ſome circumſtances, a ſpirit of conjecture was conjured up among the attendants on the embaſſy, and the preſages they formed were by no means favourable.

As ſoon as the mandarin had left the Ambaſſador, one of his Excellency's ſecretaries informed the attendants on the embaſſy, that if their proviſions ſhould be defective in quantity or quality, they were to intimate the grievance to his Excellency alone, and leave them untouched. The occaſion for this caution none of us could divine, but we ſoon found it was not given in vain, for the dinner this day ſerved up, was not ſufficient for half the number who were to partake of it. An Engliſhman cannot eaſily be reconciled to confinement, but much leſs to famine; but, in addition, we could perceive a meditated diſreſpect, and of courſe felt ſome alarm for the fate of the embaſſy. According to our inſtructions, the meat was left untouched, and a complaint preferred as directed. His Excellency having remonſtrated to the mandarin through the medium of his interpreter, in a few minutes afterwards every table was ſerved with hot diſhes, in the uſual variety and profuſion. Why this entertainment, which muſt have been nearly ready, was thus withheld, and ſo ſpeedily produced, ſerved as an enigma to exerciſe our ingenuity, but which we could never ſolve. Indeed, no other ideas could poſſibly be entertained of it, than that of an effort of Chineſe ingenuity to try the temper of Engliſhmen, which, but for the ſteps taken by the Ambaſſador, might have been productive of much miſchief to the undertaking.

Next day the preſents brought from Pe-kin were unpacked in the portico facing the Ambaſſador's apartments, they conſiſted of

Two hundred pieces of narrow coarſe cloth, chiefly black and blue.

Two large teleſcopes.

Two air guns.

Two handſome fowling pieces, one inlaid with gold, and the other with ſilver.

Two pair of ſaddle piſtols, enriched and ornamented in the ſame manner.

Two boxes, each containing ſeven pieces of Iriſh tabinets.

Two elegant saddles, and furniture, the seats of these were of doe skin, stitched with fine silver wire, the flaps were of a bright yellow superfine cloth, embroidered with silver, and enriched with silver spangles and tassels, the reins and stirrup-straps of bright yellow leather, stitched with silver, but the stirrups, buckles, &c were only plated

Two large boxes of the finest carpets of the British manufactory

These were all the presents which had been brought from Pe-kin, the rest were either too cumbersome or too delicate to be removed without much care, and were, therefore, left to be presented to the Emperor, on his return, for the winter season, to the capital of his empire.

Centinels were placed to guard these specimens of British manufacture, till the Emperor's pleasure respecting them should be known, which was afterwards notified by the attendant mandarin, with as much civility as could be expected from the supposed greatness of his office.

A mandarin of the first order, on the 12th of September, came to acquaint the Ambassador, that his Imperial Majesty would give him an audience on the 14th. This intelligence diffused hope and spirits through the whole embassy, though, it must be confessed, without any apparent cause

Orders were issued, that the suite should be ready at three on the morning of the day appointed, to accompany his Excellency to the imperial palace. The attendants were to appear in their best liveries, and the soldiers and servants, after having escorted the Ambassador, were to return, without halting, immediately to their quarters, his Excellency informing them, that he hoped the restrictions imposed on them, which were so irksome to all, would in a few days be removed by his endeavours, and every reasonable indulgence allowed them

His Excellency was splendidly dressed, in mulberry velvet, with his diamond star and red riband, and over the whole he wore the full habit of the order of the Bath Sir George Staunton was in a full court dress, over which he wore the robe and hood of a doctor of laws, with the academical cap belonging to that degree.

From the darkness of the morning, a considerable confusion arose in the intended order of the cavalcade; Colonel Benson, indeed, attempted to form a procession, which, however, was but of short duration, even such as it was, for we were soon thrown into confusion by a number of pigs, asses, and dogs, who broke in upon our ranks, and from which, in the dark, we found considerable difficulty to extricate ourselves, but as parade is useless when no one can see it, the failure was of little consequence.

As early as five in the morning, the Ambassador alighted from his palankin at the Emperor's palace, amid an immense number of the populace Sir George and Mr Staunton supported his train, followed by the gentlemen attached to the embassy.

Jehol is large and populous; very irregularly built, and lies in a valley between two mountains, the houses are low, and chiefly built of wood, and, except in the quarter contiguous to the imperial palace, none of the streets are paved.

The principal support of this place seems to be derived from the Emperor's partiality for it No river connects it with remote situations the splendid expense of a court, however, renders it rich, and in some measure commercial. The surrounding country, though not comparable to China, is in the best state of cultivation of any we saw in Tartary

As his Excellency's visit was a mere matter of form and presentation, it did not engage him long. He returned from the imperial palace before noon. The Emperor, it is said, received the credentials with a most ceremonious formality, admitting none into his presence but his Excellency, the Interpreter, Sir George and Master Staunton, with the latter of whom he appeared to be vastly delighted, and to whom he presented, with his own hands, a beautiful fan, and some embroidered purses, and likewise ordered the interpreter to signify how highly he thought of his talents.

Soon after the Ambassador's return, a number of valuable presents were received from court, consisting of rich satins, velvets, silks, and purses, and some of the finest tea of the country, made up into solid cakes by means of baking, of about five pounds each. Except such as were addressed for their Britannic Majesties, these presents were proportionably divided among the gentlemen of the suite

Next morning the Ambassador, attended only by his suite, paid a second visit to the Emperor, in order, as we understood, to attempt to open the wished-for negotiation. On this occasion he stopped several hours The interpreter gave a very favourable report of the aspect of the negotiation, as far as it had advanced, and our hopes for its success seemed to derive some confirmation from a second cargo of presents, consisting of velvets, satins, and silks, as before, Chinese lamps and valuable porcelain, and to these were added a number of calibash boxes of the most exquisite fabric A distribution was made as before, and mirth and festivity, arising from sanguine hopes of success, crowned the evening of the day.

Several mandarins visited the Ambassador on the 16th of September, and invited him and the whole embassy to attend the anniverſary of the Emperor's birth-day at court, on the morrow

Accordingly his Excellency, with the whole of his ſuite, ſet out at two o'clock in the morning, and the whole cavalcade reached the imperial palace about four. This palace ſtands on an elevated ſituation, and commands an extenſive view of the country ſurrounding it: it contains a numerous range of courts ſurrounded by porticos, none of which, however, appear very magnificent, though ſome of them are highly decorated with painting and gilding. The gardens ſurround it for ſeveral miles, and theſe are bounded by a wall thirty feet high. In the front of the palace is a fine lawn, in the centre of which is a very pleaſant lake.

As ſoon as the Emperor approached, the mandarins in waiting proſtrated themſelves, or it would have been impoſſible to have diſtinguiſhed his palankin from one of their's. No external pomp or badge of dignity, marked his dreſs or equipage, except his being carried by twenty mandarins of the firſt order. It is a favourite maxim of the Chineſe government to check ſuperfluous expenſe, and to encourage frugality and induſtry in every department. Actuated by the ſame wiſe and patriotic principle, the preſent Emperor has forbid any public joicings on his birth-day, in this leſs flouriſhing part of his empire, but ſuch unfeigned homage is paid to his dignified and amiable character, that except in his immediate preſence, and under his perſonal view, all ranks and deſcriptions of men, throughout his extenſive dominions, give a looſe to joy on this auſpicious day. He had now completed the eighty-fifth year of his age, and the fifty-ſeventh of his reign. His countenance was animated, and little expreſſive of his advanced years, his eyes were dark and piercing; and his whole air bore the impreſſion of the conſcious dignity of virtue rather than that of rank and state.—How different the sensations arising from the contemplation of this character are to those which arise from the view of a profligate European prince, we shall leave the reader to determine; we shall only say, that the Chinese evidently viewed their Emperor as the father, and not as the scourge of their country.

Our return was followed by a repetition of the same kind of presents as we received before, only varied in pattern and colour. A profusion of fruits, pastry, and confectionary, also accompanied those expressions of imperial munificence.

The next day the Ambassador went in a more private manner to have an audience of leave, as the court was soon to return to Pe-kin. At the same time, he transacted certain official business, the result of which was generally spoken of among the suite in the following terms:

That the Emperor declined entering into any written treaty with Great Britain, or indeed with any nation, as being contrary to ancient usage, at the same time he expressed the highest respect for the British nation and the King, and was strongly disposed to give them a preference in all commercial concerns, and to make any arrangements with respect to British ships at Canton for their advantage, which would not prove disadvantageous to his own subjects, but that he would not sacrifice the interests of his own people to any foreign connections, and would only continue his avowed partiality for the English, while he found it for the advantage of his own subjects, and they conducted themselves in their commercial intercourse in such a manner as to deserve it.

To evince his high personal regard for the King of Great Britain, he delivered to the Ambassador with his own hand a box of great value, containing the miniatures of all the preceding emperors, with a short character of each in verse, written by themselves, accompanied with the subsequent address

" Deliver this casket to the King your master, with " your own hand, and tell him from me, that small as " the present may appear, it is the most valuable I have " to bestow, or my empire can furnish. It has been " transmitted to me through a long line of ancestors, " and I had reserved it as the last token of affection I " had to bequeath to my son and successor, as a tablet of " the virtues of his progenitors, which I should hope " he had only to peruse to be induced to imitate; and " to make it, as they had done, the grand object of his " life to exalt the imperial honour, and advance the " happiness of his people."

This message caused no small degree of speculation among the retinue of the embassy, but none could be fully satisfied themselves, or satisfy others, with respect to the motives of the Emperor, in the present or the address. If he was concerned for the happiness of Europe, we owe him our grateful acknowledgments, and join with many others in the sincere wish that this address may never be forgotten, and that this singular present may produce that effect on the present possessor of, and the heir apparent to, the British crown, as the Chinese Emperor expected it would have produced on his son, the embassy will then prove of importance, indeed, to the British nation.

After dinner, the Ambassador returned with his whole suite and attendants, to see a play performed in the imperial palace. A temporary stage was erected, and ornamented with a profusion of silk streamers. The dramatic entertainments consisted of mock battles, vaulting, tumbling, rope-dancing, and other gymnastic amusements, which would have done no discredit to any performers in Europe. A variety of deceptions concluded this theatrical fete, one of which was the exhibition of a large bowl, in every possible position, which was immediately placed on the stage, bottom upwards, and on being lifted up again, discovered a large rabbit, which escaped from the performer by taking refuge among the audience. The spectators in general, including many of our own people, were totally at a loss to account for this deception, but to many of us, if we knew not how it was done, it was, at least, no novelty, having frequently seen the same trick exhibited by the jugglers of our own country. Other similar tricks were very dexterously performed, and amused us by their novelty and apparent difficulty The theatre made a splendid appearance, being well-lighted and well-filled with persons of distinction.

Next day, pipes and tobacco, sufficient to supply every individual belonging to the embassy, were received, and several mandarins came to pay their respects to the Ambassador In these visits we observed how little regard is paid to external appearance in China. The mandarins never varied their habits, and even the court-dresses here differ very little from the ordinary habiliments. It may be said to consist of a loose robe, falling half-way down the leg, and drawn round the neck with ribands. Over the breast is a piece of embroidery, about five inches square, finished in gold, or silk of various colours, with an exact counterpart on the back; which badges denote the rank of the wearer. The sash, which at other times is usually worn round the waist, is dispensed with at court, and the dress left to its natural flow.

We are now called upon to notice a degree of despotic authority assumed by the leader of the embassy, altogether inconsistent with the character and privileges of British subjects, and as there is reason to believe, that this assumption of arbitrary power conveyed an unfavourable impreſſion to the Chineſe of our national character, laws, and cuſtoms, to ſet this matter in a clear light, we ſhall previouſly ſtate the orders iſſued by Lord Macartney, and read to the ſhips' companies, and all perſons of every rank attached to the embaſſy, on our approaching the coaſt of China, orders which ſeemed to have been dictated by ſound policy, and a real regard to the ſucceſsful proſecution of the grand objects in view.

ORDERS, *ſealed and ſigned* MACARTNEY.

" As the ſhips and brigs attendant on the embaſſy to " China are now likely to arrive in port a few days " hence, his Excellency the Ambaſſador thinks it his " duty to make the following obſervations and arrange- " ments

" It is impoſſible that the various important objects " of the embaſſy can be obtained, but through the good- " will of the Chineſe. that good-will may much de- " pend on the ideas which they ſhall be induced to en- " tertain of the diſpoſition and conduct of the Engliſh " nation, and they can judge only from the behaviour " of the majority of thoſe who come amongſt them. " It muſt be confeſſed, that the impreſſions hitherto " made upon their minds, in conſequence of the irre- " gularities committed by Engliſhmen at Canton, are " unfavourable even to the degree of conſidering them " as the worſt among Europeans, theſe impreſſions are " communicated to that tribunal in the capital, which " reports to, and adviſes the Emperor upon all concerns " with foreign countries. It is therefore eſſential, by " a conduct particularly regular and circumſpect, to " impreſs them with *new, more juſt, and more favourable* " ideas of Engliſhmen, and to ſhew that, even to the " loweſt officer in the ſea or land ſervice, or in the civil "line, they are capable of maintaining, by example "and by discipline, due order, sobriety, and subordi- "nation, among their respective inferiors. Though the "people in China have not the smallest share in the "government, yet it is a maxim invariably pursued by "their superiors, to support the meanest Chinese in any "difference with a stranger, and if the occasion should "happen, to avenge his blood, of which, indeed, there "was a fatal instance not long since at Canton, where "the gunner of an English vessel, who had been very "innocently the cause of the death of a native peasant, "was executed for it, notwithstanding the utmost united "efforts on the part of the several European factories at "Canton to save him. peculiar caution and mildness "must consequently be observed in every sort of inter- "course or accidental meeting with any of the poorest "individuals of the country.

"His Excellency, who well knows that he need not "recommend to Sir Erasmus Gower to make whatever "regulations prudence may dictate on the occasion, for "the persons under his immediate command, as he "hopes Capt. Mackintosh will do for the officers and "crew of the Hindostan, trusts also that the propriety "and necessity of such regulations, calculated to pre- "serve the credit of the English name, and the interest "of the mother country in these remote parts, will en- "sure a steady and cheerful obedience

"These same motives, he flatters himself, will ope- "rate likewise upon all the persons immediately con- "nected with, or in the service of, the embassy.

"His Excellency declares, that he shall be ready to "encourage and to report favourably hereupon the "good conduct of those who shall be found to deserve "it, so he will think it his duty, in case of misconduct "or disobedience of orders, to report the same with "equal exactness, and to suspend or dismiss transgres-"sors, as the occasion may require. Nor, if offence "should be offered to a Chinese, or a misdemeanor of "any kind be committed, which may be punishable by "their laws, will he deem himself bound to interfere "for the purpose of endeavouring to ward off or miti-"gate their severity.

"His Excellency relies on Lieutenant-Colonel Ben-"son, commandant of his guard, that he will have a "strict and watchful eye over them vigilance, as to "their personal demeanor, is as requisite in the present "circumstances, as it is, though from other motives, "in regard to the conduct of an enemy in time of "war. The guards are to be kept constantly together, "and regularly exercised in all military evolutions, "nor are any of them to absent themselves from on board "ship, or from whatever place may be allotted them "for their dwelling on shore, without leave from his "Excellency, or commanding officer None of the "mechanics, or servants, are to leave the ship, or usual "dwelling on shore, without leave from himself, or "from Mr. Maxwell, and his Excellency expects, that "the gentlemen in his train will shew the example of "subordination, by communicating their wishes to him "before they go, on any occasion, from the ship, or "usual dwelling-place on shore.

"No boxes or packages, of any kind, are to be re-"moved from the ship, or, afterwards, from the place "where they shall be brought on shore, without the "Ambassador's leave, or a written order from Mr. Bar-"row, the comptroller, such order describing the na-"ture, number, and dimensions of such packages.

"His Excellency, in the most earnest manner, re-"quests that no persons whatever belonging to the ships "be suffered, and he desires that none of his suite, guard,

" mechanics, or ſervants, preſume to offer for ſale, or
" propoſe to purchaſe, in the way of traffic, the ſmalleſt
" article of merchandiſe of any kind, under any pre-
" tence whatever, without leave from him previouſly
" obtained. The neceſſity of avoiding the leaſt appear-
" ance of traffic accompanying an embaſſy to Pe-kin
" was ſuch as to induce the Eaſt India Company to
" forego the profits of a new market, and deterred
" them from ſhipping any goods for ſale in the Hindoſtan,
" as being deſtined to attend upon the embaſſy, the
" dignity and importance of which, in the prejudiced
" eyes of the Chineſe, would be utterly loſt, and the
" good conſequences expected from it, even on com-
" mercial points, totally prevented, if any actual tranſ-
" actions, though for trifles, for the purpoſe of gain,
" ſhould be diſcovered amongſt any of the perſons con-
" cerned in conveying, or attending an Ambaſſador, of
" which the report would ſoon infallibly ſwell into a
" general ſyſtem of trading. From this ſtrictneſs his
" Excellency will willingly relax whenever ſuch ad-
" vances ſhall have been made by him in negotiation as
" will ſecure the object of his miſſion; and when a
" permiſſion from him to an European, to diſpoſe of any
" particular article of merchandiſe, ſhall be conſidered
" as a favour granted to the Chineſe purchaſer. His
" Excellency is bound to puniſh, as far as in him lies,
" any the ſlighteſt deviation from this regulation; he
" will eaſily have it in his power to do ſo, in regard to
" the perſons immediately in his train or ſervice. The
" diſcipline of the navy will render it equally eaſy to Sir
" Eraſmus Gower, in reſpect to thoſe under his imme-
" diate command; and the Eaſt India Company have,
" by their order of the 5th of September, 1792, and
" by their letter of the 8th of the ſame month and year,
" fully authoriſed his Excellency to enforce compliance
" with the ſame regulation, among the officers of the

"Hindostan. A copy of the said order, and an extract "from the said letter, here follow, in order that Captain Mackintosh may communicate the same to his "officers His Excellency depends upon him to prevent any breach or evasion of the same among any of "his crew"

At a Court of Directors held on Wednesday the 5th of September, 1792

"Resolved,

"That the Right Honourable Lord Viscount Macartney be authorized to suspend, or dismiss the commander, or any officer of the Hindostan, who shall "be guilty of a breach of covenants, or disobedience of "orders from the Secret Committee, or from his Excellency, during the continuation of the embassy to "China.

(Signed) "W RAMSEY, Sec."

Extract from the Chairman and Deputy Chairman's Letter to Lord Macartney, dated the 8th of September, 1792

"The Secret Committee having given orders to Captain Mackintosh, of the Hindostan, to put himself "entirely under your Excellency's direction, as long as "may be necessary for the purpose of the embassy, we "have inclosed a copy of his instructions, and of the "covenants which he has entered into, together with an "account of his private trade, and that of his officers · "there is no intention whatever, on the part of the "court, to permit private trade in any other port, or "place, than Canton, to which the ship is ultimately "destined, unless your Excellency is satisfied that such "private trade will not prove of detriment to the dignity and importance annexed to the embassy, or to the "consequences expected therefrom, in which case your "consent in writing becomes necessary to authorize any "commercial transaction by Captain Mackintosh, or "any of his officers, as explained in the instructions "from the Secret Committee But as we cannot be too "guarded with respect to trade, and the consequences "which may result from any attempt for that purpose, "we hereby authorize your Excellency to suspend, or "dismiss the commander, or any officer of the Hindostan, who shall be guilty of a breach of covenants, "or disobedience of orders from the Secret Committee, "or from your Excellency, during the continuance of "the present embassy."

"His Excellency takes this opportunity of declaring also, that however determined his sense of duty makes him to forward the objects of his mission, and to watch, detect, and punish, as far as in his power, any crime, disobedience of orders, or other behaviour tending to endanger, or delay the success of the present undertaking, or to bring discredit on the English character, or occasion any difficulty, or embarrassment to the embassy, so in the like manner shall he feel himself happy in being able at all times to report and reward the merit, as well as to promote the interest, and indulge the wishes, of any person who has accompanied him on this occasion, as much as may be consistent with the honour and welfare of the public

"In case of the absence or engagements of his Excellency, at any particular moment, application may be made in his room to Sir George Staunton, whom his Majesty was pleased to honour with a commission of minister plenipotentiary, to act on such occasions."

Given on board his Majesty's ship the Lion, the 16th day of July, 1793.

By his Excellency's Command.

(Signed)

ACHESON MAXWELL, } Secretaries.
EDWARD WINDER, }

Some obfervations and injunctions of his Lordfhip, delivered at the fame time as the above, did not, however, feem to accord with the fpirit of liberty and perfonal fecurity, which accompanies an Englifhman wherever he is placed. Hitherto there had not, however, been an attempt made to carry them into execution; but now it was intimated, that all the fervants of the Ambaffador were to confider themfelves as under martial law, and that they would be punifhed according to its regulations, in any cafe of difobedience or neglect. It is true, that the experiment was never made in regard to the civil fervants of the embaffy; but the alarm which this information gave, was deeply felt and inwardly refented. To the honour of Sir George Staunton, he not only difapproved, but reprobated in very fevere terms this meafure, as repugnant to, and fubverfive of, the rights of Englifhmen, and the principles of juftice.

The order, forbidding any traffic with the natives, we believe, was punctually obferved, as far as gain was concerned; but a private in the infantry, compofing a part of the Ambaffador's guard, was reported to the commanding officer as having procured a fmall quantity of famtchoo, or fpirituous liquor, by the affiftance of a Chinefe foldier: he was immediately confined, and being brought to a court martial, of which a corporal was prefident, he was fentenced to receive fixty lafhes.

This fentence being approved by Colonel Benfon, the British foldiers were drawn up in form, in the outer court of the palace where we refided, and the offender being faftened to one of the pillars of the great portico, received his punifhment without mitigation.

The juft abhorrence excited in the breafts of the Chinefe, at this cruel conduct, was demonftrably proved by their words and looks. They expreffed their aftonifhment that a people pretending to profefs the mildeft and moſt benevolent religion on earth, could be guilty of ſuch flagrant inattention to its merciful dictates. One of the principal mandarins, who knew a little Engliſh, expreſſed the general ſentiment, "*Engliſhmen too much* "*cruel, too much bad.*"

But it ſeems as though the officers were determined, at all events, to impreſs the Chineſe with an unfavourable opinion of the Engliſh character, for it appears that Sir Eraſmus Gower, the commander of the Lion, went a ſtep farther towards alienating the affections of the Chineſe from our countrymen, for when that ſhip lay at Chuſan, a native brought a bottle of ſamtchoo on board, intending to exchange it for ſome European article, his deſign being diſcovered, the Captain ordered him to be ſeized and puniſhed with twelve laſhes, in the preſence of numbers of his countrymen, though a complaint preferred to a mandarin would have obtained the ſatisfaction neceſſary, and ſaved the appearance of arbitrary and cruel conduct.

The manners of the Chineſe, indeed, revolt at the public exhibition of theſe puniſhments they are at a loſs to reconcile European behaviour with European profeſſions. Our faith and practice, in almoſt every inſtance, appeared to them to be oppoſite, and theſe circumſtances we have had the pain to record, as well as ſeveral others which occaſionally happened, inſtead of removing unfavourable prejudices, ſeemed to legitimate and ſanction their continuance

Having previouſly been informed that the embaſſy was to proceed to Pe-kin, where its final iſſue was to be arranged, we ſet out from Jehol on the morning of the 21ſt of September, after a ſtate of impriſonment of fourteen days, for the liberty we had been encouraged to expect, was never granted.

In this place it may not be improper to give ſome account of two extraordinary rocks in the vicinity of Jehol, which the darkneſs of the morning on which we entered that city had prevented our ſeeing. One is an immenſe pillar of ſtone, about an hundred feet high, ſmall at the baſe, and gradually ſpreading towards the top, from ſeveral parts of which iſſue ſtreams of the pureſt water. This lofty object is ſituated on the pinnacle of a mountain, which adds to its ſublime effect. The upper part of this rock is rather flat, and appears to be cloathed with verdure and ſhrubs, but is totally inacceſſible. Some convulſion of nature muſt certainly have placed it here, and it is impoſſible to view it from the valley below, without the ſtrongeſt emotions of wonder and fear. The Chineſe give it the name of Panſuaſhaung, and juſtly eſteem it as one of the firſt natural curioſities of the country.

The other is rather a cluſter of rocks, whoſe greateſt height is nearly two hundred feet: theſe ſtand likewiſe on the ſummit of a mountain, and from one point of view, appear as one ſolid maſs. Perhaps the world does not produce two grander objects of the kind.

Soon after we left Jehol, we paſſed the Emperor's pagoda, where we ſaw the tributary King of Cochin China's Ambaſſador and ſuite, advancing with the annual acknowledgment.

We ſlept at the imperial palace of Callachottueng, mentioned before, where we loſt an artillery-man of the bloody flux, of which alarming malady ſeveral others among the military were ill. The attendant mandarin expreſſed great apprehenſion, leſt the Emperor ſhould hear of this circumſtance, and be alarmed on account of any contagious diſorder. The body was therefore ſent on to the next village, where we breakfaſted, and afterwards interred our companion with military honours.

This morning we received intelligence that the Emperor had left Jehol, and that it would be abſolutely neceſſary to advance two ſtages without halting, in order that the palaces might be at liberty to accommodate his majeſty's attendants. In conſequence of this notice, we reached this day Waung-chau-yeng, where we ſlept.

Purſuing the ſame route as we had done before, and re-tracing the ſame objects, our journey to Pe-kin was barren of incidents or novelty. We arrived there on the afternoon of the 26th, and took up our reſidence in the palace which had been appropriated for our uſe before we ſet out for Jehol. The morning of the 27th, Lord Macartney ſpent in examining the arrangements which had been made during his abſence, which ſeemed to meet his entire approbation; and as our ſtay here, at this period, was conſidered as certain to be of ſome continuance, every preparation and proviſion was made for the domeſtic comfort of the eſtabliſhment, and the ſplendor of the embaſſy.

The ſtate canopy was erected in the principal room of the Ambaſſador's apartments: it was made of flowered crimſon ſattin, with feſtoons and curtains, fringed with gold: the back diſplayed the arms of Great Britain; under its cover five chairs of ſtate were placed, the center one being elevated above the reſt for the Ambaſſador. At the other end of the apartment were hung whole length portraits of their Britannic Majeſties. The whole formed an appearance for an audience-chamber, equal to the conſequence of the country repreſented, and wanted no appropriate ornament.

Theſe diſpoſitions being completed, nothing remained to perfect the domeſtic eſtabliſhment, but the regulation of the different tables to be provided for the different departments of the houfehold, which it was thought beft to delay till the arrival of the Emperor in Pe-kin

Captain Mackintofh of the Hindoftan now propofed to fet off on the Monday to join his fhip, in order to proceed to Canton, there to take in his cargo for England, having feen, as he conceived, a favourable commencement of this embaffy, in which his employers had fuch a predominant intereft

On the 28th the arrival of the Emperor at the imperial palace in Pe-kin was announced by a grand difcharge of artillery.

The occupations of this day in the palace of the Ambaffador were confined entirely to writing letters for England, of which Captain Mackintofh was to take the charge, it being confidered as a fettled arrangement with the court of Pe-kin, that the Englifh embaffy were to remain during the winter, to carry on the important negotiations with which it was entrufted.

The next day his Excellency was vifited by feveral mandarins, and fome packages of broad cloths of Britifh manufacture were put in a ftate of readinefs for being prefented to the Emperor

Sicknefs at this time prevailed fo much among the foldiers attached to the embaffy, that more than half of them were unable to do duty; it was, therefore, found expedient to eftablifh an hofpital in fome of the vacant buildings within the precincts of the palace for their reception, and more fpeedy recovery.

On the 1ft of October, a mandarin requefted, in the name of the Emperor, that the ordnance prefents might be fent to the palace of Yeumen-manyeumen, where they were to be proved and examined; which, contrary to our expectations, was done by the Chinefe themfelves inftead of our own artillery men, who had been taken from England for the purpose of displaying their superiority in the science of engineering to the Emperor. The chariots and other presents were also removed to the same place, where the carpenters and the other mechanics went to hang them on their springs, their service, like that of the artillery, was, however, in a great measure dispensed with, they not being permitted to finally adjust them for representation.

The following day, the Ambassador received a formal invitation to wait on the Emperor on the morrow, in compliance with this request his excellency went in a private manner, and transacted business with the officers of state. The conference lasted for two hours, and there were no apparent reasons for supposing that the objects of the mission were not in a progressive state of success.

The Ambassador now settled the order and disposition of the tables for the different departments of the houshold, and every thing seemed to indicate a residence of some permanency at Pekin, which proved highly gratifying to us, who had no other means of judging of the probable success of the object of our embassy, than the general arrangements made for its domestic establishment.

The cabinets of British manufacture were now conveyed to the imperial residence by Chinese porters, and the presents, consisting of jewellery, plated goods, hardware, and cutlery, were now unpacked, and the whole equally divided between the Emperor and the Grand Chou-ta.

On the 5th the Emperor visited the palace of Yeumen-man [illegible], to inspect the presents which were lodged there, and [illegible] he was pleased to order eight [illegible] distributed to every European person attending [illegible] artificers, who were employed in [illegible] the carriages, and fitting up a model of an English first-rate man of war, which had been sent with the presents, described his Majesty as being about five feet ten inches high, of a slender form, but well-proportioned, and that his countenance presented a regularity of features, free from the decrepitude of age. His deportment was attractively affable, and the dignity of the prince was only displayed in the superior manners of the man. He was habited in a robe of yellow silk, and a cap of black velvet, surmounted with a red ball, and adorned with a peacock's feather. He wore silk boots, embroidered with gold, and a blue silk sash round his waste.

The opinion his Majesty formed of the presents could only be collected from their being generally received, for we could not learn that he had expressed any opinion where it could possibly be conveyed to us. Two camera obscuras were, however, returned, as being suited only to the amusement of children.

A number of bales, containing a variety of broad and narrow cloths of English manufacture, with a quantity of camblets, two barrel organs, and the remainder of such presents as were not damaged, were now removed from the Ambassador's palace by the Chinese employed on these occasions, and Mr. Plumb sometimes accompanied the presents to explain the nature and application of them, or performed that office to the mandarins, previous to their departure.

As it was now considered, as a matter of certainty, that the embassy would remain for some time at Pe-kin, the superb and elegant horse furniture which had been brought over for his Excellency and Sir George Staunton, were unpacked and got ready for immediate use.

A number of presents were this day received from the Emperor for the use of their Britannic Majesties, the Ambassador and suite.

At noon on the 6th, the Ambaſſador again went to viſit the Emperor, but on his arrival at court he fainted away, and being conveyed home, continued indiſpoſed during the remaining part of the day In the meanwhile, Sir George Staunton and Colonel Benſon diſtributed to each of the ſoldiers and ſervants, ſome pieces of ſilk, others of dongaree, a kind of nankeen, and a piece of ſilver, of about ſixteen ounces, as a preſent from his Imperial Majeſty

The optical, mechanical, and mathematical inſtruments being removed from the palace of Yeumen-manjeumen, the gentlemen and mechanics were diſmiſſed from their attendance there On a trial of the powers of ſome of the articles before the mandarins, they failed in the effects aſcribed to them, and others excited little ſurprize or admiration in the Chineſe literati who viewed them, this the good Dr. Dinwiddie and Mr Barrow immediately attributed to their groſs ignorance and obſtinacy.

A report began to circulate, that we were ſoon to quit Pe-kin. It occaſioned a conſiderable ſhare of ſpeculation, but it obtained leſs credit than afterwards appeared to be due to it the carpenters were however employed in ſtrengthening the caſes which contained the preſents for St. James s, and in the afternoon of the 7th this report, which at firſt met with only a faint belief in general, was confirmed by an order from the Ambaſſador to prepare for our departure on the Wedneſday following, being only two days notice. Our ſurprize and concern may eaſily be conceived After a variety of fatigues, we had conſoled ourſelves that we ſhould now have enjoyed ſome repoſe, but all perſonal conſiderations were abſorbed in public affairs, in which the humbleſt individual felt an intereſt. The grand objects of the embaſſy were evidently unaccompliſhed, and in our attachment to our country, its honour, and advantage, we forgot every other care.

To submit, however, we were obliged, and nothing appeared to us possible to be done but an attempt to gain a little respite, till the baggage was packed up and arranged, this seemed a reasonable demand, the attendant mandarin therefore made the requisition, and an order arrived from the Grand Choulaa to suspend our departure till Friday but judge our astonishment, when the next morning this was countermanded by the Emperor himself, and we were expressly ordered to depart on the day first intimated

It is not to be supposed that our situation could enable us to judge of the reasons on which this unexpected mandate was founded. It was reported by the Chinese, that as the business on the part of the Emperor was already completed, he was surprised the English Ambassador was not anxious to return to his own country. It was also said, that his Majesty was alarmed at the number of our sick, lest any contagion should be communicated to his subjects nor were there persons wanting who ascribed his determination to an aversion contracted against us, from the skill and ingenuity we evinced in those engines of destruction, the brass mortars, which were tried in his presence It was said he deprecated the spirit of a people, who, contrary to the avowed benign principles of their religion, had made such a proficiency in arts which seemed to contradict them all.

Many other reports of a similar nature were propagated, but the reason assigned by the Chinese government was the near approach of winter, when the rivers would be frozen, and the journey to Canton, through the northern provinces, be attended with inconvenience and crowded with impediments.

To speculate on the policy that actuated the court of Pe-kin on this occasion, would be vain, neither shall we presume to ascribe it to any misconduct or mismanagement, but the manner in which the embassy was dismissed was certainly ungracious, and mortifying in the extreme, for supposing it to be the policy of the Chinese government, that no foreign minister shall be received, but on particular occasions, and that he shall not remain in the country after he has finished his particular mission, it does not appear that the business was at all advanced which Lord Macartney was employed to negotiate, and his Lordship certainly would not have formed domestic arrangements, if he had not considered himself certain of remaining at Pe-kin throughout the winter, and of succeeding in the object of his embassy

At this time a marine, who, with three others, had been taken from on board the Lion, to fill the vacancies occasioned by the death of some of the soldiers, died of the flux, and to prevent this circumstance from being known his corpse was carried away in the night

Lord Macartney now sent his own state carriage as a present to the Grand Choulaa, who refused to accept it. It was then re-demanded, but no answer was returned to this request, and so short was the period allotted us to stay, and so much was to be done in it, that there was no time to make farther inquiries concerning it, or the reasons for the behaviour on the part of the minister by whom it was refused

The confusion arising from this sudden and unexpected event, rendered it impossible to arrange the baggage with any order. We huddled it together in the best manner that circumstances would permit Some articles which could not be packed up, or were now useless, were given to the mandarins, the natives took care to purloin a ſhare, and Lord Macartney's ſervants had the canopy of ſtate.

We ſet out on the road that leads to Tong-tchew at a very early hour on the morning of the 9th, and reached that town in the evening. Even the thoughts of being on the return to our country failed to relieve the gloom of diſappointment; and to increaſe our unpleaſant ſenſations, we met with neglect and wretched accommodations compared to what we had experienced before; for the apartments in which we were lodged here were only temporary ſheds, hung with ſtraw matting.

We have already mentioned the conduct of the Grand Choulaa, reſpecting Lord Macartney's chariot. On our arrival, however, at Tong-tchew, it had found its way thither before us, and was ſtationed oppoſite the place appointed for the reception of the embaſſy, ſurrounded by crowds of Chineſe; many of its ornaments were defaced, and it was otherwiſe injured. It was, however, drawn down to the river ſide, and a caſe being made for it on the ſpot, to ſecure it from farther injury, it was reconſigned to the hold of a junk, and finally ſent to figure at Madras.

Next morning, on proceeding to the ſide of the river, we found the junks intended for our reception. The baggage was put on board with all poſſible expedition, but not without a degree of confuſion beyond what we had yet known; for all the attention before paid to the Ambaſſador and his ſuite ſeemed now to be forgotten; things being, however, at length adjuſted, we went on board our junks, and the attendant mandarin and his party followed in ſeparate veſſels. Soon after the embarkation was completed, dinner was ſerved up; and at an early hour we retired to reſt, after a moſt fatiguing day.

On the 11th, at a very early hour, the junks were unmoored, and the fleet proceeded down the river: but as we have already given a defcription of the country through which it flows, and the local circumftances attending of it, we fhall pafs on to the period when we quitted the natural for an artificial river, indeed nothing occurred worthy of obfervation, but that though we ftill attracted the notice of the inhabitants who lived near the river, the refpectful and ceremonious attentions of our former voyage were entirely difcontinued.

On the 16th we left the channel of the river, and entered a canal conftructed with infinite labour and expenfe. The fides are mafonry throughout its extent, and at certain diftances locks, in the form of a crefcent, are erected, which confining the water to a narrow paffage in the middle of the canal, occafions a moderate fall of about three feet. The motion of the junks is accelerated in paffing thefe locks, and continues to fome diftance, and to prevent the veffels receiving any damage from ftriking againft the walls of the lock, men are always ready to let down large leathern pads, which effectually break the fhock

In the courfe of this day we paffed a number of thefe locks, whofe conftruction and effects we found invariably the fame.

For fome days we failed through a country rich in agriculture and population. We obferved plantations of the fhrub which produces the imperial and gunpowder tea. In fize and figure it refembles the goofberry-bufh. Imperial tea is the produce of the firft bloffoms, gunpowder tea is a collection of the fucceffive bloffoms as they appear.

Not only the exterior marks of refpect had been withdrawn from the embaffy by the Chinefe, but we even found our provifions deficient, both in quantity and quality. A reprefentation to the mandarin, however, procured immediate redrefs in this particular, and it was farther reported, that the ſame benevolent character had exerted himſelf with effect to do away ſome very unfavourable impreſſions, with which a Tartar mandarin had prejudiced the Emperor againſt the Engliſh, by repreſenting them as diveſted of every amiable quality, and addicted to every vice

On the 20th we paſſed numerous plantations of tobacco, a plant cultivated here in the greateſt variety, and to the greateſt extent of any country in the world. Indeed ſmoaking being the univerſal practice from infancy to old age, the quantity of tobacco conſumed in China muſt exceed all moderate calculation

Several conſiderable cities appeared at a ſmall diſtance from the canal, the garriſons from which advanced to the banks to give the uſual ſalute, and the people to gratify their curioſity.

We paſſed a number of bridges and ſeveral corn-mills, worked by water, and apparently on the ſame conſtruction as thoſe in Europe.

A lofty pagoda, of eight ſtories, opened to our view on the morning of the 23d, but not different apparently from thoſe we had before ſeen Next day we ſaw the Chineſe poſt paſs along the road on the margin of the canal. The letters are incloſed in a large bamboo baſket, hooped with cane, it is then locked, and the key is given into the cuſtody of one of the ſoldiers, who delivers it to the poſt-maſter The baſket is then ſtrapped on the courier's ſhoulders, and being decorated with a number of little bells at the bottom, they make a loud jingling when ſhaken by the motion of the horſe, and announce the approach of the poſt. Five light-horſemen eſcort the courier, and as the fleeteſt horſes are ſelected, and changed at every ſtage, the mails in China are conveyed with extraordinary expedition and ſafety.

The junks anchored on the evening of the following day in the heart of a large city, through which the canal paſſes. A continual ſucceſſion of bridges connects the banks, and theſe are guarded by ſoldiers, who ſuffer no veſſel to paſs till a mandarin has inſpected it. The fleet here received a ſalute of three guns, and a numerous body of ſoldiers lined the banks, who, wearing large helmets, and being completely armed, had a very military appearance.

We ſoon arrived at Kord-cheeaung, a city of equal magnitude with the laſt, in the center of which we ſaw a pagoda of ten ſtories, each ſurrounded by a gallery.

After paſſing ſeveral large cities in the courſe of this day's voyage, we anchored for the night at Lee-yaungoo, which was illuminated in honour of the Ambaſſador. Public attentions, indeed, begin again to be more frequent, and ceremoniouſly paid.

We paſſed the city of Kaungboo on the 26th, and found ſuch an amazing number of junks lying there that our paſſage was impeded for ſome time, and we were obliged to come to anchor, in order to give opportunity for a paſſage to be made between them. The canal winds through this place and its banks ſlope down to the water in a very beautiful form.

Every ſpot in our paſſage gave teſtimony to the exiſtence of art, and the effects of induſtry, as well as of prodigious population. On the 29th, paſſing ſeveral extenſive fields, we obſerved the peaſants ploughing; they worked with oxen, and though their ploughs were of a very clumſy form, compared with thoſe of England, the labour ſeemed to be neatly and properly executed.

A repetition of the meagre incidents that fell in our way would be tireſome. Towns, bridges, locks, and junks, fields covered with plenty, and people beyond calculation, were now common objects.

On the 30th we saw a fleet of junks laden with tea for the Canton market, nor was it an unnatural, or uninteresting observation which many of us made, that in the chance of commerce, some of their cargoes might ultimately be consigned to our own country, and arrive there before us.

The prospects around us were now constantly enlivened by pagodas and country seats, some of which were adorned with beautiful gardens, and others surrounded with the finest orchards we had ever beheld.

On the 31st in the morning, the fleet passed through a walled city, where the vast number of junks which covered its canal, justify the opinion of its extensive commerce. In its neighbourhood there are large plantations of tea and tobacco, and the next morning we passed several fields of cotton, which to us formed a pleasing and novel appearance.

The canal became much more expanded, and on the 2d of November we reached a city of great extent and trade. Several canals meet here, and on the south side of it is a bay, communicating with the Yellow river, in which the noblest fleets of Europe might ride.

The hills in the vicinity are beautifully green, their summits are crowned with pagodas, while villas and gardens adorn the lower slopes.

Passing through the bay, in which various opposite currents meet, we soon entered the river, and found ourselves again embosomed in a rich and delightful country.

Town opened on our enchanted senses after town, and no words can convey an adequate idea of the picturesque scenery that surrounded us.

About the hour of dinner, we arrived at a town of unusual magnitude and beauty, through which the river flowed for the space of three miles, the houses were uniformly built of brick, varied with a bluish-coloured ſtone, and generally riſe to two ſtories high

Here we received the military honours ſo often mentioned, and indeed it may in general be obſerved, that there was neither town nor village through which we paſſed, that had not its mandarin and its proportionate number of guards and troops, not only in China, but alſo in the remote and leſs populous regions of Tartary.

In the afternoon we anchored, for ſome time, at another conſiderable town, where the junks ſtopped to take in a ſupply of wine This town is ſituated on the ſide of a large lake, which, in ſome places, was divided only by a bank from the river on which we were ſailing.

The country ſoon after aſſumed a ſwampy appearance, the natural conſequence of ſo many rivers, canals, and lakes, which interſect it, and promote its commercial intercourſe.

The weather was cold and the mornings froſty The climate, unqueſtionably, is affected by the large bodies of water which every where abound in this part of the country We now underſtood, that it was the Yellow river on which we were ſailing, probably ſo called from ſome communications with the Yellow ſea. We paſſed ſeveral lakes, and on the 3d ſaw a number of fiſhing-boats employed in their vocations, and procured from them a ſmall fiſh, about the ſize of a ſprat, but in flavour and form reſembling the haddock On the oppoſite ſide of this lake we diſcovered a very large city, built with a dark-coloured ſtone, and roofed with tiles of the ſame hue This place appears to be about eight miles in circumference, and from the dreſs and manners of its inhabitants, we could eaſily determine was both commercial and polite. At the extremity of the wall of this city we dropped our anchor for the night

Next day we paſſed two other large lakes, and ſoon after reached the town of Kiang-fou, which is large and walled. A mandarin and his guards appeared, to give the cuſtomary ſalutes, and at each end of the line of troops, a temporary arch was erected, with a platform reaching down to the river, very elegantly adorned, to afford a landing to the Ambaſſador, ſhould he happen to be diſpoſed to ſtop At a ſmall diſtance tents were pitched, in the center of which was the mandarin s pavilion, where a collation was ready for the entertainment of his Excellency and the mandarins in our fleet But the order of the voyage prevented them from accepting this tribute of hoſpitality and politeneſs.

Beyond this, we came to another large town of ſuperior beauty, where we ſtopped to receive a ſupply of proviſions, and to be furniſhed with men to tow the junks Here we were gratified with the ſight of a number of fine women, whoſe features were beautiful and complexions uncommonly fair.

In the afternoon we paſſed a town which could not be leſs than nine miles in circumference. The walls are of immenſe height, and ſeem to be ancient Several hundreds of junks were moored along its wharfs

On the 5th we entered a large lake, adorned with a variety of beautiful iſlands, the moſt conſiderable of them contains the palace of a mandarin, with moſt elegant ſummer-houſes, plantations, and gardens, here alſo a lofty rock roſe amid the trees, and ſupported on its top a ſtately pagoda.

We ſoon entered another river, whoſe banks became highly picturesque, on which, and the adjoining heights, we ſaw a variety of villas, with gilt pyramids riſing from the roofs, which gave them the appearance of Gothic architecture.

At the city of Mee-you-mee-aung we stopped to take in the customary supply of provisions. Nature seems to have formed this place for the purposes of navigation and commerce, and rural beauty to have fixed her residence in its vicinity.

Another object here presented itself of a very different nature, and which, by its contrast, acquired additional importance. A body of soldiers were drawn up on an esplanade, the line of which extended near a mile; they were divided into companies distinguished by the variety of their uniforms, which, together with the number and colours of their standards, offered a very beautiful spectacle.

No other object, for a considerable time, attracted our notice, except a small dock-yard for building junks, enclosed in a fine grove, which formed a pleasing and picturesque scene.

The river now appeared to be proceeding boldly on into a rich, fertile country, but of more unequal surface than any we had yet seen, when, by an unexpected meander, it brought us back to the city. Here we passed through another large bridge, near a circular bastion which commanded, by its battery, every direction of the river.

On another turn of the stream we discovered a very fine hill before us, the summit of which is crowned with a magnificent pagoda, and the declivities beautified with all the decoration that could be conferred by beautiful gardens and elegant buildings. At the foot of this elevated spot are two stone gateways, which open to a walk that winds gradually up the hill to the pagoda.

This hill appears to form a part of the gardens belonging to the mandarin, whose palace is situated on the banks of the river, from whence a broad flight of steps ascends to the gate of the outer court This edifice, in its size and appearance, is suited to the dignity of its possessor, and, like other buildings of the same kind and character in China, is perfectly uniform in all its parts. The body of the house rises to three stories, and the wings are diminished to two. A paved court occupies a large space in the front, and the whole is enclosed by a wall, including a large garden, that extends to the beautiful hill, of which a very inadequate sketch has been already given

The country continued to make advances in beauty; fields full of fertility, with their shady enclosures, farms embosomed in orchards, villas, and their gardens, we had long been accustomed to behold, but now a mountain rose before us, not rugged and barren, but verdant to its very top, while innumerable herds of cattle, and flocks of sheep, adorned its sloping pastures

Another town soon succeeded, and to that a lake, surrounded by hills of the same kind, and covered with sheep and cattle From this delightful situation we passed through a lock, and between a draw-bridge into a canal, that divides another large commercial town Here we observed a brick-kiln, and a pile of bricks just made, the materials of which appeared to be a kind of sand, mixed up with the mud of the river, the kiln itself was built with the same materials, in the form of a pyramid.

In the evening we passed a large walled city, apparently similar to those we had before seen, and several pagodas being illuminated, in honour of the Ambassador and mandarins, had a very pleasing appearance amid the gloom of night

The Chinese houses are not only varied in their stile and decorations, but even the towns are in some measure marked by the colour of the materials of which they are built. On the 6th of November we entered a town of a most dismal hue, it was wholly erected of black brick, and as the houses were more lofty than those generally seen in this country, being none less than two and many four stories high, its peculiar character made the stronger impression on our minds

We passed a stone bridge of three arches, and soon after reached the mandarin's palace, a stone building of singular architecture On each side of the principal gate are two lofty walls painted red, to prevent the building from being seen but in a front view The gateway is enriched with sculpture, and the usual accompaniments of Chinese characters, it is of stone, and supports an apartment. The house itself is painted of different colours, with a stone gallery in front, and covered with a roof of the same material.

The mandarin who resided here had caused a temporary stage, or platform, to be erected, from the palace to the side of the river, in case the Ambassador, and the mandarins, should find it convenient to land. The roof of this building was covered with silk of various colours, a number of lamps fancifully adorned with gauze and ribands were suspended from it, and the floor was covered with a fine, variegated matting. He had also caused a large screen, or curtain, of this matting, to be fixed on the opposite side of the water, for the purpose of hiding some ruinous buildings, that would otherwise have disgraced the gay picture he had contrived by their deformity.

The soldiers under the command of this mandarin were of a different appearance from any we had seen, as they wore red hats with a very high and pointed crown, on the side of which was a brass plate, that appeared to be fastened with yellow ribands.

Of the elegant hofpitality of this mandarin we were not allowed to partake, by the circumftance of our voyage.

A fucceffion of towns, locks, bridges, and pagodas, appeared in rapid fucceffion for fome hours, and in the afternoon we faw a very large country refidence at fome diftance, with a lofty pagoda rifing, as it perfpectively appeared, from the center of it The tower terminated in a cupola, with a fpiral ornament rifing from the top, crowned with a ball, from each fide of which a chain hung down, till it touched the upper ftory of the building

After paffing this ftructure, the banks of the river were, for a confiderable diftance, fo high as to obfcure all view of the adjacent country

In confequence of a complaint againft fome of the captains of the junks, for embezzlement of provifions, the grand mandarin inftituted an inquiry after the fleet came to an anchor this evening . and being convinced of the truth of the charge, fentenced the culprits to be baftinadoed or bambooed, which was immediately carried into execution.

In the courfe of the next day, we had a tranfient view of Chinefe hufbandry, in the practical parts of digging, manuring, and ploughing, and from the aukward implements employed, our admiration of the fertility of the country, and the labour of the natives was increafed.

We paffed another town, the houfes of which were covered with plaifter, and many of them three ftories high, and painted black. At the entrance and the extremity of this place of darknefs, which is very large, we failed under a noble arch. We foon reached another town of the fame defcription, where many of the houfes projected over the river, and here our junks were towed by boats.

So various were the features of the river, and so frequent was the intersection of canals, that we were often at a loss to ascertain whether we were sailing on the former or the latter This, however, is of little importance, as the general outline of the country has been faithfully delineated, though to catch every object would have been impossible.

As it was intended to forward the heavy baggage from Hoang-tchew to Chusan, in order to its being conveyed by sea to Canton, arrangements were made for this purpose. A party of the gentlemen of the embassy, and servants, were to accompany it, and the Ambassador and the remainder were to proceed over land, with only absolute necessaries

The country still continued the same for some distance, but at length became more unequal, towns and villages rose in constant succession, and the pagodas on the heights seemed to multiply On the 9th the fleet was ordered to anchor in the open country near the shore, when Van-Tadge-In, the grand mandarin, visited every junk, the owners of which he briefly examined, and then ordered them to suffer the punishment of the bamboo Their crime we could never learn

Passing several plantations of tallow trees, we arrived at Hoang-tchew, on the afternoon of the 10th, when the junks were all fastened together, and every person belonging to the suite expressly forbid to land on any account Indeed, a body of Chinese soldiers pitched their tents opposite us, as if to awe us into compliance. During the time we lay here, no circumstance happened worthy of being recorded The mandarin of Hoang-tchew, who had accompanied us from Pe-kin, took his leave of us, he was a superior to Van-

Tadge-In, and had of courſe aſſumed the ſupreme direction during this part of our voyage.

The heavy baggage, which was to be ſent to Chuſan, being ſeparated from the light articles we were to carry with us to Canton, Colonel Benſon, Captain Mackintoſh, and party, ſet off to join the Hindoſtan at Chuſan, on the 5th day after our arrival; and the ſame day we alſo left Hoang-tchew, after the Ambaſſador had diſtributed ten dollars to the owner of each junk, for their reſpective crews

The Ambaſſador, accompanied by his retinue, proceeded on the 14th of November for the Green river, where we were again to embark in ſmaller junks On paſſing the city gates, the embaſſy received the cuſtomary ſalute. Between the two rivers, the diſtance could not be leſs than ſeven miles, and the whole ſpace was covered by the city and ſuburbs, and lined with ſoldiers, who ſecured us from the preſſure of an innumerable multitude of people, who crowded to ſee us The ſtreets are narrow, but well paved, the houſes two and three ſtories high, and the magnificence of the ſhops was beyond any thing we had hitherto ſeen. In commerce and population, Hoang-tchew is a city of the firſt magnitude

At noon we reached the Green river, where the Ambaſſador was received with military honours The troops were armed with helmets, and made with their accompaniments a ſplendid appearance

A triumphal arch, with a platform deſcending to the Ambaſſador's junk, had been erected for the occaſion Our embarkation was attended by a concourſe of people, great beyond deſcription. Some were mounted on buffaloes, which animal carried ſeveral at a time on its back, and appeared very docile, others were in carts, drawn by the ſame animal

Our junks were small, but very neatly fitted up, and our voyage was continued between ranges of mountains, presenting the most romantic scenery The vallies were covered with tallow and mulberry trees the former of which is remarkably beautiful

The river on which we now sailed, was, at a medium, about three feet deep the water has a green cast, and the bottom is gravelly

In the evening of the 15th, we saw the city of Zanguoa, which made a most brilliant appearance with its illuminations, and the effect was increased by numerous bodies of soldiers ranged along the banks of the river, with paper lanterns

Next day, we passed several stone pagodas, the features of the country through which we sailed, were still mountainous and picturesque, presenting often plantations of tallow and mulberry trees, and the forts and salutes became so frequent, that they grew absolutely tiresome. Indeed, so much military honour was paid to the embassy, that the salutes could only be compared to a train of wild-fire laid from Hoang-tchew to Canton, and continually exploding as we proceeded.

About three o'clock in the morning of the 17th, we were awakened by a discharge of artillery, we perceived, by the number of lanterns, that a large body of soldiers were drawn up on the shore a lighted torch was fixed to the carriage of every gun, and the bearer of each stand of colours was distinguished by a flambeau, which gave new brilliance and effect to this military illumination

In an early part of this afternoon, the fleet anchored opposite a small, but very neat town, and, in a short time, the conducting mandarin visited the junks, and distributed to the whole of the Ambassador's train, according to [illegible] [illegible] ...sents of perfumes, fans, impe-

[illegible]

On the 18th, the country changed to a fine champaign, in which numerous villages rose amidst plantations of tallow and mulberry-trees This day we passed a group of water-mills, all turned by a small cut from the river, flowing in a circular direction. These appeared to be on the European construction, and, as we understood, were employed in threshing rice

The provisions which we now received, though by no means deficient in quantity, were far inferior in quality to those we had been accustomed to receive in the former part of our journey, this defect we were given to understand arose from the nature of the country, rather than from any inattention to the comfort and convenience of the embassy Indeed, there could be no reason to suppose that the Emperor had not even been anxious to render our departure from his kingdom as agreeable as respect and exterior honour could make it.

The following day the banks of the river resumed the usual appearance, and long ranges of mountains rose into the horizon

The 20th brought us to a large and beautiful town, where we were again to disembark The scenery here might have advantageously employed the warmest pencil. The river formed a central object, on one side was the town, with its appropriate circumstances, and a military encampment in front, with all its gaudy ensigns, on the other side lofty perpendicular hills bounded the view in the most sublime stile

Having disembarked, we proceeded next day by land, some in palankins, others in sedans and bamboo chairs, or on horseback, as their fancy led them, for the attendant mandarin always consulted us on the mode in which we wished to travel, and as far as possible accommodated us. We soon reached the city of Chansoiyeng, where the Ambassador was received with due distinction. The streets of this city are narrow, and the shops which line both sides of the streets, are in the usual stile of Chinese order and splendour Leaving this, we passed another walled city, and several villages, and arrived at the city of Yoosaun, where we were again to embark early in the afternoon, here we drank of tea at the palace of the mandarin, and having stowed the baggage on board another fleet of junks, provided for our accommodation, we went on board, anxious to proceed on our voyage, which on account of a heavy rain, we could not do till the 23d

On the morning of the 24th of November, we found ourselves before the city of Mammenoa The river now ran between enormous masses of loose stone, without any continuity or connection, exhibiting the appearance of having been subjected to some convulsion of nature Some of these huge stones had been excavated into dwellings, and every interstice between them was occupied by gardens, and their attendant buildings This stupendous scenery continued for several miles, it was grand, perhaps unique in itself, and where it admitted of views into the more distant country, it produced a most delightful picture

We reached the city of Hoa-quoo in the afternoon, where much to our satisfaction, we found larger junks ready to receive us. The mandarin of the place politely sent a variety of fruits and confectionary for the use of every junk, except that which contained the soldiers. The country through which we passed was rich and fertile, a few red rocks occasionally broke the level of the scene, and a number of rice mills were at work.

The fog was so thick on the morning of the 26th, as to obscure the country, about noon it dispersed, and the eye ranged over a level extent of rice fields, interſected with villas and gardens

Our proviſions had for ſome time been very indifferent, not from neglect, but the nature of the country In proportion as we fared worſe, our Chineſe junk-men fared better, they received not only our ſuperfluity, but ſometimes almoſt the whole

The 27th preſented a novel ſcene, a village entirely built of mud, with inhabitants as wretched in appearance as their habitations were mean For this ſight we were unable to account, in a part of the country where the inhabitants ſeemed induſtrious, and the earth fertile. We this day received from the mandarin preſents of caddies of tea for every perſon in the ſuite

On the 28th the river aſſumed a formidable breadth, and as the wind was high, the waves and ſurf reſembled thoſe of the ſea We continued through the day to paſs numbers of fiſhing boats, which ſerved to vary the navigation of the ſtream.

In the afternoon of this day we paſſed the city of Tyaung-ſhi-ſennau, which, for extent and the advantages of ſituation, unqueſtionably deſerves to be reckoned one of the firſt in China Not leſs than a thouſand junks lay at anchor before it. It is built near the conflux of ſeveral rivers, and enjoys a moſt extenſive commerce, the grand mandarin of this city paid a viſit to his Excellency on board his junk, and made a variety of preſents in ſilk, porcelain, ſcarlet cotton, coloured ſtuffs, tea, and elegant ſmelling bottles.

The only novelty that preſented itſelf in the courſe of our voyage on the 29th, was a village built with blue bricks, and covered with tiles of the ſame colour Cities, pagodas, and the palaces of mandarins were now become familiar objects, but preſented nothing new, and without this deſcription would be tedious, and the reader will perhaps ſay we have already been too minute.

We paſſed two brick kilns and ſurrounding villages, and the following day we paſſed a city lying amid beautiful meadows and orchards, about two miles diſtance from the river. Beyond this the proſpect became as delightful as fancy can conceive. Mountains roſe into the horizon, foreſts waved on the ſlopes, and flocks and herds covered the vales.

Numerous cities and villages lined the banks of the river, which now expanded to a great breadth, and as the wind blew freſh, the junks ſometimes appeared to us in danger of being overſet. At this time the thermometer had ſunk to forty, and the fields were covered with froſt.

It has been remarked before, that there are no public cemeteries, except in the vicinity of populous places. Hence the country becomes a continued burial ground. Which ever way we turned our eyes, ſome trophy of death appeared, and the degree of embelliſhment it had received, marked the rank of the deceaſed. Indeed, it is not unuſual for the Chineſe to erect their funeral monuments in their life-time, and as the choice of ſituation is free, many of them become picturesque objects.

On the 1ſt of December, after paſſing Taung ſaung-au, we ſailed by the town of Saunt-y-tawn, where ſeveral ſuperb pagodas roſe above the ſurrounding groves. Numerous timber yards occupied the banks of the river, and a large quantity of timber was immerſed in the ſtream, which, as we were told, was in a ſtate of preparation for the building of junks, the principal buſineſs of the place.

We were this day ſaluted with more than uſual honour by the fort of May-taun-go, which we paſſed, as we likewiſe did a ſtately pagoda on the oppoſite ſide of the river. The cities of Loo Dichean, Morriun Dew, and Chic-a-fou, which we now approached, all lie contiguous to each other, and art and nature have united their efforts to increaſe the beauty of this charming vicinity. At a diſtance we obſerved vaſt columns of ſmoke, which roſe, as we were informed, from a porcelain manufactory.

In the evening we reached the city of Chinga-fou. Here illuminations, which were peculiarly brilliant, the firing of rockets and of artillery, took place in honour of the Ambaſſador. We received alſo a preſent of fruit and confectionary from the mandarin of the place

To note every object which arreſted and pleaſed the eye of the traveller, would fatigue the reader without informing him. Every bend of the river opened a new proſpect that gratified the ſight, to which no deſcription, however vivid, can do juſtice The ſeaſon of the year was now the moſt unpropitious for landſcape beauty, yet the charms of nature, intermixed with the veſtiges of art, imparted ſucceſſive impulſes of delight.

On the 2d of December we paſſed the city of Fie-cho-jeunau, emboſomed in plantations of trees From its apparent population, and the number of junks employed in its commerce, it appeared evidently to be ranked in the firſt claſs of Chineſe towns

The next day we had a view of ſome beautiful ruins of an ancient building, the original deſtination of which we could not diſcover, but from the remains ſtill viſible, we concluded it muſt have once been a work of no common magnificence, and it was in all probability a temple.

In this part of the empire ſituation ſeems to be duly appreciated. The villas of the mandarins, the pagodas, and even ſome of the private dwellings, are erected with a diſcriminating attention to the circumſtances of the place, and the beauty of the ſcenery.

We obſerved numbers of fiſhermen employed in their vocation with rods and lines. In lakes and large rivers, the ſame kind of bait is frequently uſed as at ſea. Nets, too, are in very comm[illegible] in ſome places bamboo canes, ſupporting a curtain of ſtrong gauze, are placed acroſs the ſtreams, and then the fiſh being allured to the ſpot by baits, are caught in nets with great ſucceſs.

On inquiry, we found that the rights of fiſhery, as in Europe, are private property. In thoſe rivers we navigated, a kind of whiting and trout were the moſt plentiful; theſe are ſold to the crews of the junks, and the demand for them is very great.

But the moſt extraordinary mode of fiſhing in this country is by birds trained for that purpoſe. Nor are hawks or hounds more ſagacious in the purſuit of their prey, or more certain in obtaining it, than theſe birds. The Chineſe call them Looau; they are about the ſize of a gooſe, with grey plumage, webbed feet, and have a long and very ſlender bill, that is crooked at the point. This aquatic fowl, when in its wild ſtate, has nothing uncommon in its appearance, nor does it differ from other birds whom nature has appointed to live on the water. It makes its neſt among the reeds of the ſhore, or in the hollows of crags, or where an iſland offers its ſhelter or protection. Its faculty of diving, or remaining under water, is not more extraordinary than many other fowl that prey upon fiſh: but the moſt wonderful circumſtance is the docility of theſe birds in employing their natural inſtinctive powers, at the command of the fiſhermen who poſſeſs them, in the ſame manner as the hound, the ſpaniel, or the pointer, ſubmit their reſpective ſagacity to the huntſman, or the gunner.

The number of theſe birds in a boat are proportioned to the ſize of it. At a certain ſignal they ruſh into the water, and dive after the fiſh; and the moment they have ſeized the prey, they fly with it to their boat, and however numerous theſe veſſels may be, theſe ſagacious birds invariably return to their own maſters, and amidſt the throng of fiſhing junks which are ſometimes aſſembled on theſe occaſions, they never fail to diſtinguiſh that to which they belong. When the fiſh are in great plenty, theſe purveyors will ſoon fill a boat with them, and will ſometimes be ſeen flying along with a fiſh of ſuch ſize, as to make the beholder ſuſpect his organs of viſion. The Chineſe repeatedly aſſerted to us, that when one of them happens to have taken a fiſh which is too bulky for the management of a ſingle fowl, the reſt will immediately afford their aſſiſtance. But while they are thus labouring for their maſters, they are prevented from paying any attention to themſ[illegible] round their necks, and is ſo contrived as to fruſtrate any attempt to ſwallow the leaſt morſel of what they take.

We alſo ſaw another fiſhing party, which conſiſted of at leaſt thirty fiſhermen, ſeated like ſo many taylors on a wide board, ſupported by props in the river, where they were angling. There was another groupe of theſe people near the ſhore, who had embanked a part of the river with ſand, where, by raking the bottom with a kind of ſhovel, they caught large quantities of ſhrimps and other ſhell fiſh.

Early in the afternoon we anchored before the city of Vang-on-chean, where the Ambaſſador received a viſit from the mandarin, and where we ſtaid about two hours; this place occupies a conſiderable ſpace, on one ſide it is bounded by the river, and on the other by a range of high mountains.

A succession of towns and villages enlivened our voyage during the succeeding day. The features of the country became craggy and elevated into hills, but fertility, in every possible situation, shewed the labour of diligent cultivation.

The appearance of indigence is by no means common in China, but this day we observed a cluster of cottages meanly constructed of logs of wood, and indicating internal wretchedness, but the eye had not leisure to give them more than a glance of commiseration, so very alluring were the charms of the surrounding country, of which the pencil of a master might communicate some general idea, but it is not in the power of language to convey any correct image even of the individual objects, much less of the picture formed by the combination of them. When we say that we saw forests, gardens, mountains, vallies, palaces, cottages, cities, villages, pagodas, and mills, with a variety of subordinate, but heightening circumstances, in one view, we certainly inform the reader of the constituent parts of the prospect, but to give him any proper ideas of their actual arrangement and relative situation, of their proportions and contrast, of their general distance from the eye, and comparative distance from each other, is beyond any exertion of description.

On the 5th the river became very shoally, and we anchored before dark to avoid the dangers of such a navigation. This day we passed the city of Yoo-jen-nau, situated at the bottom of a lofty mountain. Here we found that the river on which we had sailed, communicated with another of equal magnitude. The position of a city, at the conflux of two large rivers, readily points out its convenience for trade.

Leaving this place, the stream was divided into two streams by a beautiful islet, in which the mandarin had an elegant feat, probably for his occafional retirement.

In the evening, the city of Kaung-joo-fou prefented the moft brilliant nocturnal illumination we had hitherto feen, and this complimentary attention was heightened by a prefent of fruits and confectionary from the mandarin.

In our paffage down the river, on the 6th of December, we obferved a number of machines, with which the Chinefe water their grounds They confift of a wheel of bamboo, turned by a ftream, which throwing the water into large refervoirs, it is from thence diftributed by fluices into channels which interfect the fields.

A beautiful village, called Shai-boo, fituated on a bold elevation above the river, was the principal object in the landfcape, till the attention was called away by the pagoda of Tau-ay, the upper part of which being in ruins, gave it a picturefque and impreffive appearance, and well accorded with the character of the little burial place at its foot

The town of Whan-ting-taun was the only place of any importance we paffed in this day's voyage. Villages were, however, numerous, and fome huts again made their appearance, of the moft wretched conftruction, not being fufficient to fhelter the inhabitants from the inclemency of the weather

The 7th of December was the moft remarkable day we had yet experienced, for during our whole progrefs we faw neither city, town, nor village. A few farm-houfes were, however, difperfed over the face of the country. The banks of the river were lofty, and formed of a perpendicular barrier of red earth, ftreaked with horizontal veins of ftone, in a direction perfectly rectilinear.

This natural curiosity continued without any deviation from this regularity for several miles.

The shallowness of the river obliged us again to shift our baggage into junks of lesser burden, this caused such delay, that it was not till late in the evening that we found ourselves in the vicinity of some town or village, which we might now not have noticed, had it not been for the number of paper lanterns we saw exhibited by the soldiers, and the complimentary salute they paid us.

The weather had for some days been temperate, but the face of the country was no longer the same Barren mountains, separated by plains that seemed to defy the labour of man to produce fertility, now presented themselves on all hands. Some dwarf-trees, however, among which the camphire is said to predominate, broke the abruptness of the slopes, and here and there a village or a pagoda animated the scene.

In this place we observed several sepulchral monuments, with excavations in the rocks beneath, as receptacles for the dead. The most elevated spots, the most abrupt precipices, we generally observed, were appropriated for the repose of the dead. Whether this choice was determined with a regard to notoriety, or from any superstitious opinion, that the body might be placed as near as possible to that heaven where spirits wing their flight, we could obtain no satisfactory information. The amiable virtues, however, of the Chinese, were rendered more conspicuous by the feeling regard they uniformly appear to shew to the remains of those they have once loved or respected.

On the 9th we arrived at a city, where the embassy was to make a day's march over land, and accordingly we disembarked. The landing-place was adorned with a triumphal arch, highly decorated with silken streamers, and connected, by a platform, with a circular court, surrounded by a skreen of silk. In this place a number of horses were collected, with the choice of one of which every person in the suite was indulged for the journey of the day; but the Ambassador, with two or three gentlemen of his suite, were to proceed, as usual, in palankins The horses being selected, the cavalcade commenced their progress, and perhaps such an exhibition of equestrian exercise and grotesque dress never before amused a Chinese populace. The horses were spirited, many of the riders were new to this mode of travelling. The cries of fear, and the shouts of ridicule, were every where heard, and scarcely could we attend to the passing scene, so much were we engaged by the peculiarities of our own situation

Naung-aum-foo, through which we passed, is a large walled city; and though the river here does not admit large junks, from the very great number of smaller ones which lined its shores, we concluded it had no inconsiderable pretensions to a commercial character.

At noon we arrived at the foot of a lofty mountain, where we were obliged to dismount, having gained the ascent we passed several villages, and dined at the town of Lee-cou-au, where the road was lined with soldiers in armour, to salute the Ambassador as he passed

The women, in this part of our journey, were either educated with less reserve, or allowed a greater share of liberty, than in the country through which we had lately passed, as we frequently saw them indulging their curiosity in observing such a new and extraordinary sight as we must have exhibited.

The splendor of cultivation was exchanged for the landscape of the barren mountain; however, large patches of camphire and other trees sometimes relieved the eye.

We arrived at the gates of Naung-chin-oa, juſt as the ſun had ſunk beneath the horizon, this city ſtands in a plain, encircled on three ſides by hills, and on the fourth by the river on which we were to continue our voyage. The houſes are chiefly built of wood, in general two ſtories high, and the ſtreets are narrow, but well paved in exterior appearance and decoration, it preſerves the general character of Chineſe towns.

Soldiers lined the ſtreets to facilitate our paſſage to the mandarin s palace, a very noble building, conſiſting of ſeveral courts A ſplendid entertainment was provided for the whole ſuite, and ſuch a profuſion of lights decorated the principal apartments as are never diſplayed in Europe on an occaſion, indeed illumination, we may affirm, conſtitutes the grand appropriate feature of Chineſe magnificence.

We again embarked in the morning of the 11th of December, on board ſmall junks, correſponding with the depth of the river, and before noon we reſumed our voyage, ſailing under a wooden bridge of ſeven arches, with ſtone pillars, ſtrongly guarded by ſoldiers at each end From this point the city appears in a very advantageous view

At a ſmall diſtance from the bridge the river divides into two branches, running in almoſt oppoſite directions; on that whoſe ſtream bore us along we ſaw a large quantity of ſmall timber in rafts.

In the afternoon we paſſed a pagoda, of a more ſingular conſtruction than any which we had ſeen in our travels through the country It conſiſted of five ſtories, and terminated in a flat roof, with trees growing on it. The body of the building, from many parts of which alſo ſhrubs appeared to ſprout forth, was covered with a white plaiſter, and decorated with red paint in its angles and interſtices.

The country ſtill remained barren and mountainous, nor was its rude and dreary aſpect enlivened by any appearance of cultivation A conſiderable town, called Chang-tang, was the only place of conſequence which we paſſed in the ſhort voyage of this day.

The face of the country ſtill continued dreary, and artificial circumſtances increaſed the gloom Sepulchral monuments were the chief objects which we ſaw in the courſe of the day, the only novelty was floating rafts, with ſeveral bamboo huts, well tenanted, which we paſſed near the village of Ty-ang-koa.

On the 13th, after paſſing a conſiderable town, we came to the city of Shaw-choo, where the houſes adjoining the river appear to be ſo ſlenderly ſupported, as to threaten conſtant ruin to their inhabitants and the paſſengers. At the extremity of this city the fleet anchored, and here the Ambaſſador experienced the elegant attention of the mandarin in a very ſuperior degree.

In the evening he ſent the ſuite a very handſome preſent of china, together with a large ſupply of proviſions, we alſo, at a later hour of the evening, received a quantity of tobacco, ſome ducks cured in the manner of hams, of a very delicate flavour, together with a conſiderable quantity of dried fiſh

At this place, junks of larger dimenſions were again prepared to receive the embaſſy, and next day we paſſed through a country ſometimes varied with patches of cultivated ground, though mountainous ſterility was ſtill the predominant feature.

Towards evening we found the hills gradually approaching the river, till at laſt they ſeemed to cloſe, and admit only its courſe this gloomy ſcene continued for ſome time, as if to heighten the contraſt that was to open We now reached a mountain of immenſe perpendicular height, the upper part of which appears to project over the ſtream. Its contour is bare rock and ſhaggy foliage, and this extends for nearly two miles: its termination, like its commencement, is abrupt. At the extreme point, a pyramidical rock appears to riſe above the edge of the precipice, and this is ſeparated by an intervening plain from another enormous rock, of the ſame character, though of a different form.

As a range of hills may be ſaid to have conducted us along the river to theſe ſtupendous objects, ſo a ſucceſſion of the ſame kind continued during a courſe of ſeveral miles after we had left them; but it was the peculiar office of this extraordinary night to awaken our aſtoniſhment by the grand exertions of art, as well as by the ſtupendous works of nature; for, at the concluſion of this chain of hills, that had ſo long excluded any view into the country, we were ſurpriſed with a line of light extending for ſeveral miles over mountains and vallies, at ſome diſtance from the river, and forming one uninterrupted blazing outline as they roſe or ſunk in the horizon.

In ſome parts of this brilliant, undulating line, it was varied or thickened, as it appeared, by large bands or groups of torches; and, on the moſt conſpicuous heights immenſe bonfires threw their flames towards the clouds. Nor was this all, for the lights not only circumſcribed the outline of the mountain, but ſometimes roſe up it in a ſerpentine form, and connected, by a ſpiral ſtream of light, a large fire blazing at the bottom, with that which reddened the ſummit.

The number of lanterns, lamps, or torches, employed on this occaſion, are beyond all calculation, as the two extremities of the illuminated ſpace, taken in a ſtraight line, without eſtimating the ſinkings of the vallies, or the inequality of the mountain tops, could not contain a less distance from each other than three miles Whether these lights were held by an army of soldiers, or were fixed in the ground, we could not learn, but it was certainly the most magnificent illumination ever seen by any European traveller, and the most splendid compliment ever paid to the public dignity of an European ambassador. Successive discharges of artillery were, at regular distances, added to the honour of this superb spectacle

On the 15th the grand mandarin ordered the fleet to come to anchor, for the purpose of indulging the embassy with a view of the mountain of Koan veng-naum, one of the natural curiosities of China It has a perpendicular ascent from the water, terminating in a peak, and from the face towards the river, such enormous masses project, as apparently menace every moment to fill up the channel of the stream,

But art has heightened the curious circumstances of this extraordinary mountain It contains several caverns One of them is about forty feet above the level of the water To this there is access by a flight of steps, guarded by a rail, On reaching the top of the flight, we enter a room of good dimensions, excavated from the rock, in which stands an image sacred to Chinese devotions An artificial staircase conducts to two other superior apartments, and the whole is fitted up by the mandarin to whom the mountain belongs, in a stile of rude magnificence, corresponding to the character of the place

Proceeding through a country presenting many sublime features, we reached the city of Schizing-ta-heng about noon This place enjoys every local advantage that can contribute to render it picturesque in a high degree

Lofty banks for a confiderable fpace fhut out our view of the land, and where a cafual opening gave a wider profpect, it was not marked with any new features Similar objects occurred—varied only by fhape, or difcriminated by light and fhadow

The evening was cheered with an illumination of the diftant hills. The coup d'œil was extremely grand, but inferior to what we had witneffed before

Next day we faw a number of fteep rocks, in various grotefque forms, they were fometimes tinted with foliage, and fometimes the traces of laborious tafte, were the prevailing character of the landfcape they afforded. Among them arofe a large mountain, fhaded by an hanging foreft, which was alfo accompanied with circumftances that enlivened and adorned it. At the foot of it a road had been cut out of the folid rock, and to communicate with it, a large arch of ftone has been built acrofs a deep chafm In the centre of the wood, there is the palace of a mandarin, furrounded with detached offices, and at fome fmall diftance a temple, which belongs to it, and contains the image which is the ufual object of religious worfhip There are feveral burying places in different parts of the wood, which are the maufoleums of the mandarin's family to whom the palace belongs. It is called Tre-hou-zau

This magnificent fcene, which, on a particular turn of the river prefented itfelf, is much heightened by a contrafted fucceffion of bare and barren mountains

We now reached the city of Tfing yan-yeun, a place well fortified, and of great extent and population The number of junks which lay before it, indicated an enlarged commerce, and the timber yards on the banks of the river pointed out its principal trade Triumphal arches decorated the beach, and feveral regiments of foldiers paid the military honours as we paffed.

From this city the river takes a direct course for some miles, amidst fertile and highly cultivated meadows, and the mountains fall into the back ground.

This afternoon one of the junks was in imminent danger of being consumed by fire occasioned by a spark falling unobserved from a tobacco-pipe Indeed, where smoaking is so generally used, it is a matter of astonishment that accidents are not more frequent and fatal

On the 17th we passed the extensive village of Ouz-chouaa, where a number of manufactories appear to be established The country now resumed its fertility and beauty, and provisions became both plentiful and excellent

In the evening we reached the city of Sangs-we-yenno, where the Ambassador received every honour that the most elegant attention on the part of the mandarin could pay, or his Excellency expect The illuminations displayed here were peculiarly grand

On the following morning we passed a series of very large and populous towns, so closely connected, that we seemed for some hours to be sailing through one city of immense extent The salutes were almost incessant as we proceeded, and every place poured forth thousands of its inhabitants, though at a very early hour, to obtain a transient view of an European embassy.

We now approached the city of Tayn-tsyn-tau, a place of great importance and the most extensive trade. The suburbs lie on both sides the river for several miles, and if we may judge from those circumstances that fell under our inspection, in extent, population, and commerce, this city is only inferior to Pekin or to Canton Thousands of junks covered the river for a vast space, and scarcely had we overcome the difficulties and impediments of this crowded navigation, before we found ourselves approaching to Canton, the termination of our voyage.

Our arrival being notified at Canton, ſeveral mandarins waited on his Excellency, and theſe were ſoon followed by the gentlemen of the Engliſh factory with the Britiſh commiſſioners and Colonel Benſon. This officer brought with him the public diſpatches for the Ambaſſador, and a packet of private letters from our friends in England, together with the newſpapers which had arrived by the laſt ſhips. Thoſe only who have been ſo long cut off from any communication with the land which contained all that was dear to them, can form an adequate idea of the anxious joy we felt at opening a letter from the relative or friend we loved.

Next day we were moved into larger junks. The magnificence of the river at this place baffles deſcription. Its ſurface was almoſt covered with veſſels, engaged in trade, or attracted by curioſity. The banks were lined with ſoldiers, and covered with elegant houſes, and a ſucceſſion of forts thundered out ſalutes with almoſt inceſſant rapidity.

We reached the Engliſh factory about one in the afternoon, and both it and the Dutch factory paid his Excellency the uſual ſalute, hoiſting at the ſame time the ſtandard of their reſpective countries.

For ſome days it had been a common ſight to ſee the boats generally rowed by women. We ſometimes obſerved a child tied to its mother's back, and another at her breaſt, while ſhe was plying the oar. To a feeling mind this ſpectacle could not fail to give pain; and it may be remarked, that in Tartary, and the northern provinces of China, where the women are lamed, either by faſhion or policy, from their infant years, ſuch laborious occupations can never fall to their lot.

A temporary reſidence for the Ambaſſador and ſuite had been provided by the Eaſt India Company's ſupercargoes, and in point of accommodation and domeſtic arrangement, we found it superior to the first palaces in which we had lodged, during our long peregrination in China

As we have already given a description of Canton, we shall forbear adding any thing respecting it in this place.

For several days, during the time of dinner, the Ambassador was entertained with Chinese plays, performed on a stage erected before the windows of his apartments, and the Viceroy visited him once during his stay, which was followed by large presents of porcelain, nankeen, and sugar-candy to the whole retinue.

On the first day of the new year, 1794, his Excellency and suite were splendidly entertained by the gentlemen of the British factory The band of music which had accompanied the embassy, on the request of the factory, were permitted to enter into its service, and in a country where musements are so few and confined, it could not fail to be a valuable acquisition.

Degeneracy of manners evidently marks the character of the inhabitants of Canton, and this reflection is the more melancholy, as there is too much reason to suppose the contagion of European example has infected the simplicity of the Chinese general character, and rendered themselves objects of contempt to the Chinese government

On the 8th of January the Ambassador proceeded to Whampoa to join the ships At the same time a deputation of the retinue was dispatched to Macao, to make preparations for his Excellency's reception at that place

Whampoa, beyond which European ships are never permitted to pass, is an elegant and populous village, about eighteen miles below Canton. The river near this place is defended by a sand bank, which prevents the passage of large ships, except at high water, and two necks of land, projecting on each side of it, form the celebrated strait of Bocca Tigris

At this place Van-Tadge-In took his farewell leave of the Ambassador Our praise or censure will not reach a person of his rank, but in bestowing praise on this deservedly distinguished personage and most amiable of men, we gratify the best feelings of the human heart, and at the same time do honour to ourselves This excellent character can never be forgotten by those who experienced his assiduous care, his mild condescension, and his enlightened conduct, during a long and troublesome attendance on the embassy He held an exalted rank in the Chinese army—perhaps the highest, but no dignity of situation had rendered him inattentive to the minutest offices of duty. His mind seemed capable of reflecting honour on any rank, with the most benevolent heart he attached himself to the interests of those in whose service he was employed, he had even contracted a friendship for some, and his last adieu to the Ambassador and suite was accompanied by the tears of affection

On the 14th Lord Macartney landed at Macao, and took up his residence with Mr Drummond, one of the supercargoes of the East India Company Here the gentlemen of the several European factories have their houses as they are not permitted to remain at Canton longer than is absolutely necessary for the purpose of trade

The long intercourse which has subsisted between Europeans and the Chinese in this place, has not altered the established customs and habits of the latter The Chinese never deviate from the usages of their country, which may be considered as invariable

Without the wall is the common burying-ground of the Chinese, and in it we saw several memorials of our countrymen, whose ashes repose here. Those who die in the Roman Catholic faith have separate cemeteries. the Chinese, more liberal than the Catholics, suffer their dust to mingle with ours

Here Mr Plumb, the interpreter, though offered an handsome establishment if he chose to return to Europe, quitted the service of the embassy. He left his English friends with sensible regret, but naturally preferred passing the remainder of his days in the bosom of his family and his country.

On the 8th of March, Lord Macartney and retinue embarked for Europe, amid the salutes of forts and ships, and being joined by a large homeward-bound fleet of Indiamen, on the 17th proceeded to sea

Nothing of any particular consequence happened during our voyage We arrived at St. Helena on the 19th of June, and remained there till the 1st of July.

On the 3d of September we were seriously alarmed by running foul of a large fleet off Portland Roads, which proved to be the Grand Fleet commanded by Earl Howe Two or three of the Indiamen received some damage, but, except in this instance, our voyage was free from accident, and barren of interesting occurrence.

In the afternoon of this day we anchored safe at Spithead, after an absence of little less than two years from our native land.

In the course of the preceding narrative, it was mentioned that Captain Mackintosh, and a part of the embassy, proceeded from Hoang-tchew to Chusan

The same kind of scenery, we are informed, presented itself in the passage to Chusan as has been described in the route we made but the river itself was of a different nature from that on which we sailed, its course was occasionally broken by cataracts of a formidable aspect, and required all the ingenuity of the Chinese to contrive means to obviate the difficulties of such a navigation. Yet, ſtrange as it may appear, they apply the mechanical powers to raiſe veſſels into a higher level of the river, or ſink them to a lower: to effect which, two ſtrong ſtentions are fixed in the centre of the river, from which two large beams project over the water; to theſe blocks ſtrong ropes are attached, and the junk being well ſecured fore and aft, is in a few moments hoiſted, with all its contents, from one level to another. Perſons accuſtomed to the buſineſs are ſtationed at theſe places, and ſo certain and ſecure is their operation, that it is ſcarcely regarded as an impediment or hazard. The ſame attention, we underſtand, was paid to Captain Mackintoſh and his party, during their paſſage to Chuſan, as to the embaſſy itſelf.

FINIS.

CPSIA information can be obtained at www.ICGtesting.com
Printed in the USA
BVOW09s0548060915

416623BV00037B/703/P